Socrates and Self-Knowledge

CHRISTOPHER MO

CAMBRIDGE
UNIVERSITY PRESS

CAMBRIDGE
UNIVERSITY PRESS

University Printing House, Cambridge CB2 8BS, United Kingdom

One Liberty Plaza, 20th Floor, New York, NY 10006, USA

477 Williamstown Road, Port Melbourne, VIC 3207, Australia

314-321, 3rd Floor, Plot 3, Splendor Forum, Jasola District Centre, New Delhi-110025, India

79 Anson Road, #06-04/06, Singapore 079906

Cambridge University Press is part of the University of Cambridge.

It furthers the University's mission by disseminating knowledge in the pursuit of education, learning and research at the highest international levels of excellence.

www.cambridge.org
Information on this title: www.cambridge.org/9781107558472

First published 2015
First paperback edition 2017

A catalogue record for this publication is available from the British Library

Library of Congress Cataloging in Publication data
Moore, Christopher, 1981–
Socrates and self-knowledge / Christopher Moore.
pages cm
Includes bibliographical references and index.
ISBN 978-1-107-12330-4 (hardback)
1. Socrates 2. Self (Philosophy) 3. Self-knowledge, Theory of.
4. Philosophy, Ancient. I. Title.
B317.M67 2015
183′.2–dc23 2015014245

ISBN 978-1-107-12330-4 Hardback
ISBN 978-1-107-55847-2 Paperback

Socrates and Self-Knowledge

In this book, the first systematic study of Socrates' reflections on self-knowledge, Christopher Moore examines the ancient precept "Know yourself" and, drawing on Plato, Aristophanes, Xenophon, and others, reconstructs and reassesses the arguments about self-examination, personal ideals, and moral maturity at the heart of the Socratic project. What has been thought to be a purely epistemological or metaphysical inquiry turns out to be deeply ethical, intellectual, and social. Knowing yourself is more than attending to your beliefs, discerning the structure of your soul, or recognizing your ignorance – it is constituting yourself as a self who can be guided by knowledge toward the good life. This is neither a wholly introspective nor a completely isolated pursuit: we know and constitute ourselves best through dialogue with friends and critics. This rich and original study will be of interest to researchers in the philosophy of Socrates, selfhood, and ancient thought.

CHRISTOPHER MOORE is Assistant Professor of Philosophy and Classics at The Pennsylvania State University. He is the author of many essays in edited volumes and journals, including *American Journal of Philology*, *Ancient Philosophy*, *Apeiron*, *British Journal for the History of Philosophy*, and *Classical Quarterly*.

To the memory of Leah K. Horowitz

ἐστι καὶ χαλεπώτατον, ὥσπερ καὶ τῶν σοφῶν τινες εἰρήκασιν, τὸ γνῶναι αὑτόν, καὶ ἥδιστον ... ὥσπερ οὖν ὅταν θέλωμεν αὐτοὶ αὑτῶν τὸ πρόσωπον ἰδεῖν, εἰς τὸ κάτοπτρον ἐμβλέψαντες εἴδομεν, ὁμοίως καὶ ὅταν αὐτοὶ αὑτοὺς βουληθῶμεν γνῶναι, εἰς τὸν φίλον ἰδόντες γνωρίσαιμεν ἄν.

Aristotle

Full souls are double mirrors, making still
An endless vista of fair things before
Repeating things behind

George Eliot

Contents

Preface

The promise of self-knowledge

Philosophy has long assumed self-knowledge to be a path to happiness; but it has for just as long wondered why this might be. Some of the puzzlement devolves from self-knowledge's parent concepts. We still wonder why selfhood – personal unification and perseverance – might do us any good; and we still wonder why knowledge – truth directing our beliefs and actions – might serve us better than belief. Yet many of our anxieties about self-knowledge have their own origin. Self-knowledge introduces its own paradox, its own urgency, and its own temptation to complacence. A paradox, because we as subjects must become at once our own objects, neutral observers, and active participants. An urgency, because if we suspect that neither science, politics, nor perhaps even religion will cure our unhappiness, we might suspect that our salvation lies somewhere closer to ourselves. And a temptation, because nothing seems easier than recognizing ourselves, our nearest and most constant companion, and thus we risk always presuming more progress in our task than we really have made. Western philosophy since Thales and Heraclitus – and freshly in the past quarter century – has made serious study of self-knowledge: its avenues, its limitations, and its charms. But this study has not come to completion. In particular, the study *of* its study has only begun.

It is in this belief that I write *Socrates and Self-Knowledge*. This book contributes to the history of the philosophy of self-knowledge, and thus to the philosophy of self-knowledge itself. It does so defined by two boundaries. First, it concerns a self-knowledge that is associated historically with the name Socrates by people proximate to the historical Socrates. It is the self-knowledge that might even be said to define the image of Socrates in the Greek and subsequent imaginations. Second, it treats the self-knowledge specifically posited through Greek attempts to understand the precept "Know yourself," a precept they took seriously as a wisdom worthy of the Sages and as inscribed at the Temple of Apollo at Delphi. It is the knowledge of oneself defined as these practical contexts require, not as whatever we or others have anachronistically chosen to count as self-knowledge. Thus the following study differs from a study of other classical ideas of self-knowledge (e.g., as Aristotelian or Platonist or Stoic) and from a study of self-knowledge as a construct of modern epistemology retrojected on the past. It addresses instead how Socrates, as a key figure of Greek philosophy, talked about trying to obey the precept *gnôthi sauton*. Of course Socrates' attempts at obedience to the precept, as authors of Socratic literature had him discuss, directed his mind toward knowledge and selfhood as such, as well as much else in what we now consider Greek philosophy. Indeed, Aristotle plausibly claims that obedience to the precept occasioned Socrates' entire intellectual project. All the same, while judging where to delimit the study betokens subjective considerations – the compactness of exegesis, the avoidance of the impossibly difficult questions – I try anyway to focus on just those questions most immediately and pressingly raised by Socrates' response to the injunction.

These two restraints on the shape and size of this project – the Socratic aspect and the precept aspect – may both sound odd, fluid, even incoherent. In the remainder of this preface I shall try to make them sound more plausible.

A "Socratic" account

This book studies Classical-era views of self-knowledge associated with the name Socrates. The real man with that name, Socrates of Alopece, citizen of Athens (469–399 BC), as Aristophanes and Aristotle appear to show us, really did judge self-knowledge worth pursuing and discussing. Plato's dialogues and Xenophon's *Memorabilia* probably corroborate this historical observation. Their works, submitted to an audience who knew the real Socrates either socially or by reputation, animate a Socrates speaking constantly of "knowing yourself" and engaging interlocutors on topics of inward examination, selfhood and soul, cognition and reflexivity, and other matters related to the problems and rewards of self-knowledge. Thus we have good reason to suppose that the historical Socrates had thoughtful, articulated, and even elaborated or definitive beliefs about self-knowledge.

Unfortunately, we know practically nothing about the details of these beliefs; time and the constraints of genre have obscured their content, grounds, and implications. Aristophanes' *Clouds* aims overtly for parody; Aristotle's remarks, probably from his dialogue *On Philosophy*, survive only in minute fragments. Other good sources of information, for example the works of Phaedo or other contemporary Socratics, have disappeared almost completely. While Plato and Xenophon wrote thousands of pages about Socrates, they lack the fidelity to facts appropriate to journalists and the explanatory care proper to historiographers. These works may report, in the course of their fictive reconstructions, much truth about Socrates' views of self-knowledge; but we cannot readily perceive the parts that reveal the thoughts he really had or would commit himself to.

Our dark window onto the historical man named Socrates, son of Sophroniscus, blurs his intellectual positions. But there remain intellectual positions linked to Socrates worthy of study. Fourth-century authors depicted characters called Socrates with express and implicit beliefs articulated with a provocative degree of definition. Granted, we cannot know to what degree any literary Socrates represented accurately the historical Socrates. But we may suppose them to have been more than coincidentally synonymous. However fictional, they point somehow at Socrates himself and his defining principles.

They point in a roundabout way, crookedly, and with intermediation; this is one clear result of the scholarship on the "Socratic Problem." Some authors of Socratic literature surely strove to recreate the Socrates they knew or remembered. Others, who may hardly have known Socrates but who still prized robustness and plausibility in their representation, may have worked from the memories of friends and the depictions of other authors, endeavoring to correct for those authors' biases or argumentative restrictions. Yet others would have depicted Socrates apologetically, polemically, stereotypically, or generically. It is a truism that the supposedly Socratic beliefs these authors burnished tell us as much about the authors themselves as about the son of Sophroniscus. But these near-contemporary authors of Socratic literature lived in an intellectual and literary milieu deeply impressed by the historical Socrates and by men themselves deeply impressed by the historical Socrates, and they wrote with a consciousness of this milieu and their likely readers and critics. No author could simply depict a man of their choosing who happened to go by the name

Socrates. Each literary Socrates refers ultimately, however indirectly and partially, to some historical element of Socrates, through either the intellectual society to which Socrates contributed, or the allegiances into which his students divided, or the literary conventions writers of Socratic literature followed, or any number of other possible avenues.

Many of the extant depictions of Socrates treat the questions of self-knowledge. This fact might seem an accident of papyrus deterioration. Plato swamps our sample with his grand and excellently preserved oeuvre and obvious interest in epistemology and metaphysics. But perhaps Plato typifies a common practice of depicting Socrates talking about self-knowledge. In any case, Plato and Xenophon do develop such ideas at length, Plato doing so explicitly on many occasions.

Thus this book studies a number of Platonic dialogues and one Xenophontic text for their Socrateses' beliefs about self-knowledge. I say "Platonic" because several dialogues of interest, including *First Alcibiades*, *Rival Lovers*, and *Hipparchus*, have weathered heavy skepticism about their authorship. This book therefore approaches these texts as discrete literary and philosophical productions, not primarily as revelatory of Plato's views about Socrates. Even in so doing, it finds remarkable similarities in the ideas about self-knowledge associated with their respective Socrateses. This is despite the differences among the texts' descriptive, protreptic, analytic, or defensive goals. These similarities justify speaking of a relatively constant set of "Socratic" ideas about self-knowledge, even against hermeneutic worries about identifying a single "character" called Socrates across this range of works. That there might be such a relatively constant set of "Socratic" ideas about self-knowledge should hardly sound strange; we readily accept a core of Socratic ideas about method (constant questioning), attitude (irony and enthusiasm), virtue (its supremacy and intellectual inflection), and sociality (a deep interest in his friends' and neighbors' wellbeing). This book shows that certain ideas of self-knowledge, in part because of their connections to these other ideas, and probably in part too because of the historical Socrates' marked interest in them, remain relatively stable across these works.

For all these plausibility arguments, not much of philosophical importance ultimately depends on the constancy of these ideas across works. Nor do I argue that consistency in the Socratic literature points, as an overlapping consensus, to the actual beliefs of the historical

Socrates. It very well may, but other explanations could account for that consistency. Further, I do not insist on the robustness of this claim, that these ideas really are completely similar. Should the accounts in various of Plato's works strike the reader as incompatible, the reader should consider the explication and discussion of each work on its own terms, and should treat the book as an analysis of several admittedly distinct but individually provocative views of self-knowledge. For this sort of skeptical reader, my attempts to show commonalities across those views should be received as little more than attempts at narrative coherence. For the more sympathetic reader, however, I hope to contribute to Socratic studies while also contributing to the philosophy of self-knowledge.

A response to the "Know yourself"

I have said that this book studies just those texts where Socrates talks about the precept "Know yourself" (*gnôthi sauton*). He does so in the Platonic *Charmides*, *Alcibiades*, *Phaedrus*, *Philebus*, *Protagoras*, *Rival Lovers*, and *Hipparchus*, in Xenophon's *Memorabilia* 4, and implicitly in Aristophanes' *Clouds*. Across those works Socrates asks what the precept means, offers it as the best maxim of action to follow, claims to follow it himself, says it diagnoses a common failing, equates it with some of the cardinal virtues, and frequently identifies it as a propaedeutic to education. His remarks make clear that the precept's privileged position in moral life was universally endorsed by the Greeks but that they lacked a settled consensus about its meaning. Socrates suggests that the Greeks, in the best of circumstances, kept open the question of its implication, and of the implications of its constituent parts – whatever counts as "yourself" and whatever counts as "knowing" or "recognizing" (*gignôskein*) it. This openness was not just toward academic concept-analysis but toward this precept's legitimate action-guiding significance.

An important interpretative hypothesis, one I try to vindicate in each chapter, is that the dialogues where Socrates speaks of the *gnôthi sauton* provide material for understanding the Socratic interpretation of the injunction. References to the precept, I hold, do not simply show the speaker's fondness for cliché, idiom, or mild correction. They are not merely part of the dramatic by-play. We have many reasons, most from within the literary works themselves, to take such references as crucial to the incident and argument of those works. When we give them the weight their authors allow them, even if they do so subtly and quietly, we see the way the conversation, argument, and thematic progress inform and are informed by the charge to "know yourself." In any particular case the work as a whole might include material helpful for discerning what the precept is thought to demand, what route an effective response might take, and by what criteria that response might be judged successful.

Following Socrates' discussions of the Delphic precept fulfills two desires a student of self-knowledge might have. First, it helps tell us what occasions a concern for the study of self-knowledge. Of course, self-knowledge might simply seem fascinating, or a logical conundrum, or manifestly, even existentially, important. But I suspect that only within a complex historical context would it seem any of these; and only within those contexts could one fix a referent of this term "self-knowledge." The context for the Greeks would be the precept's concrete and traditional moral authority and thus the normative pressure to follow it. Perhaps this context is no less foreign or arbitrary than the context that spurs on research for contemporary philosophers, a context of journal articles and familiar paradoxes and the imperatives of tenure and professional success. But the Greek context of the precept, of Sage and Delphic-Panhellenic wisdom, has the chance of fitting in more broadly and snuggly with the everyday life and moral imagination of those who listened to it. Second, following Socrates' discussions of the *gnôthi sauton* lets us define the content of "self-knowledge" as only what could be interpreted as what the precept demands, given its particular role in Greek life, and thus as other than a conundrum of epistemology or metaphysics, as impressive as that conundrum may be. Part of knowing yourself would then include interpreting the meaning of "knowing yourself," which would include not only investigating the concepts "knowing" and "self" but the purposes behind the promulgation of the precept.

This procedure, studying self-knowledge only in the context of specific references to the *gnôthi sauton*, does force aside texts canonical in understanding ancient self-knowledge. I feel the strongest regret at leaving aside Plato's *Theaetetus* and *Republic*, and Xenophon's *Memorabilia* 3. (I discuss the *Protagoras*' reference to the *gnôthi sauton* in another publication (Moore 2015a). But as the concept of self-knowledge blends readily into the concepts of knowledge and self-improvement, a study of self-knowledge would soon become even more a study of the central questions of philosophy than it already must be. Such a study would demand too much from this author, and perhaps even from its readers. This book may succeed in its narrower ambit when its readers find in it cause to think again about self-knowledge with Socrates.

Acknowledgments

I tremble to take for an authorial model Marcus Aurelius, who recognized those by whom, and their characteristics by which, he came to learn to live, and thus to write. Luckily, following his lead publicly would be too awkward; this book is about ancient self-constitution, not my own. Yet I am not wholly relieved from the task. I really must mention six women without whom, even had this book been written, *I* could hardly be considered the author:

my mother: from whom my greatest good fortune comes;
my friend Leah: in the memory of whose most serious examination of self and others – including me – I wrote and rewrote every page;
my first professor at Dartmouth, Nancy Jay Crumbine: from whom I learned to talk about my education, and what is beyond myself, and also about Socrates;
my philosophy graduate advisor, Sandra Peterson: from whom I learned to write the history of philosophy, and who demonstrated an orientation to this profession I could find comfortable;
my classics graduate advisor, Elizabeth Belfiore: from whom I came to understand the meaning, promise, and ethic of rigorous scholarship; and
my wife, Kate Baldanza: from whom I have faced the truest Socratic interrogation about matters of deepest significance, and have discovered it to be filled with unimaginable fellowship and glee.

My debts for the book itself may be cited with less diffidence. I owe the topic to Josh Kortbein, my most companionable classmate, who each afternoon in graduate school brought me to the actually urgent questions of philosophy; he sketched those of self-knowledge with greatest vigor and color. Some years later, during the imagination, composition, and revision of the manuscript, Vincent Colapietro was my most genuine and constant interlocutor, and Chris Raymond talked with me joyfully about Socratic studies and read several chapters. My anonymous referees at Cambridge University Press gave powerful correctives to the structure and clarity of this book, and my editor there, Hilary Gaskin, has been an early and efficient advocate. I should also like to thank Sam Frederick and Michele Kennerly for proposing that I join their writing group in 2012–2013, during which time I wrote the book's first draft; my students Jack Bagby and Claire Griffin for edifying conversations about Socratic literature; and Chris Long for nudging me to write a book in the first place and for reading a previous version of the Introduction.

As I finished writing this book's index, my son, Solomon, entered the world. He has much yet to know of himself, and of what is good. Should the present study have taught me anything, it is to hope that by knowing the one he might know the other, and that by my care, conversation, and companionship he – and I – might be nudged just a little closer to that knowledge.

1 *Introduction: Socrates and the precept "Know yourself"*

The benefits of studying Socrates and self-knowledge

In this book I aim to reconstruct the Socratic response to the precept "Know yourself" as a view of self-knowledge that is plausible, interesting, and valuable. This view, I hope to show, has as good a chance to be true or insightful as more recent views; its complex structure and striking connections to other concepts reward more than a superficial reading or moment's reflection; and were it better known it could contribute usefully to debates about self-knowledge, to diagnosing unquestioned assumptions, to our understanding of Socrates and the origins of philosophical practice, and to our own attempts to live better lives through reason. In showing the significance of Socratic self-knowledge, I wish also to slow the continual dismissal of ancient theories of self-knowledge found among contemporary philosophers of self-knowledge. "For the ancients," a collection of recent essays begins, "self-knowledge is primarily a goal to be achieved, whereas for the moderns it is mainly a puzzle to be resolved."[1] This echoes the programmatic opening sentence of *Self-Knowledge and Self-Identity*, now a half-century old:

> The topic of this book is not nearly so lofty as its title may suggest. The term "self-knowledge" is used here, not in the Socratic sense, where it refers to something that few are able to attain, but in such a way that a person can be said to have self-knowledge whenever he knows the truth of a statement in which there is reference to himself.[2]

[1] Hatzimoysis 2011: 1. Hatzimoysis makes nothing of this difference; none of the thirteen articles in his collection mentions Socrates. The following authors mention Socrates a single time, each treating his view as obvious but not their concern: Bilgrami 2006: 274; Liu and Perry 2012: 221n3; Cassam 2014: 28n1.

[2] Shoemaker 1963: vii.

Indeed, some see the ancient attitudes toward self-knowledge not simply as different from contemporary attitudes but also as somehow less philosophically urgent. A recent review has it that self-knowledge of the contemporary sort "may not be the sort of knowledge with which the Delphic Oracle is concerned, but the whole point of the Delphic injunction was that such self-knowledge is *hard*, and philosophers haven't typically wanted to dispute that."[3] Self-knowledge has become a thorny problem in the philosophy of mind and the theory of knowledge, with questions of introspection, epistemic warrant, mental transparency, behaviorism, and truth-makers at stake. The ancient texts do not obviously address those questions.[4]

These distinctions between ancient and modern conceptions of self-knowledge rest, however, on doubtful assumptions. The first is that the term "self-knowledge" generally refers to privileged first-person access to present-tense self-directed conscious mental states, especially beliefs reportable in propositional form (e.g., "I think I will enjoy writing that").[5] That this conception is but one of a range of contemporary views, even within analytic philosophy, can no longer be denied.[6] Even were it the last view standing, the use of "self-knowledge" to name this puzzle in epistemology seems off-kilter, since few people, even philosophers, actually identify the self-directed subset of conscious ("occurrent") mental states with the "self," or believe that the ability to express incorrigibly those states exhausts the scope of "knowledge." Put differently, it is difficult to see why this problem of privileged first-person access to certain conscious states, of all the problems of mind and personhood, should receive the ancient and venerable title of "self-knowledge." Indeed, the various views of so-called self-knowledge, such as "inner sense" or "inner detection," seem more apt descriptors of their content.

[3] Smith 2012. Smith does not say what kind of knowledge is the hard kind, why philosophers of self-knowledge are not concerned with the Delphic kind of self-knowledge, or why the "hardness" of Delphic self-knowledge is the injunction's "whole point."

[4] Aristotle's *De Anima* 3.2 may be an exception; see, e.g., Caston 2002.

[5] See Gertler 2011 for a development of this position.

[6] See Moran 2001; Finkelstein 2003; Bilgrami 2006; Gertler 2011's "rationalist" mode (a conflation of several views); Schwitzgebel 2011; Cassam 2014, as well as much of the practical rationality literature, esp. Velleman 1989; Korsgaard 2009.

A failure to recognize the plausibility, interest, and value of ancient conceptions of self-knowledge is found not only among contemporary philosophers of self-knowledge. Some scholars of ancient philosophy make a related mistake. They assume that the really catchy or modish questions of self-knowledge come out of present-day "psychoanalytic" concerns, which involve "finding oneself" in a self-help, secular, getting-in-touch-with-one's-emotions fashion. It seems obvious to these scholars that the ancients lacked this therapeutic orientation when they spoke of self-knowledge.[7] And so ancient self-knowledge must, by this logic, be something distinct – presumably rather more austere, impersonal, and theoretical – from this talky and memoiristic vision of self-knowledge. Socratic self-knowledge would then be an extension of ancient epistemology and metaphysics, worthy of study for those reasons but without independent significance.

The popularity of this binary contrast, between putatively psychoanalytic and impersonal views of self-knowledge, has a number of explanations. I mention just two. Readers have often interpreted Plato as a thinker who maintained strict boundaries to the scope of knowledge, such that only changeless and impersonal universals, rather than the concrete and particular contents of human psychology, can be known.[8] Scholars have also assumed that the Delphic precept, given its Apolline context, directs people simply to observe the distinction between men and gods, or between hubris and modesty, and

[7] Annas 1985: 121–125, claims that only the modern view of self-knowledge understands it to be awareness of personal facts, "knowledge of the individual personality," which is whatever results from "thinking over one's past actions or by techniques like psychoanalysis," or from mining the "subconscious" and one's "unique and subjective point of view." Johnson 1999: 16, concludes that the *Alcibiades*' "version of self- knowledge could hardly be farther removed from … the search for a subjective, personal self that is more a matter for psychoanalysis than philosophy," for it deals not with "who we are as individuals" or as "inner selves" but with us "as rational creatures." Rowe 2011: 210, writes that "If there is 'therapy' here [in Socratic self-knowledge], it is the 'therapy' of the academic tutorial (run by a friendly, beneficent, but finally research-obsessed tutor, who thinks that finding out what the truth is [is] more important than anything else); it is not at all that of the psychiatrist's – or the psychotherapist's couch, and anyone who is tempted to assimilate the latter to Socratic practice has simply not understood Plato or, I would hazard, the original Socrates."

[8] I note that it is possible to interpret Plato this way and still think he could countenance a richer picture of self-knowledge than the binary assumed by these other authors: see Gerson 2003.

not to engage in some finer-grained self-examination. Unfortunately, even aside from the errors in these two views, assuming this binary contrast overlooks the much richer field of possible views adumbrated by the history of philosophy, and especially twentieth- and twenty-first-century approaches to selfhood, practical rationality, and authenticity. It also depends on the drastically over-simplified assumption that ancient philosophers cared little about personality, interiority, and self-consciousness.

By contrast with this common position against the philosophical importance of Socratic self-knowledge, this book argues for its broad philosophical appeal. I show that Socratic self-knowledge need not depend on controversial, outdated, or unpalatable metaphysical suppositions. It treats the "self" in a nuanced, non-arbitrary, and linguistically familiar way. It sets self-knowledge at the origins of a history of philosophy concerned with living well, orientation toward the truth, and the public debate of reasons for action. And it finds in self-knowledge simultaneously an epistemic, ethical, and practical ideal. Together these reasons suggest Socratic self-knowledge is far from an antiquarian reconstruction; it is a key legacy from the Classical Athenian philosophical period.

Some theses about Socratic self-knowledge

I have just identified the way this book endeavors to show the significance of the study of a self-knowledge associated with Socrates. I now briefly outline the book's methodological approach and philosophical conclusions. The texts that this book studies coalesce on a certain view of self-knowledge. But those texts do not explicitly state or argue for this view. Rather, they present a range of problems in understanding or pursuing self-knowledge, among them obstacles to obeying the Delphic precept. They also present material for solving these problems, or for removing these obstacles. The solutions usually differ from the way Socrates' interlocutor in the dialogue starts off thinking about self-knowledge. A fresh and improved way of thinking about it is presented dramatically, or incidentally, or gradually; but hardly ever directly. In this kind of reading of these texts we uncover this better approach to knowing ourselves in perhaps the same way that the interlocutor uncovers it: slowly, tentatively, with eyes on Socrates, and through meditation on it during and after the conversation. This tentative approach in the Socratic literature might reflect the modesty of the authors, or the imputed modesty of the literary Socrates. But it might also reflect a pedagogical insight. Being given explicit definitions of and instructions for knowing oneself might lead one to assume wrongly the ease of getting self-knowledge, and tasks assumed to be easy often seem, for all intents and purposes, already to have been completed. Leaving the instructions about knowing oneself vague and underdeveloped might have the salutary effect of encouraging some rigorous preparatory interpretative work, which work might itself prepare a person for acquiring self-knowledge.

So it may be expected that Socrates never summarizes or paraphrases his overall insights into self-knowledge, and that he has good reasons for not doing so. It is counter to that wisdom, then, that I paraphrase the view of self-knowledge I believe the texts suggest. But I am not Socrates, and do not imagine I will lead a reader to self-knowledge. For the sake of exposition I offer that Socratic self-knowledge has three faces: a metaphysical, an epistemic, and a practical face. But I do not insist on this classification. I fear that any sharp differentiation would betray the Socratic insight, beyond the obvious problem of importing technical categorization foreign to Socrates' intellectual creativity and holism.

The metaphysical thesis is that Socratic self-knowledge is self-constitution. This means that Socratic self-knowledge is not merely observatory or introspective, not merely an accounting of certain internal elements. While it may involve perception or attention, it also involves practical and determinative work. In responding to the call to know oneself, the respondent defines and endeavors to become a certain kind of self. The effort to know oneself is not simply a matter of struggling to know something that already exists, though the process does include remembering and recalling. This effort comprises, too, the making of oneself into the right sort of thing, namely a thing that happens to be susceptible or obedient to knowledge. Because self-constitution requires deciding what sort of person to become, it is normative, dependent on judgments of what is best. Because self-constitution requires becoming that sort of person, it is personal and engaged, dependent on work on one's particular beliefs, desires, and skills. So self-constitution takes a dual focus, on the general or ideal, on the one hand, and on the particular or factual, on the other. It develops certain judgments, for example about the way to unify oneself and the best ways to be, and it makes certain observations, for example about one's goals, realms of understanding, and competencies. It is not a single finely individuated intentional attitude.

The epistemic thesis, really just a reformulation of the metaphysical thesis, is that Socratic self-knowledge is knowledge to the extent that the self becomes a proper object of knowledge. In the Platonic conception – and perhaps his conception merely articulates or extends most common Greek conceptions – we know only stable and perspicuous objects. Thus coming to know oneself requires becoming more stable and perspicuous. The ideal of self-knowledge therefore involves the ideal of stabilization and clarification of oneself.[9]

Half the practical thesis is that Socratic self-knowledge comes about especially in conversation with other people. The other half is that knowing oneself is akin to, even continuous with, knowing someone else. Knowing someone else is a skillful achievement, one that takes self-application and self-work. Knowing oneself operates on a similar model. Socrates, at the end of his long speech in Plato's *Phaedrus*, urges his friend to dedicate his life single-mindedly to "love accompanied by philosophical talk," and this wish is Socrates' articulation of the practical thesis. The relation between the two halves – that self-knowledge comes about through conversation with others, and that self-knowledge is akin to knowledge of others – is explained specifically by the account of self-constitution.

Taking these theses together, this book argues that Socratic self-knowledge means working on oneself, with others, to become the sort of person who could know himself, and thus be responsible to the world, to others, and to oneself, intellectually, morally, and practically.

Witnesses to the historical Socrates' interest in the "Know yourself"

The historical record shows that Socrates in fact concerned himself with the Delphic injunction *gnôthi sauton*. Many readers assume that his radical revision of Greek moral and human concepts would have led him to understand the charge differently than others did,

[9] This thesis is anticipated by McCabe 1994, esp. 267–269, and Gerson 2003, esp. 46, though both authors focus on *Phaedo* and *Republic*, and Gerson argues, focusing on Plato, that this ideal is achieved only in a disembodied state.

placing a so-called "philosophical" spin on what had previously been either homespun or religious. In this section I canvass the evidence for the historical Socrates' interest in the precept. We get only hints of that interest's texture. In the two sections following this one I canvass the evidence for a pre-Socratic meaning or understanding of the precept, both in its use as Sage wisdom and in its inscription at the Temple of Apollo at Delphi. Only with this evidence could we even attempt to argue for Socrates' innovation. But the evidence does not bear out this claim to innovation. It in fact shows mainly that the Greeks saw knowing oneself as a profound, deceptively difficult, and self-revising practice. They recognized that the precept did not have a wholly transparent meaning, and that the precept demands interpretation and glossing before one might follow it. Socrates' deployment of the precept in his conversations very much follows this earlier culture of *gnôthi sauton* veneration and scrutiny. Of course, this continuity is tenuous, since little substantive reflection on the *gnôthi sauton* predates the Socratic period. But this brings us to the same point. The interpretation of Socratic self-knowledge must come largely from the Socratic literature itself. It cannot be determined simply by contrast with prevailing interpretations.

Aristotle wrote that the Delphic "Know yourself" set the tune for Socrates' "perplexity and search into it" (τὸ γνῶθι σαυτόν ὃ δὴ καὶ Σωκράτει <τῆς> ἀπορίας καὶ ζητήσεως ταύτης ἀρχὴν ἐνέδωκεν).[10] Aristotle

[10] *On Philosophy* fr. 1 Ross. For ἐνδίδωμι as "set the tune" (rather than simply "set in"), see LSJ s.v. ἐνδίδωμι A.VI and Aristotle *Rhetoric* 1414b20–27: "The exordium is the beginning of a speech, as the prologue in poetry and the prelude in flute-playing; for all these are beginnings (ἀρχαί), and as it were a paving the way for what follows (ὁδοποίησις τῷ ἐπιόντι). The prelude resembles the exordium of epideictic speeches; for as flute-players begin by playing whatever they can execute skillfully (εὖ ἔχωσιν) and attach it to the key-note (συνῆψαν τῷ ἐνδοσίμῳ), so also in epideictic speeches should be the composition of the exordium; the speaker should say at once whatever he likes, give the key-note (ἐνδοῦναι) and then attach the main subject" (tr. Freese 1926). The "it" (ταύτης) surely refers to Socrates' "perplexity" (ἀπορία) rather than to the "beginning" (ἀρχή) of the search: it would be odd to say that the *gnôthi sauton* set the tune for a search into the beginning of that very search, but quite plausible to say that it puzzled Socrates and gave him reasons – given its charge to "know yourself" – to make sense of (rather than to disregard) that puzzlement. Ross 1952: 78, translates accurately but with, to my ear, morose darkness: "induced in Socrates this mood of uncertainty and questioning." Guthrie 1971: 151n1, is misleading when he writes that Aristotle is "saying that it [*sc.* the Delphic precept] was the starting point of Socrates' inquiries

claims that the *gnôthi sauton* did more than introduce Socrates to a life of puzzlement, about self-knowledge at first but then about much else besides. He claims that the inscription provided the tenor for Socrates' overall puzzlement, and the tenor for the methods Socrates took to resolve it. What is this puzzlement, and what is this search? Elsewhere Aristotle identifies Socrates as noteworthy for his inquiries into the ethical life, good character, and the best ways to talk about them.[11] For Aristotle, then, Socrates' puzzlement may be about just those matters: ethics, character, and conversation. Aristotle claims that Socrates' response to the Delphic inscription "Know yourself" colored or inflected all this work. Aristotle's comment might seem bold, an incisive intellectual biography in a half-dozen words. Yet we might cede Aristotle the grounds for making it. He began his own ethical works in meditation on a temple inscription.[12] He collected precepts and maxims.[13] He wrote in particular about the origins of the Delphic inscription, and believed that Socrates visited Delphi.[14] These last facts, incidentally, give reason to think that Aristotle's judgment about Socrates came not solely through Plato's dialogues, given that Plato does not mention any visit to Delphi.[15] That Aristotle's dialogue *On Philosophy* appears to have a historical and factual character gives further reason to think that Aristotle's evidence is more than purely literary.[16] All the same, we know so little about Aristotle's specific

into the nature of man. (ἀπορίας ταύτης there [*sc.* in the passage] refers to the question τί ἄνθρωπός ἐστι, though this is not made clear by the passage as printed [by Rose or Ross])": Guthrie's "the nature of man" is really more determinate than the passage, even with the Plutarchian context, allows.

11 *Metaphysics* 987b1 (τὰ ἠθικά), 1078b17 (τὰς ἠθικὰς ἀρετάς), *Sophistical Refutations* 183b7.

12 The *Eudemian Ethics* opens with the maxim inscribed on the Temple of Leto at Delos: "The most just is finest; being healthy is best; most pleasant is to achieve one's heart's desire" (*Eudemian Ethics* 1214a7, cf. *Nicomachean Ethics* I.8, 1099a27–28). See Mikalson 2010: 95–101, for the broader context of philosophers' interests in inscriptions and dedications.

13 Searby 1998.

14 *On Philosophy* frr. 2, 3, 5, 8 Ross.

15 Plato appears to deny that Socrates left Athens except on military campaign and, according to most manuscripts, once to the Isthmus (*Crito* 52b, *Phdr.* 230c–e). But Diogenes Laertius reports on Ion of Chios' authority that Socrates visited Samos (DL 2.23), a claim defended by Jacoby 1947: 9–10, and Graham 2008, in particular against Calder 1961, 85, and Woodbury 1971. This suggests that Socrates traveled more than his character in Plato's works implies.

16 On the historical character of the dialogue, see Chroust 1975.

understanding of his philosophical grandfather. We may infer only that Aristotle takes Socrates' intellectual journey to have been both founded on and textured by his response to the *gnôthi sauton*, and that this journey concerned itself most notably with investigating the best way to come to and talk about living well. (Proclus repeats this lore 800 years later: Socrates "began his impulse towards philosophy by coming upon the Pythian inscription and considering it to be the bidding, as it were, of Apollo himself.")[17]

Aristotle comments neutrally about Socrates: he gives an intriguing bit of biographical information but does not explicitly endorse Socrates' attitude toward investigation.[18] Our source for Aristotle's comment, however, treats the mere association of Socrates with the *gnôthi sauton* as an endorsement of "knowing oneself." Plutarch is defending his philosophical commitments, and thereby his forebears, against the harsh charges of the Epicurean Colotes (*c.* 320–after 268). Colotes has claimed that Socrates investigates absurd and trivial matters (*Against Colotes* 1118c). He has laughed at Socrates for "seeking out what a human is" (ζητοῦντα τί ἄνθρωπος ἐστι) and for "brashly asserting that he does not know it" (νεανιευόμενον ... ὅτι μηδ' αὐτὸς [αὑτὸν] εἰδείη).[19] Plutarch does not cite Colotes' sources. We might at first suppose that he has read Plato's *Phaedrus*, *Theaetetus*, or *Apology*, but in none of these does Socrates explicitly claim that he seeks out the nature of man and yet does not know it. In any event, Plutarch does not impugn Colotes' fidelity to his sources, or the sources themselves. He makes three other responses.

Plutarch's first response is to argue in several ways for the importance of self-knowledge. Heraclitus presents his having "sought out myself" (fr. 101 DK) as some grand and somnolent (μέγα τι καὶ σέμνον) achievement. Plutarch then relies on his own status as high priest at Delphi to observe that the *gnôthi sauton* "seems the most divine" (θειότατον ἐδόκει) of the Delphic inscriptions. He mentions Aristotle's comment about the centrality of the *gnôthi sauton* to Socrates. He later adds that one could hardly hope to gain knowledge of anything else were

[17] Proclus, *Commentary on Alcibiades I*, 5–6, tr. O'Neill 1971.

[18] Matthews 2003 argues that Aristotle came to value perplexity in philosophy differently than Socrates did. Lear 1988 argues that Aristotle's philosophy culminates in a kind of self-knowledge.

[19] This text, proposed by Pohlenz, is from Einarson and De Lacy 1967, followed by Kechagia 2011: 300.

he to avoid gaining knowledge of the most important aspects of himself. Plutarch's second response is to reveal the preexisting Epicurean commitment to the investigation of human nature, and thereby to charge Colotes with hypocrisy or crass ignorance. Plutarch notes that Epicurus writes and talks about the "being of soul and the origins of the human race" (περὶ οὐσίας ψυχῆς καὶ τοῦ ἀθρόου τῆς καταρχῆς). Since the soul is the most authoritative principle of the human, a search into the soul amounts to a search into human nature. So Epicureans must themselves value seeking out what a human is. Plutarch's third response is to point out that Colotes should have recognized the difficulty in seeking out the nature of soul. His Epicureans claim that the material of soul is something hot, breathy, and airy, but when it comes to accounting for its functions, that by which it "judges, remembers, loves, hates – how, in sum, it reasons and calculates," they plead that there is no name for it. No doubt this may be so, but their silence shows their confusion, and thus the ubiquitous challenge for all those seeking to discover the nature of the soul, and by extension, what a human is.

Plutarch concludes, contra Colotes, that Socrates should seek himself (ζητῶν ἑαυτόν), that Colotes' philosophical commitments entail his accepting the value in doing so, and that there should be no surprise if Socrates claimed not yet to have finished the task. Of course, Plutarch's argument rings strongly forensic. He conflates, without argument, knowing what a human is with knowing oneself and knowing the material basis of the soul. But the confidence and urgency of his responses to Colotes, and more importantly Colotes' focused choice of charges, show that the search for self-knowledge had become emblematic of Socrates.[20]

Both Aristotle and Colotes came of age decades after Socrates' death, and so they may have come to know of him, and his supposed commitment to following the *gnôthi sauton*, only through the prisms of the Socratic circle's reports – and those of its opponents. But one witness to Socrates' interest in self-knowledge could have known him directly, sharing nearly thirty years of an Athenian adulthood with him.

[20] On the Epicureans' particular interest in Socratic self-knowledge, see Riley 1980; Kleve 1983; Long 1988; Brouwer 2008. On Colotes' use of Socratic ignorance to settle contemporary scores, see Vander Waerdt 1989: 253–259; Ioppolo 1995, 98–106; Warren 2002.

This is Aristophanes (*c.* 446–*c.* 386). His *Clouds* appears to show that Socrates characteristically bandied about the precept "know yourself." The play's protagonist, Strepsiades, proves an indifferent student but an effective mimic. He fails to learn Socrates' lessons but remembers Socrates' words well. This is apparent when Strepsiades tries to convince his son to take his place at Socrates' school, the *phrontisterion*. Over several dozen lines he repeatedly parrots Socrates' language, to comic effect: he appeals to Fog and Whirl, scorns traditional beliefs in Zeus, laughs at archaic thought, announces that he has secret new thoughts, and vaunts the value of education.[21] Pheidippides calls his father out for such unfamiliar language, and asks from whom he got it.[22] Strepsiades admits he gets his terms from Socrates (830), a man he says he holds worthy of respect despite his peculiarities (833–837). Pheidippides asks, "What would someone even usefully learn from those people?" (840), meaning Socrates and the school's co-director Chaerephon. Strepsiades responds:

> Seriously? However much wisdom (σοφά) people have. And you'll know yourself, how unlearned and thick you are (γνώσει δὲ σαυτόν ὡς ἀμαθὴς εἶ καὶ παχύς). (841–842)

Strepsiades goes on to echo Socrates' grammatical training and show off his Socratic-style dress (847–859). Then Socrates enters, and, with some hesitation, accepts Pheidippides' discipleship.

Most of Strepsiades' lines in the passage 814–859 exactly repeat Socrates' remarks earlier in the play. Even his remarks about wisdom (σοφά) and the content of the self-knowledge (ὡς ἀμαθὴς εἶ καὶ παχύς) echo Socrates. Socrates tells Strepsiades to attend closely "whenever I toss up something wise" (ὅταν τι προβάλωμαι σοφόν, 489), and when Strepsiades balks, Socrates says that "this man here is unlearned and barbaric" (ἄνθρωπος ἀμαθὴς οὑτοσὶ καὶ βάρβαρος, 492). Only one phrase does not explicitly repeat something Socrates has said: that being with Socrates will bring Pheidippides to know himself (γνώσει

[21] Oaths to meteorology: 814, 828, echoing 264–266, 269, 291, 380, 424, 627; scorning Zeus: 818–827, echoing 247–248, 252, 365–367, 380, 423; ridiculing archaic thought: 821, echoing 238 with 137; new secret thoughts: 824, echoing 258 with 140, 143; value of education: 822, 826, echoing 369. Lineation and text is from Dover 1968.

[22] 816–817, 829, 832–833, 840, 844–846.

δὲ σαυτόν). The fact that this phrase is new draws attention to it; the fact that everything else Strepsiades says repeats Socrates suggests that even this repeats him, either his real or his imagined off-stage person.[23] Aristophanes thereby seems to associate the advice to gain self-knowledge with Socrates. He may even be associating the precept *gnôthi sauton*, as so worded, with Socrates. Strepsiades' dig at his son's education does not, after all, grammatically require the reflexive pronoun σαυτόν ("yourself"), since the verb γνώσει ("you will know") can take the indirect question "how ignorant and thick you are" alone. This passage may therefore represent the earliest attribution of the *gnôthi sauton* to Socrates.[24]

Beyond attribution of the precept to Socrates' characteristic mode of talking, we might find a hint of a gloss on the Socratic use of the precept. Strepsiades' insult to his son, that he will come to recognize the extent to which he has not learned (ἀμαθής), and cannot readily learn (παχύς), gives important content to the *gnôthi sauton* as Strepsiades attributes it to Socrates. He does not say that Pheidippides will learn that he is mortal, or that he has some position in the cosmic order, or that he must take divinity more seriously.[25] Instead, Strepsiades says that Pheidippides will come to assess two central and related aspects of himself: his education and his educability. Strepsiades' harshly negative evaluative language implies that his son will learn more than mere facts at Socrates' school. He will realize that he is badly off in these two ways. When he realizes that he is badly off, he will seek to rectify his imperfections; this is implied by Strepsiades'

[23] Perhaps Strepsiades does echo Socratic speech as viewers of the *Clouds* hear it, since forms of αὐτός and reflexive pronouns are associated with Socrates. Socrates is introduced as αὐτός, and Strepsiades asks, τίς αὐτός; (219). Just earlier, Socrates' student refers to the *prôktoi* of Socrates' other students studying astronomy αὐτὸς καθ' αὑτόν (194). See Havelock 1972: 10–14, on reflexives in this play.

[24] Scholars sharing the view that this passage alludes to the *gnôthi sauton*, but without making the argument I have made, include Taylor 1911: 172; Wilkins 1917: 102; Havelock 1972: 14n38; Denyer 2001: 191; Jeremiah 2012: 188. The discussion of the *gnôthi sauton* in Tortzen 2002 does not mention this instance of it.

[25] On these views of the meaning of the *gnôthi sauton*, see, e.g., Wilkins 1917: 12–22, and 1929: 1–10, 49–68; Nilsson 1948: 47, 55; Defradas 1954: 269; Courcelle 1974: I, 12; Burkert 1981: 148; Tränkle 1985: 23; these will be discussed more below.

(admittedly self-interested) hopefulness about his son's coming to learn to speak (859–887). Coming to know oneself is evaluative, and so includes wanting to improve oneself. Strepsiades articulates Socratic self-knowledge in the negative terms that Plato's *Apology of Socrates* characterizes as knowledge of ignorance (21b4–5, d6, 22d1). There, Plato's Socrates expresses gladness that while he lacks the wisdom of craftsmen, he also lacks their unlearnedness (μήτε τι σοφὸς ὢν τὴν ἐκείνων σοφίαν μήτε ἀμαθὴς τὴν ἀμαθίαν, 22e3–4), and so he keeps going around asking people questions about virtue. Here, Strepsiades' claim that Pheidippides may learn "however much wisdom people have" (ὅσαπέρ ἐστιν ἀνθρώποις σοφά) parallels the Platonic Socrates' observation that he has discovered himself to have at most a "human wisdom" (ἀνθρωπίνη σοφία, *Apol.* 20d8), where this wisdom prompts continued self-improvement. "Wisdom" (σοφία) in the *Clouds* usually means thoughtfulness (Aristophanes' playwrighting: 522; Nestor and his ilk: 1057), good judgment (the primary trait of the audience: 520, 526, 535, 575, 899), and intellectual success (the primary trait of members of the *phrontisterion*: 94, 1202, 1207; Euripides and other poets: 1370, 1378).[26] Aristophanes' Socrates urges a self-knowledge that recognizes the distance between one's ideal and one's present position, and that motivates self-improvement toward that ideal.[27]

This interpretation of the "Know yourself" may seem castles in the sky given Aristophanes' parodic goals. But it is hard to see what besides historical reality would explain Aristophanes' attribution to Socrates a characteristic interest in "knowing oneself." It certainly seems possible for Aristophanes to have noticed such an interest. And as we have seen, Plato and Xenophon develop this interest in their literary dialogues, Aristotle cites Socrates' engagement with it as significant to the history of philosophy, and Colotes treats it as emblematic of Socrates' intellectual obscurantism.

The Socratic commitment to self-knowledge is not surprising; many readers of ancient philosophy have taken Socrates to have vaunted the Delphic precept. The background conditions of that interest have occupied far fewer readers. To those we now turn.

[26] Only on two occasions does it mean mere "cleverness" (764 with 773, 895).
[27] The three previous paragraphs follow §§2–3 of Moore 2015b.

The earliest witnesses to the challenge "Know yourself"

Ion of Chios (*c*. 480–*c*. 421) cites the *gnôthi sauton* as a popular saying in one of his tragedies.[28] That he likely knew Socrates well might disqualify him as an impartial witness to its meaning.[29] All the same, he provides the earliest extant explicit reference to it.

> This "know yourself" is a saying not so big, but such a task Zeus alone of the gods understands (τὸ γνῶθι σαυτὸν τοῦτ᾽ ἔπος μὲν οὐ μέγα | ἔργον δ᾽ ὅσον Ζεὺς μόνος ἐπίσταται θεῶν). (Fr. 55 *TrGF* = Plut. *Dem*. 3.2, *Cons. ad. Apoll*. 116d)

In following Snell's *TrGF* (1971), I print the version found twice in Plutarch. There are also two later and alternative formulations, both from commentaries on Plato's *Alcibiades* 129a, with material consequences for our interpretation of the tragic fragment. Olympiodorus quotes it this way: "This 'know yourself' is not so big in its words, but in its practice Zeus alone of the gods understands" (τὸ γνῶθι σαυτὸν ἐν λόγοις οὐδὲν μέγα, | ἔργῳ μόνος δὲ Ζεὺς ἐπίσταται θεῶν, *In Alc*. 129a). An anonymous scholar quotes it with a modified second line: "but in its practice only god understands it" (ἔργῳ δὲ μόνος τοῦτ᾽ ἐπίσταται θεός, scholion on Plato's *Alcibiades* 129a).

Translators have often translated ἐπίσταται as "knows how" rather than "understands" (as I have above) and so produce "only Zeus among the gods knows how to do it."[30] Their translation implies that Zeus, though not the other gods, knows *how* to know himself. This is a strange interpretation, given that nearly everywhere else in Greek literature knowing oneself is a human action. The exception, discussed more below, is Prometheus, but it is an exception that proves the rule. In the relevant play, Prometheus, who is told to know himself, has already been displaced by a god and restrained by strength and might. We might think that the fact that literature does not record gods being told to know themselves means only that they do not need to be told it; they already know everything. According to Solon, for example, Zeus gets the knowledge of humans that would count for themselves as self-knowledge, namely, looking into and revealing their

[28] On his dates see Jacoby 1947; Ion death precedes Aristophanes' *Peace* of 421 BC, per 832–835; and his first tragedy was either 452 or 448.

[29] Jacoby 1947: 11; Fletcher 2007; Graham 2008.

[30] Gagarin and Woodruff 1995: 74, and similarly Denyer 2001: 211.

hearts (θυμός, fr. 13.27–28 West, cf. ἐκφάνειν νόον, fr. 34.3 West); by contrast, humans tend toward self-ignorance (fr. 13.33–42) and fail to apprehend (νόησαι) the unseen measure of reflectiveness (γνωμοσύνης) (fr. 16).[31] But if Zeus already knew himself, it would be pointless to say that he knew *how* to know himself. A more difficult problem with this interpretation of επίσταται as "knows how" is that it excludes all gods but Zeus from knowing themselves, and yet it is unclear what could possibly stop most but not all gods from knowing themselves.[32]

So since no infinitive verb follows ἐπίσταται, I take it to mean "understand," in the sense of "comprehend" or "appreciate."[33] Thus the reference to Zeus serves only to underline the difficulty of knowing oneself: nobody recognizes how difficult it is but for the greatest of all beings. So much for the second line. The first line notes the popularity of the precept. The suggestion is that the maxim is often used or taken lightly – too lightly. Sure, it is only a few words, not some grand pedagogical pronouncement; and probably some people think it can be accomplished with little difficulty. But in truth it is a big deal. It is not easy to know oneself. Indeed, it is an extraordinary project to take on. This passage does not let us speculate on the content of these two interpretations of the precept, the popular "easy" reading and the oft-forgotten "difficult" reading. We can thus make only several conclusions. First, the character speaking in Ion's tragedy, whoever he or she was, acknowledged two opposed readings; second, something about self-knowledge proves very troublesome; and third, self-knowledge probably ought to be sought, despite the obstacles we find before it. Fourth, by the date of this play, certainly before 421, the precept *gnôthi sauton* had become an item for reflection on the stage, and thus in the intellectual milieu. Indeed, in Plato's *Protagoras*, set around 440 BC, Socrates says that the precept is "repeated by everyone" (πάντες ὑμνοῦσι, 343b3).[34]

Statements about the great task and significance that obeying the *gnôthi sauton* involves came at some point to be attributed to

[31] See Owens 2010: 196–199 and Long 2009.

[32] Tortzen 2002: 2–3, translates "but it is a task which Zeus is the only god to undertake" and unconvincingly argues that the saying does not refer to the Delphic inscription.

[33] Cf. LSJ s.v. II.

[34] On the date of the *Protagoras*, see Wolfsdorf 1997; 2008, 66.

the sixth-century Sages.[35] Late sources record that Thales, Chilon, and Pythagoreans stated that self-knowledge is the hard thing to get.[36] We cannot recover whether those men ever really made those claims, or whether they were the first to do so. In fact, the earliest accounts explicitly linking the *gnôthi sauton* to Sages or other mortals come not until Plato, a century and a half later. In the *Protagoras*, Socrates calls the precept *gnôthi sauton* one of the "first fruits" of Sage wisdom (ἀπαρχήν, 343b1), and interprets Simonides' song to Scopas, the one that references Pittacus' claim about the difficulty of being good, as part of the competitive traffic in Sage wisdom.[37] In the Platonic *Hipparchus*, Hipparchus (d. 514), a contemporary of Simonides' (556–468), competes with the imagined authors of the *gnôthi sauton* and other chief precepts for educational relevance, ordering that his own precepts be inscribed around Athens (228e1–229b1; this dialogue will be discussed in this book's Conclusion). As noted above, Aristotle and his students tried to get clear about the origins of the Delphic inscriptions. In the generations following, studies of the *gnôthi sauton* became remarkably popular; but these studies are now lost, and so too any hope of establishing the date by which popular or elite culture attributed this precept to the Sages.

Fortunately one early reference to knowing oneself might support a sagely provenance of the precept by the end of the sixth century. Stobaeus cites Heraclitus, who died early in the fifth century, to have written a fragment on self-knowledge:

> All people have a share in knowing themselves and being sound-minded (ἀνθρώποισι πᾶσι μέτεστι γινώσκειν ἑωυτοὺς καὶ σωφρονεῖν). (*Flor.* 3.5.6 = 116 DK)

This fragment has often been athetized since Schleiermacher, usually on the grounds that the wording is more Socratic than Heraclitean.[38]

[35] On the Sages see Tell 2010; Kurke 2011.

[36] Thales: DL 1.36 (δύσκολον), Suda s.v. Θαλῆς = θ 17; Chilon: DS 9.10.1, Suda s.v. γνῶθι σαυτόν = γ 333; Pythagoreans: Iamblichus, *Life of Pythagoras*, 18.83 (τὸ χαλεπώτατον).

[37] See Moore 2015a on this passage.

[38] E.g., Heidel 1913: 714; Kirk 1962: 390; Marcovich 1967: 88–96; Pradeau 2002: 271; and more cautiously, Bywater 1877; Dilcher 1995: 21n30.

But these grounds are poor, and more recent work accepts the fragment.[39] Heraclitus may very well allude to the *gnôthi sauton* precept; his interest in self-knowledge is usually accepted on the strength of his "I searched out myself" (ἐδιζησάμην ἐμεωυτόν, fr. 101 DK).[40] We need only interpret his claim as being simultaneously straightforward and ironic, as befits Heraclitus.[41] On the one hand, fragment 1/6 seems to be saying that people actually can obey the imperative, thanks to their human capacity. On the other hand, it seems to charge that they probably overestimate their facility to do so, and such overestimation blocks the serious and challenging effort to achieve genuine self-knowledge.[42] Supporting this interpretation is the ambiguity of μέτεστι, which can mean both "possess actually" and "have a right to."[43] This ambiguity allows the fragment to allude both to the easy and to the difficult senses of "knowing yourself," and thus even to the popular Sage precept.[44] It is worth noting that Heraclitus here draws a connection between knowing oneself and exercising *sôphrosunê*. He elsewhere treats *sôphrosunê* as deeply important to human life: "to exercise *sôphrosunê* is the greatest virtue and wisdom, to speak and act truly, perceiving according to nature" (σωφρονεῖν ἀρετὴ μεγίστη καὶ σοφίη ἀληθέα λέγειν καὶ ποιεῖν κατὰ φύσιν ἐπαίοντας).[45] This connection is discussed below.

The only other use of the phrase "know yourself" before Socratic literature is from the middle of the fifth century. It is in the *Prometheus Bound*, sometimes attributed to Aeschylus and dated between 456 and 424.[46] Oceanus has come to visit Prometheus, who is fettered to the mountain, and says that he wants to be helpful (284–297), and that having seen Prometheus' punishments, he wishes – with all due respect

39 E.g, Bollack and Wismann 1972; Barnes 1982: 57; Robinson 1987; Tonelli 1993; McKirahan 1994; Mouraviev 1999; Graham 2010: 146–147.

40 The meaning of this fragment is debated; Robinson 1987: 147, summarizes five possible interpretations.

41 Kahn 1979: 6–8, 89–95; Mackenzie 1988a.

42 This latter observation is also made by Gerson 2003: 31.

43 LSJ s.v. II. See Dilcher 1995: 21.

44 Granger 2004: 7–10 (despite 13–14), suggests without this argument that Heraclitus would have been deeply influenced by the wisdom of the Seven Sages.

45 See Kahn 1979: 116–123.

46 For cautious and condensed remarks on authenticity, see Conacher 1980: 141–174 and Podlecki 2005: 195–200. Aristophanes' *Knights* (424 BC) alludes to the play; Mt Aetna erupted in 479 or 475 (alluded to at 363–372).

to Prometheus' wide-ranging mind (ποικίλῳ) – to give him advice (παραινέσαι, 307). He starts:

Know yourself and adopt new | habits: for there is even a new leader among the gods (γίγνωσκε σαυτὸν καὶ μεθάρμοσαι[47] τρόπους | νέους: νέος γὰρ καὶ τύραννος ἐν θεοῖς). (309–310)

Oceanus does not stop here, which he might had "knowing yourself" implied something obvious even to Prometheus. Instead, he glosses his remark over the next seventy lines.[48] This suggests that he takes it to be a common but in fact not so easily understood precept.

The first piece of explanation follows what may be an explanatory καί: "adopt new habits." This verb, μεθαρμόζω, appears only several other times in tragedy. Near the beginning of Sophocles' *Electra*, Orestes, having just heard from the Delphic Oracle, tells his tutor to "set aright" his plan, in case he has misinterpreted the Oracle (31). In Euripides' *Alcestis*, Admetus cheers that his and his wife's lives are now set aright (1157). Oceanus thus develops the idea of knowing oneself in terms of remaking oneself – one's "turn" or "character" (τρόπους) – for the better. Recent events demand that Prometheus reorganize how he lives. This "fix yourself up" reading is supported by another point: because Prometheus is himself a god, Oceanus cannot be telling him to recognize his humanity.[49] He is being told, as we

47 Most MSS have the verb in active voice, μεθάρμοσον, which would mean "correct your new habits," but Page 1972 prints the middle voice, presumably because Prometheus does not yet have new habits. Either way, the focus is on the adjective νέος.

48 Contra Tortzen 2002: 3, who thinks that Oceanus' remark is a simple proverb, even an idiomatic phrase with the most mundane sense of "look at yourself," and Denyer 2001: 191: "when the maxim is addressed to Prometheus, it is immediately glossed as enjoining him to get used to the fact that there is a new and powerful rule of the gods." Irby-Massie 2008: 134, takes it to echo both the Delphic inscription and Heraclitus' fr. 101, but does not develop the thought, and in fact focuses on the theme of inquiry-into-nature rather than self-inquiry. Long 1958: 236, 250–252, notes the Delphic resonances here, especially in light of the play's double reference to μηδὲν ἄγαν (72, 327) and "platitudes" (ἀρχαι', 317), and Prometheus' oracular speech.

49 Podlecki 2005 ad loc. recognizes a paradox but with uncertain effect: "*come to know yourself* seems intended to echo the Delphic maxim, where it implies, 'become aware of your human limitations' (but Prom. is precisely and self-avowedly *not* human) ... On Okeanos's lips this and the following line ring platitudinous, and therefore hollow." Podlecki 1969 made clearer the ways in which Prometheus fails to know himself despite thinking he does.

would say, to get his act together. The inchoative γίγνωσκε suggests the long and ongoing process this would require.[50] As Oceanus' speech continues, he emphasizes that Prometheus' speech outruns what is appropriate. He warns against Prometheus' "hurling harsh and sharpened words" (311), his "excessively high-speaking tongue" (318–319) and his "vain tongue" (329). He tells Prometheus to "be quiet and not [to] talk excessively boldly" (327), and to "expunge (ἄφες) what passions (ὀργάς) you have" (315). Thus Oceanus treats "knowing oneself" as curtailing inaccurate and irresponsible talk, and as, in effect, unifying one's actions and desires by ceasing some and eradicating others. Oceanus observes that Prometheus makes statements inconsistent with his current situation.

Prometheus responds unhappily, asking Oceanus to leave him alone, and telling him that any overtures to Zeus on his behalf would be wasted; Oceanus should simply watch out for himself (σοι μελησάτω … πάπταινε δ'αὐτός, 330–334). In response, Oceanus apparently reiterates his very first advice: "you made your neighbors thoughtful much better than you did yourself" (πολλῷ γ' ἀμείνων τοὺς πέλας φρενοῦν ἔφυς | ἢ σαυτόν, 335–336). That this observation effectively reiterates the γίγνωσκε σαυτόν is suggested by its position again as first remark of this speech and by the duplication of the second-person reflexive pronoun. It suggests that "knowing oneself" involves making oneself thoughtful. Knowing oneself must be active, practical, rational, and constructive.

The remainder of Prometheus' exchange with Oceanus continues in the same vein. Prometheus tells Oceanus that there is nothing he can do to help (340–376). Twice Prometheus uses the second-person reflexive pronoun, as though to recall Oceanus' double use: "calm *yourself* and get out of the way" (ἀλλ' ἡσύχαζε σαυτὸν ἐκποδὼν ἔχων, 344), and "save *yourself* in whatever way you know how" (σεαυτὸν σῷζ' ὅπως ἐπίστασαι, 374). The second use appears to echo the *gnôthi sauton*.[51] Remarkably, after this long speech, Oceanus' first words once again echo the γίγνωσκε σαυτόν, both in language and in their emphasis on language and self-transformation. At the beginning of a gnome-rich stichomythia, Oceanus begins: "Thus, Prometheus, don't you recognize (γίγνώσκεις) that words are doctors of an ill anger?" (377).

[50] Scott 1981 ad loc.; Long 1958: 250 translates "endeavor to know thyself."

[51] Long 1958: 252–253, also notes these frequent echoes of line 309.

Between his two requests that Oceanus stay away, Prometheus cites a particular reason for leaving him alone: Oceanus risks bearing collateral damage. That Oceanus, whether despite or because of his sympathy, faces risk, Prometheus reasons from analogy, first from his brother Atlas and second from the famous Typhon, an early adversary of Zeus.

> That child of earth too, inhabitant of Cilician caves, hostile, monstrous (δάιον τέρας), with a hundred heads – I saw and pitied him as he was violently overcome – Typhon furious for war, who stood against all the gods, hissing terror with dreadful jaws ... intent on the violent ruin of tyranny. Zeus' unsleeping bolt came to him ...; it hit him out of his lofty boastings (ὅς αὐτὸν ἐξέπληξε τῶν ὑψηγόρων κομπασμάτων); he was struck to the very heart of his being (φρένας ... εἰς αὐτάς) ... Useless now ... his body lies ... crushed beneath the roots of Etna ... from which rivers of fire will one day erupt to devour the broad fields of fertile Sicily with savage jaws: such is the anger (χόλον) Typhon will send boiling upward in red-hot bolts of blasting fire, a storm none may approach. (351–371, tr. Collard 2009)

Typhon parallels an unreconstructed Prometheus: standing against Zeus, boasting loftily, body fettered to earth, still seething in anger. Typhon lacks control over his fate, and this causes turmoil to those around him.[52] Prometheus wonders whether he too lacks self-control. The play shows later that he does have some control, thanks to his partial foreknowledge of Zeus' future. But here he shows that he worries that he might never come to know himself and harmonize himself to the new order. As it turns out, Typhon as an emblem of the failure to know oneself returns in the Socratic literature.

The *gnôthi sauton* appears before Socratic literature, then, only in the work of Ion of Chios, Heraclitus, and the author of the *Prometheus Bound*. A full study of the theme itself would have to include Sophocles' *Oedipus Tyrannos*. But this play does not cite the maxim as precisely as these others do; at least, it does not use a reflexive pronoun. So I will make only the briefest of remarks. Jocasta says to Oedipus, "Oh ill-fated one, may you never come to *know who you are*" (ὦ δύσποτμ', εἴθε μήποτε γνοίης ὃς εἶ, 1069). The king's mother is right, in one way: Oedipus' recognition of his familial identity will reveal his

[52] For more on Typhon/Typhoeus, see Chapter 4.

culpability for patricide and his city's curse, and his incestuous marriage and fatherhood. So distant from his noble self-conception as a leader of integrity and persistence, his realization of this true history might shatter him utterly. Jocasta's wish, as mother and wife, acknowledges that Oedipus' self-constitution may not abide or assimilate such contrary facts; it would be better for him to remain in ignorance. But in her warning against self-knowledge she is also wrong. Oedipus' failure to recognize his over-confidence, his shaky reliance on cleverness, and his irascibility are themselves partly responsible for his bad end. In other words, while self-knowledge in a biological-legal sense could be irreparably damaging, self-knowledge as the recognition of Oedipus' commitments and goals could be beneficial. The progression of the play dramatizes the way these two images of self-knowledge cut against each other.[53]

Socrates may have been an adult when each of these other works – excepting Heraclitus' book – were publicly performed, and even Heraclitus' book he says he read (DL 2.22). Thus the texts above reveal the milieu into which the historical Socrates' thinking about self-knowledge came about, and eventually even that of his students and the writers of Socratic literature. It is worth repeating the patterns found among those texts. The saying "Know yourself" must have had some sufficiently common casual sense but simultaneously a lining of more profound meaning, a lining which prompted reflection and warning. Heraclitus and Oceanus connected it to *sôphrosunê* and control over one's beliefs and actions. Ion, the Sages, and Prometheus treat it as profoundly difficult or at least a grand task hardly undertaken lightly.

As we have seen, none of these earliest references to the *gnôthi sauton* have linked it explicitly to Delphi. Yet the Socratic texts often do. Because these earliest non-Socratic references to the precept usually go unremarked when scholars aim to make sense of Socratic self-knowledge, the meaning of the precept is usually evidenced instead from its supposed Delphic provenance. The Apolline Delphic meaning

[53] On the theme of avoiding self-knowledge see Aristotle's example of its ironic deployment, *Rhetoric* 1395a18–35. See Kaufmann 1979: 102–135; and Jeremiah 2012: 148, for a range of interpretations of the *Oedipus* connected to self-knowledge, though not the present one. Thein 2011: 172–175, discusses the Sphinx's riddle of man in the context of the *Oedipus* in relation to the *Alcibiades*.

is the one from which Socrates is usually thought to have innovated. So we now turn to the Delphic inscription itself.

The Delphic inscription

Though archaeology does not prove it, literary evidence claims that somewhere at the entrance of the Temple of Apollo to Delphi stood several inscribed maxims, including the *gnôthi sauton*, and an "E." Plutarch, who served as high priest of the Delphic sanctuary, found the meaning of this E most mysterious, and indeed modern scholarship has focused on it over the other inscriptions, for it seems most connected to the cult background of the site.[54] These studies have made mostly incidental remarks about the *gnôthi sauton*, treating it as, for example, an instruction of ritual preparation.[55] But some authors have considered the meaning of the *gnôthi sauton* directly, and have thus taken it to have more than cultic value. Martin Nilsson writes that while the Delphic inscription *gnôthi sauton*, "for us, signifies the need for self-knowledge, for its own time it meant, 'know that you are human and nothing more' ... [and that] an impassable barrier stands between gods and men."[56] Walter Burkert reads it similarly: the injunction, "as has long been recognized, is not intended in a psychological sense or in the existential-philosophical sense of Socrates, but in an anthropological sense: know that you are not a god. An ethics of the human emerges, but it is closer to pessimism than to a programme for human progress."[57] The humbling function of the "Know thyself" is put most vividly by Parke and Wormell in their work on Delphic oracles: "the Greek was all too ready to humanize his deities and stand on easy terms with them. But Delphi, while providing access to the divine, did much to stress its transcendence."[58] We may note similarities between this Apolline meaning and Socrates' views as commonly understood from Plato's *Apology*, and this could seem to support the claim that Socrates came through and out of this tradition, whether breaking with it or simply developing it.

[54] Griffiths 1955 gives the clearest account of the literature.
[55] Roscher 1901: 99; cf. Roscher 1900.
[56] Nilsson 1948: 47, 55; similarly, Defradas 1954: 269; Griffiths 1955: 244.
[57] Burkert 1981: 148; similarly, Courcelle 1974: 12; Tränkle 1985: 23.
[58] Parke and Wormell 1956: 420.

The problem with these views about the meaning of the Delphic *gnôthi sauton* is that they are asserted with inadequate evidence. They follow two lines of reasoning. One is to rely on what historians of religion know about the cults of Apollo, supposing that the inscription's placement on the Temple of Apollo gives it an Apolline imprimatur. The other is to infer from the apparent meaning of other Delphic precepts, of which there were supposedly several proximate – μήδεν ἄγαν ("nothing in excess") and ἐγγύη, πάρα δ' ἄτη ("pledge, and ruin is near") – and, by some historical time, many more in the vicinity. Yet neither actually illuminates the meaning of the *gnôthi sauton*. We know too little about the occasion of its inscription at Delphi, as we may now see.

In Plato's *Protagoras*, Socrates claims that the Seven Sages dedicated the first fruits of their wisdom at Delphi (343b). He says this in the context of imagining that the Spartans practiced philosophy before anyone else, doing so by condensing their ingenuity into brief, baffling statements.[59] This means that Socrates takes the *gnôthi sauton* to capture in the briefest way the prevailing Sage wisdom. Its placement at the Temple of Apollo at Delphi indicates public recognition of its great value.[60] Socrates acknowledges no special Apolline or anti-hubristic meaning. On the contrary, the competition between Sages in the promulgation of wisdom (343c), and the Spartan-philosophical desire to stump listeners, suggests an appreciation of striving.

An interesting variant of this story comes from Plutarch, half a millennium later, in *On Garrulity* 17. He attributes the decision to inscribe the *gnôthi sauton* on the temple to the Amphictyones, the leaders of the sanctuary.[61] Like all Greeks, he says, these leaders admired brevity, and so instead of setting down Homer's *Iliad* and *Odyssey*, or Pindar's paeans, they decided on the most compact of speeches, namely *gnôthi sauton* and its siblings. Plutarch does not mention the authorship of the precepts, but he suggests that the Delphic leaders wanted to

[59] Herodotus states that the Spartan Dieneces was remembered for his brief and memorable sayings (7.226); Aristotle also speaks of a category of Λακωνικὰ ἀποφθέγματα (*Rhet.* 1394b35).

[60] This is the view adopted by Broad 2007: 18 ("lest visitors doubt their arrival at the epicenter of wisdom").

[61] On Plutarch's selective sensitivity to the facts of Delphi, see McInerney 2004; Plutarch called his own Pythian Essays "first fruits" (ἀπαρχάς, *On the E at Delphi* 384e).

display the best products of the Greek mind. After all, Homer's epics are not generally taken to represent the Apolline perspective. Pindar's paeans would certainly reflect the Delphic self-image, and the view that gods may avenge human transgression, but they do not have a primary goal of dissuading people from hubris except in the anodyne way of encouraging peace and justice.[62] It is worth noting that, from a chronological perspective, Plutarch's story could be true. The *gnôthi sauton* would be inscribed after Pindar's earliest paeans and the public admiration of Homer's epics. Pindar wrote his paeans presumably after 500.[63] Hipparchus began public performance of Homer's *Iliad* and *Odyssey* around 520.[64] Both types of works may have been inscribed on stone tablets as dedications at temples.[65] These dates would put the Amphictyones' decision in the early part of the fifth century. This would be compatible with most of our other evidence about the Delphic inscription, as we will see.[66]

In Plato's *Charmides*, Critias tells a story fundamentally different from the *Protagoras*' Socrates' or Plutarch's in *On Garrulity*. Critias claims that the inscriber of the *gnôthi sauton* put the phrase on the Temple not to honor the god or regale visitors with wisdom, but to serve as the god's greeting to visitors. As a greeting, he says, it means *sôphronei* ("be sound-minded/disciplined"). Critias gives this odd gloss without explicit argument and without describing the nature of a greeting; but he does recognize its oddness, a precept being used as a greeting. He admits that the other inscriptions found at Delphi do

[62] On the encouragement of peace and justice, see Rutherford 2001: 37, 82–87; on Pindar's alliance with Delphi, 179; and on the gnomic ending of *Pa.* VIId, reading μάλα πρᾶξον [δι]καίως, "act really justly," 172, 209–210.

[63] See Rutherford 2001: 192, 231, 274, 284, 331, for the range of possible dates for extant paeans.

[64] Plato *Hipparchus* 228d7 and other evidence at Davison 1955: 7; see West 1999 for the explosion of interest in Homer's two epics in the last quarter of the sixth century.

[65] For paeans, see Rutherford 2001: 144, 177; the *Homeric Hymn to Apollo* was displayed in the Delian Temple to Artemis (West 1999: 381–382). It would not be absurd to inscribe parts of the Homeric epics on the Temple of Apollo; the neighboring Athenian Treasury had the complete Athenian laws on it.

[66] A conflict is with the dialogue *Hipparchus*, which has Hipparchus competing with the explicitly "Delphic" *gnôthi sauton* by inscribing his own precepts on roadway herms. Since Hipparchus died in 514, the inscription would have to predate it, though perhaps not by much – if, for example, its recent inscription there incited his competitive desire to inscribe his own herms. The anachronism, at any rate, would be small.

give advice, and specifically distinguishes them in this respect from the *gnôthi sauton*. In fact, he says, the Temple has these advice-giving precepts just because later inscribers mistook the *gnôthi sauton* for a piece of advice. What Critias means to be doing we will pursue at length in Chapter 2. The point relevant here is twofold. First, Greek bafflement about the meaning of the *gnôthi sauton* had reached such a climax by the Socratic period that Critias' analysis, even if ostentatiously iconoclastic, could plausibly contribute to its recovery. Second, and relatedly, even were *gnôthi sauton* really to mean *sôphronei*, the Greeks had no unanimous opinion about the meaning of *sôphronei*. Just in *Charmides* alone, for example, the charge was offered to mean "be calm and collected," "be modest and bashful," "do your own," and "do what is good." A simple consequence of these two points is that Greeks did not construe the *gnôthi sauton* as having an obvious and clear Apolline meaning; otherwise, Critias would have had to make at least a cursory dismissal of it.

Again, Plutarch follows up on the Platonic story. His character Ammonius, in the dialogue *On the E at Delphi* (17.392a) – a text which revels in Greek uncertainty about the origins of the Delphic sayings – calls the *gnôthi sauton* a greeting for those approaching (προσιόντα) the Temple. Ammonius does not cite Critias or Plato, and does not support this interpretation. His silence suggests that Plutarch finds a tincture of plausibility in the account in its own terms. Again, Plutarch forgoes discussion of any obviously Apolline meaning.

Other ancient authors provide a range of alternative accounts. Diogenes Laertius cites a certain Antisthenes, who in his *Diadochê* (*Successions*) says that Phemenoê, the first Pythian priestess at Delphi, is responsible for the saying.[67] Porphyry cites unnamed historians in favor of Phanothea, a different Pythian priestess.[68] Diodorus Siculus tells a story similar to Plato's *Protagoras* in historical detail but elaborated in its exegesis:

> When Chilon came to Delphi, he thought to dedicate to the god the first-fruit, as it were, of his own wisdom (συνέσεως), and engraved upon a column these three maxims: "Know yourself"; "Nothing in excess"; and the third, "Pledge,

[67] DL 1.40 with Strabo 9.3.5 for the identification of the priestess. Diogenes Laertius possibly refers to Antisthenes of Rhodes, *c.* 200 BC; see Rives 2004: 49–51, for bibliography on the question.

[68] Stobaeus *Flor.* 21.26.

and ruin is near." Each of these maxims (ὑπάρχον), though short and laconic (βραχὺ καὶ Λακωνικόν), displays deep reflection (μεγάλην ... τὴν ἀναθεώρησιν). For the "Know yourself" exhorts (παραγγέλλει) us to become educated and to become reasonable (φρόνιμον): for in such a way may someone know himself, either because it is chiefly those who are uneducated and thoughtless (ἀλόγιστοι) that think themselves to be very sagacious (ἑαυτοὺς συνετωτάτους ὑπειλήφασιν) – and that, according to Plato, is of all kinds of ignorance the worst – or because such people consider wicked men to be virtuous, and honest men, on the contrary, to be of no account; for only in this one way may a man know himself and his neighbor – by getting an education and a sagacity that are superior (περιττοτέρας). (9.10.1–2, tr. Oldfather 1989, modified)

According to Diodorus, then, one of the Seven Sages caused the *gnôthi sauton* and other precepts to be written at the Temple, not for any specially Apolline reason but to combat people's ignorance of their own ignorance by encouraging their self-education. Several paragraphs later, Diodorus returns to the *gnôthi sauton* and makes three additional points: he reiterates the brevity of the saying; he explicitly distinguishes "Know yourself" from "Nothing in excess," thereby preempting claims that "Know yourself" means something like "be as moderate as human nature allows"; and he asserts that the three sayings are together adequate wisdom for a human life (9.10.3–6).

Proclus, five centuries later, abandons the sage accounts altogether and focuses on the religious context:

For as the public notice warned those entering the precincts of the Eleusinian Mysteries not to pass within the inner shrine if they were profane and uninitiated, so also the inscription "Know Thyself" on the front of the Delphic sanctuary indicated the matter, I presume, of ascent to the divine and the most effective path towards purification, practically stating clearly to those able to understand, that he who has attained the knowledge of himself, by beginning at the beginning, can be united with the god who is the revealer of the whole truth and guide of the purgative life, but he who does not know who he is, being uninitiated and profane is unfit to partake of the providence of Apollo. (*Comm. on Alc. I.*, 5, tr. O'Neill 1971)

Proclus says that the *gnôthi sauton* tells people how to prepare to benefit from god's salvation.[69] He recommends not humility but

[69] We lack evidence that the Delphic inscription copied the practice of local initiation rites; my thanks to Radcliffe Edmonds for discussion on this point.

taking the first step to knowledge (knowledge of oneself) before taking subsequent steps toward knowledge (knowledge of the future and the nature of the world). Olympiodorus, in his own commentary on Plato's *Alcibiades*, makes a humbler claim: the inscription told people, most of whom came to the Delphic Oracle to ask about their children or about leaders and wars, that they should pay attention to themselves first. He likens this Delphic advice to the Egyptian habit of putting mirrors in front of their temples.[70] The idea appears to be that success comes more readily from correcting one's own faults than from getting hints about external events.

Time shrouded the Delphic inscription with the salutary combination of mystery and profundity.[71] Greek forgetfulness about its real origins became, by Plato's time, an advantage, allowing the setting of stories suitable for their particular lessons without forcing an interpretation. The fact that authors by Plato's generation did not consider the inscription to have a particularly Apolline meaning does not prove that it did not; they may have forgotten its original intention. But these authors produce explanations of the precept's meaning that are just as plausible as the contemporary assumption that it is Apolline. And the earliest authors abide by a principle of minimal speculation at least to its meaning.

The archaeological evidence for Sage inscriptions at Delphi, while provocative, proves not to resolve the central problem of interpretation.[72] Nevertheless, it is worth setting out what is known, to clear up confusion. The inscription's exact location might inform us about its connection to cultic, prophetic, touristic, or Panhellenic aspects of the Temple of Apollo. Pausanias says that it was "in the fore-temple," the area on the platform in front of the cella (ἐν τῷ προνάῳ, 10.24.1). Before him, Diodorus Siculus said it was "on some pillar" (ἐπί τινα

[70] *In. Alc.* 8.15–9.19.

[71] Fontenrose 1978: 294, is right to call "Know thyself" an "unclear command." Croesus, he notes, thought it meant to know his identity, in particular his name; and others knew it was a maxim not easy to understand. He notes further: "it may mean 'Know your place in the world,' 'Know that you are a man,' 'Know your true self' (which also can be given several meanings, including the psychoanalytic), among other possible interpretations." He does not give the source for these potential meanings.

[72] Wilkins 1917: 1–11, and Lipsey 2001: 229–257, offer general though incomplete accounts.

κίονα, 9.10.1). Plutarch, presumably the best-positioned source, unfortunately says no more than that it was "written on the sanctuary of Pythian Apollo" (τῷ ἱερῷ τοῦ Πυθίου Ἀπόλλωνος … ἐπέγραψαν, *On Garrulity* 17). We know less about its date of inscription. It must have been put up before Plato wrote his dialogues, and dramatic plausibility would put it before Socrates' adulthood, for Socrates in the dialogues of Plato and Xenophon speaks of it as already established.[73] An early temple of Apollo at Delphi burnt down in 548 BC, and a new temple and façade, probably in part funded by the Athenian aristocratic and anti-tyrannical Alcmaeonids, went up, likely in several efforts, sometime in the last half of the sixth century.[74] Many scholars date the inscription to this period.[75] This dating makes the claims about the Seven Sages' explicit decision to inscribe it impossible, but would be consistent with the inscription being inspired by Sage wisdom; it would have to be several decades later if the Amphictyones really decided on it over Pindar's paeans. It seems sensible to set the period as between 525 and around 450, not itself an implausible seventy-five years during which Delphi would have been asserting itself as a center of wisdom.

If the precept reflected something other than Apolline religion, one possibility is that it reflected the genre of wisdom promulgated in other Sage sayings inscribed at Delphi. Suppose for the sake of argument that the other sayings more readily yield clear meaning. We have long known of Sosiades' 147 inscriptions of the Seven Sages, cited in Stobaeus (3.125–128 Wachsmuth–Hense).[76] But until the last century, scholars could not show a connection to Delphi, or at least they could not date one. An inscription in Thera, dated to the fourth century, contains at least the two most famous inscriptions, and several others badly damaged.[77] In 1906, a panel of fifty-five mostly two-word precepts – many but not all matching those on Sosiades' much longer list,

[73] Contra Tortzen 2002: 3–4, who dates it as late as the writing of the *Alcibiades* or to the extreme of the reconstruction of the temple after 373 BC.

[74] See Childs 1993: 415–441, and Neer 2007: 247–251.

[75] E.g. Wilkins 1917: 6; Burkert 1981: 148; Bowden 2005: 70.

[76] This list does not include the *gnôthi sauton* or *eggua para d'atê*, but does include *mêden agan* (38).

[77] *Inscriptio Therae insulae*, *IG* XII 3, 1020. Dated and reconstructed by Hiller von Gaertringen, and attributed to an ephebe's gymnasium; see Oikonomides 1987: 72, fig. 4, for an image and a convincing new reconstruction of the first two lines.

and in approximately its order – was found in Miletopolis (Turkey), probably from a gymnasium. Epigraphy dates it from around 300 BC.[78] In 1966, archaeologists found the base of a stele in Aï Khanum (Afghanistan), which stele probably held around 140 precepts.[79] The base contained the final five precepts from Sosiades and an epigram from Klearchos, probably a student of Aristotle's. That epigram states:

> These wise commandments of men of old
> stand dedicated in the most holy Pythian shrine
> From there Klearchos copied them very carefully
> and brought them in the shrine of Kineas to shine far around it.
> (tr. Oikonomides 1987)

As a student of Aristotle, Klearchos would have gone to Delphi in the few decades around 300 BC. We can thereby date to the years before 300 a panel containing many inscriptions attributed to the ancient wise men. In fact, we might have to suggest many years before 300 to allow time for enough bad copies to circulate that Klearchos would want to visit Delphi for a good copy.

Scholars have heretofore not established the date of this panel's first appearance. But in his analysis of the stele, Roberts convincingly reconstructs a precept from the one remaining part of the stele, the lower-left corner: φιλόσοφος γίνου ("become a philosopher").[80] This precept is forty-eighth on Sosiades' list, and its position on the stele suggests that it is at the bottom of the first of three columns. This precept provides an important temporal point. Such a precept could hardly be coined, much less promulgated, before the second quarter of the fourth century. Before that time, the word ΦΙλόσοφos did not have the widely appearing honorific quality or the settled connotation that such a precept would require.[81] Of course, the panel at Delphi

[78] Hasluck 1907: 62–63, *Syll.* 3 §1268.

[79] Analyzed by Robert 1968, and related to a papyrus, P. Univ. Athen. 272, by Oikonomides 1980 and 1987.

[80] Robert 1968: 430–431 and fig. 6. This precept is not found on the Miletopolis panel. My argument is in contrast to Oikonomides 1987: 68, who seems to assert a sixth-century provenance of the sayings.

[81] I argue this in ongoing research. Another precept, σοφίαν ζήλου ("emulate wisdom," Sosiades' twenty-third), echoes the Academic accounts of Pythagoras' explanation of philosophy; these accounts were formulated, though perhaps not first established, by Plato's student Heraclides Ponticus. Naturally, they could themselves reflect Sage wisdom.

could have undergone growing versions; the one Klearchos checked in Delphi may have been a late draft. But if the position of a precept on the list correlates with its date of accession to the list, then φιλόσοφος γίνου would have been a relatively early addition. The Temple of Apollo at Delphi was rebuilt in 373 when the earlier temple fell to an earthquake. I conjecture that a panel containing φιλόσοφος γίνου postdated that rebuilding. Of course this tells us nothing about the existence or nature of a shorter version of the panel predating 373; but then we know nothing about it at all.

This history of the *gnôthi sauton* at Delphi has a negative and a positive conclusion. The negative conclusion is that we know very little about the disposition of the *gnôthi sauton*, and whatever other precepts came to accompany it, before 373. Thus we do not know how people understood it or how they related it to other precepts. The positive conclusion is that by 373, though surely for decades before, the *gnôthi sauton* was assimilated to a tradition of Sage precepts.[82] This favors the interpretation of Socrates in the *Protagoras*: the *gnôthi sauton* was dedicated to the god in celebration of its wisdom, not because it construed Apollo's or his priestesses' beliefs with perfect aptness. That someone would think to make such a dedication has a parallel in Heraclitus' dedication of his book of obscure and fragmentary writings to the sanctuary of Artemis (DL 9.6), most notably among other dedications by leading intellectuals.[83]

The consequence for understanding Socratic self-knowledge is this: we cannot establish how, if at all, Socrates reinterpreted the precept from its original, early, or Delphic meanings. But we can be sure of the precept's enormous importance. Its inscription at Delphi, whether representing the best of Greek wisdom or announcing Apollo's wishes, is imprimatur enough, vindicating our studying it against those who treat it as a mere folk saying. Uncertainty about its origins increased its apparent pertinence for philosophical reflection. The proliferation

[82] Hippias of Elis, perhaps slightly younger than Socrates, probably collected Sage precepts in his *Sunagogê* (Plato, *Hippias Major* 285d, Athenaeus 13.608–609, Clem. *Strom.* 6.15.1–2); see Węcowski 2009.

[83] Someone dedicated Hesiod's poems, written on lead tablets, on Mount Helicon (Pausanias 9.31.4), poetic works by Alcaeus and astronomical works by Eudoxus were written at Delos, the poems of Aristomache at Delphi, an astronomical table by Oenopides of Chios at Olympia, etc.: see Rouse 1902: 64–66.

of inscriptions of Sage wisdom, some of them seemingly derivative of the *gnôthi sauton*, speaks to the precept's grip on many Greeks' moral imagination.

When we study Socratic self-knowledge, then, we will not be able to assume a background or traditional meaning of the precept. We will have to rely largely on the material our authors of Socratic literature provide us. Fortunately, the *gnôthi sauton* shows up in some of the densest and most richly creative literature from the Classical Athenian period, and so this material is the best to work with.

Some common but dismissive views of Socratic self-knowledge

It has long been understood, among both ancient and contemporary scholars, that Socrates cared centrally about self-knowledge.[84] But Socrates' estimation for knowing himself has not always convinced readers to esteem it as much as he has. Sometimes we may blame definitional niceties. For example, in his recent study of "ancient philosophies as ways of life," John Cooper claims that "issues about self-knowledge" are "of peripheral interest." He speaks of Socratic self-knowledge only in the context of Socrates' disavowal of knowledge in Plato's *Apology*. In the ensuing pages, however, he summarizes Socrates' activity as self-examination, the commitment to virtuous actions, modesty in speaking about the content of human value, and an open-ended search for truth, particularly in the practice of life.[85] These, we will see, turn out partially to constitute the search for self-knowledge. Thus the derogation of self-knowledge may amount to a terminological dispute, a result of an overly narrow view of self-knowledge. But scholars have often foregone the study of self-knowledge for reasons other than accepting a narrow referent of the concept. Many have thought its pursuit a conceptual dead-end, a misleading formulation of the Socratic project, or at best the opening move in the long game of the pursuit of truth.

[84] For example, Ballard 1965; Guthrie 1971: 147–153; Warnek 2005; Foucault 2006; Nightingale 2010; Rowe 2011. For interest in self-knowledge around Socrates, see Long 2001 and 2014.

[85] Cooper 2012: 59–61.

For some, self-knowledge is impossible. This view can start from the putatively Platonic knowledge–belief discontinuity: knowledge is of unchanging universals alone; the self is the soul; the soul is not an unchanging universal; thus there can be no knowledge of the self.[86] It can also start from a view of metaphysical psychology: beliefs constitute the self; but examining a belief alienates the belief from oneself; so examination cannot be of the self; so there can be no knowledge of the self.[87] Others resist attributing to Socrates an impossible mission; he may very well have good reasons for searching for self-knowledge. These people diagnose the impossibility argument as wrongly assuming that selfhood cannot be an unchanging universal. Perhaps it could be. It could be selfhood as such, or soul as such, or rationality, or divinity. This recuperation of self-knowledge maintains a familiar use of "knowledge" at the price of rejecting a familiar (personal, idiosyncratic, individual) use of "self."[88]

Whether impossible or possible, some believe that talk of self-knowledge is, for Socrates, actually otiose. Julia Annas, for example, thinks that the concept really does not do much work. Self-knowledge, a recognition of one's "station and duties," as she interprets it, coincides with the knowledge of justice. So we should talk about justice, as we do, for example, in the context of the *Republic*.[89] Of course Socrates does in fact use the language of self-knowledge, but perhaps only because talk of "knowing yourself" has rhetorical or sentimental efficacy. The conversational value of that language does not legitimate any analytic value. There might be challenges in the study of justice, too, but they depend on issues perhaps more tractable than the referent for "selfhood" or the possible objects of knowledge.

[86] Westra 1992; Werner 2012: 80; Gerson 2003: 4, 39, 50, etc., argues that self-knowledge is impossible for embodied persons but is possible once a soul is disembodied.

[87] Woolf 2008: 33–37. At 37n68, Woolf admits that Socrates, in the *Phaedrus*, implies that he still does seek self-knowledge, but Woolf avoids reconstructing Socrates' perspective on his own activity, in particular how Socrates would assess Woolf's argument about the impossibility of self-examination. It will be relevant later in my discussion that Woolf does not distinguish between beliefs as "impressions," psychological entities, and as "commitments," norms of action and thinking.

[88] See especially Johnson 1999, addressed in Chapter 3.

[89] Annas 1985.

For all this pessimism about the value for Socratic philosophy of "self-knowledge" as familiarly conceived, plenty of readers do accept the possibility and usefulness of self-knowledge. But many qualify that usefulness. They treat it as preliminary to the real business of philosophy and the pursuit of truth and happiness. They take it as the recognition that one lacks knowledge where one had thought there was knowledge, a recognition prefatory for research, but not itself the recognition of the true and the good. As Proclus observed, one starts by purifying oneself with self-knowledge, but one does not end with it.

These familiar dismissals of self-knowledge all have something right about them. The self is hardly a promising candidate object for knowledge. As a fluxing and inconstant thing – coming to be and passing away, comprising multiple parts moving in diverse directions – one's self could hardly be known, should we know only stable and unified things. Until it becomes more stable and more unified, a person may perceive momentary aspects of it, or have opinions about it subject to immediate change without notification, but those perceptions or opinions could not count as self-knowledge; they could at best be called questionable reports about passing psychological elements. The counterpoint to the impossibility argument – the argument that rescues self-knowledge by replacing a "personal" self with something "impersonal" – gets something similar right: a robust self-knowledge surely aims beyond the mundane and messy factuality of oneself. As one sees the term "self" as an honorific, as referring to something great and good, and as one reflects that the other highly valued elements of this world have an impersonal character, it becomes reasonable to think that the acquisition of self-knowledge edifies because it assimilates something universal to one's idiosyncratic self. These highly valued elements of the world tend to be sharable, even intersubjectively defined or discovered, and thus impersonal rather than personal. In the respect that self-knowledge aims for this common object of knowledge, it is like justice or knowledge of the good; it may even coincide with them. "Know yourself" is as provocative as it is because by "self" it means something more than we usually conceive. To the extent that self-knowledge still has a personal component, it does involve intensive and possibly painful self-scrutiny, self-inventory, and self-evaluation. Successful completion of those activities allows philosophy's forward momentum.

Some sympathetic views of Socratic self-knowledge

Even with their elements of truth, however, these dismissive or reductive views of self-knowledge minimize the importance Socrates gives to self-knowledge. In their desire to avoid attributing to Socrates some biographical or psychoanalytic view of self-knowledge, they swing too wide. Troubling questions remain. Were self-knowledge impossible, why does Socrates talk so much about it? Were it about something impersonal, why does he frame it in terms of the very personal charge *gnôthi sauton*, rather than as "know rationality" or "know the nature of the soul"? Were it a redundant or misleading term, why does he not eliminate it entirely? And were it simply propaedeutic, why does he not make absolutely distinct the stage of philosophy subsequent to the successful acquisition of self-knowledge?

Several recent scholars have found a way to take Socrates' attention to the personal aspect of self-knowledge seriously and without reducing it to the mundanely biographical. Andrea Nightingale draws attention to Socrates' proclaimed knowledge of ignorance in the *Apology*, for example, and his concern to bring himself and his interlocutors to *aporia*. She distinguishes this self-directed knowledge from expert skill or the tentative confidence that dialectical exchange may produce. She calls this self-knowledge a sort of "self-reflexive awareness," in particular of one's "epistemic limitations." It "constitute[s] a kind of ethical wisdom," and therefore acquiring it is a boon.[90] Revisiting the idea that the self is the most rational part of oneself, but that "oneself" refers to one personally, Sara Rappe has argued that Socratic self-knowledge takes shape as the cognizance of oneself as a particular knower. Recognizing oneself as a knower, as sensitive to and directed by the truth, forces one to accept that one's actions and teachings must have certain kinds of warrant. Justification will be to objective standards. Self-knowledge thus devalues subjective preference. This replacement of self-interest with a passion for the absolute good rewards the painful and annoying self-searching with the happiness consequent

[90] Nightingale 2010: 11–16. Not only is it not always clear how knowing one's ignorance could be possible or beneficial, on which see Burger 1981; Benson 2003: 35–36. It is hard to know exactly what Socrates' position about his knowledge of ignorance is; see Lesher 1987; Graham 1997; Forster 2007; and Fine 2008 (arguing that Socrates never explicitly makes the contradictory statement that he knows that he does not know anything).

to moral knowledge.[91] Voula Tsouna tries to broaden this view: the self-knower knows not only that she is a knower, but also that she is such-and-such a type of person, with such-and-such degrees of virtue, courage, obligation, and so forth. Tsouna pushes back toward the ideal of knowing one's factual person in its diverse and significant qualities.[92] M.M. McCabe, in a series of papers over the past twenty-five years, has argued that Socratic self-knowledge concerns less the puzzles of self-consciousness than the revision of and deep commitment to one's rational and ethical principles:

> It requires, certainly, intellectual acuity, a good sense of where inconsistencies may lie, a clear view of the domain. It requires reflective detachment, too, the ability to look at a group of claims or beliefs and assess their coherence. But it requires more: the courage to persevere, to acknowledge failure, to live with the knowledge of one's own ignorance; and the courage to stick to a thesis that seems unpopular, to care less about the views of others than one's own. It requires both the commitment to what goes deep with oneself; and the willingness to see that this may after all be deeply mistaken. It requires a serious commitment to subject-related self-knowledge itself, and a willingness to insist on that throughout the hard, even impossible, process of coming to know, and coming to know that, and what, one knows.[93]

The central idea these authors identify is that in seeking self-knowledge one works to acknowledge key aspects of oneself: one's ignorance, one's epistemic capacities, one's moral traits, and one's deepest commitments. It turns out that such acknowledgment may change one for the better.[94] Knowing yourself in a sufficiently robust and dynamic way is a crucial mode of self-improvement. Naturally, there are queries for this view, especially about the way it captures the sense of "selfhood" (seemingly vaguely or too concretely); the connection between

[91] Rappe 1995; cf. Gerson 2003, who claims to be studying the "Platonic" rather than the "Socratic" perspective, and thus links it to Plato's purported commitment to soul-immortality and forms.

[92] Tsouna 2001: 43–44.

[93] McCabe 2011: 176; see also Mackenzie 1988b and McCabe 2007a, 2009, 2010, 2013.

[94] This perspective makes so-called "Socratic intellectualism" more plausible, by showing, contrary to some formulations (e.g., Reeve 2013: 47–48), that the knowledge sufficient for virtue may in fact influence "the condition of one's desire structure or will," because this knowledge involves more than the knowledge of the "definitions of virtues."

knowing something (seemingly epistemic) and changing oneself (seemingly non-epistemic); and the way by which one would know oneself through Socratic engagement (seemingly without knowledge). But these questions may be answered with broader reflection on the sort of thing self-knowledge really could be.

Self-knowledge and self-constitution

As it is in contemporary philosophy of self-knowledge, even if not always admitted, the severe challenge in ancient philosophy is to identify the "self" of self-knowledge. What does the Delphic inscription want a person to know? To whom or what does the precept address itself? One possibility assumes an essential similarity among all objects of knowledge. Facts and people – familiar objects of knowledge – preexist any effort to know them. Their coming to be known depends on their existence as items in the world. Understood on this model, the self would be something in the world independent of one's attempts to know about it. Options include one's soul considered as a life-force, one's belief-set, or the network of rights and obligations in which one lives. Should the self be some natural thing, bundle, or state of affairs, a series of tough questions arises in the process of obeying the *gnôthi sauton*: What thing, bundle, etc., exactly is the self to recognize? How do we know this to be so? How do we come to learn about it? What obstacles hinder our learning? And what good does coming to know it do us? These questions match the questions we ask about any scientific field where we aim to learn about a phenomenon whose existence we suspect or can demonstrate.

But this is not the only way to imagine the self toward which the inscription directs one's knowledge. Something properly considered a "self" may not fully preexist any effort to know it. The "self" may need to be completed, not just found. The imperative to know yourself may prompt construction, not just discovery. Selfhood would be aspirational, an accomplishment, where creative success would be determined by linguistic or moral convention, not by the already-established order of the world. The obstacle to knowing oneself then would not immediately be a matter of finding oneself in the dark, as it were, but of there not yet being a self to find. Once someone attains selfhood, perhaps the self is thereby manifest for the knowing. Like a slowly built bird's nest, with twigs and leaves and string, some found *in situ*, others found in the world, pieces bent and rebent into the best – the right – shape, it would become increasingly visible, needing no special work to find it. On this view of the self, new questions arise: what should eventually count as the self; what materials go into the constitution of the self; and why should we come to create a self at all that did not already exist in complete form?

This second possibility may seem to strain the interpretation of the *gnôthi sauton*: "know something that is not yet there." It demands something that, by hypothesis, most people cannot do. It asks for an effect of bootstrapping, bringing oneself about by oneself. It assumes a perfectionist, dynamic view of the self, one distant from the view many people may accept about the way they are. It breaks from colloquial uses of the instruction "know *this*." It exaggerates the depth of the usual charge to "know yourself" as a reminder to calm down, ease up, or be the right size for one's britches. The first way to interpret the kind of object of knowledge the "self" might be – something already there for the knowing – may seem to avoid these difficulties. While the first possibility has the problem of leaving quite unspecified that to which "self" refers, at least it is something that already exists, and this, it would appear, at least limits the scope of specification.

For all this, the second possibility, that selfhood is aspirational, coheres with the way selfhood is talked about in existentially fraught contexts. At least this is what theorists of self-constitution argue. They wonder about the differences between adult humans on the one hand and children or animals on the other. Why do we hold adults responsible for their claims and their actions? That is, why do we say that they mean what they say or what they do, and think that children or animals cannot mean it in the same way?[95] The answer usually involves saying that for non-adults, speech is practically an imitation of what they have heard, or a repetition of conditioned linguistic behavior, or the mostly inarticulate exclamation of emotion; and that their action is an elaborated response to an impulse or inclination or feeling, a behavior activated no more from within than from external stimuli or coercion. More abstractly, we attribute speech and action in animals and children to *parts* of them: to drives, or mechanisms, or processes. We therefore attribute responsibility to the parts that have caused the questionable (e.g., insincere, tactless) speech or the problematic (e.g.,

[95] This perspective is emphasized in Schapiro 1999; Lovibond 2002.

harmful, heedless) behavior. If the speech or behavior must change, those parts become the object of reformation. In adults, by contrast, we attribute moral responsibility to so-and-so *herself* or *himself*, not just to some combination of his or her psychological parts, and demand, if necessary, that *she* or *he* change. And we think it is right to do so. So the self is, somehow, a moral status beyond the assemblage of parts we accept as causally relevant in children and animals.

Thus selfhood seems to come from maturation and the development of agency or autonomy. We might call this "becoming a person," where "personhood" contrasts with being a machine or a mere organism. Theorists of self-constitution care about what happens in maturation and the development of agency, autonomy, and personhood; or put in other words, what preconditions underlie attributing selfhood – linguistic and practical responsibility, and thereby also intellectual and moral responsibility – to some human being. A typical answer explains how certain of one's beliefs and desires become "one's own," rather than merely active within parts of one's body. This can be seen as winnowing them down, selecting only the appropriate and consistent ones, or as owning or owning up to them, accepting and committing oneself to them rather than merely abiding their proximity. "These are my close friends; those are weird roommates I'll tolerate until they move out." Harry Frankfurt focuses on desires: selfhood involves having second-order desires about the first-order desires that are to constitute our will. Without preferences about the desires that our actions come to satisfy, we can be described only as unorganized bundles of desires, with the desires themselves, not ourselves, as responsible for the actions that satisfy them.[96] Christine Korsgaard, also focusing on desire, speaks of authorizing certain of our inclinations – the ones that pass tests of universalization – as reasons for action. Precipitated from this murky pool of urges and wishes comes a unified and solider core of reasonable motivations to action.[97] Other authors focus on beliefs. Richard Moran, for example, observes that though we accumulate, quite accidentally, broad swaths of beliefs, many with unknown or unsatisfactory epistemic value, maturation involves testing the plausibility and truth of our beliefs, and committing ourselves to the good ones, or to reforming those susceptible to improvement. Incoherent prejudices give way

[96] Frankfurt 1988. [97] Korsgaard 1999, 2009.

to coherent well-grounded opinion or knowledge.[98] Of course, for self-constitutionalists, selfhood is more than coherent and acceptable sets of desires and beliefs. Selfhood may involve subtle practices of unification and coordination.[99] But even those practices exist essentially to furnish opportunity to evaluate judgments of value (desire) and truth (belief).

Self-constitutionalism thus provides an avenue for thinking about selfhood that is sensitive to questions of responsibility and development; but it does so at a theoretical cost. It must confront a paradox whose nature the concept "self-constitution" itself advertises. How could a bundle of impulses and beliefs unify themselves unless there were something unified to do the unifying – the sorting, judging, owning up to, etc. – already at play in the human being? Put more simply, who or what does the constituting? The nest hardly builds itself. Who or what counts as responsible for doing it? Tamar Schapiro argues for a piecemeal expansion of selfhood through playful imitation of (adult) selfhood. Children imagine being adults who have unified personae and systems of value. With enough practice, they come to instantiate some of those unifying ways of being a person.[100] This argument plausibly recounts the childhood intersection between purposive action and causally determined process. But it does not explore the precise mechanism for shifting responsibility from the part to the unified self. It also appears to assume that the child starts out with at least a minimum amount of selfhood – that is to say, control over one's parts – from which to expand. These difficulties are not unique to Schapiro's view. To give a totally robust account, Frankfurt, for example, would have to explain how we come to take our desires as interesting objects of desire, and how those second-order desires come to reflect or constitute plausible long-term projects. But these theorists need achieve total robustness only if they were shown that selfhood, as they conceive it, is impossible, on grounds, say, that it neither exists at a child's birth nor can be increased from zero. Barring that, they can point to the usual progression of people's lives, from not responsible for their words and deeds to responsible for their words and deeds, from a contingent collection of beliefs and desires to a systematically sound person of

98 Moran 2001.
99 Schapiro 1999; Bratman 2000; Larmore 2010.
100 Schapiro 1999: 731–734.

knowledge and commitments. The task of the self-constitutionalist is to show what accounts for and perspicuously describes this increase in what we call selfhood.

This account of self-constitution relates to self-knowledge in several ways. Self-knowledge will have as its object the self that is constituted. The charge to "know yourself" will necessitate simultaneously constituting yourself. But constituting oneself will also take much self-reflection: on one's actual beliefs and desires; on what one finds true and choiceworthy; on one's progress toward realigning and rectifying those beliefs and desires. Naturally, there is a reciprocal process here. As one's beliefs and desires become more sharply defined and more stable, the more observable they will become. With the approach to selfhood, the more knowable that (proto-) self becomes. Likewise, the more one reflects on one's beliefs and desires, the more readily one will be able to certify or reject them. Thus the closer one is to knowing one's proto-self, the closer one comes to selfhood. Self-constitution and self-knowing perfect themselves in time and together. Knowing oneself is not just awareness of one's present states; that awareness is a kind of quasi-knowing of one's quasi-self. But it is also not just a reflection on one's completely unified selfhood; it includes, as a matter of investigation and discovery, the elements soon to be making up one's self.

What one knows when knowing oneself

From the perspective of self-constitution, it comes to look like "knowing yourself" means "knowing your *self*," where the "self" is whatever accounts for someone being responsible. But this is highly abstract, and hardly clarifying about the sort of object of knowledge under consideration. Sarah Rappe, as mentioned above, interprets "knowing yourself" as "knowing yourself *as a knower*"; this is also Lloyd Gerson's view.[101] The plausibility of the view comes minimally from the assumption that if you can *know* yourself, then being a self involves being able to know. The charge spelled out means that you should recognize that you are someone who can recognize and respond to significance and the logical obligations of truth. The recognition of an ability is underwritten by your actual ability. This epistemic formulation has

[101] Gerson 2003: 4, 39, 45–46, 50.

moral and practical relevance, since we can speak of your knowing your moral obligations and your abilities in interpersonal interpretation on the one hand, and knowing your competence for various skilled actions on the other.

But this formulation may sound overly epistemic, almost too Socratic in its intellectualization of selfhood. This was Tsouna's concern, and while the concern may not be merited, the concept is certainly made less appealing by a constrained view of knowledge. Equally abstract but less epistemic is the view that "know yourself" means "know your ideal self." This cannot mean, however, that one simply pictures an ideal self, because then this is not *oneself*, but a possible way to be; this would be enjoined as "know the heights of human perfection." It must mean something more personal: "decide on your ideal self; become it; and know that future yourself." This version clarifies the double vision that self-knowledge requires and aims to bring together: knowing something possible for oneself, and knowing something actual about oneself. But it still gives little content to selfhood as such.

Above I spoke of knowing one's desires and beliefs. Since desires are judgments of what is good for oneself, and beliefs are judgments of what is true, we could also speak of knowing what is good for oneself and of knowing what is true. We all desire such knowledge; but we wonder how that object of knowledge could coincide with selfhood. It seems much too broad, much too impersonal. The answer circles back on our previous discussion. We hold people responsible for their actions when we think they have acted on desires they mean to have and to act on, and when their actions depend on beliefs that they have good reason to accept as true. We think they are more responsible the more they have deliberated on their desires and beliefs, the more those desires and beliefs become central to their ongoing activities. We strongly identify actions as coming from someone when they come from their central commitments; those central commitments reflect a person's judgments about what is, over the long term, good and apt for them. What ultimately strikes a person as good depends on their reflection on candidates for choiceworthy pursuit, and what ultimately strikes a person as true depends on their reflection on candidates for correspondence with the world.

Self-constitution depends on the coherence of belief and the coordination of desire; one becomes a self the more true (or at least consistent) beliefs one has and the more legitimated (or at least prioritized) desires one has. So knowing oneself, at the limit point of selfhood, involves having true beliefs, which is knowing what is true, and having good desires, which is knowing what is good.[102] This "transparency" – knowing what one believes by discovering what is true – looks, unfortunately, to conflate the personal and impersonal perspectives. Or worse, it seems to replace the personal with the impersonal perspective. It seems a species of the gargantuan Stoic view that knowing the whole precedes, or suffices for, knowing oneself. This worry is misplaced. For it is *my* desires and *my* beliefs that allow *my* actions for which *I* am responsible. I am not an encyclopedia, for as full of knowledge and judgment as an encyclopedia may be, it remains an impersonal repository; nothing in it determines actions or underlies its responsibility. By contrast, an impersonal perspective in the context of human self-knowledge allows a freedom from one's given feelings and assumptions; the impersonal perspective provides room for a creative expansion of one's commitments and goals. The verb in the Greek *gnôthi sauton* – *gignôskô* – can mean "recognize" or "acknowledge." Just so, we might think the Delphic injunction encourages recognizing oneself as (personally) responsive to the (impersonal) claims of truth and goodness. To recognize this requires becoming actually responsive to those claims; and such actual responsiveness requires both insight into the claims (through investigation) and real change in light of that insight.

The self-constitution approach to self-knowledge finds special appeal in the Platonic context, which emphasizes stability as a criterion of knowability. We know more what changes less. Our stable beliefs are at less risk of becoming false, and they fit more thoroughly into a complex of other stable beliefs. This transparency view of self-knowledge – that we know what we believe by investigating the truth about things, and believing what we find – works to tie otherwise mercurial beliefs to immutable reality. This does not straitjacket us as people; rather, it allows us to act in constructive, concerted, broadly oriented ways.

The specifically Socratic pursuit of self-knowledge may even give sharp insight into the nature of self-constitution. Socrates, in his pursuit of conversation, emphasizes responsibility for the things one says. Being properly a self involves meaning what one says, understanding

[102] McCabe 1994 and Gerson 2003 emphasize belief.

how it differs from the other things one could say, and taking seriously its consequences for oneself and one's conversations. We exist as people largely in conversation with others – or at least under the obligation to talk if called upon – and so our selfhood depends largely on our ability to account for our actions, our views, and our attitudes.

Knowing oneself and knowing another

The saying *gnôthi sauton* twists a common question, "Do you know him?" or a common recommendation, "You should get to know her!" by replacing a non-reflexive with a reflexive pronoun.[103] Our knowledge of other people determines how well we can trust them, rely on them, empathize with them, learn from them, or enjoy their company. Our projects often depend on others, whether for pleasure, efficiency, or sheer feasibility. Some people we struggle to know and eventually fail: those who act differently from day to day, who claim to believe one thing but then another, who deny having any particular preferences or beliefs or intentions or attitudes. But those with whom we have frequent intense conversation, where we get clear about each other's views, push each other for the justification of those views, and see the active effect of holding those views, these people we can come to know. In knowing them, we can predict what they will do, understand what they are doing, and help them to make sense of what they, and we together, have done. We can do this because we see some of their desires and beliefs; and because we have good reason to think that they try to coordinate their desires and substantiate their beliefs, we can infer those desires and beliefs we have not explicitly observed.

Coming to know oneself is surprisingly like coming to know someone else. In the Socratic literature Socrates often makes the otherwise odd claim that with knowing yourself comes knowing the person you have been talking with. He is making three related points here. First, self-knowledge comes through conversation. We seem to reveal our beliefs and desires more readily – including their entailments and exclusions – when someone we trust asks us than when we ask ourselves. Perhaps we notice contradictions, and feel moved to eliminate

[103] Jeremiah 2012 argues that the use of a reflexive, especially in the sixth and early fifth century, would have a marked status as against the more ancient middle voice.

them, more readily when someone we admire finds them than when we inquire within ourselves. Whatever the reason, Socrates regularly notes the benefits to self-understanding that mutual discussion and critique bring about. He identifies this through frequent analogies to mirrors, and the dialogues often highlight the moment of greeting and acknowledgment at the beginning of a conversation. Socrates' second point is that knowledge of other people also comes through conversation. This is unsurprising; we could hardly know about people's reasons for action, or their fine-tuned beliefs, simply by observing their behavior. We must ask them pointed questions. His third point is the really interesting one. The process of knowing oneself just *is* the process of knowing someone else. This means that self-knowledge cannot be purely or even mainly introspective. It is conversational and exploratory.

There is one important difference between self-knowledge and other-knowledge. Self-knowledge involves self-constitution. Thus it involves choices, determinations of what to believe and to value. This can be done only for oneself. Of course, such determinations of one's beliefs often rely on recommendation and encouragement and opportunities organized by others; and thus so too the self-directed determinations by one's friends depend on your encouragements. But ultimately self-constitution and self-knowledge are a personal responsibility. Yet this is consistent with the observation about conversation. Continued participation in the conversation is also a personal responsibility.

Sôphrosunê and self-knowledge

The core Greek virtue *sôphrosunê* is a matter of exercising discipline, being sound of mind, and integrating, tempering, or moderating the potentially divergent desires one might have. Scholarship has claimed that *sôphrosunê* has had a traditional association with self-knowledge.[104] But the character of this relationship is complicated. In Heraclitus' fr. 116, for example, the καί of γινώσκειν ἑωυτοὺς καὶ σωφρονεῖν could be either explanatory or additive. Heraclitus might simply identify *sôphrosunê* with knowing oneself, or he might point out that *sôphrosunê* has a status similar to that of knowing

[104] North 1966, though contrast Rademaker 2005: 335N6Y.

oneself but a different content. Aristophanes associates Socrates with self-knowledge and against the traditional education obsessed with a conservative form of *sôphrosunê*.[105] Prometheus is accused both of not knowing himself and of not yet knowing how to be *sôphrôn* (σύ γ' οὔπω σωφρονεῖν ἐπίστασαι, *Prometheus Bound* 982). The *Charmides* proposes and rejects a series of definitions of *sôphrosunê*; its possible identity to "knowing yourself" and self-knowledge gets by far the greatest attention. Both the *Alcibiades* and the *Rival Lovers* explicitly equate *sôphrosunê* and knowing oneself, along with a range of other capacities. In the *Phaedrus*, a dialogue about self-understanding and self-development, whereas both of the earlier speeches explicitly praise *sôphrosunê* (231d3, 237e3), the long last speech appears to praise *mania*, treated as *sôphrosunê*'s opposite; but this appearance is probably deliberately misleading.

Throughout this book we will pay detailed attention to the relationship between the virtue and self-knowledge. We can at least say here the obvious, that the relationship shows that self-knowledge shares features with a virtue, a disposition to act in certain ways, and thus with something to be improved. We might even say that coming to know oneself must mean developing a certain competence in self-control and self-mastery, a kind of intellectual coherence, and unification.

Non-Socratic self-knowledge

We have too little evidence to determine whether the Socratic mode of self-knowledge differs in principle, conception, or model from those of his contemporaries. If we expanded the search, we might find interesting contrasts in the Stoics, Cicero, Augustine, and Neoplatonists. But the growth of self-conscious philosophy, political change, and Christianity partially explains those contrasts; and their discussion exceeds the scope of this work. We have for the Socratic period mainly two kinds of information about non-Socratic views of self-knowledge. The first is the fact that Socrates' interlocutors often have inchoate views about self-knowledge, especially that getting it is easy. In the coming chapters I speculate on these interlocutors' mistake. The second kind of

[105] *Clouds* 962, 1006, 1027, 1060, 1061, 1067, 1071; the earlier uses are the Better Argument's; the latter uses are the Worse Argument's echoes and criticisms of those earlier uses.

information we have about non-Socratic views of self-knowledge is the references to "knowing yourself" discussed above, and several references to it in Plato and Xenophon in non-Socratic settings. As we will see, the precursors to Socrates' views on self-knowledge end up having views similar to Socrates'. Of course, Plato's and Xenophon's views may have been influenced by Socrates', or at least by the same cultural material by which Socrates was influenced.

Plato cites the *gnôthi sauton* three times in non-Socratic settings. In his *Laws*, the Athenian proposes that the Magnesian city founders modify inheritance laws. Men near death, in severe psychic strain, should not dictate the disposition of their property. They have, the Athenian says, no vision beyond the day (ἀτεχνῶς ἐφήμεροι), and they struggle to recognize their best interests about their property or about themselves, per the Pythian (Delphic) inscription, especially when harassed by legatees (923a4–8). In the *Timaeus*, Timaeus explains the division of labor between visionaries, who utter inspired divinations, and the interpreters of those divinations. He appeals to the ancient saying (πάλαι λέγεται) that "doing one's own things, and knowing oneself, are for the sound-minded man (σώφρονι) alone appropriate" (72a7–8). Inspired persons may conduct divine knowledge to men but fail to know what they mean by what they say. In the *Seventh Letter*, Plato scolds those who have copied his ideas and presented them as their own; these people do not know who they themselves are (341b). These three usages are consistent, as we will see, with Socratic usages, but they do not provide the richness of context the Socratic usages do.

Xenophon cites the Delphic imperative twice in non-Socratic works. In the *Hellenica*, he records Thrasybulus' challenge to some Athenians about their supposed superiority over the rest of the Athenians:

> "I advise you," he said, "men of the city, to know yourselves (γνῶναι ὑμᾶς αὐτούς). And you would know (γνοίητε) [this] most, were you to figure out (ἀναλογίσαισθε) on what grounds (ἐπὶ τίνι) you have such confidence (μέγα φρονητέον) that you try to rule over us. Are you more just? But the populace, being poorer than you, has not yet done any wrong to you for the sake of money, and yet you, being richer than all of them, have done many execrable things for the sake of profit. And since nothing of justice belongs to you, look whether you ought to have confidence in your courage. And what better judgment of this should come about than the way we have made war against one another? But you might claim to excel in mind (γνώμῃ), you who have a wall and materiel and money and Peloponnesian allies, and who

have been squashed by those having none of these. But do you indeed think to take confidence about the Spartans? How, since they have given you over like a barking chained dog; in this way they have given you to this wronged populace and they leave and head out." (2.4.40–41)[106]

Thrasybulus charges these men with self-ignorance. They exaggerate their virtue, courage, intelligence, and social cunning. In every department they "think [too] big." They have failed to reason correctly about themselves. Thrasybulus implies that they ought to think through the grounds for their self-assessments. This reflection, taking into account comparative data, would cause greater self-knowledge. Such self-knowledge would amount to calibrating their public personae to the reality of the situation.

In the *Cyropedia*, Croesus tells Cyrus about his experiences at Delphi. Croesus admits that he started out incorrectly. One time he persuaded the Oracle to tell him whether he would have sons, and it said that he was to have them; but one died and the other was mute. So he asked how to live happily, and it responded, "Knowing yourself, Croesus, you will go through [life] (περάσεις) being happy" (7.2.20). Croesus thought this would be easy, because "while it is possible to know some people, and impossible to know others, I believed that every person knows himself, what he is" (ἑαυτὸν δὲ ὅστις ἐστὶ ... εἰδέναι, 21). This was true to some extent; when he recognized himself to be inadequate to fight against Cyrus, he got safely away (22). But he broke down in the face of his own wealth and an overgrown self-regard caused by gifts, flattery, and claims of his utter human superiority by people wanting him as their leader (23). This failure of self-knowledge caused him to forget his fighting inadequacy, and he lost, and was punished (24). Croesus charges himself with insouciance about the Delphic injunction. He let his reputation – an outside factor – stand in for his actual self. His failure of self-knowledge, and thus his failure of happiness, amounted to a failure to recognize what he really was.

Structure of the book

Like Croesus, Socrates' interlocutors have not thought well enough about the best way to obey the *gnôthi sauton*. They might be excused;

[106] Munn 2000: 418n8, discusses the scholarship on this speech's historicity.

it is not clear how to go about knowing oneself, or even that it is possible or useful. The works of Socratic literature concerned with the *gnôthi sauton* take on these difficulties. I organize the following chapters accordingly. I generally focus on the source of the *aporia* about obedience to the *gnôthi sauton*, and then look for a solution that the conversation, arguments, and actions of dialogue offer up. As it turns out, each dialogue suggests that by looking at self-knowledge as self-constitution, we may dissolve, avoid, or alleviate those problems.

Chapter 2, on Plato's *Charmides*, addresses most directly obstacles to self-knowledge. After extracting Critias' view of self-knowledge, Socrates finds that self-knowledge so conceived looks impossible; and even worse, on the assumption that is possible, it would still be quite useless. Critias' view appears to assume a reflexivity with an impractically tight back-bend. And were the problem of reflexivity straightened out, Critian self-knowledge would still seem void of content, concerned with "knowledge" itself but with nothing that knowledge is characteristically of or good for. This impossibility and uselessness, however, stands against Socrates' interest in self-knowledge, evident in the very dialogue, and the approving citation of the inscription at the Temple of Apollo at Delphi. To resolve this tension, I argue that Socrates' claims of impossibility and uselessness actually diagnose the nature of self-knowledge as Critias himself conceives it. He conceives knowing oneself too much on the model of visual perception, and thinks of self-knowledge's objects as pieces of knowledge. He should conceive it instead on the model of interpretation and judgment, and think of self-knowledge's object as oneself, a person. In other words, whereas Critias sees self-knowledge as a mode of epistemic inventorying, appropriate to a conscientious and clear-eyed property manager, the dialogue points to self-knowledge as a mode of self-possession, a constituting oneself as a person able to direct oneself toward publicly testable truth and goodness. This is coextensive with the virtue *sôphrosunê*. I support this view by focusing on three parts of the dialogue. First, Critias analyzes the *gnôthi sauton*, as mentioned above, as a greeting and not a piece of advice. He does not integrate this frankly baffling analysis well with his later discussion of self-knowledge, to his disadvantage, because, when we see it in a broader context, his idea about a Delphic "greeting" shows remarkable insight. A greeting is a way of acknowledging another person as appropriate for conversation; and conversation is at the heart of self-constitution. Second, in the conversation with Charmides, Critias' young ward, Socrates keeps asking Charmides to look inside for his reputed *sôphrosunê* and his convictions about its nature. He does this five times. Each time, however, Socrates presents that inward look as less perceptual and less internal, and by contrast more evaluative and more social, a testing of the beliefs Charmides could potentially commit himself to. These first two elements of the *Charmides* – treating the *gnôthi sauton* as an acknowledgment prefatory to conversation and Socrates' encouragement to Charmides to decide conversationally what he should believe – prepare us to read the third element more critically, Socrates' discussion with Critias about the meaning of "knowing yourself." This discussion notoriously switches among nearly a dozen apparently or questionably equivalent permutations on that formula. Each formulation has a certain plausibility to it. But it is in the course of this conversation that self-knowledge comes to seem impossible or useless. The dialogue's prior attention to recognition of other people and of one's make up suggests promising responses to the problems of impossibility and uselessness. That is, self-knowledge is possible, and useful, only when self-knowledge is coordinated with maturation, the appreciation of and attempt to deal with one's fields of ignorance, and striving for rational and moral responsibility.

The Platonic *Alcibiades*, the subject of Chapter 3, avoids the *Charmides*' dilemmas. It treats self-knowledge as possible, useful, and even urgent. In the *Charmides*, the journey to self-knowledge nearly capsizes on the impossibility of visual reflexivity. By contrast, in the *Alcibiades*, Socrates helps his friend understand self-knowledge precisely on the model of an eye seeing itself, in a reflective surface. In the *Charmides*, even were self-knowledge attainable, as a second-order knowledge it would seem to prove idle, since the goods of life are produced by first-order knowledge alone. Again by contrast, in the *Alcibiades*, Alcibiades heartily assents to self-knowledge's benefits for the entirely practical political power he seeks. After all, he needs to know what he really desires, what actions and knowledge those desires require, and what aspects of himself he needs to work on. But the *Alcibiades* reveals its own problems for self-knowledge. The one continually noted by Alcibiades is the *way* by which one comes to self-knowledge. This depends, of course, on the content of self-knowledge. Unfortunately, the content of self-knowledge is quite unclear. Julia Annas takes self-knowledge to be – or to be knowledge of – justice. Others take it to be knowledge of something impersonal, selfhood, divinity, or rationality as such. Thus self-knowledge would be, in some respects, ethics, metaphysics, theology, or philosophy of mind or logic. But these deflationary views of the object of self-knowledge in the *Alcibiades* come from a too-circumscribed study of the dialogue. They focus mostly on its final discussion of the *gnôthi sauton*, analogized to the self-seeing eye. They generally ignore the earlier two discussions of the *gnôthi sauton*. By consequence, they work without a textured idea of the self. This chapter studies all three discussions of the *gnôthi sauton*. The first identifies the importance of reflecting on one's desires; the second, the importance of thinking about the nature of selfhood; and the third, the connection between talking rationally with others, recognizing one's status as a knower, and determining which possessions are one's own, a connection characterized by *sôphrosunê*. Alcibiades is to prepare for political participation and just dealings by coming to constitute himself as a person, where this means knowing his desires, knowing himself as a self, and knowing himself as a knower, and he is to do all this in conversation with Socrates or others like him.

Chapter 4 addresses the *Phaedrus*, a dialogue akin to the *Alcibiades* in depicting amatory seduction and men avid for public address. Unlike the *Alcibiades*, however, not all readers recognize the *Phaedrus* as a meditation on self-knowledge. It seems focused principally on love, rhetoric, the soul, or on philosophy as division, collection, and the contemplation of the forms. Yet this may contain the most profound analysis of self-knowledge in our three dialogues so far. Four strikingly puzzling episodes suffice to reveal this. First, and most famously, Socrates claims that his range of intellectual activities is curtailed by his failure yet to obey the Delphic precept to "know himself." But Socrates does not say what has slowed his progress, and why it takes, even in his age of maturity, such single-minded devotion. Colotes, as we noted above, simply doubted Socrates' claim; and Christopher Rowe, for example, assumes that Plato himself came to that sort of knowledge. The dialogue shows, however, that Socrates has good reason to call the task unfinished. This is not just because of a particularly complicated or dynamic structure of the soul, but because of the nature of self-improvement: the taming and reorienting of one's desires and the realizing and realigning of one's beliefs. Second, moments after calling his task of self-knowledge incomplete,

Socrates says he wonders how he differs from the mythological monster and Zeus' last contender to rule, Typhon. Socrates says nothing more of the object of his self-knowledge, suggesting that this comparison alone gets at something important; but what? Many have read this passage as concerned with the status of myth: Socrates just disavowed his commitment to myth-rectification, but since he will go on to liken the soul to a charioteer and team, imagery familiar from mythology, he must find some uses of myth legitimate. Unfortunately, this does not explain his appeal to Typhon in particular. Prometheus' reference to Typhon in the *Prometheus Bound* and the monster's appearance in a crucial quotation of poetry in Aristophanes' *Clouds* (329–338) give a clue. Typhon represents the possibility that humans can neither constitute nor improve themselves, lacking decision-making agency over their proclivities, behaviors, and attitudes. Socrates' query about his similarity to Typhon reveals his basic concern: whether he is amenable to self-improving, that is, self-constituting action. In the third puzzling episode in the dialogue, Socrates reworks the *Alcibiades*' mirror-scene. In the Palinode, Socrates describes the recipient of a person's love provoked to love himself by his own beauty reflecting off the person who loves him and being struck by it. If this explanation for the reciprocal feelings of love by appeal to an unwitting narcissism is not strange enough, Socrates' speech goes on to say that the recipient does not understand the source of his newly provoked love. His failure at self-recognition occurs simultaneously with his dawning love, and it is this dawning love that eventually brings him to self-growth. This odd counter-picture to the cognitive reflection in the *Alcibiades* – there, transparent, rational, self-knowing; here, opaque, aesthetic, self-ignorant – represents the struggle of self-knowledge. One begins like a statue, with little knowledge, self-possession, or reason, and only in time, in engagement with another, does one come to understanding. The fourth puzzling episode in the *Phaedrus* is a puzzle of *sôphrosunê*: *mania*, in the Palinode, has grown ascendant. Perhaps in devaluing *sôphrosunê* Socrates has a new or better idea here about the way humans grow up; perhaps he has tempered his intellectualism and gained faith in the irrational and appetitive. Whether Socrates rightly appreciates the power and significance of the feeling and impulse of *erôs* or not, however, we should forbear from concluding that Socrates has changed his attitude about *sôphrosunê*. Dominic

Scott has already shown that the argument for the importance of *mania* to philosophy, as adumbrated in the Palinode, proceeds invalidly, and Socrates is to be expected to realize that. Just as importantly, I argue that the speeches treat *sôphrosunê* inadequately, as a kind of calmness or diffidence. The *Charmides* has already shown this inadequacy. Just as the "vulgar" (pleasure-induced) virtues in the *Phaedo* (68d–69c) have more estimable doubles, the inadequate *sôphrosunê* has a more estimable ideal, one that remains essential for self-knowledge and philosophy. The second part of this chapter investigates a way Socrates suggests that one comes to know oneself: on the model of an activity he disowns, myth-rectification.

Chapter 5, on the *Philebus*, fits this book's narrative because Socrates refers to the *gnôthi sauton* halfway through the dialogue. He theorizes that comedy amounts to our finding self-ignorant people funny – those who have not obeyed the Delphic imperative. He then says that what holds for the dramatic genre holds for all of life. He gives this account ostensibly to show the pervasiveness of mixed pleasures, and it seems an odd digression. A dialogue mostly empty of allusion to cultural activity pauses at spectator-theory; why? I argue that Socrates in effect links self-knowledge to a normative picture of selfhood. His doing so here is no mere digression. A step back shows that Socrates has directed much of the conversation toward questions of self-knowledge. A most pressing one recalls the *Charmides*. Protarchus claims that the life of reason alone, lacking all pleasure, would appeal to nobody; Socrates accepts this claim. We have argued through this book for the importance of self-knowledge; but without pleasure, self-knowledge seems a pair of mirrors reciprocally reflecting their reflectivity to infinity, an absolutely empty reflexivity, pure but hardly choiceworthy. To prevent the desertification of the self-knowing subject, we water it with pleasure. The *Philebus* suggests that humans need pleasure for the flourishing life; but also that pleasure cannot be merely mixed in. I analyze Socrates' argument that pleasure becomes part of a person's life, and thereby makes that life worth living, only through self-knowledge. Pleasure must be recognized and integrated into one's life, and this is done through a range of self-reflective cognitive capacities. That the characters in the dialogue talk often of the philosophical puzzles of selfhood and the unity of the person gives support to the view that self-knowledge as self-constitution plays a central role in the good human life.

Chapter 6 turns from Plato to Xenophon. The latter's *Memorabilia* 4.2 appears to give an impoverished view of Socratic self-knowledge, as "knowing your powers." Readers have inferred from this that Xenophon fails to recognize the perplexities around self-knowledge. This would mean either that Xenophon did not completely understand Socrates, or that Plato's writings on self-knowledge outran Socrates', or that Socrates spoke of self-knowledge differently around these two men. I show that we need not decide between these historical claims, because *Mem.* 4.2 does not present Socratic self-knowledge as "knowing your powers." In fact, a careful rereading of this section shows that Socratic self-knowledge in Xenophon is remarkably similar to that found in our other texts. It is connected to knowing justice, self-commitment and self-possession, knowing the good, knowing other people, and having scrutinizing and reforming conversations.

Chapter 7, the Conclusion, begins with a reading of the *Rival Lovers*, the dialogue with the most explicit description of a problem-free and self-constituting self-knowledge. This allows a summary of the main points of Socratic self-knowledge. But I then turn to the *Hipparchus*, where Socrates says that the Athenian tyrant Hipparchus replaced the *gnôthi sauton* with his own pithy practical wisdom. This dialogue has wanted a plausible interpretation, but, as I show, conflict between the most recent published readings depends on differences in their authors' assessment of the value of the *gnôthi sauton*. These difficulties may in fact symbolize the difficulties in studying Socratic self-knowledge. But the more important inference from this dialogue is the possibility of dismissing the value of "knowing yourself." I return to the apparently good reasons for abandoning "self-knowledge" as simply too vague and for preferring concrete questions about the way we know our beliefs, our abilities, the fact or conditions of our existence, or our consciousness. If not too vague, then too capacious: if self-knowledge means becoming a good person, then this is all of philosophy, or anyway much of it. Or a word too much: if self-knowledge ends up meaning "really know," as "becoming a knower" might suggest, asking about it is asking the basic questions of epistemology. Or assuming the existence or possibility of a self. Or giving insufficient weight to the centrality of self-deception, spontaneity, and plurality to human wellbeing. I respond to these concerns, and reiterate the value in thinking about Socratic self-knowledge.

2 Charmides: *on impossibility and uselessness*

Two problems with self-knowledge

In the *Charmides*, self-knowledge confronts its most fundamental pair of obstacles in the Socratic literature. Socrates concludes, after lengthy discussion with Critias, that self-knowledge may very well be impossible. He further concludes that, even were it possible, it might very well be unbeneficial. Should these conclusions be sound, they would have catastrophic consequences. They would undermine all pursuits of self-knowledge; they would impugn the dignity of the Sages and Delphic leaders who command people to know themselves, showing them up as thoughtless time-wasters; and they would require a new assessment of Socrates as the famed exponent of self-knowledge.[1] The possibility of such dire consequences also, however, prompts revisiting the arguments and assumptions underlying them – arguments and assumptions made by Critias and granted by Socrates in the second half of the dialogue. Revisiting these arguments requires, in addition, reflecting on the rest of the *Charmides*. On the suspicion that Socrates does not actually reject the fact or value of self-knowledge, we might suppose that he hints somewhere at an alternative.[2] We might look for a sketch of some picture of self-knowledge counter to – and more productive than – the assumptions made about it in the argument for its impossibility and lack of benefit. These assumptions involve picturing self-knowledge as separable in principle from the persons knowing themselves, and by consequence, as knotted into a suffocating reflexivity. In truth, however, neither Critias nor Socrates ever defines

[1] Were the *gnôthi sauton* really to have the imprimatur of the god, then the god would be lying; and this would overturn one of Socrates' deepest beliefs (*Apol.* 21b4, 21b7, 21e7, 22a8, 23a7).

[2] This is akin to the method urged by Tuozzo 2011: 4–51, namely that Socratic "elenchus" has goals beyond showing his interlocutors their inadequacies; but I do not use Tuozzo's language of "positive elenchus."

self-knowledge with adequate clarity; despite the many permutations that the concept "knowing oneself" undergoes, none seems to define it in terms familiar enough to capture our – or the Greeks' – sense of self-knowledge. Fortunately, other aspects of the conversation in the *Charmides* give a more stable and valuable, if not more explicit, image of knowing oneself. This image involves taking self-knowledge as a matter of knowing oneself as one knows another, through conversation, by understanding what one ought to believe and desire, and with the goal of constituting oneself as a social and mature individual. Where this new image comes from, and how it improves upon the other, will occupy much of this chapter. First, however, we must look more precisely at the obstacles that the *Charmides* sets up, which it does presumably to encourage a serious revisiting of self-knowledge.

Self-knowledge appears to be impossible under two formulations of self-knowledge.[3] The first formulation of self-knowledge takes it as purely reflexive, a knowledge of knowledge and of nothing else, not even of the usual objects of (first-order) knowledge, whatever it is that a person might learn. On the unstated but plausible assumption that knowledge is structurally similar to perceptual or intentional states, like seeing, hearing, desiring, or fearing, what holds for the latter with respect to reflexivity may very well hold for the former. Yet seemingly no perceptual or intentional state takes only itself, and not its usual perceptual or intentional objects, such as color, sound, pleasure, or danger, as its object. So we have reason, based on this analogy, to doubt that knowledge could take only itself and not its usual objects as its object. Further, knowledge seems necessarily relative to something else, namely, what it knows. But other relatives, including being larger than, double than, heavier than, and older than, cannot be so related to themselves. This is because they would have to embody both their own nature (being larger than, etc.) and also the nature of that to which they are relative (being smaller than, etc.), and here this compresence of opposites is conceptually impossible. In yet other relatives, like sight, their having to embody the nature of that to which they are relative (being colored) would simply be odd, since sight – whether as process, or activity, or event – does not seem itself to be colored. Thus

[3] Tuozzo 2011: 209–226, is especially valuable on the analysis of the first formulation.

knowledge, or knowing, would need to have the very quality of that which is known; and the track-record for this being the case looks bad.

The second formulation of self-knowledge understands self-knowledge more actively and personally, as knowing what one knows and what one does not know. Yet this formulation also looks to have no possible referent, because – if we individuate knowledge by its particular object – it is not by self-knowledge that you know what you know, but by the first-order knowledge itself. At best self-knowledge could tell you what state counts as an instance of knowledge, and thus *that* you know something; but this "that" is opaque, not transmitting the ability or content that the knowledge is of. Socrates notes incidentally, at the dialogue's end, that the notion of knowing what you do not know seems, on the face of it, simply paradoxical. So the arguments for the impossibility of self-knowledge depend on failures of reflexivity and failures of transparency.

The lack of benefit afforded by self-knowledge is also inferred in two ways. The first argument for the lack of benefit is a direct consequence of the second argument for impossibility. Second-order knowledge, where it exists, looks to have no benefit. This is because only first-order knowledge is useful: medicine produces health, construction produces houses. Self-knowledge is a second-order knowledge – whether as knowledge of knowledge, or knowing what one knows, or knowing that one has some knowledge – and so it cannot be useful. The second argument stands out as even more devastating. True, only first-order knowledge is useful, but actually only one kind of first-order knowledge is beneficial: the knowledge of good and bad. Knowledge of knowledge is not the knowledge of good and bad. And even if as a second-order knowledge it oversaw the first-order knowledge of good and bad, the failure of transparency mentioned above would prevent it from being beneficial even at one remove. Thus knowledge of knowledge – or in other terms, self-knowledge – is unbeneficial.

I have paraphrased these arguments against self-knowledge from a rather more circular and confusing conversation between Socrates and Critias. In this paraphrased form, they may not appear so very impressive. We may even wonder why Critias accepts them. We might attribute his acceptance of them – or his failure to deny them – to the blurriness of a meandering conversation and the suggestive force of Socrates' loaded questions. Or an inadequately articulated and thus unexamined picture of self-knowledge may have held Critias in its thrall. But neither the conversational ambiguities nor Critias' inadequacies allows us simply to dismiss these seemingly weak arguments against self-knowledge's possibility and benefit. After all, the doubts are common, and their resolution less simple than it might seem. It may be even trickier to see how the *Charmides*, with its Socratic conversation, offers a way to account for self-knowledge that allows for it to be possible and beneficial, and that simultaneously awards it the honorific "self-knowledge." All the same, I believe that with the resources of the *Charmides* we can both diagnose the arguments against the viability of exhorting people to know themselves and also salvage a promising picture of self-knowledge. The title of the dialogue points to the face of this picture, the young man Charmides himself. The dialogue is about the means by which he must come into himself as a responsible adult. It is a picture of intellectual and moral maturation, what we have earlier called self-constitution.

The *Charmides* is essential to the study of Socratic self-knowledge because it deals directly with the most essential difficulties; but it also puts the question of self-knowledge into a uniquely rich context. The dialogue depicts Socrates' first substantial conversation after his return from a multi-year military campaign in the early 420s, and in the process conjoins Socrates' ethical, epistemological, social, and political concerns. He confronts, on the one side, his democratic friend Chaerephon and, on the other, his aristocratic, eventually tyrannical, associates Charmides and Critias.[4] The talk about self-knowledge amounts to a testing of Critias' definition of *sôphrosunê* – discipline or sound-mindedness – as knowing oneself; this follows and precedes attempts at equating *sôphrosunê* with composure, diffidence, propriety, prudence, the knowledge of knowledge and ignorance, and, indirectly, the knowledge of what is good and bad.[5] Because all these dispositions overlap to a degree, self-knowledge looks to fall in with all these possible glosses of *sôphrosunê*. This itself presents coming

[4] On Chaerephon, see Moore 2013a; on Charmides and Critias, see Tuozzo 2011: 53–90.

[5] Socrates never takes up Aristotle's definition of *sôphrosunê* (*EN* 1117b24–1119b20), concerned with control over one's appetites, nor the ideas of self-mastery and appropriateness found elsewhere in Plato (*Symp*. 196c5, *Rep*. 389e, *Laws* 710a, *Grg*. 503d–508c, *St*. 309a–311c); cf. North 1966 for the full range of meanings in the Classical period. For attempts to explain these absences, see Benardete 1986: 9–15; González 1998: 41–61; Reece 1998; Schmid 1998: 2–14; Tuozzo 2011: 101–112.

to know oneself as maturation, the rational selection of appropriate behavior. The conversation hardly keeps strictly to definitional inquiry, of course; throughout it Socrates links talk about *sôphrosunê* to talk about beauty and sex, knowledge and its criteria, grammar and logic, pedagogical and investigative methodology, and the deep psychological expectations people grow up with and burnish in their associations with others. Because questions of self-knowledge occupy the core of the dialogue, we realize that these other strands of thought pertain to understanding self-knowledge too.

This chapter begins, naturally enough, with Critias' stunning interpretation of the *gnôthi sauton* inscribed at the Temple of Apollo at Delphi. It is the longest and most peculiar attempt to explain the inscription found in the Socratic literature. Socrates neither affirms nor denies the account. Several commentators have argued that it simply undermines Critias' credibility as a productive interlocutor. These arguments are not persuasive. I argue instead that this seeming digression actually enunciates a key aspect of the Socratic understanding of the *gnôthi sauton*: one should acknowledge others and oneself as persons worthy of conversational engagement. The recognition of personhood and one's suitability for dialectical exchange is a principal move in knowing oneself as an authoritative epistemic agent – that is, as a knower and a self.

In the subsequent section, I show that Socrates uses his series of definitional exchanges with Charmides, and then Critias, to modify the way we think about knowing oneself – these exchanges are the sorts of conversational engagement to which the Delphic inscription must pertain. At first, Socrates commands an introspective procedure: peering within one's present-moment consciousness. When Charmides cannot say what he wishes to be able to say, Socrates gives him a different command, asking for a reflexive attitude with greater mediation and interpretation. In each of several further commands for self-revelation, Socrates gets farther away from bodily, perceptual, and localized self knowledge and closer to a procedure reliant on public discussion of theses plausibly worthy of personal acceptance. He shows that a person best knows his commitments – what he takes to be good and true – through the mutual testing of plausible ideas. Of course this procedure involves more than testing one's own preexisting commitments; it also proposes theses that, on the basis of a person's deepest commitments, he may find good reasons to accept. These beliefs and desires are not simply possessions of something prior or more substantial that can also be known – some "self," for example; they are all that can be known, and therefore, so I argue, are what the self to be known is. This means that we become – and come to know – who we are through conversation about beliefs we may not even yet hold.

I turn then explicitly to the obstacles to self-knowledge. First, I diagnose the agreements that lead to the supposed impossibility of reflexivity and transparency. Socrates hints repeatedly that these agreements deserve a fresh reappraisal. I recall that the Delphic command addresses us as human beings, not as disembodied instances of knowledge. So even if knowledge in its bare state cannot self-apply, as seems to be the case for other intentional or relative states, and even if knowledge does not see through other instances of knowledge, there are presumably various ways for *a person* to know her knowledge. Second, I diagnose the agreements that lead to the supposed uselessness of self-knowledge. As with the other set of agreements, Socrates nods to the importance of going back over them. Again, trouble arises when one forgets that the Delphic inscription commands that we know *ourselves*, not knowledge specifically. As we learn in the section that analyzes the increasingly social definitional exchanges, we count more as a "self" the more we can act on the basis of knowledge of what is (held in one's conversations to be) good and what is true: that is, on the basis of good desires and true beliefs. When we act on the basis of whim, error, or ignorance, we hardly attribute these actions to ourselves; we attribute them instead to such foreign causes as these. Knowing oneself thus has two aspects, as Socrates' conversation suggests: determining whether you know what is good (in certain realms) and determining whether you know what is true (in certain realms). Determining whether you know what is good in some realm allows you to act with benefit, even if the benefit of this knowledge is derivative on actually knowing *how* to act in that realm. Similarly, determining whether you know what is true in some realm – which is knowing whether you have knowledge there – allows you to decide whether you can act in various cases, even if the benefit of this knowledge is derivative on actually knowing whether it would be *good* to act in this case. Knowing the good, and knowing your knowledge, are mutually dependent for living well.

The conclusion of this chapter reviews the contributions of the *Charmides* to our investigation into Socratic self-knowledge, bringing together the dialogue's attention to acknowledgment and conversation, talk about meritorious ideas, and coming to know what is good and what one knows as the two-track route to successful living. The biggest problems to Socratic self-knowledge have been relieved. In subsequent chapters we will see the smaller though still insidious ones, and their solutions.

Critias and the Delphic inscription

Critias, cousin of the eponymous Charmides and eventual oligarch, is the one who brings up the Delphic *gnôthi sauton* in this dialogue. He appeals to it in support of his third definition of *sôphrosunê*, as "one's knowing oneself," the definition that occupies his and Socrates' attention for nearly the whole of the dialogue's second half. He does not simply free-associate to a familiar or authoritative moral charge. He defends his view. Critias claims that *gnôthi sauton*, inscribed on the Delphic temple, actually means *sôphronei*, "be disciplined," and thus these commands' results, self-knowledge and *sôphrosunê*, are the same. Socrates does not assess Critias' argument about the precept's Delphic meaning. Instead he tests whether the apparent equivalences to self-knowledge – for example, knowledge of knowledge and ignorance, or knowing that one has knowledge – are possible and beneficial in the way *sôphrosunê* is. We will turn to this testing in a later section. Socrates' turn away from the details of Critias' Delphic story to the value of the definition itself has some importance. It suggests that he accepts the story as a somehow edifying, even if strictly untrue, disquisition on the meaning of the Delphic inscription. This is what justifies close scrutiny of it. When we give it that scrutiny, we will find that it highlights the role of acknowledgment and conversation in a way that recalls the opening drama of the dialogue. This opening drama suggests that self-recognition and self-knowledge, and subsequent moral and intellectual maturation, come only through conversation.

It is worth starting by seeing how Critias comes to claim that *sôphrosunê* is self-knowledge. Though he presents it as a new definition, it follows plausibly from his previous (inadequately supported) definitions. When he goes on to defend this new definition, his reasoning is hardly compelling, but has a certain charm and resonance nevertheless.

The route to a definition

Socrates begins his search for a definition of *sôphrosunê* with three suggestions offered by Charmides, a young and handsome man esteemed for his *sôphrosunê* (157d3–8). In fact, Socrates began his questioning as an investigation into whether Charmides really is *sôphrôn* (157a5–159a10; discussed in the next section). When Charmides fails to defend against refutation all three definitions he proposes, however, Charmides cedes the conversation to Critias. This transfer makes sense; Critias already claimed to know that Charmides exemplified *sôphrosunê* and also provided Charmides with his third definition (161b5).

Critias begins by retrying this third definition of *sôphrosunê*, "doing one's own things" (τὸ τὰ ἑαυτοῦ πράττειν, 162d5–6). When he cannot sustain his views against Socratic pressure, even with complex linguistic maneuvers and appeals to Hesiodic authority, he modifies his view to "doing good things" (τὴν ... τῶν ἀγαθῶν πρᾶξιν, 163e10). But a consequence, that a *sôphrôn* person could do good things without realizing it (164b11–c2), and thus without realizing that he was *sôphrôn*, looks quite impossible to Critias (164c7), and so he drops this definition, too, occasioning the self-knowledge definition. But before we look at that definition, the dialogue's fifth and most significant, we should note that Critias, despite his confident rejection of his "doing good things" definition, does not explain his rejection. He must believe that the definition's adverse consequence, being *sôphrôn* without realizing it, is universally unacceptable. He might accept something like the following reasoning. A person acts well only when he knows what is good, and more specifically when he knows whether his own actions are good. If he did not know whether his actions were good, he would be acting well only accidentally. If everyone always intends to act well, acting well only accidentally would mean *acting* only accidentally. If a person acts intending to attain some good, but fails to attain the good, then he has not acted as he intended, and if acting is intentional behavior, then he has not acted. So failing to know whether his actions are good amounts to failing to act. He would instead be, for all intents and purposes, flailing about, or at best engaging in stereotyped behavior. The *sôphrôn* seems, if nothing else, a person who *acts* (wholeheartedly) rather than flails about (erratically), who is in control of his actions rather than controlled by his accidental impulses. A consequence of knowing that one does good things – with the addition, of course, of knowing what counts as *sôphrosunê* – is knowing that one is *sôphrôn*.

Upon recognizing the inadequacy with his definition that *sôphrosunê* is "doing good things," Critias could have added two words and tried "knowing and doing good things." He does not, and drops the language of "doing" and "good" altogether. His adoption of the definition "knowing oneself" is odd, for it bleaches out the talk of action and value that is presumably central to talk of *sôphrosunê*. But perhaps Critias' reformulation makes sense. Critias might take "knowing that one is *sôphrôn*" to summarize "doing and knowing what is good"; he might take "knowing oneself" in turn to summarize "knowing that one is *sôphrôn*." The first formulation, "doing and knowing what is good," might strike him as an inelegant and inadequately unified definition, and he and Charmides strive to follow norms of good definition (cf. 159b5, 160e4–5). The second formulation, "knowing that one is *sôphrôn*," might strike him as simply circular when taken as a definition of *sôphrosunê*, defining something in terms of itself. Thus "knowing oneself" might strike Critias as a happily Socratic formulation, and remind him of the *gnôthi sauton*, which he knows has cultural weight. This reasoning might of course trouble some people, if it equivocates on "being *sôphrôn*": in the middle step ("knowing that one is *sôphrôn*") it means "knowing and doing good," and in the conclusion, it means "knowing oneself." But if "knowing oneself" is elliptical for something like "knowing and doing good, and thus being an agent, and knowing it," then the equivocation is harmless. In any event, this reasoning might be worth trying out.[6]

Critias does not try it out. He neither notes the simple addition he needs to make to his second definition nor explains the relationship between it and his third definition. In fact, he even blurts out that he would happily retract any mistake they might find in his earlier claims (164c7–d2, 165a8–b3). He does not isolate that mistake, and, as we have seen, he need not retract anything except the claim that doing good things itself constitutes *sôphrosunê*; he really just needs to add something. Surprisingly, then, while Critias seems to have a reasonable idea about *sôphrosunê* or even self-knowledge, he seems not to know the reasons for the idea that make it good. He cannot know that he

6 See Tuckey 1951: 23–26; van der Ben 1985: 41–42; and Tuozzo 2011: 178–185, for alternative reconstructions.

really knows, rather than just surmises, the definition; he has given a useful answer accidentally. He apparently lacks the very *sôphrosunê* and self-knowledge the nature of which he expounds. Critias' ignorance of the straightforward implicit reasoning in his reformulation becomes most evident in his next remarks. He decides in fact to explain his equation of *sôphrosunê* and knowing oneself. And yet he does so in just about the strangest possible way.

Apollo's greeting as explanation

In support of his third definition, Critias turns to the fact that the *gnôthi sauton* is inscribed at the front of the Temple of Apollo at Delphi. Critias asserts that this inscription represents the god's salutation to visitors. This view differs from the traditional supposition, that it simply advises visitors (164d5–165a8). Critias explains how this traditional supposition could have come about. Gods speak rather riddlingly (164e9), and so they would say something other than what they mean. According to Critias, the most apt salutation for the god would be *sôphronei* (164e3, e8). The inscription *gnôthi sauton* would be the riddle that refers to *sôphronei*. Thus, Critias concludes, "one's knowing oneself" (τὸ γιγνώσκειν αὑτὸν ἑαυτόν) is the same thing as *sôphrosunê* (165b4).

Critias' thinking here is baffling. None of his assumptions is more plausible than the resulting equation of *sôphrosunê* with self-knowledge, especially since that equation might have been common knowledge since at least Heraclitus' time. Critias assumes that the temple, or its god, greets its visitors; he assumes that a god would obviously welcome guests with the greeting "be *sôphrôn*"; and he assumes that a god would say "know yourself" to mean "be *sôphrôn*."

Because Critias' reasoning seems to do no useful explanatory work, many readers have come to suppose that Critias wants merely to show off his sophistic rhetoric, his interpretative acumen, his aping or assimilation of Socratic interests, or his cynical view of theological mythology.[7] Others have ignored Critias' intentions and thought that Plato includes this story about the Delphic inscription (as well as the scene with Chaerephon at the dialogue's beginning, 153b2–c7)

[7] Bruell 1977: 165; Benardete 1986: 25–27; West and West 1986: 36n45, 39n48; Schmid 1998: 36–38; Lampert 2010: 186–190.

to presage the *Apology* story of the Delphic Oracle.[8] None of these dismissive explanations, however, considers Critias' account in close detail. Nor do they take seriously the fact that were Critias influenced by the Socratic culture of interest in the *gnôthi sauton*, he could be a good source of information about it. Because of Critias' connection with Socrates, the evidence that he articulates good if unexplained ideas, the literary fact that this discussion is at the center of the dialogue, and the reality that we have a reference to the *gnôthi sauton*, a term so significant in the Socratic literature, we have reason to take his remarks seriously.[9]

Critias never entertains, even to dismiss, the idea commonly retrojected onto the inscription, that it warns visitors to remember their limitations or place as they enter the god's domain. He also denies that it merely pronounces some helpful advice (165a1–5). His key claim is that the inscription serves as opening words to those entering (προσρῆσις, 164d7, 8). A *prosrêsis* is used to address someone – whether familiar or not – as a person with whom one might have conversation.[10] As the Athenian Visitor says in the *Laws*, one should nearly always "address" (πρόσρησιν) a slave with an "order" rather than with the standard greeting due to free persons, because the standard greeting causes those exchanging it to become "familiar" (προσπαίζοντας) (777e5–7). Critias thereby treats the inscription as an expression of acknowledgment, an admission into possible rapport. Since a *prosrêsis*

[8] Bruell 1977: 142; Woolf 2008: 23.

[9] Critias has long-standing membership in Socrates' circle of "philosophy" discussants (implied at 153c7). He has trained Charmides to answer definitional questions "in a word," in the Socratic fashion (159b5, cf. 160e4–5). He cites Hesiod as evidence, just as Socrates cites Homer, and he draws Prodicean distinctions (163b2). He understands that holding certain commitments prevents him from holding other commitments, preempts claims of inconsistency (164d1–2, 165b1–3), and asks for agreement (165b3–4). He even identifies undue simplifications (165e3–166a2, b7–c6). Landy 1999 offers further, if at times tenuous, arguments for Critias' connection to Socrates. Schmid 1998: 37; Press 2002; and Lampert 2010 observe that Critias got his ideas from Socrates, but think that he corrupted or misunderstood them.

[10] At the beginning of the *Statesman*, Socrates observes that a young man and friend of Theaetetus is also "called" and "addressed as" (κλῆσις … πρόσρησις) "Socrates" (258a1); he says that one ought to "be eager to recognize (ἀναγνωρίζειν) those akin to us by talking to them." The right *prosrêsis* can contribute to praise (*St.* 306e7), even if that praise is misplaced (*Soph.* 239a10). Tuozzo 2000 and 2011: 186–188, also draws attention to the function of greeting and conversation in this passage.

introduces conversation, and conversation depends on the willingness and sensitivity to listen, respond, and adapt to what others say, and the ability to entertain new and potentially worthwhile ideas, together the ideal qualities of a mature person, a *prosrêsis* stereotypically acknowledges personhood.[11]

Two scenes of recognition and conversation

That we should take Critias to be bringing up greeting, acknowledgment, and their relationship to conversation gets evidence from the early part of the *Charmides*. There Plato presents two counterbalanced scenes of recognition, conversational introduction, and their delay. The first scene opens the dialogue. Socrates, discharged from the army at Potideia, has hurriedly arrived at the palaestra (ἥκομεν … ἀφιγμένος … εἰσῆλθον, 153a1–2). There he discovers many that he knew (γνωρίμους), and some he did not yet know (ἀγνῶτας, 153a6). All who notice his entrance welcome him (ἠσπάζοντο, 153b1). Chaerephon does so most vehemently, running toward him, grabbing his hand, and asking him how he survived the battle (153b2–6). Socrates goes on to greet Critias and his companions (153c8–9), answer all their questions about the war, and ask his own questions. He is especially interested in talking about the state of philosophy – as a circle of particular kinds of conversation – and of promising young candidates for membership in their philosophical circle (153d2–5). From Socrates' energetic and easy reunion springs the conversation depicted in the dialogue, one presumably helpful to all his companions.

Against this set-piece of recognition and the fast recovery of rapport, Socrates narrates Charmides' later entrance. Socrates has just inquired after the rising stars of beauty and wisdom. Then, Critias looks to the door, seeing some youths entering (εἰσιόντας … εἰσιόντες, 153d5–154a4). They are Charmides' advance guard, and pay attention to nobody but themselves. Soon Charmides himself enters (εἰσέρχεται, 154b7; εἰσῄκει, c4). He greets nobody, and nobody greets him in turn; all are stunned, in love, astonished, and in noisy confusion

[11] Contrast Benardete 1986: 27, who says that the *gnôthi sauton* "is purely formal and does not require one to do anything more than echo it when one hears it. It is just a polite version of 'Mind your own business.'" Benardete later gives it more content when he says, quite gnomically, that it means "Be knowledge." (I am not sure whether this would be an inspiring or rude greeting.)

(θαυμαστος ... ἐρᾶν ... ἐκπεπληγμένοι ... τεθορυβημένοι, 154c1–3). They stare at him as though he were a statue (ἄγαλμα ἐθεῶντο, 154c8). Even Chaerephon cites only the beauty of Charmides' face and body (εὐπρόσωπος, 154d2; τὸ εἶδος πάγκαλος, d5). There is no acknowledgment here, only aesthetic or sexual infatuation. No rapport ensues. Indeed, Socrates can speak to Charmides only once Critias manages a ruse, pretending to his ward that Socrates will cure the young man's headache. Despite that, at first Charmides does not even want a conversation. Though he sits next to Socrates (155c5), and gives him an irresistible (ἀμήχανόν, 155d1) look, he does not greet Socrates, instead asking whether Socrates is the one who knows the cure and then to write it down (156a1–2), presumably to work on it alone.[12] He treats Socrates totally instrumentally. It is not until Socrates jokes about Charmides' failure to gain rapport with him – wondering whether Charmides will act with persuasion or not (156a3) – that Charmides laughs, calls Socrates by his name, and acknowledges that he already knows Socrates (156a4–8).[13] Socrates says that he is glad about the familiarity, because it will allow him to speak more freely (παρρησιάσομαι, 156a9–b1). With this frank speech Socrates can eventually diagnose Charmides as needing more conversation, a diagnosis to which Charmides, in the end, happily submits (176a6–c2).

Critias' story about the Delphic inscription reads more forcefully seen against these two introductory scenes of entering and acknowledging. Greetings give us the chance to reacquaint ourselves with each other as sharers in the human experience, express our pleasure at our reunion, and open ourselves to questions and answers. In the absence of greeting, those already present are ignored (as absent or uninteresting), and those who enter are objectified (as items for visual consumption or gossip). Thus for Apollo, or Apollo's syndicates, to greet the temple entrants is to acknowledge their aptness for communication and to express openness to conversational interchange.

[12] Cf. McAvoy 1996: 84.

[13] Contrast this account of Socrates' remark about persuasion with Tuozzo 2011: 111–112, who observes that persuasion appeals to the benefits that the audience would receive from some course of action.

Greetings that are not advice but urgings-on instead

Greetings have this deep social and ethical use, whatever their specific words. But they do take specific words. The traditional human greeting, Critias says, is "rejoice" (χαῖρε). Critias warns against taking greetings as advice. In the case of *chaire*, then, the greeting is not to be understood as recommending to those that do not find joy in their lives to do so. Critias does not explain his reasoning. Perhaps he thinks that such recommendations would be presumptuous or paternalistic. This would start conversations off badly. All the same, greetings are phrased as recommendations, indeed as commands. Fortunately, between the greeting and the advice or command is a middle speech-act: an "urging each other on" (παρακελεύεσθαι ἀλλήλοις, 164e2). This exhorts the addressees to do what they are already doing. Socrates thematizes the word *parakeleuesthai* in the *Phaedo* – interestingly, in the one place in this dialogue about knowing oneself where he explicitly admits to doing philosophy, and where he describes what he takes as his defining occupation. Socrates says that a dream had often told him to work on music and make an effort. He used to interpret that dream, he says, as "urging on and encouraging what I was [i.e., continuously] doing, just as those cheering on runners do, encouraging this, making music" (**παρακελεύεσθαί** τε καὶ **ἐπικελεύειν**, ὥσπερ οἱ τοῖς θέουσι **διακελευόμενοι**, καὶ ἐμοὶ οὕτω τὸ ἐνύπνιον, ὅπερ ἔπραττον, τοῦτο ἐπικελεύειν, μουσικὴν ποιεῖν, 60e8–61a3). Socrates uses three words that share the –κελευω stem, each expressing a speech-act that is not quite a command (cf. *Chrm.* 176c2–3). Cheers and other shouts of encouragement tell people to do what the speaker thereby acknowledges they are already doing. So urging someone on encourages her to do what she already tries to do, and points out that one realizes she already tries to do it, and affirms it. Saying "Good day" or *chaire* wishes your listener to have a good day, without implying that she is not already doing so, and admits to your realization that your listener has the capacities for having, and is trying already to have, a good day or opportunity for rejoicing. We might explain the importance of greetings to conversation by observing that the recognition that one wishes a continued good or cheerful day is what allows conversation to ensue, just as a farewell is an invitation to future conversations. Each party to the conversation is to expect that whatever questions, criticisms, or ideas he provides the other are spoken in the spirit of contributing to each other's efforts to have a good or joyous day. As our real-life experience shows us, many people fail to greet us at all, or fail to greet us well, and this sort of slight, while often overlooked, is real and disappointing. Acknowledgment of others is difficult, even in the form of a greeting, as difficult as having good conversations is.[14]

Critias explains that it is appropriate to greet, but *chaire*, despite being what humans say to one another, is not the correct greeting (164e1). It is better to say *sôphronei* (164e2–4). Critias does not explain why. A fair guess is that *chaire* seems to Critias to depend on hedonistic assumptions, and that the god would abjure such superficial measures of wellbeing.[15] Indeed, the author of the Platonic *Epistle III* makes a similar argument, in a remarkable parallel to this passage:

> Plato to Dionysius, rejoice (χαίρειν):
>
> Would I thus be addressing you (ἐπιστείλας) with the best greeting (προσρήσεως)? Or should I rather, in accord with my habits, write "Do well" (εὖ πράττειν), as I usually address (προσαγορεύειν) my friends in letters? For indeed even you, as the ones on your embassy to Delphi announced, addressed (προσεῖπες) the god flattering him with this expression, writing, so they say: "Rejoice (χαῖρε) and preserve the pleasant (ἡδόμενον) life of the tyrant!"
>
> But I would urge on (παρακελευσαίμην) no man with this invocation (κλήσει), nor indeed any god, to do this: regarding god, because I would be assigning (προστάττοιμ') what is against his nature, for the divine sits far from pleasure and pain; and regarding a person, because pleasure and pain beget much harm, bringing stupidity, forgetfulness, foolishness, and hubris into the soul. And let these be the things I have said about addresses (προσρήσεως). You reading these things, however you wish to accept them, in that way accept them. (315a8–c10)

"Do well," the author's stated preferential form of address, is in fact the salutation found in the twelve other Platonic letters. *Epistle XIII* even explicitly identifies this form as idiosyncratic to Plato (360a2).[16]

[14] We admire people who set us at ease, take our company seriously, and look after our wellbeing. McCabe 2011: 179n9, is mistaken, I think, to treat proper acknowledgment as categorically simpler than knowing oneself.

[15] Argued by Witte 1970: 98 and Tuozzo 2011: 186–187. But it is not generally observed in *Charmides* scholarship that *chaire* is addressed to the god by a visitor to his or her sanctuary (like Delphi), requesting that the god take pleasure in one's visit, offerings, song, and so forth: see Race 1982: 8–10; MacLachlan 1993; Rutherford 2001: 76.

[16] Hackforth 1913: 52–68, 188, accepts Platonic authorship of both *Ep. III* and *XIII*.

It means perhaps something akin to *sôphronei*. The important point is that Plato (or his imitators knew that he) took seriously the implication of "rejoice" as a salutation, associated it with pleasure, and associated pleasure with its attendant problems. It would be better, the letter-writer says, to invoke people with "do well" because then this invocation, which is an urging and an assigning, would be more suitable.[17]

Whatever Critias' reasons for rejecting *chaire*, he claims that the god would want to encourage his visitors to *sôphronein*. Doing so would urge his visitors on in a pursuit to which they should already find themselves committed. This coheres with our interpretation of Heraclitus' fr. 116, that people already have or seek self-knowledge to some extent, but must keep at it diligently. For the Temple at Delphi to express such a salutation allows conversation to ensue. And if conversation conduces to being *sôphrôn* (as the *Charmides* seems to show; cf. 176b5–8), *sôphronei* would be an especially apt way to build rapport for conversation. The goodwill it expresses, in hoping that the person greeted may persevere and succeed in becoming *sôphrôn*, would lead to just the sort of activity that would support such success.

The greeting "Know yourself"

Critias says that the Delphic greeting means *sôphronei*; but of course the Temple nowhere says that. The inscription is in fact ΓΝΩΘΙ ΣΑΥΤΟΝ. Critias takes these two commands, or urgings-on, as "the same" (ταὐτόν, 165a1). His inference from "do good things" to "know yourself" by way of the implicit addition of "know what is good" and the corollary "know the goodness of what you're doing" suggests that he takes the greeting to mean "Know and do what is good; and know that you know this." Given that salutations acknowledge people, and that *gignôskein* can mean "recognize" or "acknowledge," the god

[17] Similar reasoning is given in Plutarch's dialogue, *On the E at Delphi* 17. Speaking of the "E," another inscription on the Temple of Apollo at Delphi, Plutarch's Ammonius says "It is an address and salutation (προσαγόρευσις καὶ προσφώνησις) to the god, complete in itself, which, by being spoken, brings him who utters it to thoughts of the god's power. For the god welcomes and addresses each one of us as we approach (προσιόντα οἷον ἀσπαζόμενος προσαγορεύει) him here with the words 'Know Yourself,' which certainly is in no way of less import than 'Rejoice' (χαῖρε); and we in turn reply to him 'You are' (εἶ)" (tr. Babbitt 1936, modified).

seems to be acknowledging a visitor by urging him to acknowledge himself. Granted, this is not the most perspicuous way to put it. We might rather say that the particular formulation of *know yourself* highlights the speaker's wish to applaud and encourage the self-reflective part of being *sôphrôn*, and hope that the coming conversation conduces to such self-reflection. It might very well conduce to that, to the extent that the conversation takes on questions about what is good and what is not. The salutation could also encourage acknowledging oneself as a potential object for transformative conversation. Knowing yourself requires assuming a certain pliability and capacity for improvement. In both cases, greetings open up rapport by acknowledging the possibility of conversation. Conversation involves both question and answer, discovery and criticism, entertainment of ideas and the development or rejection of those ideas. The chance to participate in a conversation thereby involves the chance to improve oneself. The proper encouragement of such conversations, by expressing good will and shared hopes, is important, because conversations will sometimes seem to work at cross-purposes to one's goals. Some, like the one depicted in the *Charmides*, may even seem to show that the interlocutors know so little about *sôphrosunê* as to undermine any hopes of finding it. Greeting someone with *gnôthi sauton* or *sôphronei* promises that the coming interaction will aim to cause them to know themselves more and to grow in *sôphrosunê*.

Critias' gloss of the *gnôthi sauton* has two instructive absences. The first is his lack of interest in the second-person pronoun in the classic saying (σαυτόν). He thus addresses neither the nature of selfhood nor the paradoxes of reflexivity. While this could reveal Critias' incautious hermeneutical procedure, it could just as well show that we need not always take the grammar of a precept so seriously. Critias may be thinking here – though presumably not later – that self-knowledge, while reflexive, is not best understood in its guise of *sôphrosunê* through its reflexivity. After all, three of the previous four definitions of *sôphrosunê* forewent reflexive language: quietness, modesty, doing good things. Here, knowing oneself is being *sôphrôn*, and more particularly, knowing and doing what is good; in brief, "doing well" or being virtuous. This is self-oriented but not self-focused, in the way that self-mastery is not most notably mastery over oneself but mastery that makes one a self (a master *at* something).[18]

[18] Kosman 1983, 2012.

The second instructive absence is Critias' obscurity in his distinction between the *gnôthi sauton* and the two other most famous Delphic inscriptions, "nothing too much" and "pledge, and ruin is near" (165a3). He claims that the latter two precepts do serve not as riddling salutations but instead as useful advice (συμβουλὰς χρησίμους, 165a6–7). He does not assimilate them to self-knowledge or *sôphrosunê*. This suggests that Critias dissociates self-knowledge and *sôphrosunê* from moderation, on the one hand, and from self-sufficiency, on the other hand. Perhaps he thinks the commands these precepts imply – "Don't do too much" and "Don't pledge yourself" – are, in their negative formulation, too passive, and that salutations should encourage salutary activity.

Critias understands the *gnôthi sauton* as a way of acknowledging someone's aptness for conversation, where conversation may conduce to self-knowledge and *sôphrosunê*. He implies that people are already trying to know themselves, and that they may be encouraged to keep doing so. The proximity of this digression to his earlier claim that *sôphrosunê* involved doing one's own things, and doing good things, and perhaps even knowing what is good, suggests that he thinks that the conversations enabled by the salutation could promote these elements of *sôphrosunê*.

Ways of knowing oneself

Critias' story gives way to the assessment of his newest definition of *sôphrosunê*. It is here that self-knowledge runs into its biggest problems, its possible non-existence and uselessness. As we have already seen in outline at the start of this chapter, these problems may prove surmountable. Some of the most compelling evidence against the reality of these problems comes from Socrates' exchange with Charmides. In it, Socrates gives a sequence of instructions to Charmides to discover something about himself: whether he is *sôphrôn*. As we have seen in the previous section, knowing whether one is *sôphrôn* seems to represent not just a part but the whole of knowing oneself. Socrates' earliest instructions to Charmides emphasize introspection and other forms of inward perception. As Socrates refutes the notions of *sôphrosunê* that these forms of "looking inside" generate, his later instructions increasingly abandon "empirical" modes of search and replace them with increasingly conversation-based evaluation of ideas.[19] Contemporary philosophy observes that this method depends on the "transparency" thesis: that we know what we believe by deciding what we should believe; our beliefs are transparent to our understanding of the world.[20] Our beliefs, after all, are not mere clutter to be shuffled and pruned; they are active commitments to the truth as best we see it. (Desires are active commitments to what is good as best we see it.) Treating the search for self-knowledge as inward looking fails to acknowledge belief's normative character. Neither Charmides nor Critias will know themselves, and reap the benefits the Delphic inscription could conceivably provide, simply by grasping images inside themselves. This positive lesson about and picture of self-knowledge provides a counterpoint to the abstruse content of the literal talk about self-knowledge in the dialogue's second half.

As Socrates provides a picture of self-knowledge increasingly connected to public debate of ideals and rationality, he does not thereby abandon the core of self-knowledge as *knowledge of self*. He does not transform self-knowledge into knowledge in general, for example. Instead, he helps his audience, and by extension the dialogue's reader, revisit what self-knowledge, and thus selfhood, might be. Selfhood looks to be connected less to the impressions and forces located in one's mind, and more to that for which one is responsible, one's commitments.

Procedure 1: admission

Socrates asks Charmides about *sôphrosunê* for two reasons. First, Critias has said that Charmides possesses more than anyone his age (157d1–7), and Socrates would like to know whether this is true. Second, which remedy Socrates must use to relieve Charmides' headache purportedly depends on Charmides' possession of *sôphrosunê* (157d3, 158b5–c2). Socrates will not diagnose Charmides by looking at him or by relying on others' testimony. He takes another tack. He simply asks Charmides to say himself whether he agrees with Critias – that he excels all others in *sôphrosunê* – and to say whether he has it (αὐτὸς οὖν μοι εἰπὲ πότερον ὁμολογεῖς τῷδε καὶ φῂς ἱκανῶς ἤδη

[19] Most commentators conflate the methods, e.g., Landy 1999: 187; but West and West 1986: 6, is an exception.

[20] Evans 1982: 225; Moran 2001.

σωφροσύνης μετέχειν, 158c2–4). In asking his two-part question in this way, Socrates focuses on the first-personal aspect of self-knowledge.[21] *Sôphrosunê* is something a person possesses, in their soul. It would seem, therefore, to be known only by the person himself (αὐτός). It would also seem knowable and admitted to (φῄς) immediately. This picture of self-knowledge assumes the unmediated, uninterpreted, and unimpeded presence to mind of all one's psychic states.

This procedure, and the associated picture, yield mixed results. They certainly get Charmides to attend to himself, with such self-consciousness that he blushes and glows (158c5–6). This might itself represent something like *sôphrosunê* or the related *aidôs*. But it does not bring him to answer either part of the question about his possession of *sôphrosunê*. Charmides feels strong pressures not to answer in either way. Disagreeing with Critias would show him – and his other admirers – up (158d3–5). Since a disagreement with Critias would also amount to speaking against himself, a strange enough thing to do, he would, further, bewilder those around him (ἄτοπον αὐτὸν καθ ἑαυτοῦ τοιαῦτα λέγειν, 158d2). On the other hand, agreeing with Critias that he exemplifies *sôphrosunê* would involve self-praise, which could very well be grating (ἐμαυτὸν ἐπαινῶ, ἴσως ἐπαχθὲς φανεῖται, 158d4).[22] Charmides is in a bind. This does not mean that Charmides does not know whether he has *sôphrosunê*. It is possible that his diffidence prevents him from saying what he knows. It is also possible, of course, that his diffidence obscures his nature even from himself. Whatever it is, Charmides' failure to follow Socrates' instructions means that we cannot count on a person revealing, or being able to reveal, himself simply because he is the one with the traits to reveal.

Procedure 2: introspection

To save Charmides from his embarrassed bind while still trying to get him to reveal himself, Socrates takes a new tack. He starts by saying twice that he would like to investigate with Charmides (κοινῇ ἂν εἴη σκεπτέον εἴτε κέκτησαι εἴτε μὴ ὃ πυνθάνομαι, 158d8–e1; ἐθέλω σκοπεῖν μετὰ σοῦ, e3). Charmides tells Socrates to consider how best to investigate;

21 Contrast Bruell 1977: 144, 152.

22 The strangeness and irritation of these two self-directed attitudes seem to presage the strangeness and irritation of self-knowledge.

Socrates parrots his words back, that the following seems the best way to investigate (158e6). Socrates sets out the way:

It is clear that if *sôphrosunê* is present to you (πάρεστιν), you can form some opinion about it. For, I suppose, its being inside you (ἔνεστιν) – if it really is – would necessarily furnish (παρέχειν) a certain perception, which would give you a certain opinion about it, as to what *sôphrosunê* is and what qualities it has (ὅτι ἐστὶν καὶ ὁποῖον τι) … So given that this at any rate is what you think (τοῦτό γε … ὃ οἴει), since you know how to speak Greek, surely you could also say the very thing that appears to you (αὐτὸ ὅτι σοι φαίνεται)? (158e7–159a7)

Socrates' recommended method treats *sôphrosunê* as some internal item, but unlike the assumption of Procedure 1, not an immediately present one. Introspection has intermediary stages. If some trait, *sôphrosunê* for example, is present in a person, it is perceptible; if perceptible, one can have an opinion about it; opinions concern a thing's nature and qualities; one's ability to speak allows one to articulate those beliefs; so if Charmides can articulate the type of thing *sôphrosunê* is, he and Socrates could guess (τοπάσωμεν, 159a9) that he possesses *sôphrosunê*.[23]

Socrates' system deploys assumptions from a naïve mechanistic psychology. It sounds like an argument from an earnest but reductionist theory of consciousness. We know about ourselves by having beliefs responsive to perceptions caused by our constituent aspects. Since we obviously know facts about ourselves, how else could we come by them? We just check and see! But this "see–think–utter" view of the mental echoes no other Socratic remarks in the dialogue. Nor do any of the characters in the *Charmides* evaluate the productivity of this route to self-knowledge. All we get is Charmides' failure to support his proposal occasioned by this set of instructions: the claim that *sôphrosunê* is a kind of quietness.[24] His failure does not directly

[23] Van der Ben 1985: 23–24, makes clear that Socrates is not asking Charmides to give his view *of* the thought (as though Charmides might misconstrue his own thought, which the translation of Lamb 1927: 27 would allow), but just to enunciate his thought.

[24] On the value of this definition, see Kosman 1983; Dusanic 2000: 59–60; McCoy 2005: 140–142; Tuozzo 2011: 157–161. West and West 1986: 26n28, note that Socrates always proceeds quietly and slowly,

impugn the method of introspection. Charmides may really have seen inside himself that *sôphrosunê* was quietness but simply lacked a strong defense of the thesis.[25] Socrates, after all, does not verify the "quietness" definition by asking about the nature of Charmides' perception or the way his belief about that perception arose. He instead inquires of Charmides whether his definition comports with other beliefs he holds. The failure of the method does not, however, speak very well for it. Had Charmides seen *sôphrosunê* within himself, one would expect he could have defended his understanding of it better and differently than he did, or at least more persistently. Had he not seen it, on the grounds that he lacked it, one would expect him to have withheld an answer. Socrates does not return to this model of introspection in anything that follows. This most strongly suggests he thinks it lacks promise.[26]

especially in contrast with those around him, and that readers of dialogues must proceed slowly. See *St.* 306d and 307a for a diagnosis of the difficulties Charmides runs into.

[25] He may even have seen that it was quietness by noting his own reluctance before speaking (καὶ ὅς τὸ μὲν πρῶτον ὤκνει τε καὶ οὐ πάνυ ἤθελεν ἀποκρίνασθαι: ἔπειτα μέντοι εἶπεν, 159b1–2); cf. Benardete 1986: 19–20, who notes, however, that that reluctance might not itself have manifested *sôphrosunê*, but that the slowness of Socrates' refutation might.

[26] That is not to say that the model is phenomenologically implausible; see the *Philebus*: "from memory and perception come opinion and the attempt to have an opinion to us" (ἐκ μνήμης τε καὶ αἰσθήσεως δόξα ἡμῖν καὶ τὸ διαδοξάζειν ἐγχειρεῖν γίγνεσθ', 38b12; cf. 39a1–7). All the same, Woolf 2008: 21, takes Socrates' investigative method here as explicit evidence against simple first-person authority. Charmides can report only his *opinions* about his internal realm, and as such Socrates can refute those opinions; thus both have only third-person access. Bruell 1977: 152–153, wonders whether Charmides should be so sure that even were he to have some perception, his opinion would correctly identify it as *sôphrosunê*, and whether he should be so sure that he has no opinions that do not come from internal perceptions. He observes that Charmides could think that "being quiet" involves avoiding self-assertion and instead giving someone else's view; were this so, Socrates' introspective method would be stymied. McCoy 2005: 138–140, gives a sunnier interpretation of this passage: "Socrates is still interested in Charmides' delving deeply into his soul to explore what he *really* thinks"; "while a person might have a correct 'sense' what σωφροσύνη is, she might not immediately be able to transform that perception into language," and this person is only partway to the goal of virtue.

Procedure 3: inference from external appearance

The method just discussed assumes that self-knowledge comes about by locating internal traits and thinking about what they are. The next method Socrates offers depends on self-reflection and inference. He replaces multi-stage direct access with a sort of multi-stage indirect access. Socrates starts by telling Charmides to apply his mind (προσέχων τὸν νοῦν, 160d5–6), the general idiom for concentrating or paying attention. He then says to look to himself for the nature of *sôphrosunê* (εἰς σεαυτὸν ἐμβλέψας, 160d6). The meaning of this claim is obscured by a textual crux. I printed the OCT's ἐμβλέψας, but the oldest manuscripts print ἀπεμβλέψας and ἀποβλέψας. The common meaning of these readings appears to be: "focus on yourself as you would focus on someone else."[27] Socrates thus tells Charmides to determine the nature of *sôphrosunê* by looking at himself in the way he would determine something by looking at someone else. This is not perceiving the trait per se, but understanding a person who has that trait. Socrates has moved beyond the "inventory" picture of self-knowledge, where one looks for some particular property or mental content and can speak about it, to a "social" picture of self-knowledge, where one understands oneself just as one understands a face-to-face companion. This is familiar from real life, where we regularly notice the feelings, beliefs, and commitments that our friends express through their faces, and infer from what we see to how they are.[28]

Socrates goes on to specify this interpretative approach: "Reflect on the sort of person the presence of *sôphrosunê* makes you (ἐννοήσας ὁποῖόν τινά σε ποιεῖ), and what sort of thing it is that would produce a person like that (τοιοῦτον ἀπεργάζοιτο)" (160d6–8). Upon having had these thoughts, Charmides is to collate (συλλογισάμενος, 160d8) them and then express how they *seem* (given that their reality is ultimately hidden). This multi-stage reasoning allows thorough self-investigation (πρὸς ἑαυτόν διασκεψάμενος, 160e2–3). Rather than looking at

27 See Murphy 2007: 220 on the crux. He defines the possibilities as follows: ἀποβλέπω, "look at from a point of observation, scrutinize"; ἐμβλέπω, "look at in the face"; ἀπεμβλέπω, a neologism probably meaning "look away from everything else into your own face/eyes."

28 Woolf 2008: 22, again treats this new method as explicit evidence against Socrates' belief in first-person authority. So it may be; but I aim to show the advice it gives about the *kind* of third-person access one might strive to have toward oneself.

sôphrosunê itself, or thinking about the perception it causes, and then enunciating what one sees or believes, Socrates recommends working backwards. Think about your personal qualities – perhaps those manifest to others, such as blushing, downcast eyes, and so forth – and then figure out what underlies them.

This routine brings Charmides to define *sôphrosunê* as shame and bashfulness (160e3–5). Though Charmides does not give the reasoning for his proposal, he seems to have thought that the noble bearing typical of the *sôphrôn* person involves deep fears of social impropriety. He may have come to think this through his own experience. In this dialogue Charmides shows himself to be susceptible to blushing self-consciousness in the face of self-assertion; self-assertion is a quality easily taken as hubris or overreaching. Perhaps, then, Charmides was thinking about the proclivities that could cause the hesitance for which his elders honor him. He might have inferred that his susceptibility to embarrassment and shame had the most active role.[29]

Charmides' identification of *sôphrosunê* with shame falls apart in about six short steps (160e9–161b2). In his refutation, Socrates deploys the new interpretative approach almost ostentatiously, explicitly inferring from a person's nature to the nature of their traits. In doing so he makes overt what Charmides may have used implicitly to come up with his definition. As Socrates reasons, *sôphrones* ("disciplined people") are good men; whatever does not produce (ἀπεργάζεται) good things is itself not good; *aidôs* sometimes does not produce good men (it is "no good for needy men," per Homer); but *sôphrosunê* always makes (ποιεῖ) good those in whom it is present; and so *sôphrosunê* is not *aidôs*. We may leave aside the details and validity of this baldly convoluted argument; Charmides readily accepts the refutation (161b3).[30] The problem with Charmides' definition of *sôphrosunê* as shame seems clear enough. He has generalized too quickly from one set of experiences to an overall claim about *sôphrosunê*. He did not take into account all his beliefs about shame, or his

[29] Interestingly, Socrates told him to discern this "manfully," and then says that he did do so (ἀνδρείως … πάνυ ἀνδρικῶς, 160e1–2).

[30] See van der Ben 1985: 28–32, for detailed reconstructions. Schmid 1998: 25–29 and McCoy 2005: 142–146, for whom the argument is important, address it only in general terms. Lampert 2010: 172–173, and Tuozzo 2011: 161–165, also note that the refutation follows the pattern Socrates asked Charmides to follow.

desire to respect Homer's judgment (who wrote the verse purportedly impugning shame). In other words, while he has started to think about *sôphrosunê* in light of larger interpretative skills and his personal habits, he is still thinking about it in too great an isolation from his many other commitments.

Procedure 4: testing of one's avowals

Immediately upon having his "shame" view refuted, Charmides says he remembers yet another view. He says he has heard that *sôphrosunê* is "doing one's own things" (τὸ τὰ ἑαυτοῦ πράττειν, 161b4–6). Socrates examines this view too, and again Charmides cannot defend the thesis. He accepts Socrates' narrow construction of "one's own things" as including one's name and one's cloak. But he also accepts that there is no impropriety, no failure of *sôphrosunê*, in writing somebody else's name, or weaving a cloak for someone else. So on this narrow construction, he cannot defend his definition of *sôphrosunê* as "doing one's own things" (161d1–162a8). Charmides has a sketchy and unreflective view of ownership and of the ways some instances of ownership are more or less private, individual, or personal than other instances of ownership.

Before this exchange, Socrates had encouraged Charmides to seek self-knowledge in a series of three ways: speaking for himself; introspecting mental objects; and inferring internal reality from external appearance. At the start of this exchange, Socrates encourages a fourth way. He suggests testing the propositions he already accepts. One's avowals reveal one's beliefs, judgments, and other commitments. By testing our avowals, we test our beliefs, and thereby test whether we can stand by those beliefs. If our beliefs withstand examination, we can say we know their truth, and that we know them, and that, therefore, we know what we stand for, and in this way at least we know ourselves. The three previous routes to self-knowledge treated the self as something empirical and inner to be publicized – either directly, or through perception and judgment, or through inference and abductive reasoning. This fourth route also treats self-knowledge as concerning something inner to be brought out, but not exactly as empirical. This inward element is something normative, the beliefs one is willing and able to take responsibility for avowing. Such an ability includes understanding one's avowals; and understanding them means making sense of them in light of one's other avowed beliefs; only some beliefs make sense in such a light; and so one would responsibly avow only those beliefs that could cohere with one's other beliefs. So one does not avow just any old inner impressions (the empirical picture); one avows those impressions deserving of the name "beliefs".

There is some danger, however, in speaking of "one's avowals," and therefore in knowing which avowals represent or constitute who one is. After all, we have just seen that Charmides fails to appreciate the ambiguity in the general phrase "one's own things" (τὰ ἑαυτοῦ). He did not recognize the differences in the ways things associated with oneself by the genitive may be considered owned by, controlled by, used by, or otherwise exclusively or partially linked with oneself. Of course, neither does Socrates analyze the concept of ownership here, or even tell Charmides that he should think about it. He leaves the problem implicit. But it is only shallowly implicit. The conversation has already brought up the challenges in assigning avowals to a person. It should not surprise us that the question of the owner of an avowal arises in the *Charmides* at the moment that the definition is about doing one's own things.

Charmides wants to test the "doing one's own things" view as a view that someone else has put forward (λέγειν ὁ λέγων, 161b7). Socrates suspects aloud that Critias or another wise man is the speaker. Critias immediately denies that Charmides heard it from him. Charmides then asks whether it matters who spoke it. Socrates says that it does not: only the truth matters. Charmides is relieved to have replaced the task of assigning responsibility – which he thinks he himself would have to perform – with that of epistemic evaluation, which he thinks Socrates will have to undertake. But as soon as it seems that avowals may be divorced from speakers, Socrates reverses course. For "doing one's own things" seems to be a riddle, something someone would say when deliberately intending to foil a listener. The speaker must have had something else in mind than the surface meaning when he gave the definition. So judging the definition requires discerning what the speaker himself really meant (161b8–d2). An avowal like this cannot be divorced from its avower.

Once Socrates finishes refuting the "doing one's own things" definition, he reiterates his view that the speaker must have spoken riddlingly. He now explains why he thinks this. The speaker is presumably not a simpleton (162a10), and so he would not have meant to say something so obviously unsupportable. Charmides amplifies this, saying that his source seemed quite wise (162b2). Indeed, Charmides reinforces this sense that avowals must be owned if they are to be avowed properly when he admits that he does not know what the definition means (162b6–8). In an important way, he could not have avowed the definition, and so could not have meant it, or believed it, or known it; he at most could echo it, uttering it as someone else's avowal.

Charmides seems unhappy, nonetheless, at the failure of this definition. Perhaps he had put some stock in its speaker, and in the self-evidence of the definition itself. Even if he could not have understood the statement (it being too confusing, for example), he could have believed that he could treat the statement as something he believed. As a consequence, in an act of vengeance, he wonders aloud whether even Critias – who Socrates assumes originated the definition – knew what he meant by it (162b9–10). He forces Critias to come to the statement's defense:

> he [Critias] seemed to get angry at him [Charmides], just like a playwright gets angry at an actor who recites his lines badly [*sc.* the poet's: τὰ ἑαυτοῦ]. So he looked him in the eye (ἐμβλέψας) and said: "Is that what you think, Charmides? That if you don't know what whoever said *sôphrosunê* is doing one's own things could have meant, then he doesn't know it either?" (162d3–8)

With the imagery of playwright and stage-actor, Socrates again shows that statements do not belong equally to all who utter them. They belong more to those who mean them, who better understand them. (This view is consistent with Socrates' view of poets in Plato's *Apology* and *Ion*. Since poets do not understand their own lines, they are in important ways not the owner of those lines; they carry god's words to an audience.) Thus unless we understand our beliefs, they are – perhaps surprisingly – not our beliefs. This is why it matters who avows a statement. Someone who avows something has at least a chance of understanding what he says, and thus an investigation of that statement becomes an investigation of that person. The statements that are one's own are those one accepts as true; and to accept something as true entails understanding it enough to resist critical onslaught.

Taking a statement as true, and thus as one's own, and thus as constitutive of oneself, does not demand that one has invented the concept on one's own. It could have been heard from elsewhere, but then made one's own by reflection or habituation.[31] Charmides' echo of Critias' definition is illicit, not because it was first said by Critias, but only because Charmides did not see whether it has any meaning for himself. Socrates underlines the legitimate path to adoption. Rather than making Critias affirm that he originated the definition that *sôphrosunê* is doing one's own things, he asks whether Critias "concedes" and "accepts the statement" (συγχωρεῖς … παραδέχῃ τὸν λόγον, 162e2–3, cf. e6). Critias does, and therefore they can go on to test it. This fourth mode of getting self-knowledge is testing the beliefs that one accepts. The beliefs that belong to a person are those he concedes he takes to be true.

In the following discussion, Critias responds to Socratic pressure by repeatedly modifying what he claims he holds to be true (162e7–163c1). Socrates accepts Critias' modifications, but pleads with him to make precise and plain what he is saying (163d6–e1). He also says, after Critias frequently wonders whether Socrates disagrees with what he is saying, that "we're not yet going to investigate how it seems to me, but what you are now saying" (163e7). This prompt works, and Socrates eventually shows Critias that his views seem to entail that a *sôphrôn* person could be ignorant of his *sôphrosunê*. Critias so little likes this consequence that he says he would rather take back his earlier agreements, the ones that imply this consequence, than admit that a *sôphrôn* person might be ignorant of his *sôphrosunê*. Critias thereby sorts through and picks out the beliefs that he thinks more likely to be true than the others, and thus more closely associates with himself.

Procedure 5: testing plausible ideas

In time, however, Socrates refutes Critias so often that Critias grows balky. He accuses Socrates of arguing incorrectly (165e2, 166b7). Critias finally grows frustrated enough to exclaim that Socrates is "trying to refute him, having given up on what the argument is about" (166c8). At this point, Socrates tries a fifth method of directing his

31 McCoy 2005 attends to Charmides' weakness for relying on others' moral authority, but she should emphasize the reasonableness of accepting, for testing, others' good ideas. Lovibond 2002 calls this learning to speak seriously.

interlocutor to gain self-knowledge.[32] Whereas the fourth method encouraged testing the beliefs one could claim already to accept, the fifth encourages testing just *any* plausible idea, even an idea one has never expressly advocated. This is in a sense the most aspirational of all forms of seeking self-knowledge. It investigates what one *could* accept, and thereby who one *could* be.

When Critias asks whether he needs to convince Socrates further that *sôphrosunê* is knowing oneself, Socrates responds that Critias acts toward him as though "I claim to know what I ask, and that, should I wish it, I would agree with you." But the truth is, Socrates says, that "I search (ζητῶ) with you each time there is a proposition, on account of my not knowing." Socrates admits to wishing to search (σκεψάμενος) before announcing any agreement or disagreement. He asks for time while he searches (ἕως ἂν σκέψωμαι). Critias accepts the agreement, urging on his search (σκόπει δή). Socrates says, using the present, "I am searching" (καὶ γὰρ ... σκοπῶ), and proceeds to ask questions (165b5–c4). The ensuing questions, through his perplexity expressed up to and near the dialogue's end (166c8–e2; ἐξ ἀρχῆς ἐπισκεψώμεθα, 167a9), must constitute his search, a thinking-aloud in common. The comically repeated terms for searching reinforce the fact that investigating one's beliefs depends on conversational deliberation about the best possible or least inconsistent beliefs.[33]

Socrates seems to prefer testing candidate beliefs and endorsing the acceptable ones rather than testing beliefs he already thinks he endorses but may fail to be able to continue endorsing. This is a good idea if it is hard to give up beliefs one has already put time into accepting; moreover, the ideas one already has may be from a needlessly limited subsection of all belief-worthy ideas. Socrates says that Critias should not think that Socrates engages in refutation

> for any reason other than the one for which I would also question myself thoroughly (διερευνῴμην) about anything I say – namely, the fear that at some point I'll get away with thinking that I know something when I don't know it. In fact, that's what I claim to be doing right now – looking into

[32] Benardete 1986: 10 notes that it is "only when introspection is not an ingredient in the discussion that *sôphrosunê* is defined as self-knowledge."

[33] Admissions of ignorance and subsequent searching are the main theme of McAvoy 1996; see 64n1 on this passage.

> the argument (τὸν λόγον σκοπεῖν) most of all for my own sake, and perhaps even for the sake of my friends. Or don't you think it's a good shared by just about everyone, when each thing shows itself as it is? ... Then take heart, my blessed friend, and respond to the question as it presents itself to you, leaving aside whether Critias or Socrates is the one being tested. Pay attention to the claim itself, and look into (σκόπει) whatever comes out of its being tested. (166c8–e2)

Socrates has not given up on the criterion of sincerity or courageous self-revelation that we find throughout the Socratic literature. He simply modifies the scope of that sincerity. Critias should answer questions honestly but with indifference to any supposed original ownership. He should say what he thinks about the posited definition. He need not say at the moment whether the posited definition is his own. Socrates says that he wants to know the details about, and the success of, various definitions (cf. 165b6–c4). This knowledge helps him ensure that he does not falsely assume he knows what those definitions mean and how true they are. Socrates' use of reflexive language here suggests the importance of this stance toward self-knowledge. It may be doubted that Socrates faces much risk of carelessly accepting theses. Still, he faces the risk theoretically. More importantly, he must model to Critias, Charmides, and the others in their circle the norms of proper self-examination.

The remainder of the conversation stays at this level of putatively impersonal but authentically engaged discussion. It is by this means that Socrates brings Critias into perplexity (169c3–d2), and by this means Socrates puts momentum back into the argument (169d2–5). It is even by this means that Socrates finally if indirectly floats a new definition of *sôphrosunê*, that it is knowing what is good and bad; but this is a definition he does not pursue (174c1–3). Thus of the five modes of getting self-knowledge that have been adduced by Socrates in the course of this dialogue – self-expression, introspection, inference from public comportment, testing one's preexisting views, and testing plausible views – the fifth, the most social and least perceptual, seems the most promising. This method depends most on conversation, on appeal to deeply held but shared commitments, and on innovation and discovery. Knowing oneself amounts to learning what is best to believe and to desire, which amounts to learning who one ought to be, and becoming it.

Just as the opening of the dialogue presaged Critias' ideas linking knowing oneself with the acknowledgment of persons, the opening also presages this refinement of methods of seeking self-knowledge. In the opening pages, everyone feels awe toward Charmides' physical appearance. Chaerephon says that the feeling for beauty would intensify if they saw his body and not just his face. Socrates does not ask Charmides to strip.[34] He suggests that they look at (ἐθεασάμεθα) his soul instead, to see whether it is beautiful and good. They will look at it by means of discussion (διαλέγεσθαι).[35] Charmides is well suited for this kind of display (ἐπέδειξάς), since he already has the skills appropriate to discussion, philosophy and poetry (154d5–155a8). From the start, Socrates shows that self-knowledge is sought through conversation.

Two obstacles to self-knowledge

We have so far seen two avenues for making sense of the *gnôthi sauton* in the first half of the *Charmides*. The first makes explicit reference to the precept: it is a divine greeting, acknowledging a person's aptness for salutary conversation. The second does not make explicit reference to the precept, but deploys a range of self-oriented epistemic language: one comes to know oneself more through public testing of ideas than through any kind of direct or perceptual introspection. Both avenues hold promise. People can in fact be greeted, and enter into salutary conversation. People can in fact learn in conversation about what they would believe and defend. All of this is possible and beneficial; but does this mean self-knowledge is possible and beneficial? Or does it mean only that something like self-knowledge, but not self-knowledge itself, is possible and beneficial? These questions arise from the course of the dialogue's second half, which casts self-knowledge into direct doubt.

[34] We see the importance of the language of "stripping" to self-knowledge in *Clouds* and *Phaedrus*, on which see Moore 2015b; see also *Alc.* 132a6, *Prot.* 352a1–b1, *Tht.* 169a8–b4, *Menex.* 236d1, *Ion* 535b5. On this passage in the *Charmides* see Bruell 1977: 144; McAvoy 1996: 66, 90, 97.

[35] By ignoring the fact that the stripping requires one-on-one conversation, Benardete 1986: 12–13, mistakenly claims that "Charmides' own individuality would disappear with the uncovering of his *eidos*," and thus generalizes to the claim that "self-knowledge cannot mean knowledge of the self, as a unique bundle of particular features, but it must refer to a class-knowledge." In fact, self-knowledge involves a dynamic interplay between particular and ideal.

In fact, while the critique of the definition of *sôphrosunê* as self-knowledge far exceeds in complexity and depth the critique of the earlier definitions, it works in about the same way. In most of them, the argument proceeds by assuming that *sôphrosunê* is always good, and then showing that the proposed definition is not also always good. "Quietness" often proves worse than "alacrity"; "shame" is not good for a needy man; "doing one's own things" forbids doing things for other people that it would be good to do; "doing what is good" is not obviously good for the doer if he does not know he is doing it. So in this last argument, the benefit of self-knowledge is thrown into doubt in two ways. First, if self-knowledge cannot exist, then there would be nothing there to benefit someone. Second, even were self-knowledge to exist, since it would be different from any possible source of benefit, it could not itself be beneficial.

Readers of the *Charmides* often feel some resistance to accepting the arguments against the earlier definitions of *sôphrosunê*. We might also feel some resistance to accepting the argument against the self-knowledge definition of *sôphrosunê*. In this section, then, I set out those arguments and try to identify the problems with them, and the significance of those problems. I suggest what Socrates may want us to think about self-knowledge in light of the agreements that got him to questioning the possibility and benefit of self-knowledge, and what his uncertain judgment about that hints at.

Impossibility

Before his account of the meaning of the Delphic inscription, Critias defines *sôphrosunê* as "knowing oneself" (τὸ γιγνώσκειν ἑαυτόν, 164d4). In his conclusion, he redefines it as "oneself knowing oneself" (τὸ γιγνώσκειν αὐτὸν ἑαυτόν, 165b4). In both instances, he speaks of an action, knowing or recognizing. Only in the second instance, however, does he indicate that this action has a subject (one defined, of course, only by its knowing). I mention this because his ensuing conversation with Socrates comprises a sequence of reformulations, two of which Critias suggests on his own, the others to which Critias assents, and this sequence pays only flickering attention to the knower who knows himself. In the first five reformulations of "oneself knowing oneself," for example, only the third retains a reference to the subject:

1. Socrates: knowing something, at least (γιγνώσκειν γέ τί, 165c4–5)
2. Socrates: some knowledge of something (ἐπιστήμη τις ... καὶ τινός, 165c5–6)
3. Critias: a knowledge of *oneself* (... ἑαυτοῦ, 165c7, cf. d7–8, e1)
4. Critias: the only knowledge of the other kinds of knowledge and itself (ἡ ... μόνη τῶν τε ἄλλων ἐπιστημῶν ἐπιστήμη ... καὶ αὐτὴ ἑαυτῆς, 166c2–3, cf. e5–6)
5. Socrates: a knowledge of ignorance and of knowledge (ἀνεπιστημοσύνης ἐπιστήμη ... καὶ ἐπιστήμης, 166e7–8).

Each of these transformations is on its own interesting. The first treats the self as "something" (τί), not necessarily something reflexive, and coordinates knowing oneself with other kinds of knowing. The second provides a nominal formulation that emphasizes distinctions between kinds of knowledge and the fact that knowledge always has an object.[36] The third shows that Critias accepts the shift in epistemic terminology,[37] and opens himself up to be asked about the object of the knowledge that is *sôphrosunê*.

[36] For the relationship between *gignôskein* and *epistêmê* in Plato's works, see Lyons 1963: 151–228; for the difficulty in determining the meaning of specific uses of *gignôskein*, Fine 2008, esp. 83–84; and for a useful hypothesis about the use in *Charmides*, Morris 1989. Bruell 1977: 166–168, says that this agreement "collaps[es] ... the distinction between recognizing or knowing in some loose sense and science [which has a 'strict'] sense," but he does not justify or explain this claim; similarly, Taylor 1927: 53, and Benardete 1986: 27–28. Avnon 1995: 306–307, supposes that *gnôsis* would be more immediate, private, and pre-linguistic than *epistêmê*. West and West 1986: 30n34 and 36n46, take a more moderate stance, observing that *gignôskein* is inchoative and not stative, and that *epistêmai* easily refer to "different branches of learning." Tuozzo 2011: 193–194 takes an even more moderate stance, and suggests that the switch to *epistêmê* allows Socrates to explore and compare the relationship self-knowledge has with other forms of craft-knowledge. Tuckey 1951: 30–31, also notes that *epistêmê* reminds one of Socratic virtue, but thinks that the idea of a "craft" of oneself is ludicrous, and therefore that Critias has not appreciated the content of Socrates' terminological shift.

[37] Taylor 1927: 53–54, does not have evidence that Critias "is virtually confusing the direct acquaintance with one's own individual strength and weakness really meant in the Delphian inscription with the 'science' of the psychologist. He is taking it for granted ... that to know psychology and to have a profound acquaintance with your own 'heart' are the same thing." Tuckey 1951: 39, believes that Critias misunderstands Socrates' question. Wellman 1964: 110–113, finds the inference from *gignôskein* to *epistêmê* to be unremarkable, but on the basis of an unexplained assimilation of practical to reflexive knowledge.

It is the fourth transformation that is really interesting. The reflexive pronoun changes in gender, from ἑαυτοῦ to ἑαυτῆς. This represents a shift from the knowing agent's "oneself" to the intentional state's "itself." This is a valid shift when the person (αὐτόν) knowing himself is defined only by his knowing; thus for the person (αὐτόν) to know himself is for the knowing to know itself. Further, his knowledge knows not only itself; insofar as it, or he, is exclusively knowledge, it, or he, knows knowledge generally. By consequence it, or he, knows all individual instances of knowledge (τῶν … ἄλλων ἐπιστημῶν) to the extent they are knowledge.[38] Critias does not limit these instances of knowledge to those known, as it were, by the self-knowing knowledge; the knower of knowledge could also know other people's knowledge.

Thus Critias' shift to impersonal formulations of self-knowledge is consistent with personal formulations. But consistency does not imply perspicuity or explanatory fecundity, and it does not guarantee that Critias will remember that the Delphic inscription is directed at people. Further, Critias does not specify what "one's knowing" is as an object of knowledge or as the substance of a self-knowing person. It could be pure rational activity, or could include non-rational and bodily elements, like desires, senses, and other abilities. It could be only the ideal aspects of one's knowing, or it could include the idiosyncrasies and relations attendant on the particular instances of knowing.

Socrates' two subsequent formulations refocus attention on the personal quality of self-knowledge. The fifth formulation introduces knowledge of ignorance. On the one hand, this might be a logical consequence of knowing knowledge; what is not knowledge is its opposite.[39] On the other hand, mentioning ignorance brings with it the usual context of ignorance: a person. We might speak impersonally of knowledge, to get clear on its subject, or formal structure, or relation to other types of knowledge. But we would hardly ever speak impersonally of ignorance; we want to know, instead, *who* is ignorant, why *that person* is ignorant, and what

[38] Woolf 2008: 24–25, treats knowing knowledge as "discerning a certain formal property of the subject's belief-set, namely its structure"; similarly Taylor 1927: 54; Bruell 1977: 177, 188; Chen 1978; Benardete 1986: 28. Wellman 1964: 111–113, claims that it concerns "an aspect of the problem of self-consciousness," without evidence.

[39] Cf. Benson 2003: 36–40; Murphy 2007: 225–226.

effects will befall him. By dropping the reflexive pronoun Socrates simplifies the formulation, but also brings the personal back to mind.

Socrates' next formulation confirms the suspicion that this fifth formulation represents his re-acknowledgment of the personal context of self-knowledge.

6. Socrates: the *sôphrôn* man, he alone will know himself (αὐτός … ἑαυτὸν γνώσεται) and will be able to examine (ἐξετάσαι) what he happens to know (τί … τυγχάνει εἰδώς) and what not, and will be able likewise to investigate (ἐπισκοπεῖν) in others what someone knows and believes (οἶδεν καὶ οἴεται), on the condition that he knows (οἶδεν), and what, in turn,[40] he thinks he knows, when he does not know. … And this is *sôphronein* and *sôphrosunê* and one's knowing oneself: knowing what one knows and what one does not (τὸ εἰδέναι ἅ τε οἶδεν καὶ ἃ μὴ οἶδεν). (167a1–7)

Here Socrates speaks of people concerned to investigate each other,[41] in particular to know what various things they and others know and about what things they are respectively ignorant. This is knowing oneself if who we are is defined by those epistemic norms against which we can and cannot act successfully. Socrates is a Greek speaker (he knows the norms of the Greek language, and follows them), not a cobbler (he does not know the norms of shoe-repair), etc. False or unsubstantiated beliefs, and the effortful discernment of what one in fact knows, are aspects of human life. Because self-knowledge is parallel to other-knowledge, self-knowledge must be no more direct than other-knowledge; it must be achieved only through the route by which we know what others believe and know – by talking with them and listening and watching them.

The significance of the personal angle is confirmed by the similarity between this passage and Socrates' most memorable self-description in the *Apology*.[42] "I am aware (ξύνοιδα ἐμαυτῷ, 'know with myself') that I am wise neither greatly nor modestly" (*Apol.* 21b5–6, cf. ἐμαυτῷ …

[40] Burnet 1903 reads αὖ, following Bekker; B and T have αὐτός, "he himself"; Buttmann (followed by Tuozzo 2011: 202) reads αὖ τις, "someone in turn"; presumably all refer to the τις (someone other than the *sôphrôn* man) at 167a3.

[41] See Tarrant 2000a and Goldman 2004 on Socrates' use of ἐξετάσαι and other words of examination.

[42] This is widely noted: Tuckey 1951: 65–66; Santas 1973: 120; McKim 1985: 63; West and West 1986: 39n49; Kahn 1996: 193; Schmid 1998: 59; Benson 2003: 35. This reference becomes an interpretative crux, because in the

ξυνῇδη οὐδὲν ἐπισταμένῳ, 22d1). A moment later he says: “I thought to myself that I am wiser than this [political] man: for perhaps neither of us knows (εἰδέναι) anything fine or good, but he thinks he knows something, not knowing it, but I, just as I do not know anything, do not think I know it” (21d2–6).[43] Plato’s allusion helps us keep a palpable connection between an increasingly impersonal idea, knowledge knowing knowledge, and the quotidian but important personal idea of knowing what one knows and, especially, does not know.[44] Socrates clarifies what he means by “knowing what one knows and what one does not” (τὸ εἰδέναι ἅ τε οἶδεν καὶ ἃ μὴ οἶδεν). He means:

7. Socrates: knowing [concerning] what one knows and what one does not know, <that one knows [it?] and> that one does not know [it?] (τὸ ἃ οἶδεν καὶ ἃ μὴ οἶδεν εἰδέναι <ὅτι οἶδε καὶ> ὅτι οὐκ οἶδεν). (167b2–3)

Knowing oneself means being able to identify that one knows the particular fields that one knows and fails to know certain other fields.[45]

It is at just this point that Socrates says that he suspects self-knowledge is impossible. Despite his emphasis on the personal formulations, however, the definition of self-knowledge that expresses his suspicions depends quite explicitly on a version of Critias’ impersonal formulation (ὅπερ σὺ νυνδὴ ἔλεγες, 167b10):

8. Socrates: some one knowledge, which is a knowledge of nothing except itself and the other kinds of knowledge, but is also a knowledge of ignorance (μία τις ἐπιστήμη, ἣ οὐκ ἄλλου τινός ἐστιν ἢ ἑαυτῆς τε καὶ τῶν ἄλλων ἐπιστημῶν ἐπιστήμη, καὶ δὴ καὶ ἀνεπιστημοσύνης ἡ αὐτὴ αὕτη, 167b10–c2).

Apology Socrates treats self-knowledge as possible and valuable, but here the course of the argument suggests it is impossible and not valuable in the way knowledge of good and evil (the having of which knowledge Socrates disavows in the *Apology*) is.

43 On these passages, with 22e7–23b4 and 20d6–e3, see Fine 2008.

44 See also *Tht.* 200a8–c4.

45 Benardete 1986: 29, reads without the emendment ὅτι οἶδε καὶ made by the later manuscripts and argues that this passage focuses on knowing that one is ignorant: this is the most remarkable element of Socratic self-knowledge. But Murphy 2007: 223, gives strong textual reasons in favor of the emendment. It seems that Socrates, in the *Apology*, wanted to know both *whether* his interlocutors had knowledge of certain fields, and if they did, *what* the content of that knowledge was. See Benson 2003 on the puzzles this fact generates.

This formulation differs from earlier ones in that it makes explicit that the only object self-knowledge takes is itself, other kinds of knowledge, and absences of knowledge. As Socrates explains shortly thereafter, this is a knowledge of no learning (μαθήματος, 168a6). It is meant, all the same, to represent Critias' formulation. On the basis of some analogies, this formulation comes to seem to pertain to some impossible attitude (ἀδύνατον, 167c6).

Socrates reasons first from vision, the act of seeing (ὄψις, 167c8–d2). Critias does not think there could be a seeing that sees no color (the usual object of seeing) but that sees only itself and other instances of seeing. Critias surely believes, rightly so, that seeing is practically defined as a sensitivity to color. Socrates reasons identically from hearing (167d4–5). He generalizes to all perceptions (αἰσθήσεις, d7–9). He then goes through five other attitudes – desiring (ἐπιθυμία, e1–2), intending (βούλησις, e4–5), loving (ἔρως, e7–8), fearing (φόβον, 167e10–168a1), and believing (δόξαν, a3–4) – none of which makes any sense to Critias should they take only themselves and their absences for their objects, not their usual objects. This tells badly against knowledge's taking only itself and not the knowable as its object (a6–8). Socrates does not investigate the relations between knowledge and the perceptions and intentional attitudes; the assumption is that they are similar enough. All the same, while admitting the oddness (ἄτοπον, 168a10) of a knowledge that takes no learning as its object, only itself and other instances of knowledge, Socrates warns against concluding yet (μήδεν γὰρ πω διισχυριζώμεθα) that it is, for all its strangeness, impossible; they ought to search still more (ἔτι σκοπῶμεν, 168a10–11). Thus his mitigated pessimism leads to the second part of the argument for impossibility.

Whereas the first part of the argument demonstrates the improbability of a perception or intentional attitude that takes no standard object, the second part demonstrates the improbability of a relative state having both its own quality and the quality of that to which it is relative. Socrates begins with quantitative differences. Something that is "larger than" is necessarily relative to something that is "smaller than." But if it were relative to itself, the thing that was larger than itself would also have to be smaller than itself. But this is impossible (168b5–c2, e4). The same holds for being double (c4–7), being more (c9), being heavier (c9–10), and being older (c10). Socrates then returns to hearing and sight. Hearing is relative to a sound. For hearing to hear itself, it would itself need to make noise (168d3–8). Seeing, likewise, would see itself only if it were colored (d9–e1). Socrates suggests that these possibilities are hard to accept (168e4–5, 169a1). So if knowledge were like the quantitative differences, it could not be reflexive; if it were like the perceptions, many would doubt it could be reflexive. Thus these two arguments make the impossibility of knowledge of knowledge, at least as Socrates presents Critias' formulation, as likely as not (cf. 175b6–7).

From here Socrates proceeds to the next impossibility argument. He concedes, for the sake of the argument's momentum, that there could be a knowledge of knowledge (169d2–5). He accepts that this concession seems to mean that oneself knowing oneself (γιγνώσκων που αὐτὸς ἑαυτὸν, 169e5–7) is possible. But he says that this concession does not seem to enable his later, personal formulation – knowing what you know and do not know – to which Critias also acceded (169d5–9). He makes a brief argument supporting his view (170a6–d10). A knowledge of knowledge could at most recognize what counts as knowledge. Insofar as the objects of knowledge differ, for example health from house-building, what knows those objects does not differ *qua* knowledge. So while a knowledge of knowledge could distinguish between an instance of knowledge and an instance of non-knowledge, it could not distinguish between two instances of knowledge in terms of their object. First-order knowledge is not transparent to second-order knowledge. Second-order knowledge cannot know what the object of the first-order knowledge is. It can only know *that* the first-order knowledge *is* knowledge. Socrates goes on to confirm these conclusions by arguing in the other direction, that only a doctor could know whether someone else is really a doctor (170e1–171c10). Thus a concession about the possibility of knowledge of knowledge does not entail the possibility of knowing what you know and do not know. Indeed, the opacity of knowledge looks to make this impossible.

Possibility

Socrates repeatedly says and implies that though a knowledge of knowledge looks to be impossible, and even were it possible, knowing what one knows and does not know looks impossible, he and his interlocutors should check these claims again. As we have already seen, he says that while some candidate reflexives may raise "serious doubts" (ἀπιστεῖται σφόδρα, 168e4, 169a1) for some, they may not for others. He lists among these doubtful but not obviously impossible reflexives hearing and vision, and two new reflexives, "movement moving itself" (κίνησις αὐτὴ ἑαυτὴν κινεῖν) and "heat burning [itself]" (θερμότης κάειν, 168e9–10). These two reflexives have at least some plausibility.[46] And as for Socrates himself, he says – using self-reflexives, we may note – that he does not trust himself to have sorted out all these issues (οὐ πιστεύω ἐμαυτῷ ἱκανὸς εἶναι ταῦτα διελέσθαι, 169a7–8; οὔτ ... ἔχω διισχυρίσασθαι, b1; cf. 173a3–5). His continued concessions for the sake of the argument's momentum give force to Socrates' faltering commitment to his conclusions (171d1–6, 172c7–d1); if the impossibility results were so certain, advancing to the next step would have little point. Socrates even ends the conversation doubting his conclusions altogether (175e5–6). So it is worth thinking through the ways Socrates might imagine the conversation could have gone more productively.[47]

Let us start with the first argument for impossibility. Socrates and Critias agreed that it would be a very strange type of perception or intentional attitude that took no normal object, only other perceptions or intentional attitudes. They also agreed that it would be impossible, or at least doubtful, for a relative state, even if it were to take normal objects, to have the relevant properties of its normal objects. In the case of seeing, for example, it would be very strange for the seeing to see nothing colored; it is also doubtful that seeing itself is colored. We might have good reasons for agreeing with both claims.

Yet Socrates also gives us reason to think about ways to minimize the decisiveness of these two claims. I noted above Socrates' admission to have a reflexive attitude about his own attitudes: he has a belief (lack of trust) about a belief (the distinctions between different kinds of relative states) (169a7–8). Earlier, when Socrates asked Critias about the intentional attitudes, he asked him for his intentional attitudes

46 See *Phdr.* 245c5–a2; *Laws* X 896a; Aristotle on Alcmaeon in *De Anima* 405a30–32 (though at *De Motu* 1–2, Aristotle argues against the possibility of absolute self-motion); Moore 2014a; Bruell 1977, 174–175. Eisenstadt 1981: 127, argues that "self-moving" and "self-burning" (mentioned adjacently) are "a kind of hendiadys for ἔρως," depicted dramatically early in the dialogue when Charmides sat next to Socrates: he felt "the burning sensation of erotic excitement," and the "transport of his soul." Eisenstadt seems to imply that both reflexives are possible.

47 Cf. Carone 1998: 276; Halper 2000: 311–313; Benson 2003: 42.

about those attitudes. He told Critias to "consider" (σκοπῇς, 167c5, d7, 168a11) what he thinks about them, see how it "seems" (δόξει, 167c5, c8, d2, e1), "think about" (ἐννόει, 167c8), "assert whether" (φαίης, 167e7, 168a6), and "notice" (κατανενόηκας, 167e10). Socrates even asks for Critias' views about "beliefs" (δοξῶν); and by eliding the verb he seems practically to highlight the fact that he is asking for Critias' beliefs about belief (168a3–4), and thinks this question could yield an answer.[48]

Earlier in the dialogue, Socrates also indicated that he could see that people were seeing. The dialogue begins with Socrates noticing that his friends at the palaestra saw him coming (εἶδον, 153b1). He soon observes Critias looking toward the door and seeing Charmides' train enter (ἀποβλέψας ... ἰδών, 153d5–154a1). Once Charmides arrives, Socrates says he was fascinated by the number and intensity of gazes on the young man (προχέσχον τὸν νοῦν ... ἔβλεπεν ... ἐθεῶντο, 154c1–8). Charmides gave him an irresistible look (ἐνέβλεψέν τέ μοι τοῖς ὀφθαλμοῖς ἀμήχανόν, 155c8–d1). Many of the most dramatic episodes in the dialogue are the times when Socrates sees some pointed seeing (εἰς τὸν Κριτίαν ἀπέβλεπεν, 162b11; ἐμβλέψας αὐτῷ, 162d4). So it certainly seems possible to see that at least other people are seeing.

What happens in the conversation, therefore, seems to belie the conclusion of Socrates' arguments about knowledge of knowledge. It does so in two ways. The first is by suggesting that believing, seeing, and the other perceptual and intentional attitudes do have the qualities of the objects of those attitudes. Seeing is visible. Perhaps it is not visible considered just as seeing, if seeing is a psychic process occurring in the eye or the mind. But considered just as seeing is to consider it in abstraction from human seeing. Human seeing involves more than invisible psychic processes. It involves eyes open and directed, pupils contracting and expanding, heads turning and following, emotional expressions playing across faces, remarks acknowledging one's attention. All this makes seeing seeable. Of course, seeing this way requires that I be a human, with experience looking at parts of a person's face and body, and experience with my own seeing. With a mirror I could see my own seeing. Perhaps I can even see my own seeing without a mirror. It is with vision that I can determine that my eyes are open, that I am seeing, that I am seeing a particular person. When I see a

[48] Cf. Benardete 1986: 29–30; Morris 1989: 52–53.

new and interesting sculpture, I *see* that I am seeing it, with fresh sight, as we say, aware as I am of the aesthetic experience.[49] As Aristotle argues, though, I can see that I see only because I am a complete person, not merely a pair of eyeballs.[50] In any of these cases, the seeing I see is colored.[51] Unlike the greater, which cannot be greater than itself because it would have to be smaller than itself but is not, seeing can see itself when the seeing is colored. It is colored when considered in its human context. Perhaps I am not seeing the psychic process itself, but so what? Seeing, in humans, comprises more than a psychic process; it is a social, intellectual, and bodily affair. Fearing is similar: fear as a psychic process might not itself be dangerous or liable to be painful, but fear humanly incarnated can be frightening, if it leads one to act irrationally, erratically, or otherwise dangerously. Thus there is in principle no obstacle, on the basis of the nature of relatives, to knowledge taking knowledge as its object, if that knowledge were humanly embodied. Thus even if knowledge of knowledge – taking those instances of knowledge in perfect isolation – were impossible, knowledge of knowledge in a person seems very likely possible.

Socrates' claims about seeing instances of seeing also diagnose a problem with Socrates' Critian formulation of self-knowledge. Critias is perhaps wrong to think of self-knowledge as a knowledge of knowledge and of nothing else.[52] He may feel that the uniqueness of self-knowledge's object gives it dignity, an aristocratic hauteur separate from other kinds of messy and mundane knowledge. But dignity does not justify cutting self-knowledge off from all other epistemic

[49] This self-conscious seeing is an accomplishment, not merely an immediate and conceptually necessary response; McCabe 2007a: 11 and 2007b are misleading in this respect.

[50] Aristotle *De Anima* III.2; Kosman 1975; Osborne 1983; Caston 2002; McCabe 2007b.

[51] See also *Tht.* 184d with Roochnik 2002: 47. Halper 2000: 312, thinks that we should recognize the *disanalogy* between perception, which depends on materiality, and knowledge, which depends on the immaterial, purely intelligible realm, and that Plato means for us to think of self-knowledge in terms of knowing the forms (which, when we know them, instantiate themselves as knowledge; thus our knowing the forms is knowing knowledge). He also says that understanding the discussion of knowledge in Plato's *Republic* would instantiate knowledge of knowledge. Unfortunately, nothing in the dialogue, as I can tell, hints at the value of thinking about forms.

[52] This is called the "exclusionary principle" by Politis 2007 and 2008 and Tuozzo 2011.

states. We can see instances of seeing, but that is because we can see color. We might be able to know other instances of knowledge, but that is because we can know the knowable.

The purported impossibility of the knowledge of knowledge is alleviated once we accept that self-knowledge can know the normal sorts of objects. This acceptance also alleviates the purported impossibility of knowing what we know. Some commentators observe that this alleviation seems not altogether necessary. Socrates still accepts the possibility of knowing what counts as knowledge, and despite his worries, this is an important aspect of self-knowledge.[53] If who we are depends on our knowledge – what we can treat as a reliable guide for action – then we should care what counts as knowledge. I address this issue again, in the section on benefit. All the same, Socrates treats knowing *that* one has knowledge as a lesser achievement than knowing *what* one has knowledge about. (Presumably the greater achievement includes the lesser.)

If self-knowledge were merely about something's counting as knowledge, it might seem impossible to *see through* the knowledge. Yet this seems to imagine that we could know whether something is knowledge simply by assessing its formal structure. But this is misleading. We determine whether we know something by testing our belief that we have knowledge. To test whether we know a proposition to be so, we see whether we believe it, and whether it is true, and whether we have good reasons for believing it. We determine whether we believe it by reconsidering the reasons for holding it, and determining whether those reasons move us. We determine whether it is true in the same way: assessing the evidence and our background understanding. So for a proposition, we know whether we know it simply by, as it were, coming again to find that we know it. Thus knowing our knowledge treats the first-order knowledge as transparent.[54] The same holds for non-propositional practices. I know whether I know carpentry by trying it and seeing whether I do it correctly, flexibly, and in whatever

[53] Carone 1998: 270n5, 283, says that knowing the formal requirements of knowledge (e.g., "the principle of non-contradiction, systematicity, and ... the rules of logic") implies knowing "the psychological conditions of virtue." See also Morris 1989 and McCabe 2011.

[54] Compare McCabe 2007a. McCabe 2011 focuses on self-knowledge as working on one's commitments to truth and rationality. Mackenzie 1988b combines the focus of those two papers.

other ways are dispositive of competence in some skill. I know what I know how to do by doing it.

Critias is right to agree that I know carpentry through knowledge, not through a second-order knowledge of knowledge. Thus my second-order knowledge of knowledge does not do woodwork. Indeed, where bare knowledge is concerned, second-order knowledge is totally otiose. It is only a human who would want to know what she knows. She could want this only if she could forget or misunderstand what it is that she knows. She can recall what she knows not by training her second-order knowledge on her first-order knowledge but simply by trying to exercise her first-order knowledge, or by remembering times when she did exercise her first-order knowledge, or by talking to people familiar with what she has learned and done. These routines require the embodiment, complexity, and social context of a human being.

Uselessness and benefit

Socrates suggests one benefit produced by knowing what counts as knowledge. A person with this kind of knowledge of knowledge would gain a pedagogical advantage. He "would learn more easily and palpably all that appears to him, because in addition (πρός) to that which he learns, he would behold-in-addition (προσκαθορῶντι) the knowledge (ἐπιστήμην); and others, in turn, he will examine more finely regarding that which he himself has learned" (172b4–7). Whether this is so or not is open to question. But this question really is moot, Socrates says, since this pedagogical benefit pales in comparison to the benefits they had expected from self-knowledge.

Two big benefits have been squashed. First, all goods Socrates and Critias can think of come from first-order knowledge; since knowledge of knowledge has no authority over any of that first-order knowledge, no good comes from it.[55] Second, it is not even clear that first-order knowledge is useful in itself, and so it might do no good to know what

[55] Politis 2007 and 2008 argues that Critias sees knowledge of knowledge as exclusively about *which* instances or kinds of knowledge one has; Socrates leaves open the possibility that knowledge of knowledge includes knowledge of the good. Relying on the *Republic*'s sun-analogy, Politis argues that knowing the good may include knowing oneself (as enabled to have knowledge *by* the good). I agree, for different reasons.

one knows and fails to know, and even what others know and fail to know (171d6–172a3, 173a8–d3). Shoemakers make shoes without knowing, as shoemakers, whether a person ought to wear them. Pilots transport passengers across a bay without knowing, as pilots, whether their passengers ought to go there. Only knowledge of what is good and bad determines what a person ought to do, and therefore only it conduces to happiness. To the extent that knowledge of knowledge or self-knowledge differs from knowledge of good and bad, it does not conduce to happiness (174d3–7, 175a6–8).

As with the impossibility results, Socrates encourages revisiting these arguments. He claims, at the conversation's end, still to believe that *sôphrosunê* is a great good (175e8–176a1). Perhaps it is therefore not "knowing oneself"; but perhaps, too, knowing oneself is not so neutral a state. This latter possibility suggests that we see whether we can identify something mistaken in the agreements about self-knowledge's failure to provide any benefit. We might ask ourselves, then, two questions. What good could knowing what you know and what you do not know provide, were this possible, that differs from the good provided from the individual topics of knowledge? And must we take self-knowledge to differ from knowledge of the good and bad?

The first question yields the negative answer "nothing" only when we think of ourselves as a single instance of knowledge. The doctor gets no important benefit from knowing she knows medicine beyond the benefit she gets from practicing medicine. Whenever she is practicing medicine well, she is benefiting; when she is not practicing medicine, *as doctor* she is not doing anything. She starts practicing medicine when a patient is set before her. But we as humans are not single instances of knowledge. We know a range of different things, and lack knowledge about a range of different things. We are not always presented with that one thing on which we ought to work. We must decide what to do with ourselves, either by picking between multiple options, or by seeking out activities. We have to take an active stance toward our lives, rather than a merely passive one. Further, not only are we people who know and fail to know; we are also people who have beliefs, true and false ones, about what we know. Those beliefs incline us to act in ways that would deploy our knowledge, were we to have it. But were we not to have the knowledge, we might still try to act, and do so unsuccessfully. So knowing what we know and fail to know is beneficial to us in helping us, first, plan and be active in the world, and second, determine whether our beliefs about what topics we know are valid. Of course this value redounds only to people, beings with temporal extension, a small place in the world, multiple but limited abilities, and often misplaced confidence about the abilities they do have.

We can see this in another way. There is no problem with the doctor practicing medicine. The problem is with the person who *believes* he knows medicine practicing medicine. The self-knowing shoemaker realizes – by knowing what he knows and does not know – that he does *not* know medicine. He acts with self-knowledge by not even trying to practice medicine; and because he does not waste his time failing to practice medicine, he can actually go on to make shoes. Self-knowledge is this kind of "knowledge in addition," a knowledge that allows one to act on one's knowledge.[56] This is what makes one aware of one's failures and successes, and, presumably, encourages improvements.

The references to Socrates' *Apology* self-description help recall this function of self-knowledge. We might call this function "modesty": recognizing what one *does not* know.[57] It seems likely that Socrates brings Critias to *aporia* on the recognition that Critias does *not* see self-knowledge as modesty, but instead as something independently valuable. But it is valuable only in the context of knowing and failing to know the things one knows and fails to know.

This picture of personhood, encouraged by Socrates' talk of doctors and pilots and so forth, suggests that who we are is dependent on what we know. We simply *are* (incomplete, limited, often mistaken) knowers. So to know what we know is knowing ourselves rightly and abandoning self-misconceptions. But determining whether we in fact know something – rather than just believe it – requires that we test our beliefs against reality, or consistency, or experts, or other good conversationalists. In the process, we are liable not only to find out whether

[56] A remarkable seven times in the latter part of the dialogue Socrates uses *pros*-prefixed words: προσέχων ("to hold next to," 160d5), προσφέρῃ ("to bring up to," 165b7), προσεπίστηται ("to know in addition," 170b8), προσποιούμενον ("to procure additionally," 170e1), προσκαθορῶντι ("to behold besides," 172b6), προσδίδαξον ("to teach besides," 173d9), and προσποθῶ ("to desire besides," 174a10). This is a hint, I think, to think of *sôphrosunê* and knowing oneself as a helpful addition.

[57] It might also be called "resource," recognizing despite one's modesty what one does know. See Belfiore 2012 on the way Socrates recognizes that he knows *ta erôtika*.

we do in fact know it, but also to increase our knowledge about it. So coming to know what we know should increase what we know, at least in the areas in which we believe we might have knowledge. If selfhood is a matter of knowing, coming to know oneself makes one's "oneself" more of a self.

The second question, whether self-knowledge differs from knowledge of the good and bad, yields the answer "yes" only when we think of self-knowledge as knowledge of knowledge, and the knowledge which constitutes us as a purely practical and value-free knowledge. If the picture described in the previous two paragraphs is right, then personhood involves knowing what you know and do not know, so that you can navigate a complex world and puncture a complex self-image. But unless you know what actions (deployments of knowledge) are good, then all this rationality and realism is for naught. Yet let us consider self-knowledge in Critias' initial, Delphic formulation, "oneself knowing oneself." This formulation treats self-knowledge as a first-order knowledge. It allows investigating the relationship between two potential objects of knowledge, the self and what is good. These objects of knowledge appear different, but they need not so appear. To know what is good is to know what to desire, what to pursue, what to do. That means acting on the basis of the reasons that one accepts as the best reasons. It means not having to try to act on the basis of erroneous reasons, or on no basis at all. In these imperfect situations, it is the error, or nothing in particular, that grounds an action. In the perfect situation, it is one's acceptance of the good that grounds the action. It becomes possible to say that it is oneself who is responsible for one's actions. So to know the good is to be a self; it is just those norms of good action – as opposed to urges and mistakes – that one knows when one is a self. So to know the good is to know (because one finally is) oneself.

Both arguments for the uselessness of self-knowledge dissolve when we assume a richer picture of the people who might know themselves. Socrates' conversation with Charmides and Critias, as we saw in the section on the "Ways of knowing oneself," tries to urge Socrates' friends to think about themselves, and self-knowledge, in this richer way.

Conclusion

This chapter has brought together three related lessons from the *Charmides*. The injunction *gnôthi sauton* can be seen as an acknowledgment that the person greeted may come to know himself, in particular through conversation and reciprocal testing. Socrates' sequential suggestions to Charmides, and then Critias, about ways to know whether they know something, and what they know, show that the most effective way is through conversation and reciprocal testing. The paradoxes of higher-order knowledge can be resolved when we see that thinking about ourselves as a whole, as knowers who know and fail to know various things, who meet and fail to meet various epistemic criteria in various places, is itself of deep importance when we want to rely on what it is we do know. The details of the conversational method Plato depicts throughout the dialogue show that it is, again, through conversation and reciprocal testing that we come to have this second-order knowledge, this knowledge that makes our knowledge, or our ignorance, available.

This chapter shows, in particular, the connection between one's knowledge of one's ignorance, and self-knowledge in general.[58] Self-knowledge merely manages, or examines, what we already have. It is at best "additional." But so too Socrates in the *Apology* calls his merely human knowledge – his recognition that he lacks wisdom, the most estimable divine knowledge – worth little or nothing. From that divine perspective, perhaps *sôphrosunê*, and Socratic self-knowledge, really are worthless; but so too then would be courage for the immortal, justice for the blessed, and piety for the gods.[59]

So self-knowledge makes a person, in a community of interlocutors, more human. The next chapters develop the ways it does so. Here we have seen how two ways of opposing the value of "knowing oneself" – that it is impossible and that it is useless – urge us to think of self-knowledge not as a reflexive perception but as a matter of aspirational self-constitution. This aspirational self-constitution involves constituting ourselves as knowers who can deploy that knowledge and avoid acting on mere conceits of knowledge, and constituting ourselves as selves who can act on the basis of the knowledge of what is good.

[58] This is a familiar thesis; cf. Coolidge 1993; McAvoy 1996; and McCabe's essays cited in n. 54.

[59] Cf. Mahoney 1996; Carone 1998; Stern 1999. McKim 1985 and Ketchum 1991 find it worthless even from the mundane perspective.

3 Alcibiades: *mirrors of the soul*

New problems

The *Alcibiades* foregoes the *Charmides*' conundrums about self-knowledge. Whereas in the *Charmides*, Critias fails to defend either the possibility or the profit of self-knowledge, in the *Alcibiades*, Socrates encourages Alcibiades to see self-knowledge as an urgent necessity. Alcibiades' aspirations to great power, to be tested in the coming days, demand that he learn to know himself. Whatever obstacles to self-knowledge exist, they exist in Alcibiades' reluctance to admit his need for it and, should he admit it, in his confusion about how he should ever attain it. Thus the drama of this dialogue, on its surface a parody of amatory seduction,[1] does not concern whether Socrates or Alcibiades vindicate the importance of the imperative "Know yourself." It concerns whether Alcibiades will accept Socrates and the imperative he presses on him, and when he eventually does accept him and it, whether and how Socrates will help him obey it.[2]

Socrates eventually helps him obey the Delphic precept by appeal to a model. He says that really the only useful model for one's responding to the "Know yourself" is an eye's responding to the precept "See yourself." An eye cannot see itself on its own. It always sits behind its own visual field. To see itself, its visual appearance would have somehow to get in front of itself. This is possible, Socrates shows, without its splitting in two. It can use a reflecting surface, presenting itself to

[1] Belfiore 2012: 31–67, gives a careful account of this "erotic" seduction, and Dillon 1994 describes later Platonist interpretations of this erotic seduction (connecting the *Alcibiades* to *Phaedrus*). Gordon 2003: 11, calls it "philosophical seduction." Daniel Parra 2010 and Lauriello 2010: 240–253, observe the troubles Socrates faces in this pedagogical encounter (the former locating them in Socrates' immaturity as a teacher and Alcibiades' self-love; the latter in human irrationality); Finlay 1994 tries to understand Socrates' interest in Alcibiades.

[2] Alcibiades asks three times (124b7–c2, 127e3–4, 132b4–5).

itself at a distance. With this paradigm, Socrates says, we can understand a person knowing himself. It simply takes a reflecting surface that presents, at a distance, the knowable appearance of the person to himself.

This model brings to mind the *Charmides*' own analogy between vision and knowledge. In that dialogue, far from being the only analogy for the possibility of self-knowledge, it serves as a leading example of its impossibility. Socrates wonders whether sight (ὄψις) can see itself. It cannot, because sight registers only color, and sight itself has no color.[3] Socrates provides no way around it, and in fact shows that other modes of perception suffer the same difficulty: the process lacks the quality to which it is uniquely sensitive. Socrates is not utterly skeptical, and he recommends that they all think again and harder about reflexive processes, but he does not help Critias or the others at the palaestra do so.

Though the *Alcibiades*' optimistic model for knowing oneself looks strikingly similar to the *Charmides*' pessimistic model for self-knowledge, there is an obvious difference. In the *Alcibiades*, Socrates asks how an eye and a person, using their respective powers, could apply those powers to themselves (the eye and the person). In the *Charmides*, he asks how the powers themselves, seeing and knowing, could apply themselves to themselves (the seeing and the knowing). The *Charmides* is about knowledge knowing itself; the *Alcibiades* about a knower knowing himself. At least from the vantage of these two dialogues, the second formulation seems the more productive one, the more human one, the one that best satisfies the Delphic injunction.

Still, we cannot say that the conversation of the *Alcibiades* makes an advance over the *Charmides* in Socrates' studies of self-knowledge. The action of the *Alcibiades* predates that of the *Charmides*. More importantly, the characters, their problems, and Socrates' goals differ. Critias comes to the attention of Socrates, lately returned from a several-year absence, as a person who needs his definition of *sôphrosunê* shown up. By contrast, Alcibiades appears to Socrates as an excellent conversational companion, with this companionship not as yet developed,

[3] Though see Caston 2002: 762, and Denyer 2001: 232–233, on the ambiguity of ὄψις, which can refer "not only to the pupil and other organs of sight (LSJ s.v. ὄψις II.c–d) but also to more or less anything connected with vision: the sensory capacity itself, its operations, and its objects."

and so Socrates needs to convince Alcibiades that his goals require it. Rather than baffle his interlocutor (who already likes the notion of self-knowledge), in the *Alcibiades* Socrates entices his interlocutor (who as yet does not). Whereas in the *Charmides*, Socrates presents to his interlocutor a conceptual problem about self-knowledge (how to understand it), in the *Alcibiades* he presents his interlocutor with a personal problem about self-knowledge (how to desire it).

The fact that Socrates does not at this moment of first contact confront Alcibiades with the conceptual problems of self-knowledge does not mean, however, that he does not present Alcibiades with the kernels of the problems he will have to think back over on further reflection or in later conversations. Such problems as Socrates sets – or that the author gives to his readers – go to the heart of the scholarly and even quotidian concerns about self-knowledge. In some sense they are more compelling than the problems in the *Charmides*, which many take as far-fetched and the result of a particularly obtuse Critias. These problems seem like actual difficulties in understanding what self-knowledge is. I note three of them here.

The first kind of problem is that the concept of self-knowledge looks otiose. As presented in Julia Annas' 1985 paper, which inspired new investigations into self-knowledge, self-knowledge, as the *Alcibiades* presents it, is reducible to the knowledge of justice. Knowing yourself amounts to knowing your station and duties in the world; but this is precisely what knowing what is just amounts to. Knowing what is just might be itself difficult, but at least *that* is the difficulty. The self-pertaining formulation of "self-knowledge" does little work beyond engaging with Alcibiades' self-regard.

The second kind of problem is that the concept of self-knowledge looks misleading. The concept's origins in the precept "Know yourself" suggest that what you know in knowing yourself is something particular, idiosyncratic, localized, and perhaps secret to yourself. But as Socrates' extension of the self-seeing eye analogy seems to show, self-knowledge in fact takes as its object something impersonal and abstract. Self-knowledge is less a matter of personal discovery than one of theology, metaphysics, and at best a theoretical rational psychology. Knowing yourself really means knowing about reason and god. Knowing about reason and god might be itself impressive, but that is what is impressive. The formulation of "self-knowledge" involves a redefinition of selfhood, from individual to transcendental nature.

The third kind of problem – in uncertain relation or contradiction with the first two – is that self-knowledge as Socrates recommends it looks ineffective or even inhibitory. Alcibiades wants the ability that will both allow him to speak to his city about war and peace and help him to triumph over the kings of Sparta and Persia for Aegean supremacy. Yet it is not clear how his knowing about a transcendental self – or potentially more concretely, about reason and god – would give him the practical leadership skill he needs. Indeed, we might even suspect from Socrates a perverse intellectual sabotage. The long effort such a study would require of Alcibiades, combined with the change in attitude a successful study of selfhood, justice, and the divine could cause, might very well lead Alcibiades to give up on his quest for world domination. He would realize that true power rests not in political rule but in, say, self-mastery. Alcibiades' goals require that he get self-knowledge for their attainment; having gotten self-knowledge, he renounces those goals. Self-knowledge would cause a certain turning toward oneself and away from one's standing goals.

This chapter confronts these problems. It shows that while the problems are formulated on the basis of reasonable observations, the wrong inferences have been made from those observations. Self-knowledge is in fact a productive concept, about something familiarly personal, and apt for Alcibiades' goals of power. Self-knowledge overlaps with justice, as it does also with *sôphrosunê* and wisdom, but this apparent unity of virtue does not eliminate the conceptual value of self-knowledge itself. The emphasis on knowledge and on selfhood, emphases absent from other virtues (or their names), has interpretative benefit. Likewise, getting self-knowledge requires reflecting on the nature of selfhood, rationality, and excellence. But that is because these provide ideals of good structure and reasoning that a person might decide to adopt and commit his or her idiosyncratic self to. Knowing what is good in general depends on knowing also what is good for oneself. Anyway, Alcibiades is to study more than the good; he is also to study Socrates and himself. Finally, the pursuit of self-knowledge may open Alcibiades up to a critique of his particular plans. Even so, it is his desires that he critiques and works on, and it is his judgment that he deploys. So he as much develops himself as gives himself up in the process. By the end of the conversation depicted in the *Alcibiades*, Alcibiades looks hardly ready to reject his original plans. No doubt this is because the tutelage has barely begun. But it may also be that Socrates neither intends nor expects self-knowledge to bring Alcibiades to alienate himself from his guiding cares.

In the *Alcibiades* Socrates cites the Delphic *gnôthi sauton* three distinct times (124b1, 129a2–3, 132c10), more often than anywhere else in the Socratic literature.[4] The result here is that he gives three distinct though complementary analyses of its import. Thus this chapter proceeds by studying each of those analyses. In fact, most previous studies of self-knowledge in the *Alcibiades* have given only partial or limited interpretations because they have not taken all three into account.[5] All three contribute to Socrates' single goal, getting Alcibiades' commitment to further conversation of a certain variety. The first two are important in their own right; but they also prime the way Alcibiades, and the reader, should hear or read the third. They present the natural contexts for talking about self-knowledge. Those contexts are the importance of assessing and understanding one's most-cared-for desires and the concomitant responsibilities. The three discussions of self-knowledge treat in turn knowing one's desires, knowing the nature of selfhood, and knowing oneself as a knower. Together they treat self-knowledge as constituting oneself as a unified person, with coherent and transparent desires and beliefs, desires and beliefs for which one is responsible. This means that Alcibiades' desires will not vanish but instead become his own; his beliefs may be shared but become his beliefs; and he is to become a more stable, knowable, tractable individual, but not so as to etherealize himself onto the theoretical plane.

My view in this chapter is that for Socrates, "Know yourself" means something much more than it is usually granted. Nicolas Denyer says that the injunction originally exhorted us to "know our limits and our place in the world, rather than, for example, 'to be in touch with our emotions' ";[6] Benjamin Rider says that the god at Delphi "emphasized humility, knowing your place and business, and recognizing your human limitations … The cardinal sin against Apollo … was

[4] Tortzen 2002: 12, thinks that this dialogue did the most to popularize the saying and its connection to Delphi. Bluck 1953: 48–52, judges the dialogue to be part of a wave of renewed interest in the Delphic inscription. Lineation and text from Denyer 2001 unless noted.

[5] Foucault 2006 (partially) and Werner 2013 excepted.

[6] Denyer 2001: 191, 236, both about 124b1; at 222 he says it means knowing one's intellectual limits; at 238 "knowing what [one's] strengths and weaknesses are," and at 239, "appreciat[ion of] my position in the world." He does not explain the relation between these accounts.

hubris, believing and acting as if you are more or better than what you are."[7] Yet neither gloss makes sense across Socrates' three discussions. Socrates never challenges, and indeed appears to ratify, the breadth of Alcibiades' passion, which amounts basically to ruling the known world. Socrates' association of the self with the divine or godlike in the climactic scene of the dialogue does even less to sustain a sharp distinction between humans and the gods. All the same, Socrates does counsel coming to appreciate what one's desires do in fact involve and commit one to, seeing that one's knowledge stops shorter than one probably imagines, and distinguishing that for which one is responsible from that for which one is not.

The *Alcibiades* contributes to this study a new set of questions about self-knowledge, but though it takes an approach distinct from that of the *Charmides*, it pulls the reader toward the same conclusions. The value of this shared conclusion might seem doubtful. Since Schleiermacher, the evidentiary value of the *Alcibiades* has come under question.[8] This is despite the fact that ancient teachers took the dialogue as Plato's best introduction to his Socratic project.[9] Of course, it is just this fact, that it is "an excellent introduction to philosophy," that the editors of the standard English Plato translations use as potential evidence against Plato's authorship: "The clearest argument against Plato's authorship is probably that Plato never wrote a work whose interpretation was as simple and straightforward as that of *Alcibiades*."[10] I hope this chapter, and the literature I cite within, belie the claim that this interpretation is simple. Quite the opposite looks more true. Anyway, many scholars do now accept the *Alcibiades* as Platonic;[11] many others find it admirable irrespective of authorship.[12]

[7] Rider 2011: 399, influenced by what is now Reeve 2013: 1–17.

[8] Schleiermacher 1836. More recent skeptics: Bluck 1953; Slings 1999: 163–164; Tarrant 2000b: 119; Joyal 2003; Smith 2004; Kurihara 2012.

[9] *Alcibiades* as introductory Platonic text: Diogenes Laertius 3.62, Olympiodorus *In. Alc.* 10.18–11.6; Proclus *In. Alc.* 11; Iamblichus *Proleg. Phil. Plat.* 219.24–29 Hermann; Albinus *Prologus* 5 (with Annas 1999: 27); see generally Tarrant 2000b: 92–93, 118–123; Segonds 2003: x–lxxxviii.

[10] This is Hutchinson's introduction to *Alcibiades* in Cooper 1997: 558; he says that acceptance of the dialogue's authenticity is a minority position, and that the dialogue may have been written by an "Academic philosopher in the 350s." This text marks the *Alcibiades* in the Contents with the signification "It is not generally agreed by scholars whether Plato is the author of this work."

[11] Jirsa 2009 gives the best rebuttal to recent skepticism about authorship.

[12] E.g., Guthrie 1971: 150–153, 157; Joosse 2014.

For the purpose of this book, of course, authorship matters little. What matters more is that the author articulates a Socratic perspective on self-knowledge. That the author does, and what it is, are what I hope to show here.

It is worth noting one more feature of the interpretation of this dialogue. The *Alcibiades* shares an interpretative difficulty with the *Charmides*. Critias and Charmides came to their ends in oligarchic coups against Athens (cf. *Chrm.* 176c7–d5). Alcibiades comes to his own less-than-admirable end during the Peloponnesian War. Socrates hints that something might pull him away from Socratic conversation (*Alc.* 135e6–8). Is this a problem with Socrates' vision of self-knowledge? Has Socrates even exacerbated Alcibiades' taste for power, or at least failed to step in when he could? I doubt the author wishes to argue this. He probably wishes to do indirectly what Xenophon does explicitly, to explain Alcibiades' slip from Socrates' influence (*Mem.* 1.2.39–47).[13] It would take a grimly vindictive author to try to show that Socrates' shared pursuits of justice and rationality explained Alcibiades' depressingly riotous middle age. As it is, I leave the historical questions aside, assuming that the author means to depict in his dialogue a thoughtful rather than a perverse picture of self-knowledge, one worth studying and treating as a candidate for our own projects of self-improvement.

That I do not step into the psychological history of the post-Periclean age does not mean, however, that this chapter considers arguments in isolation from those speaking them. Everything Socrates does and says in the dialogue contributes to helping Alcibiades understand that living as he hopes to depends on his acceding to further Socratic conversation. Such conversation presses him for his views, helps him assess the commitment he has toward his purported beliefs, and reveals the nature and import of his desires. It also teaches him how to have conversations, take responsibility for his assertions, and act more like Socrates. It embeds the central Greek wisdom of "knowing yourself" into questions of moral development and civic maturation. In so doing it implies that knowing oneself includes figuring out, for yourself, what knowing oneself even means. It means something much more complex and challenging than commonly assumed.

[13] Cf. Sanders 2011.

Knowing one's desires

Socrates first mentions the "Know yourself" at the end of his longest speech, five-eighths of the way through the dialogue. He had been contrasting Alcibiades with his competition: not his age-mates in Athens but the kings of Sparta and Persia. Alcibiades had underestimated them, doubting their substance and maturity of character (120c4–5). Socrates' speech, touching on the nobility and purity of these kings' ancestry, the richness and system of their education, and the grandeur of their wealth, ends with an image of the Spartan queen: she would puzzle over (θαυμάσαι) Alcibiades' pretensions. How could he have any hope to contest (διαγωνίζεσθαι) with her country? He could not. Socrates concludes:

> But, my blissful friend, obeying me and the Delphic inscription, know yourself, that they [*sc.* the kings] are your opponents, not those whom you suppose; we should excel absolutely none of them, except by care and skill alone; if you will be lacking in these, you will also be lacking in the acquisition of a name among the Hellenes and the barbarians, which you seem to me to love as nobody loves anything else. (124a8–b6)

The casual reading of this passage makes it look like Socrates is saying that knowing oneself means knowing one's true social or political peers, or at least not having false views about the environment in which one acts. But this seems an overly narrow gloss on both the Delphic inscription and this passage.[14] The grammar shows that Socrates glosses "know yourself" with the entire passage.[15] The passage contains three demands. Together they constitute Socrates' first reading of the *gnôthi sauton*.

[14] Reductive readings are found in Foucault 2006: 35, 52, who calls it the "weak form" of the Delphic injunction, "simply a counsel of prudence"; Gill 2007: 98, who supposes that Alcibiades "probably interprets [this advice] in the traditional sense of recognizing his strengths and weaknesses in relation to others"; Belfiore 2012: 33, that Alcibiades is to recognize his mistakes about his true desires; Gordon 2003: 13–15, 20–21, that Socrates means to "redirect" Alcibiades' concerns from bodily and material effects to his "true self," his soul (cf. Ambury 2013: 258–262, from appearance to transcendental forms).

[15] Socrates gives specifies the γνῶθι σαυτόν with a relative clause (ὅτι ...) that he then extends with two additional relative clauses (ὧν ... ὧν ...). The OCT's full stop before the last relative could just as well be another high dot.

First, Alcibiades must discover and articulate to himself what he really loves (ἐρᾶν). This exceptional desire is for fame throughout the Greek and non-Greek world. Alcibiades must recognize that he does not simply desire dominance in Athens. Second, Alcibiades must recognize what his love obligates him to, given the external situation. Here it is surpassing (περιγενοίμεθα) those best positioned to have the reputation he desires. So he must know something about the Spartan and Persian royalty. Third, Alcibiades needs to develop the abilities appropriate to satisfying his desire: care and skill (ἐπιμελείᾳ ... καὶ τέχνῃ). Being able to know yourself involves knowing how to do what you intend to do.

Knowing oneself is the compound of these three aspects. It means acknowledging your commitments – what you believe best or desire most to do – by recognizing what they involve. It means treating them as specific normative pressures to engage in certain actions. Far from warning Alcibiades against hubris, as many readers have assumed the *gnôthi sauton* does, Socrates uses the Delphic inscription to ratify the intensity of Alcibiades' passions. His passions are not to be eradicated, denigrated, or transcended; they are to be recognized, developed, and taken seriously. Nor does Socrates encourage Alcibiades to know himself in the manner of a passive observer, or to know his limits whether intellectual or otherwise, or to know about the nature of the soul or mortal being.

That Socrates does not give some unfamiliar gloss to the Delphic precept is not, in the end, so surprising. In this passage he identifies his own advice with the advice of the inscription (πειθόμενος **ἐμοί τε καὶ** τῷ ἐν Δελφοῖς γράμματι). This passage is Socrates' peroration to a long speech, and the long speech a cap to the back-and-forth conversation preceding it. He seems therefore to be summarizing all his remarks, and all the ways he has been speaking, as what the Delphic precept means. But if Socrates identifies his advice with the precept's advice, he must understand the precept to advise what he would advise. It is practically a commonplace that Socrates advises knowing what you intend to do before you do it, and to adopt those beneficial practices that would improve your ability to know what you intend to do.

Someone might argue that because Socrates means to seduce Alcibiades into continued conversation, he has to coax him with a palatable, accessible view of self-knowledge. This makes a fair guess about Socrates' psychological assumptions. But it would be excessive to accept a supposed inference from this claim, that Socrates starts with a view of self-knowledge that he eventually discards or disowns. Alcibiades mentions an "easy" view of self-knowledge in a later section of the dialogue, but he does not link it to the view mentioned here. In fact, the self-knowledge mentioned here is not particularly easy to acquire; Alcibiades certainly has not yet gotten it, or even thought about getting it.

Socrates' seductive gambit might be seen better against the long speeches of diagnosis he has just presented to Alcibiades. Socrates shows that it is appropriate for a lover to help draw out his beloved's "true self," by drawing out what is actually appealing, desirable, and admirable to him. So as Socrates asserts that self-knowledge involves knowing the scope and texture of one's true desires, and as he encourages Alcibiades to spend time with him, he also shows Alcibiades that he, Socrates, can help Alcibiades know the scope and texture of his true desires, by spending time together. Socrates, standing silently by Alcibiades, mirrors Alcibiades (103b2–104c6, 104d6–105c6, 109d1–5). This image finds its theoretical version later in the dialogue, discussed below. So Socrates' view of self-knowledge here both articulates the point of the previous parts of the conversation, and provides a concrete example for the mirror-analogy.

Knowing selfhood

Socrates' next use of the *gnôthi sauton* comes five pages later. Alcibiades has come to admit his confusion about the nature of justice. He asks what to do (127e3). Socrates replies with a question: "What is caring for oneself?" (τὸ ἑαυτοῦ ἐπιμελεῖσθαι, 127e8). Alcibiades thinks that caring for oneself (αὑτοῦ) means caring for whatever belongs to oneself (τῶν αὑτοῦ, 128a2–3). Alcibiades' view is plausible for several reasons. The time one spends on self-care, in bathing, dressing, and outfitting, goes mostly to caring for one's personal effects. Indeed, it is hard to know what else to care for besides one's effects; if there is anything internal at all, it is presumably perfectly adequate to itself. All the same, Socrates pulls Alcibiades away from this view. As Socrates argues, we care for shoes with shoe-repair, but feet with medicine. The practice of caring for something's belongings differs from the practice of caring for the thing itself.[16] What then is the "oneself" for which

[16] Johnson 1999: 4–6, discusses difficulties in this argument; still, it propels the conversation to the next point.

Alcibiades is to care apart from his appurtenances? If one's money, or body, or reputation are, paradigmatically, the shoes, what is the foot? Alcibiades cannot say. Socrates asks with renewed urgency: "Would we ever know what skill makes someone better, being ignorant of what ever we ourselves are?" (τίς τέχνη βελτίω αὐτόν, ἆρ ἄν ποτε γνοῖμεν ἀγνοοῦντες τί ποτ ἐσμὲν αὐτοί; 128e10–11).[17] Why would Socrates think this? As a heuristic, he brings back the Delphic inscription:

Socrates: Is it really so easy "to know oneself," and was whoever put it up on the temple in Pytho [*sc.* Delphi] so dumb; or, is it something difficult and not belonging to everyone?

Alcibiades: To me, Socrates, often it seemed to belong to everyone, but often at other times it seems utterly difficult.

Socrates: But, Alcibiades, easy or not, this is how things stand: if we knew this [i.e., about knowing *oneself*], perhaps we'd know about caring for ourselves; but if we were ignorant, we never would.

Alcibiades: So it is.

Socrates: Come then, how might the self itself (αὐτο τὸ αὐτό)[18] be discovered? For in this way we perhaps would discover what we ourselves are; while still being in ignorance of this, it would be, I suppose, impossible. (129a2–b3)

This passage augments Socrates' picture of the Delphic injunction in several ways. First, even Alcibiades realizes there are opposed senses of knowing yourself. There is the easy, banal sense. Alcibiades sees himself as hungry for greatness. He knows this without effort. He does not feel adrift, or uncertain, or opaque to himself. So this superficial form of self-knowledge must involve merely feeling, merely registering, one's appetites and wishes. It involves perceiving one's actual descriptive psychological states. What then is this contrasting "utterly difficult" (παγχάλεπον) sense? It would be insulting to assume the person inscribing the *gnôthi sauton* were so base as to mean something so

[17] Denyer 2001 ad 128e10–11 conjectures ἄνθρωπον in place of the MSS' αὐτόν, with the argument that scribes often mistook abbreviations of ἄνθρωπον ("human being") for shorter words. The choice makes no difference to my discussion.

[18] Denyer 2001 ad 129b1 and Allen 1962 translate "the itself itself." The MSS also have αὐτο ταὐτό ("the same self"), and one quotation has αὐτο τοῦτο ("this self"). 130d5 repeats these textual problems. Gill 2007: 98–104, emphasizes that this is a "double intensive," meaning the "essence" of something, but he worries too much about imputations of reflexivity, as Gerson 2008 observes.

superficial. Indeed, were everyone to start out with self-knowledge, as they would on the superficial reading, the command would be pointless. Since Alcibiades recognizes that the inscriber must have some point, he realizes that he often lacks awareness about the meaning of the *gnôthi sauton*. Alcibiades must suspect that the injunction calls him to some task whose nature he cannot even conceive. Part of the work of self-knowledge, then, is giving up the delusion that we've done the work already, or that we could do it easily if only we felt like it. This deeper sense of self-knowledge requires more than introspection or autobiography; giving an account of oneself may, seemingly paradoxically, require someone else's help even in making sense of the request.

Second, Socrates says that the self that one knows coincides with the self for which one cares. Because Socrates only ever speaks of care for individual objects – like for Alcibiades – the self we know must also be individual. It must also be improved by attendance or degraded by neglect. This appears to rule out an impersonal, abstract, or immutable self. This is a piece of evidence against the interpretation of self-knowledge as, ultimately and primarily, knowledge of reason or god itself.

Third, Socrates says that they might (ταχ') come to understand self-knowledge by understanding "the self itself" (αὐτὸ τὸ αὐτό), or "selfhood." Not only is Socrates' term here, a bare double intensifier, unprecedented; his reasoning too is elusive, why he thinks that knowing something abstract, what selfhood is, helps with knowing an individual object of care. A hint may come by looking to the "itself" in the phrase "beauty itself," which points to that configuration of traits that accounts for all beautiful things being beautiful. By analogy, a discovery about selfhood is a discovery about whatever accounts for all selves being worthy of being called selves. This is a serious question. But Socrates does not say that by knowing the self itself they would have self-knowledge. He says instead that by knowing the self itself they might "discover what we ourselves are" – and presumably discovering precedes knowing. As it turns out, Socrates and Alcibiades never discuss what selfhood ultimately amounts to.[19] Socrates directs the conversation elsewhere, to the nature of man, a passage in which, of body, body–soul complex, and soul alone, soul wins out. Socrates reflects that they were investigating into the nature of each thing (αὐτόν)

[19] Cf. Gill 2007: 106–107.

rather than into the "self" itself (νῦν δὲ ἀντὶ τοῦ αὐτοῦ αὐτὸν ἕκαστον ἐσκέμμεθα ὅτι ἐστί, 130d4).[20] Nevertheless, Socrates' hesitant suggestion that we understand the Delphic precept by understanding selfhood is provocative. It relates knowing oneself to knowing something about selfhood construed formally. For Socrates, the term "self" unites every instance of "myself" and "yourself" as instances of selves.[21] Failure to understand the meaning of "self" undermined Charmides' argument that *sôphrosunê* is "doing one's own things." In general, our concepts of responsibility, intention, and agency depend on a coherent notion of selfhood.

These three features together mean that Socrates suggests that knowing oneself is more difficult than feeling or expressing one's prevailing passions; it is coincident with caring for oneself; and it is dependent on understanding what the "self" means, not simply assuming it is one thing or the other. These three features present important insight into the distinctiveness of Socratic self-knowledge. They articulate the normative or formal requirements of self-knowledge more sharply than the previous picture did. The previous picture acknowledged that self-knowledge is more than a descriptive analysis of oneself at a moment in time; it is an elaboration of the expectations and requirements implicit in one's present-moment beliefs. This picture makes more precise the sort of abstract topics Alcibiades would have to know.

As part of the seductive affair, Socrates is moving Alcibiades, not quite through a bait and switch, to terrain where Alcibiades will feel uncomfortable going on his own. He, like most of us, simply lacks any articulated and contextless views of "selfhood." But as a matter of responsibility – for our words and deeds – we do have inchoate views of that selfhood. Socrates is showing Alcibiades how he can come to understand not just his own desires but also his more theoretical but inchoate or submerged beliefs with the help of good friends. Socrates is also showing how love may require joint attention to matters of shared interest.

[20] For this text and reading see Johnson 1999: 7.

[21] Cf. Allen 1962: 189. Foucault 2006: 38, 52–53, 67, claims that Socrates is saying that the self and thus the subject is reflexive. This is not an implausible inference but at this point Socrates seems to emphasize unification more than reflexivity. Selfhood, he seems to be saying, has boundaries of some sort, and self-knowledge involves delineating those boundaries.

Knowing oneself as a knower

A difficulty only now

Socrates' final discussion of the Delphic inscription comes three pages before the dialogue's end. Though Socrates and Alcibiades bypassed the inquiry into the nature of the self itself, settling for the simpler question about man (130c3), they take this answer as sufficient for their purposes, presumably Alcibiades' pedagogical seduction. They infer, "plausibly" (ἔοικεν), says Alcibiades, that knowing oneself means knowing one's soul (130e7–8). Since "soul" has been defined only as that which "rules" the body (ἄρχουσα, 130a1–c3), knowing about oneself would mean knowing about ruling. This might itself seem adequate for Socrates' and Alcibiades' purposes, and self-knowledge would be knowledge of the good for others, a result we see later in dialogue (133c21–23).[22]

Still, while this is an interesting implication and shortcut, it is not one that Socrates and Alcibiades dwell on. They go on to infer that caring for oneself is also caring for one's soul (132c1–2). Of course, Alcibiades had asked for the *way* to know oneself, and so Socrates reasks his question: how are we to know our souls most palpably (τίν ... τρόπον γνοῖμεν αὐτὰ ἐναργέστατα 132c7)?[23] After all, "once we know this, so it seems, we will also know ourselves" (ἐπειδὴ τοῦτο γνόντες, ὡς ἔοικεν, καὶ ἡμᾶς αὐτοὺς γνωσόμεθα, c8–9). In response to his own question and the justification for that question, Socrates returns with renewed urgency to the Delphic inscription:

> By the gods, that well-speaking Delphic inscription, which we just recalled – do we understand it? ... I will tell you what it looks to me that it means and advises us (ὅ γε ὑποπτεύω λέγειν καὶ συμβουλεύειν), this inscription. For it seems there are hardly any models (παράδειγμα) of it, except in terms of sight alone ... Think about this: if to our eyes, just as when advising men, it said: "See yourself," how would we take its exhortation (παραινεῖν)? (132c9–d7)

Socrates' first reference to the Delphic inscription (124b1) treated knowing oneself as important but without any obvious problems.

[22] Guthrie 1971: 151–152 seems to take this view.

[23] Denyer 2001 ad loc. argues that αὐτά refers to soul, body–soul complex, and body; even if this made sense in the argument's progression to the mirror-analogy, the present concern is solely with knowing one's soul.

Indeed, the content of and path to self-knowledge seemed largely set out in Socrates' speech about Persia and Sparta and in the moral of his story. His second reference (129a2–3) allowed that it might be difficult to achieve but identified no specific hindrances; Socrates implied only that they would have to understand the "self itself" that self-knowledge took as at least part of its object, and that the inscriber would not have put the inscription there if everyone practically already had self-knowledge. Only here, at the third reference, does Socrates impute some deep mystery to the Delphic inscription. He implies that self-knowledge's reflexivity makes the idea perplexing. Only by considering another reflexive state, an eye's self-seeing, might we understand that for which self-seeing is a model, self-knowing. In less than a page, Socrates sketches the way that self-seeing – as in a mirror, or in an another's eye, or in the best part of another's eye – points the way to self-knowing as in another's soul, indeed the best part of another's soul, or something similarly "reflective."

Because of the compression, elision, and even ambiguity of Socrates' sketch, not to mention problems in the manuscript tradition, and the suspicious fact that Socrates simply lays out this view without first working up Alcibiades' confusions, we need to give close attention to the structure of the argument. The first part of the argument is Socrates' choice of model.

The model of a self-seeing eye

Socrates' choice of model for knowing oneself is not perhaps so self-explanatory, and its multiple effects are not perhaps so obvious. I here address the supposed need for a model, the usefulness of this model, and the intriguing ethical considerations the model suggests. Addressing these observations in this order will bring to light some implications of Socrates' choice of model.

As I mentioned above, not once did the conversation about knowing oneself and self-knowledge suggest, before Socrates' remark at 132c9–d7, that reflexivity causes conceptual or interpretative problems. Socrates strove to convince Alcibiades that he needed to pursue self-knowledge, not that, despite appearances, he could if he wanted. Socrates' deflection of Alcibiades' questions concerning the way to proceed in self-care and self-knowledge was explained by his intention to bring Alcibiades further into self-recognition and humility, rather than by any implication that he was selling potentially non-existent goods. The first appeal to the Delphic inscription suggested that self-knowledge is reflexive in a quotidian way: we seek to know, and can succeed in knowing, our particular desires, implications or conditions of those desires, evaluative norms, and our fields of ignorance. Socrates' conversation with Alcibiades reveals that such reflexivity happens.

Usually we would point to a model of reflexive activity when we fail to understand something confusing in the operation of some other reflexive activity. Socrates' first two discussions of self-knowledge as knowledge of one's commitments and knowledge of the nature of selfhood suggested no such confusion. Thus the model of reflexive activity hints that Alcibiades *should* take the reflexivity of self-knowledge seriously, and as a conceptual difficulty. Alcibiades must recall that when he knows himself, it is him, or from his vantage, "I," that he is to know, not some alien or impersonal thing. Of course few people on reflection think that their commitments and the nature of selfhood are truly alien. To the extent that these notions may be spoken of without reflexive language, however, it may be easy to forget that one's understanding of them is an understanding of oneself, and that, to the extent that one is responsible for oneself, one is responsible for them. So though the conversation had not yet articulated the logically confounding puzzles of self-knowledge, the model's implication that it should be taken as logically confounding helps bring out the practical significance of self-knowledge. Self-knowledge concerns transforming *oneself*, and without self-knowledge, it is oneself who fails to live well.

Socrates uses the model to focus Alcibiades' attention on self-knowledge's concern with himself. This fact does not in itself, of course, explain the usefulness of this particular model.[24] It would seem that models clarify a murky phenomenon by appeal to a clearer phenomenon. But self-seeing is not obviously simpler than self-knowing. The *Charmides* made it totally puzzling, by treating of sight itself. In the *Alcibiades*, it is less puzzling but puzzling nevertheless. Socrates queries not self-seeing vision but a self-seeing bodily organ, the eye. Eyes themselves are colored, and thus may be the proper objects of

[24] It is often observed that the Greeks associated knowledge and perception: see Bluck 1953: 47; Denyer 2001 ad 132d3; Bartsch 2006: 43–47; *Tht.* 151e4.

vision.[25] This introduces a new problem. Not only is vision only of colors; it is also of what is in one's limited visual field. Eyes are behind, or outside, their own visual field. So an eye's self-seeing is confounded by its location. Thus the model for self-knowledge, having started out not so puzzling, has become more puzzling.

As it turns out, Socrates shows Alcibiades that an eye may come to see itself, when aided by something reflective in its visual field, as would be familiar from pieces of polished metal or bodies of still water. Socrates does not account for the optical or ocular details; studies of the Greek science of vision suggest they would be complex.[26] The phenomenon of mirror reflection occurs, all the same (cf. *Rep.* 596d8), and is not itself especially puzzling. A self-seeing eye seems for a quick moment perhaps as confusing as self-knowledge, but with a little change of perspective, it hardly seems worth puzzling over. This may be in part the point of the model. Self-knowledge can be made to seem confusing, when we see it as reflexive in an overly tight way, but as a totally familiar phenomenon when we change our perspective slightly.

The most interesting aspect of Socrates' choice of model is the ethical content of the charge to "see yourself" (ἰδὲ σαυτόν, 132d6). There may seem to be, of course, no ethical content at all. Telling an eye to see itself would seem a matter solely of mechanics. Yet this is not how Socrates presents it. He gives at least four reasons to think about it differently. First, though in his first reference to the visual *paradeigma* Socrates treats the eye as seeing itself (αὑτόν ἰδεῖν, 132d8), in the very next remark, he asks what *we* look at (ὁρῷ**μεν**) in order to see *both* it (ἐκεῖνό, the eye) and, simultaneously, ourselves (ἅμα ἂν καὶ ἡμᾶς αὑτούς, 132e2, cf. 133a1). So the "see yourself" is only incidentally addressed to the eye; it is really addressed to a person who looks both at his eye

[25] Denyer 2001 ad 132d3 makes the interesting observation that though eyes have a distinctive look, and so can be seen, ears do not have a distinctive sound, and so would not be heard. But this is mistaken. Eyes are visible only in the correct conditions, namely when light of a moderate brightness strikes them and a mirror is close and clear enough. Ears can be heard in correct conditions, namely when wind of a moderate strength strikes them and the sound either passes directly to the hearing canal or via an echo. The point is that reflexivity depends on particular external conditions.

[26] For discussion of ancient Greek mirrors and theories of reflective vision, see Gosling 1973; Denyer 2001: 231–233; Bartsch 2006: 59–69, with bibliography at 18n3 and 40n77; Belfiore 2012: 57–59; Wohl 2012.

(or eyes?) and at himself. Second, Socrates treats the command to see oneself not as a trivial matter, a direction for the eye to try to look, but as "counsel" and "exhortation" (συμβουλεῦον ... παραινεῖν). These terms Socrates and Alcibiades use elsewhere in reference to Alcibiades' goal of giving political advice (107b12, 108e6–7). It is people who are advised and urged on, not bodily organs, and they are advised for some good to them. Third, Socrates has drawn a parallel between the counsel that the Delphic inscription gives people – and that others in turn use in its name, as Socrates has done twice already in this dialogue – and the counsel some imaginary inscription would give an eye (ὥσπερ ἀνθρώπῳ, 132d5). The counsel to know oneself is not simply a matter of mechanics, and so too neither would the counsel to the eye be. Finally, the command to the soul, to know itself, is actually a command to a person.[27] Thus the parallel command, to the eye, to see itself, would also be a command to a person.[28]

What then could be this ethical content tied up with a command to see oneself? There are two familiar uses of the command: a negative charge, and a positive encouragement.[29] The negative charge would be to "observe how badly you are behaving." Charmides' claims that *sôphrosunê* is quietness or modesty suggest that the trait of character depends on seeing yourself as others might see you, and restraining yourself accordingly. In the *Clouds*, the Better Argument's brief for *sôphrosunê* (962) dwells at first only on restraint in activities that could be seen or heard (963–983). Similarly, the charge could mean "see what you are actually doing, not what you merely think you are doing," and thereby counsels realism about one's potentially questionable self-image (cf. *Chrm.* 158c7–160e4).[30]

27 Cf. 130e2–5: "When Socrates speaks using a speech to Alcibiades – not to his face, it seems, but to Alcibiades – he makes speeches; and that is the soul."

28 Hutchinson's translation, in Cooper 1997, captures this sentiment – "If the inscription took our eyes to be men and advised them" – at a loss of transparency about the Greek. Lamb's "suppose that, instead of speaking to a man, it said to the eye of one of use, as a piece of advice" is more transparent at the price of a misleading contrast.

29 This contrast pervades ancient discussion, as Bartsch 2006: 2–3, 16–41 shows.

30 The later history of philosophy associated Socrates with ethical advice phrased in the language of mirrors. Diogenes Laertius 2.33 says that Socrates recommended the young constantly look at themselves in a mirror, "so that, if they are beautiful, they may become worthy of it; but if they are ugly, they may cover over their bad looks with education" (cf. 3.39, for a similar story about Plato). Apuleius *Apology* 15.8–15 treats the tale with greater attention to

We might call the positive encouragement, by contrast, the ethical narcissist interpretation. The sense is "look at yourself, rather than at others." Here the encouragement is to keep one's visual, surface-level attention self-directed. In this vein, Denyer notes Prodicus' allegory about Heracles' choice of lives.[31] That story treats "wanting to see, and to be seen, and trying to do both at once by looking at herself, [as] among the most striking features of Vice." Denyer quotes Xenophon's version:

> [Vice] held her eyes wide open; she wore a gown through which her charms could most easily shine forth; she kept looking down at herself; she looked out also to see whether anyone was gazing at her; and often she would even inspect her own shadow [a sort of mirror-image]. (Xen. *Mem.* 2.1.22, tr. Denyer 2001: 231)

Vice took every approach to self-seeing: gauzy or loose clothing, a self-directed glance, the vicarious enjoyment of others' attention, and appraisal of her own image. Denyer continues by noting that the mirror (κάτοπτρα), the technology by which an eye might see itself, is "an oriental luxury" and is "unmanly," wielded by Aphrodite but not by Athena, goddess of wisdom.[32] The person proud of his looks and personal effects (perhaps like Alcibiades: 104a3–6, e7, using ἰδεῖν and ἑώρων; 131c6–7) would follow the charge to "see himself" as a way to become confident about his success.

The parallels between seeing oneself and knowing oneself may extend to the bivalent ethical content. We might imagine that there are two valences of knowing oneself. The ethical narcissist charges one to "know oneself, not others," and to bask in one's propitious

self-consciousness: "Is not Socrates the philosopher reported to have enjoined upon his students to contemplate themselves frequently in a mirror, so that those among them who were self-satisfied with their beauty might above all else take care that they did not disfigure the attractiveness of their body by bad character traits, but those who thought they were less good-looking might take pains to conceal their ugliness with the praise of their virtue? To such a degree did the wisest of all men use the mirror for the inculcation of good character" (tr. Bartsch 2006: 19; see her 18–20). Confusingly, just as Stobaeus recorded an account attributing the *gnôthi sauton* to the Sage Bias, he also records an account that attributes to him a version of this advice: "Consider, just as you would in a mirror, your actions, so that you may adorn the beautiful, and hide the shameful" (3.21.11).

[31] Denyer 2001: 231. [32] Ibid.

background and resource. Alcibiades seems at obvious risk of such aristocratic hauteur based in passive self-admiration. The negative charge, on the other hand, presses a responsive, active self-scrutiny, one open to failure and inadequacy. Saying "Know yourself" would criticize someone for acting in ignorance of his ignorance, or for failing to appreciate the scope of his beliefs and desires, or, put generally, for careless action, thought, and talk. It would be a charge against an indifference to the truth and the standards of responsibility for oneself. This charge may have no traction against people who want to be indifferent to truth and the standards of responsibility, who want to act whimsically, arbitrarily, or otherwise with no rational mediation between their impulses and their actions. But then again, Socrates shows that Alcibiades does not abide irresponsibility or failures of planning, and so even Alcibiades feels the force of the charge to know himself. Thus while there could be an ethically neutral recommendation to "know yourself" – to acquire certain facts about your position or metaphysical nature – Socrates' parallel with the "counsel and exhortation" to a person to see himself, an obviously ethically charged command, suggests understanding "know yourself" as ethically charged as well.

As we see, then, Socrates' model of a self-seeing eye is not simply the "only" (μόνον, 132d3) parallel for self-knowing. It introduces a not-yet-thematized interest in the reflexive, and it suggests that the "solution" to the puzzlement the reflexive causes might be completely commonplace. Most importantly, it encourages thinking about the critical sharpness any such reflexive charge might carry. There may be an interesting perceptual or psychological puzzle in understanding reflexivity, but the significance of the puzzle pales relative to the ethical significance of the charge.

Two kinds of reflection

For all the weight Socrates' choice of models bears, he does not belabor it. He enters directly onto the solution. The eye sees itself, and we see ourselves, Alcibiades knows, in mirrors and their like (132e1–4). Yet eyes themselves contain something mirror-like. So an eye may see itself, and the face of which it is part, in another eye. Indeed, the reflection occurs in the eye's most reflective part, which is the very part of the eye that has the excellence of the eye, seeing (ἀρετή … ὄψις, 133a1–b6).[33] Just so, Alcibiades comes to agree, a soul knows (γνώσεσθαι) itself by looking into (βλεπτέον) the best part of another's soul, or into something like it (καὶ εἰς ἄλλο ᾧ τοῦτο τυγχάνει ὅμοιον ὄν, 133b10). Just as the eye's most reflective region exercises its excellence, seeing, the soul's most reflective part exercises its excellence, wisdom, which is knowing and reasoning (ἀρετή, σοφια … τὸ εἰδέναι τε καὶ φρονεῖν, 133b9–c2). So self-knowledge, on the perceptual model, involves the soul "seeing" itself – and presumably our seeing ourselves – in the best part of another's soul, the part that involves knowledge.

This opens two questions, about the necessity of a partner in knowing, and about the connection between knowing and seeing. We have already asked, in the subsection above, why Socrates appeals to the eye model. The eye cannot see itself directly because it is a physical organ that registers light received from outside itself. There is no immediate reason to think that knowing requires a physical organ that registers ideas from its outside alone; our access to memories, bodily sensations, and thoughts suggests otherwise. Accordingly, we have no immediate reason to think that the perception model matches the cognitive model adequately. Three explanations might suffice to vindicate the relevance of Socrates' model. Olympiodorus believes that Alcibiades has so (metaphorically) blinded himself, giving himself up to irrational activity, that he simply cannot turn his attention to himself; he is activated only by external stimuli.[34] A second possibility is that while many instances of self-knowledge are not absolutely reflexive, where the instance of knowing does not actually take itself as its object, only something else that belongs to a person's "self," there are in fact other instances of self-knowledge that are absolutely reflexive, and these are the ones that need intermediation (cf. *Chrm.* 166a4–b6). A third possibility is that knowing oneself goes especially well when two people are involved, and so Socrates wants to recommend it, even if self-knowledge could be attained following some other model. Perhaps partnership, even if

[33] Socrates never says that the eye reflects better than other kinds of mirrors, but he gets Alcibiades to agree that in order to see itself, an eye *must* look (βλεπτέον) to another eye, not just to any reflecting surface (133b3); this comes to disagree with 133c8, the start of the problematic passage, where Socrates says that mirrors are better in three ways than eyes.

[34] *In Alc.* 8.2–12, 271.12–16, and similarly Proclus *In Alc.* 20.16–21.9; see Tarrant 2007.

not absolutely necessary, is, from the perspective of anthropology, very helpful.[35] Whichever it is, it is clear that Socrates wants to emphasize for Alcibiades the social production of self-knowledge.

The other question concerns the degree to which Socrates uses the language of vision when talking about self-knowledge. He says that the soul knows itself by "looking" (133b8), and he repeats this language three more times (βλέπων, 133c5; βλέποντες, c13; ὁρῷμεν, c16). This use of perceptual language obscures the proper activity of the soul. Indeed, Socrates only twice mentions that the soul is to "know" (γνώσεσθαι, 133b8; γνοιή, c6) itself, at the beginning and end of the main argument. So Socrates says nothing about what this knowing, likened to seeing, amounts to. Thus this parallel, while suggestive, leaves more to find out about self-knowledge. Perhaps, however, Socrates' decision not to break free of his model is suggestive in another way. Vision has a passive aspect, considered as the way one receives visual information. But it also has an active aspect, either as active scrutinizing, when someone looks at or for something, or as self-transformation, when someone comes to see something. Basking in one's looks shares more in the passive aspect; discerning and repairing the problems in one's comportment shares more in the active aspect.[36] Just so, perhaps one may know oneself in a more passive and a more active way, either as an idle introspecter or as an energetic self-carer. Socrates' conversation with Alcibiades would seem to suggest treating his favored mode of self-knowledge as the active form.

Rationality and divinity

These ambiguities in the nature of self-knowledge, and the imagery behind them, might seem provocative enough to direct Alcibiades,

[35] See *Magna Moralia* 2.15: "For it is the most difficult thing, as some of the wise have said, to know oneself, and also the most pleasant (for self-knowledge is pleasant). Yet we are not able to see ourselves from within ourselves. The fact that we cannot do so is clear because we criticize others for things that we do not notice when we do the same things ourselves. This happens through good will or passion; and this blinds many of us with regard to correct judgment.) Just as, therefore, whenever we want to see our own face, we look at it by gazing into a mirror, in the same way, whenever we want to know ourselves, we can do so by looking at a friend. For a friend, as we say, is a second 'I' " (1213a, tr. Bartsch 2006).

[36] This is a simplified view of looking, leaving out, for example, "gazing," "peeking," "staring," "objectifying," "emulating," and so forth; Bartsch 2006 describes some range of these in ancient literature.

should he now accept the importance of self-knowledge, to engage in further conversation with Socrates. Yet Socrates heightens the stakes, and gives a few more details about the parallel. How many more details depends on the way we judge the *Alcibiades*' famed textual crux. All manuscripts agree on the following seven lines. The aspect of the soul that exercises wisdom and knowledge, Socrates suggests, is more divine (θειότερον) than any other aspect. Being "more divine," it is thus like (ἔοικεν) the divine or god (133c1).[37] Socrates has hereby shifted the register of his language from the intellectual ("wisdom," "reason," "knowledge," human "excellence") to the theological. This shift is not unprecedented; Socrates has earlier mentioned "the god," in reference to his divine sign (103a5–6), and other dialogues present him as likening intellect to the divine.[38] But the purpose of this shift is not immediately apparent. Socrates goes right on to draw the consequence. Someone looking to it (τοῦτο: apparently the divine in or of the soul), coming to know (γνούς) the whole of the divine (πᾶν τὸ θεῖον) – glossed as "both god and reason" (θεόν τε καὶ φρόνησιν) – will also most know himself (ἑαυτὸν ἂν γνοίη μάλιστα, 133c4–6). Just as an eye reflects best off the purest – and perhaps thereby most perceptually acute – pupil of another's eye, a soul reflects best off the purest source of wisdom, the divine, god, and reason. The parallel is clear enough. Self-knowledge happens best with the partner best in terms of human excellence.

Of course this leaves important matters to be explained. How does a purer source of wisdom, so pure as to have a divine status, help someone else get more self-knowledge? How is the "whole of the divine" and "god" related to the intellectual part of an individual person's soul? Is it the *character* of that part of the soul; is it somehow *manifest* in that part of the soul; or has Socrates suggested moving *beyond* an individual soul? And in any event, how is one to *know* any of the divine, much less the whole of it?

Eleven more lines, only in manuscripts seen by Stobaeus and Eusebius, aim perhaps to answer some of these questions.[39] In these lines, Socrates continues:

[37] MSS TW print θείῳ (divine), B prints θεῷ (god); see Johnson 1999: 10nn22–23.

[38] See Denyer 2001: 234–237, for references.

[39] Eusebius *PE* XI 27.5, Stobaeus *Ecl.* III 21.24 (differently than in Eusebius), and others influenced by them. See Tarrant 2007 for discussion. Lamb 1927 omits these lines without mention.

Socrates: So then, just as mirrors are clearer than the reflecting surface in the eye, and purer and brighter too, so too wouldn't the god happen to be purer and brighter than the best [aspect] in our soul?

Alcibiades: It would at least seem so, Socrates.

Socrates: Looking to the god we would make use of that finest reflecting surface, and of human matters, to the virtue of soul, and in such a way we would most see and know ourselves.

Alcibiades: Yes. (133c8–17)

These lines answer no questions about the means by which one knows the god, nor advance more than a merely metaphorical explanation for the improvement in self-knowledge these better reflective surfaces provide. Indeed, they mostly restate the implications of the preceding analogy. They do, however, answer one question, and add one odd piece of information. God is purer and brighter than the best in the soul; this suggests that god is separate from the soul. This could mean that self-knowledge comes ideally from contemplation not of another person's soul but of god as distinct from anybody's soul. (Perhaps looking at another's soul is, practically speaking, a necessary first step for seeing the god beyond that soul, but there is no evidence for that view here.) In this view, self-knowledge does not really require another person's soul. The talk of another person's soul, and then of its intelligence, would then serve only to explain the importance of divinity. This passage, after all, even rejects the idea that an eye needs another eye to see itself, since it identifies clearer mirrors than pupils; the image of the other eye served only to explain the importance of reflectivity.

The odd addition is what follows Socrates' remark that, in looking to the god, we would make use of that finest reflecting surface. He adds: "and of human matters, [looking] to the virtue of soul" (καὶ τῶν ἀνθρωπίνων εἰς τὴν ψυχῆς ἀρετήν). This addition appears to make one of two types of concession.[40] It could be saying that in seeking self-knowledge we in fact look to two different reflective surfaces: to god, in the case of non-human matters, and to the virtue of soul, in the case of human matters. Sure, god is brighter and purer, and so perhaps are cosmological, theological, or otherwise spiritual matters, all

[40] Denyer 2001 ad 133c13–15 claims that the translation of which mine and Hutchinson's in Cooper 1997 are examples is even more awkward than his suggestion, which he admits itself awkwardly drops the parallel between

of which pertain to self-knowledge. But as far as human matters are concerned, which are also important to self-knowledge, looking to god is to look too far away; one must look instead to the murkier surface of the soul's virtue, presumably reason, knowledge, and wisdom. Or modified slightly, self-knowledge might have two conjoined aspects, a knowing of oneself *qua* divine matters and a knowing of oneself *qua* human stuff; the two sorts of mirrors are individually necessary and only together sufficient for self-knowledge. The alternative type of concession would not involve positing two separate reflecting surfaces. Socrates' remark could be implying that god and virtue are the same, and "virtue" is the name for that surface when we speak of human matters. The contrary implication above, that god is brighter than the best aspect of the soul, could simply mean that god is the ideal of human virtue, never instantiated but theoretically equivalent.

This theological speculation feels foreign to the dialogue. Even were it not so foreign, the dubious passage seems to add nothing concrete beyond an implication that god is external to soul.[41] It is better to see what follows.

Sôphrosunê *and ownership*

Most accounts of self-knowledge in the *Alcibiades* end at Socrates' account of souls knowing themselves in a most reflective – that is,

the two uses of εἰς: "So, if we were to look at God, we would be using that most splendid mirror, of human life in particular, in order to make our souls virtuous." It is true that Socrates goes on to say that having self-knowledge is equivalent to being *sôphrôn*, and thus virtuous, but nothing in the imagery of the eye suggests that seeing and knowing oneself would make one virtuous, or that we would know and see ourselves best *if* we had virtuous souls (though again I think it is true, and that Socrates would agree). Further, the inclusion of "of human life in particular" makes one wonder whether different beings would seek self-knowledge more successfully elsewhere. In any event, Denyer 2001 ad 133c8–17 thinks these lines are post-Platonic intrusions, given the infelicities of language.

41 Tarrant 2007 argues that the main debates about this passage in late Antiquity concerned the internality (non-Christian) or externality (Christian view) of god with respect to soul. He also notes that Neoplatonists seemed never to take this passage as evidence for an "assimilation to the divine" view, citing Alcinous' *Didascalicus* 28, 181.21–42. Bluck 1953: 46, interprets the preceding lines as a position about "a generic or universal likeness between one innermost 'self' and another," but he thinks this is a non-Platonic view and athetizes the whole dialogue accordingly.

rational and divine – surface.[42] But Socrates does not stop here, or change topics. He goes on immediately to remind Alcibiades that they agreed that knowing oneself is the same as being sound-minded (σωφροσύνην, 133c18, cf. 131b4). This in turn amounts to knowing, of our belongings, which are good and which are bad (εἰδέναι τὰ ἡμέτερα αὑτῶν κακά τε καὶ ἀγαθά, 133c21–23). As part of this knowledge, we also come to know which things are our belongings, and which things our belongings' belongings (133d1–9). This means we come also to know other people's belongings (133d10–e5), and thus, more generally, the belongings, or affairs, of the city (133d7). Drawn by mention of the city to the topic of leadership, Socrates then says that without self-knowledge one would not know one's actions and mistakes, presumably whether the actions are right (134a2–9), and thereby one would not prosper (134a13–14) or impart virtue to the citizens (134c1–2).

This turn to ethics and politics in a cascade of benefits due to self-knowledge is a stunning departure from talk of mirrors and god. Socrates returns briefly to talk of the divine in his recapitulative but textually suspected remarks at 134d1–e7 and in his apparent reference to his daemonic sign at 135d6.[43] By and large, however, he focuses on Alcibiades' need to gain self-knowledge if he is to become just and thereby live well. Yet the transition from seeing and knowing, in 132d5–133c17, to judging and owning, in 133c18–134c2, is deeply puzzling. The earlier passage purports to explain how one gets self-knowledge; the latter passage purports to explain the benefit of self-knowledge so attained. And yet if self-knowledge is to be attained through reflection on the most divine part of someone else's soul, or even on the divine itself, it is unclear how anything those methods would impart would give a person the particular skill of being *sôphrôn* and the particular knowledge to discern what belongs to whom, and how good those belongings are.

[42] This transition is almost never addressed. Bartsch 2006: 52, is a standard case: she makes absolutely no mention of it, and misleadingly states that "we are left with a definition of self-knowledge that cannot be pushed further than the soul's recognition that it is divine," ignoring the subsequent page of discussion; similarly, Joosse 2014.

[43] The passage at 134d1–e7 is deleted by Carlini 1964 and Cooper 1997, who translates it as follows:

Socrates:	And if you and the city act with justice and self-control (σωφρόνως), you and the city will be acting in a way that pleases God (θεοφιλῶς).
Alcibiades:	That seems likely.

The transition would be especially puzzling if we took the "self" to be discovered as an "impersonal" self, one that transcends anybody's individual personality or commitments and is instead rationality as such. Such a view of self-knowledge has been put forward recently by David Johnson. He encourages such a view by noting something peculiar about the writing of the *Alcibiades* itself: it is, he says, dramatically bland. But there is an explanation for this blandness:

> Socrates shows that we are ultimately to be identified first with our souls, then with the intellectual part of soul, and then ... with the divine intellect which is God ... [T]he self is ultimately impersonal, rational, and universal, and no one, not even Alcibiades, will ... stand out as a unique individual. The characterization and drama of the dialogue are limited for a reason, then: we are to get beyond such externals.[44]

Johnson observes that by identifying the pupil as the most reflective part of the eye, Socrates has also identified the part that never differs across eyes: though people have different color irises, pupils are always black. So to look at someone's pupil is to see something common, not particular. Also, since the pupil "possesses the virtue of the eye," to see a pupil is to see *seeing*. Since I am myself seeing when I see this *seeing*, to look at someone's pupil is again to see something common, not particular. Just so, the ideal rationality of souls is identical, and souls reflect off other souls only to the extent that those other

Socrates:	And, as we were saying before, you will be acting with a view (ὁρῶντες) to what is divine and bright.
Alcibiades:	Apparently.
Socrates:	Of course, if you keep that in view, you will see and understand yourselves and your own good (βλέποντες ὑμᾶς τε αὑτοὺς καὶ τὰ ὑμέτερα ἀγαθὰ κατόψεσθε καὶ γνώσεσθε).
Alcibiades:	Yes.
Socrates:	And you will act properly and well.
Alcibiades:	Yes.
Socrates:	And if you act that way, I'm prepared to guarantee your prosperity.
Alcibiades:	And I trust your guarantee.
Socrates:	But if you act unjustly, with your eyes on (βλέποντες) what is dark and godless, as is likely, your conduct will also be dark and godless, because you don't know yourself.
Alcibiades:	That's likely.

[44] Johnson 1999: 2. This view is found again in Bartsch 2006: 49–55.

souls are acting rationally; and thus souls too, in looking at themselves in other souls, see what is common to all souls. Socrates' argument continues, and for Johnson it further supports the impersonal view of self-recognition. The intellectual part of the soul is the most divine, Socrates suggests. God, it seems, is nothing but rationality. This makes god the best reflecting surface. But, as Johnson implies, it would also be, in a sense, the best filter, reflecting back nothing but one's rationality. (In this it would differ from unnervingly precise vanity mirrors!) Johnson concludes that this passage reveals concern not for "who we are as individuals" or as "inner selves" but for us "as rational creatures."[45]

In this view, self-knowledge is recognizing the best thing about us, our rationality. There is no doubt that this is a crucial element of Socrates' view. But Johnson's position cannot be the whole story.[46] He does not explain Socrates' move from his talk of the self as an object of care to the self as equivalent to impersonal rationality or god;[47] these seem inconsistent. Johnson might believe that Socrates uses two incommensurable senses of "self," something to be cared for and something deeper and more pristine, but then many of Socrates' arguments in the dialogue would fail, as instances of equivocation.[48] Johnson also states that Socratic conversation allows interlocutors to identify what they believe and about what they are ignorant, but he does not explain the connection between self-confidence or self-ignorance and self-knowledge.[49] Most importantly, Johnson has argued that, according to the eye-analogy, contemplation of some

[45] Johnson 1999: 8–16; quotation at p. 16.

[46] Both Rider 2011 and Belfiore 2012 also challenge the argument in Johnson. Rider notes that we come to know human nature "as instantiated in [one]self as an individual" (399, 401); the maxim conventionally means recognizing one's *own* place (399); Plato tends, as in the eschatological myths of the *Phaedo*, *Gorgias*, *Republic*, and *Phaedrus*, to speak of souls as individuals (400); the self may include non-intellectual and thus private aspects (400); if we needed only to see what *some* rational soul looks like, we would not need to look at our reflection (401); self-knowledge involves discovering one's fields of ignorance, what one really wants, and what one's potential is (408). Belfiore acknowledges that the attribute "god-like" could apply to any desire for the greatest power, and that the discussion of it alludes to a Sappho poem (60, 64); because Socrates and Alcibiades have distinct goals, their souls differ.

[47] Johnson 1999: 3.

[48] Bartsch 2006: 51, notes the discontinuity but makes nothing of it.

[49] Johnson 1999: 9.

exemplification of pure rationality, whether in a good interlocutor or in god, is a necessary condition for knowing oneself (fully). But he has not shown that such contemplation is a sufficient condition for self-knowledge. After all, if I am to know what my desires commit me to – the meaning of self-knowledge suggested by the first reference to the Delphic inscription – I must reason about them rationally, and to do this I must maintain before my mind's eye, as it were, an ideal of rational reflection. This might not, however, be all of it. While I could know myself as an individual only in the context of knowing the ideal of rational reflection, or of unification (the *auto to auto*), or of the norms of self-identity, I may also need to know about my particular beliefs and desires, and the fact that I am alone responsible for my actions.[50] Socrates' reference to "seeing yourself" as seeing one's face and oneself contributes to thinking so.

If we do not think that the model of the self-seeing eye requires thinking of self-knowledge as knowledge of some impersonal item, then the transition from the reflective view of self-knowledge to the equation of self-knowledge and the correct discernment of ownership becomes less puzzling. The equation of self-knowledge and *sôphrosunê* is not unfamiliar. Self-knowledge is not simply any knowledge about oneself. It must be what one would be *charged* to get, and this would be knowledge concerning one's self-improvement, and thus one's level of goodness.

Socrates' first inference from *sôphrosunê* is to knowing the goodness and badness of our belongings. Our belongings – specified simply by a genitive pronoun – presumably include everything from property to pleasures, looks to ideas. These are the things one is committed to nurturing or maintaining: certain objects, ideas, practices,

[50] Johnson 1999 cites the *Phaedrus* in connection with the *Alcibiades* in support of his view that "Socrates would have us pursue self-knowledge not by considering who we are as individuals but by asking what sort of creatures we are" (15). He does so by adducing the Palinode's description of a lover looking to his beloved, in whom he sees his patron god, and to his god itself (14). The god is the model toward which the lover strives and aims to help his beloved strive (251a–253a). Johnson does not stress enough, however, the result of this striving. The result, of course, is the perfection of the individual *as* an individual in a relation with another person. It is an explanation for lovers' attraction only to certain beloveds and for the way the passions of love cause an improvement in both the lover and the beloved. This will be discussed in more detail in Chapter 4.

employments, goals. (We will see another version of this argument in Chapter 5 on the *Philebus*.) At the moment one reflects on the value of one's belongings, one reflects too on one's possession of one's (putative) belongings. To commit to owning something is to judge it as good to own.[51] Self-knowledge is not a matter of identifying the person who owns some piece of property,[52] but with deciding whether to identify *with* something that *could* be one's property. It may be difficult to disown some potential belongings, one's body for example, but Socrates' point is that it is up to us (our "soul") to decide to what extent we want to take responsibility for anything. In noting that self-knowledge allows one to know what belongs to *other* people, and thus who *they* are, and what *they* judge to be good and bad, Socrates implies that self-knowledge amounts to this sort of judgment of value and commitment, and since both I and others are loci of such active judgment and commitment, self-knowledge must be concerned with individual valuation. This is easy to accept when we think of the self in self-knowledge as the sum of one's commitments, and knowing them to mean making true judgments about them (for example, as worth maintaining).

This has yet to explain Socrates' reference to knowing oneself in other souls, or knowing oneself in the god that is rationality. Eyes see themselves in other eyes, or in bright mirrors, because those reflecting surfaces send back their precise forms and put them just where eyes can best see: in front of themselves.[53] Likewise, people learn and think best in the most familiar situation, talking to someone in front of them. Since people can understand each other, they can bounce their ideas coherently and clearly among themselves. People are, so to say, better reflectors than books (the source of self-knowledge to which Euthydemus, whom we will meet in Chapter 6 on Xenophon, committed himself). Just as the medium for sight between eyes is light, the medium between souls must be conversation. Souls reflect off one another through their intellectual virtues, knowing and reasoning. Presumably this means that the more rigorous the knowledge and reasoning, the better the reflection; as far as conversations go, the more nimble and precise one's interlocutor, the

[51] This is not to encourage envy or theft; it is bad to try to own something that is not yours to own.

[52] Denyer 2001 ad 133d1–3 seems to think this, prejudiced as he is by a simplistic view of the Delphic imperative.

[53] Gill 2007: 108: "the two pupils resemble each other in having *active* capacities." See Belfiore 2012: 59–64.

better able people are at learning what that interlocutor is saying. The divine is perhaps located in one's particular interlocutor, and in oneself, to the extent that the interlocutor and oneself know and reason.[54] As the interlocutors refine the speeches through which they come to know their own and each other's selves – making them more consistent, more plausible, more precise, more responsive to the epistemic and practical demands the world sets on them – they refine themselves. They become more perfectly rational and wise, capable, presumably, of exercising their capacities excellently.

Seeing the rationality and divinity of one's own soul conduces to *sôphrosunê*, perhaps by providing an ideal of thought worthy and coherent enough to follow.[55] This excellence controls one's judgments about particular matters: what one owns, and the quality of those things. So the better – the more rational and divine – one's reflective soul is, the more *sôphron* one becomes, and the more precise one's individual, personal commitments may be. Socrates suggests that acknowledging one's rationality and one's unity – both of which may be so laudable as to be divine – is a crucial part of knowing oneself. Socrates is telling Alcibiades to unify himself, and to make himself rational, if he wants to achieve his particular purposes. Gaining self-knowledge is a matter of becoming properly the distinct person one wants to be.

A young man's coming to know himself

This survey of the *gnôthi sauton* in Socrates' long persuasive gambit presents three faces of self-knowledge. The first is the face of

[54] Gill 2007: 109–110, calls this looking to another person and to the divine the "triangular" model, and in presenting it he advances a theory similar to my own. Croiset 2002: 57, claims that knowledge of the divine *precedes* our judging ourselves or others; he thereby seems to think that looking to the divine is necessary but not sufficient for self-knowledge. Lauriello 2010: 248–251, connects this passage with Xenophon *Memorabilia* 1.1.11, 16, claiming that Socrates connects the study of quotidian affairs with theological and cosmological matters, and concludes that "morality itself, and our attraction and concern with it as something good in itself and for us, can only be fully soluble with such gods." This is a provocative claim but not one for which this passage gives adequate evidence.

[55] Lauriello 2010: 249, states, from a different perspective, that "self-knowledge necessarily follows from the examination of justice because that examination pertains to one's own private good and the city's," but takes up a richer view of self-knowledge in 253–254.

authenticity, acknowledging one's commitments. This takes investigation of one's desires, the practical or worldly obstacles to those desires, and the commitment one has to those desires in light of the obstacles. The second is the face of self-constitution, becoming a self rather than a plurality or disunity. This takes reflection on the nature of unification, ownership, and responsibility, and caring for oneself in a way that may engender such consolidation. The third is the face of rational maturation in conversation, holding oneself and one's interlocutor accountable for what each says and thereby improving one's understanding of whatever one may stand for, a mode of *sôphrosunê*. To put these together in the epistemic language of the Delphic inscription, seeking to know oneself means seeking to become both a better knower and a more knowable self. The language of virtue would suffice as well. "Be *sôphrôn*," it could say; that is, be virtuous, be a master of oneself, know what is good.

This rich account of self-knowledge makes sense in the dramatic context of the dialogue. Alcibiades approaches adulthood (103a4, 105b1, 110a2–8). He has lived long enough to have absorbed both the dominant values of the democratic fifth-century Athens and the particular self-confidence of his family: a youthful zeal, a model in his guardian Pericles, and an extraordinary lineage (104a6–c1). The dialogue's first half shows that absorption is the right word; Alcibiades never sought out or intended to learn anything (109d1–113c1). Alcibiades has not reflected on the way he can represent, simultaneously, the political and ethical norms of fairness and equity (110b1–c2), on the one hand, and his personal norms of entitlement and aspirations to power (113d1–e4), on the other hand.[56] He has not thought about the content of his desire to rule; after all, ruling Athens, or any municipality, takes imparting virtue to the citizens (134c1–2), but he claims not to have studied this pedagogical mode or content. Alcibiades' success, dependent on self-knowledge, cannot stop at the mere observation of his desires, or at humbling himself to the task, or at appreciating human nature. He has not known himself until he has acknowledged what his ultimate goal is, what it amounts to, and what it requires of him; and to figure this out may take an integration or reappraisal of

[56] Gordon 2003: 18, makes a similar point in terms of Alcibiades' upbringing under Pericles.

his desires. He may have to order them by some principle. Integration will at least partially constitute his self-knowledge.

Socrates does not urge quiescence or modesty of purpose, even if we suspect that Alcibiades' turn to reflection would result in this. It certainly would not serve Socrates' seductive purposes. Admonishing Alcibiades to seek self-knowledge means urging him to grow into his desires, making those desires realizable. We might wonder why one should work so hard to understand the desires that one has simply absorbed, through society, through one's family, or in any other fortuitous way. In other words, we might wonder why Socrates would, in his seduction, encourage those traits he would not obviously approve of. He might seem to be urging Alcibiades to limit himself to working with accidental and indeed inauspicious material. Probably this worry is what motivates readings of the Socratic *gnôthi sauton* as telling people to find their true self in divine rationality, an unsullied font of selfhood. But there is no *content* in this conception: it tells *how* to be, namely, rational, but not *who* to be. Alcibiades is to come to be, and has to come to be, Alcibiades; in an important respect, he cannot become anything else. Socrates talks with Alcibiades, not somebody else, and it is Alcibiades, not someone else, whom he loves. To be a person is to value certain things; and to be a person worthy of the nominalized reflexive "oneself" takes coordinating those values in logically consistent and experientially plausible ways. We can of course change, but we change *ourselves* when we do so within the framework of our commitments.

There is one other way that this rich account of self-knowledge reflects the course of the conversation between Socrates and Alcibiades. Socrates urges Alcibiades to spend time with him, nothing else. He gives no reason to think that future conversations will differ significantly from the present one. The one depicted in the *Alcibiades* has Socrates asking questions, Alcibiades answering, and then Socrates causing them both to reflect on his answers. He even frequently thematizes this conversational method. "I ask if you have in mind what I claim you have in mind" (106b11, with b1–c2). Or again:

Socrates:	Simply answer the things I ask.
Alcibiades:	No, but you yourself speak.
Socrates:	What? Don't you most want to be persuaded [that justice and expedience coincide]?

Alcibiades: Oh, completely.
Socrates: Then if you say that these things are the case, won't you most have been persuaded?
Alcibiades: It seems so to me
Socrates: Then answer! And if you yourself don't hear yourself (αὐτὸς σὺ σαυτοῦ ἀκούσῃς) that just things are also expedient, do not believe anything else [that I say].
Alcibiades: I won't, you know, and I'll answer. (114e2–9)

Socrates shows Alcibiades to associate his speech with his convictions (cf. 112d11–113c1). Socrates continues this even further, quoting Euripides (*Hipp.* 350–353) and reinforcing the point that Alcibiades made the claim, not Socrates, and so Alcibiades has only himself to blame. By talking we learn what we believe. Alcibiades learns that he must take responsibility for the things he says and the entailments of those statements. He must acknowledge his commitment to the validity-preserving power of inference, and to the consequences of his beliefs. He must own up to the reality of his inadequate maturity, and at the same time accept the sovereignty of his own diagnostic capacity.

Alcibiades' reflections on his answers cause him to recognize his ignorance. He discovers that he sometimes wavers in confusion, where his words and their import seem to split apart (116e3–118b8). This failure to know what he means, an experience he at first does not even recognize, comes to appear as mistaking what he believes for what he knows.[57] So in conversation with Socrates, Alcibiades comes to understand his desires more thoroughly, he newly appreciates what they commit him to, he abandons certain ideas about himself and the conceptual structure of the world, and he directs his actions toward a specific goal.[58] We can assume that the conversations the men take up in the future could cause similar changes. The implication is that coming to know oneself is the same as having the kind of conversations and reactions depicted in the dialogue.

[57] οὐκ οἶδ ἔγωγε οὐδ ὅτι λέγω, 116e4; δέδοικα … ἔγωγε ἤδη περὶ ἐμαυτοῦ, 117a1; τοῦτο … ἀγνοεῖς τὸ πάθημα τί ἐστιν, 116e6; οὐ μόνον ἀγνοεῖς τὰ μέγιστα, ἀλλὰ καὶ οὐκ εἰδὼς οἴει αὐτὰ εἰδεναι, 118b1–3; cf. 127d6–8.
[58] See Belfiore 2012: 36–51, for details.

Conclusion

The analysis of self-knowledge presented here leaves many questions open about the *Alcibiades*. Why does Socrates risk developing Alcibiades' audacious goals? Why does he use the language of divinity more bluntly here than he does in similar works of Socratic literature? What topics of conversation might Socrates intend to bring up in future engagements with Alcibiades?

As the analysis of self-knowledge opens these questions up, it also provides a new avenue to answer them. Rather than supposing the pursuit of self-knowledge takes theological or metaphysical assumptions foreign to Alcibiades' or Socrates' practical goals, we can see it as directly involved in both friends' goals.

In this chapter, Socrates showed self-knowledge to require inquiring into what one knows, to see whether one actually knows it. In future chapters, we see the development of several important concerns. How quickly can one attain self-knowledge? In the *Phaedrus*, Socrates suggests not quickly at all. Not everyone seeks political power; most people simply want some pleasure and avoidance of pain. Can we see self-knowledge as connected to this basic desire? The *Philebus* argues that we must: pleasure is either worthless, or harmful, without self-knowledge.

4 Phaedrus: *less conceited than Typhon*

Alcibiades and Phaedrus

The *Phaedrus* and the *Alcibiades* both depict one-on-one interactions between Socrates and a younger man, conversations parodying amatory seduction.[1] In both cases, the younger man wants to become excellent in public address, and in both cases he meets an unsavory end, having first gotten involved in the scandals of 415.[2] Alcibiades appears to care more for power and charm than for intellect and study, but his commitment to Socrates and his investigative conversations to some extent belie that appearance. Phaedrus shows a capacious delight in learned speech of all types, and he seems captivated by the use of language for its magnetic appeal. Socrates aims with both men to have them scrutinize the conditions underlying the power of rhetorical display, to decide whether they have met those conditions, and to think about their goals in wielding that power.

Despite these similarities, whereas all readers treat the *Alcibiades* as about self-knowledge, many do not treat the *Phaedrus* similarly. The dialogue is usually taken to concern love, rhetoric, and *psychagôgia*.[3] In part this is reasonable, since Socrates urges Phaedrus to pursue, not self-knowledge, but philosophy. "Philosophy" in the *Phaedrus* looks to be concerned with something other than self-knowledge, including contemplation of the really real, collecting and dividing the natures of things, seeking knowledge rather than appearances, or at the most

[1] Mueller 1957: 50, thinks Socrates means to seduce Phaedrus, but see Yunis 2011: 7–10, in rebuttal.

[2] On Charmides' involvement in the mutilation of the Herms, see Tuozzo 2011: 86–88. On Alcibiades' involvement in the enactment of the Mysteries, see Munn 2000: 96–126.

[3] "Self-knowledge" is mentioned neither on the back cover nor in the index of Rowe 1986 or Yunis 2011, nor on the back cover of Waterfield 2002 or Rowe 2005.

nuanced, cultivating the right kind of socio-erotic conversational relations.[4]

A closer look at the *Phaedrus* shows, however, that the *Alcibiades* and the *Phaedrus* also share a concern for self-knowledge. In the first place, both reference the Delphic "Know yourself" as part of an important lesson. This is obvious in the *Alcibiades*, as we saw in Chapter 3. There, Socrates closes his most impressive speech with a peroration on knowing oneself, and twice elsewhere pauses the conversation to mention and gloss the Delphic precept. In the *Phaedrus*, the significance of the lesson on the *gnôthi sauton* is highlighted by its abrupt appearance early in the friends' meeting. After Phaedrus tells Socrates that he just got hold of a speech written by his literary inamorato, Lysias, and that is well worth discussing, they seek a spot to get comfortable and talk about it. As they walk, Phaedrus thinks he sees a spot noteworthy in Athenian mythic history, where Boreas seized Oreithuia. Socrates points to the actual location, and then, in response to Phaedrus' curiosity whether he believes that the events the story narrates actually happened, he digresses at length on myth-rectification (τὸ ἐπανορθοῦσθαι), the skill that explains the source of such stories. At the digression's end, Socrates claims that, despite knowing about myth-rectification, he does not practice it.

> For these things I have no leisure at all. The cause of it, my friend, is the following. I am not yet capable, in line with the Delphic inscription, to know myself. (*Phdr.* 229e5–6)

Socrates explains what he means, and then makes an ostentatious return to talking about the natural scenery. Socrates' outburst about self-knowledge is part of the least narratively explicable set-piece in the dialogue. Though Socrates uses myth again in the dialogue, the talk about myth-rectification was not expressly occasioned by Phaedrus' question, seems not to demand talking about self-knowledge, and does not return. Socrates' claim that he has yet to obey the Delphic inscription is one of the few places in the *Phaedrus* where Socrates makes an explicit remark about himself. The Delphic reference obviously has some impact on Phaedrus, who soon makes his own reference to Delphi (235d9).

[4] "Philosophy" and related words are mentioned fourteen times in this dialogue.

A shared reference to the Delphic injunction is not, however, the only way the *Alcibiades* and the *Phaedrus* share a concern for self-knowledge. The *Alcibiades* deploys a mirror-analogy, both explicitly and as an implicit formulation of Socrates' relation to his younger friend. Both the analogy and its dramatic counterpart had parallels in the *Charmides*, where Socrates treats of the counter-example of vision seeing itself and makes frequent reference to his interlocutors' looking each other – and themselves – in the eyes. The parallels carry forward to the *Phaedrus*. The narrator of Socrates' "Palinode" speech explains how an object of someone's genuine love comes to reciprocate that love. The beloved and his lover spend increasing time together in talk, activity, and physical contact, for example in the gymnasium (255b3, 8). The beauty of the beloved emanates.

> Then it is that the springs of that stream which Zeus as lover of Ganymede named "desire" flow in abundance upon the lover, some sinking within him, and some flowing off outside him as he brims over; and as a breath of wind or an echo rebounds from smooth hard surfaces and returns to the source from which it issued, so the stream of beauty passes back into its possessor through his eyes (διὰ τῶν ὀμμάτων), which is its natural route to the soul; arriving there and setting him all of a flutter, it waters the passages of the features and causes the wings to grow, and fills the soul of the loved one in his turn with love. So he is in love (ἐρᾷ), but with what, he is perplexed (ἀπορεῖ); and he neither knows (οἶδεν) what has happened to him, nor can he even say what it is, but like a man who has caught an eye-disease from someone, he can give no account of it (πρόφασιν εἰπεῖν), and is unaware (λέληθεν) that he is seeing himself in his lover as if in a mirror (ὥσπερ δὲ ἐν κατόπτρῳ). (255c1–d6, tr. Rowe 1986, modified)

This mirror-like experience between budding lovers is, like the mirror-like experience between friends in the *Alcibiades*, part not just of a process of self-recognition, but of a process of self-improvement. Granted, there are some differences. The *Alcibiades* emphasizes the reflection off an eye; this dialogue emphasizes the eye as the recipient of an image of itself. The *Alcibiades* only hints at erotic seduction with the model of "Seeing yourself" and "looking yourself in the face"; the *Phaedrus* makes the sexual element explicit. Reflection in the *Alcibiades* has as its content language and reason; the *Phaedrus* treats it as beauty, desire, and love. The *Alcibiades* passage expressly relates the best part of the soul, via rationality, to the divine; the *Phaedrus* passage sets the reference to the gods in an earlier passage. These distinctions stem obviously from their functional differences, the *Alcibiades* containing encouragement of Alcibiades to share in conversation with Socrates, the *Phaedrus* explaining the profound benefits of "philosophical" love in general. But a closer comparison between them might enrich our understanding of both.

Even aside from the *Alcibiades* connection, the dialogue has obvious relevance to the study of self-knowledge. In some respects it might contain the most profound analysis of self-knowledge among the three dialogues we have so far discussed. This is because Socrates speaks of people in their concrete reality, in the context of political and social persuasion and favoring the earthier language of "soul" over the logically or grammatically austere "self" (or by contrast, the ideal language of "soul" over the mundane "self"). Phaedrus, who prizes language and its use above all else, must modify his relation with it, and thus with himself; knowing himself is knowing how he stands, and ought to stand, with respect to language. The Palinode is about more than lovers and beloveds; it describes, in a mythic register, the striving careers of souls, and captures, for anyone who has grown in love of somebody, the texture of that experience. Outside of the Palinode, Socrates gets Phaedrus to accept that the success of rhetoric depends on knowing about individual souls – their form and their proclivities – and yet Socrates admits that this task is extremely difficult. It would not be tendentious to say that while the *Phaedrus* ostensibly depicts the protreptic to philosophy that Socrates gives, in speech-discussion and conversational form, to Phaedrus, a protreptic connected to Phaedrus' love for verbal performance and composition, what Socrates really wants is for Phaedrus to join him in active obedience to the Delphic inscription, and that the discussion of love and rhetoric shows Phaedrus how to obey it.

This is of course not an unprecedented thesis. Charles Griswold took self-knowledge as the organizing theme of his 1986 study, *Self-Knowledge in Plato's Phaedrus*. He was preceded by Gustav Mueller's article (1957), which claimed that the dialogue's real theme is self-knowledge, and that Lysias' narrator lacks self-knowledge. But this article was too short to develop its theme. Since then, a number of studies have taken up questions of self-knowledge.[5] For all their

[5] Ballard 1965; Ferrari 1987: 6, 12, 24, 59, 121–124, 147–148, 164, 193; Warnek 2005: 141–169; Werner 2012: 35–43, 85–87, 258–271; Rapp 2014.

value, however, they tend to the diffuse, not treating self-knowledge as a well-defined problem. Christopher Rowe writes, for example, that "For Socrates, 'knowing oneself' seems to have meant recognizing the importance of one's soul, of one's spiritual or moral health, by contrast with the body, i.e. ordinary material concerns; Plato now reads the injunction against the background of a developed psychological theory."[6] Griswold, referring to Socrates' remark about the Delphic "Know yourself," says that "the kinds of things Socrates is asking here about himself seem to have nothing to do with 'epistemology' or 'philosophy of mind.' At this state 'self-knowledge' means understanding oneself as 'this particular person' in a very general, quite everyday and prescientific sense."[7] These works conflate "self" and "soul," and give too little consideration to the self-improvement side of self-knowledge, convinced perhaps by the Platonic context that self-knowledge must be principally knowledge of something always and already universal.

This chapter is in two parts. In the first part, I work out four puzzles; the solution to each advances the book's argument that Socratic self-knowledge is self-constitution. The first of these puzzles is suggested by the first quotation in this chapter: why precisely cannot Socrates yet know himself? The second is about the most famous passage in the literature on Socratic self-knowledge, and asks: why does Socrates compare himself to the monster Typhon? The third is about the mirror-analogy in the second quotation of this chapter: what are we to make of the fact that the beloved, looking to the reflective surface that is his lover, in fact fails to see himself? The fourth is about the meaning of the Palinode and its apparent vaunting of *mania* and rejection of *sôphrosunê*: if self-knowledge is equated with *sôphrosunê* throughout the Socratic literature, how are we to think about this apparent rejection of self-knowledge to make space for enthusiastic irrationality? As we learn from these four passages, for Socrates, coming to self-knowledge is coming to increasing acknowledgment of one's guiding norms and the recognition that one can in fact be guided by those norms. Humans can know themselves not just because they have a reflexive consciousness but because they are adaptable and determinable by what they come to judge as good.

[6] Rowe 1986: 141. [7] Griswold 1986: 43.

In this chapter's second part, I return to the context of Socrates' remark that he cannot yet know himself, the discussion of myth-rectification. I argue that though he dismisses myth-rectification as a kind of work for which he has no time, he describes it to provide a model for his own coming to self-knowledge.

Four puzzles

Socrates' present inability

Socrates says that he cannot spend time rectifying myths because he is not yet able (οὐ δύναμαί πω, 229e5) to follow the Delphic inscription and thus to know himself. This problem differs from those we saw in the *Charmides* or *Alcibiades*. Socrates does not say that it is impossible to know himself; he does not say he needs to convince himself about the value or necessity of knowing himself; he does not say that he is perplexed about the best way to know himself. He simply gives a negative self-evaluation about his progress, and implies that he has to keep working at it.

The Epicurean Colotes, as we saw in the Introduction, considered Socrates to be joking or lying when he complained that he did not know himself, presumably referring to Socrates' remark in the *Phaedrus*. Plutarch defended Socrates against these accusations. But an alternative explanation is that self-knowledge is simply impossible, and so we should not wonder that Socrates has so far failed to know himself. While some commentators on Plato do think self-knowledge is impossible, in this context they would have to construe Socrates as either irrational, pursuing what he knew could not be attained, or ignorant, pursuing what he did not know could not be attained. Few people, as far as I know, are willing to make either claim.

A more sensitive proposal is Charles Griswold's; he gives the most direct attention to this question, and so is the one most worth considering in detail. He offers three reasons for Socrates' inability yet to know himself. First, "a person can always become something more, or different, than he presently is … [and this] entails that self-knowledge is not terminable so long as one lives." Second, "the soul is genuinely difficult to know, for it seems to be, among other things, both simple and complex." Third (though Griswold treats this as an extension of the second reason), "That Socrates does not know himself reflects the inability of any human being to know himself perfectly."[8] In other words: we change; we are complicated; we are impossible to get exactly right. Each of these claims seems true. But perhaps they do not completely account for Socrates' claim not yet to know himself. I take these issues in turn.

The first explanation for Socrates' concession points to human dynamicity and the impermanence of our characters. Griswold gives as an example that "a philosopher can become wiser or can degenerate into a sophist."[9] But there are several difficulties with accepting this explanation for Socrates' inability yet to know himself. First, one's changing is in fact consistent with a sort of self-knowledge, namely momentary or temporary self-knowledge. Even should Socrates fear future change, nothing stops him from knowing himself now. Because he surmises he may change again, he will free up time in the future to recalibrate his self-knowledge. But Socrates does not say in the *Phaedrus* that he is exercising forethought and thereby keeping his time free; he says he cannot yet know himself, meaning *now*. This means that Socrates does not know himself now. Perhaps he has recently changed, and has had inadequate time to catch up in self-knowledge. But Socrates' phrasing suggests he has never known himself. This means that he is not simply updating his self-knowledge. Further, were it possible to know oneself at least for a while, Socrates would not need to make such a blanket refusal to engage in myth-rectification (the context in which he mentions not yet being able to know himself); he could instead claim to have only sporadic opportunities to work at it. Of course, a rebuttal to this line of argument observes that I have assumed intermittent rather than constant change, with moments to catch up in self-knowledge; but Socrates could be always and continuously changing. Then he would never have a chance to catch up. Yet this very inability undermines the rebuttal. Socrates implies that he still strives to know himself. He even expresses some optimism. He does not say that he hopes simply to maintain the same level of partial self-ignorance. Were he always changing, he would be a rower in a too-strong current, and should give up, saving his energy for some other task, or keep at it,

[8] Griswold 1986: 43. [9] Ibid.

though acknowledging his plight. A generous interpretation of his remark requires that we make his intentions plausible.

There is a basic problem with explaining Socrates' inability yet to know himself by appeal to ineluctable change. It casts altogether in doubt the value of getting self-knowledge. In a life of constant change, whatever self-knowledge we might settle upon would have a quickly effaced value. This explanation also assumes an artificially narrow definition of self-knowledge, as something that goes out of date whenever a person becomes wiser. This disqualifies one's more stable structural or constitutional aspects from being objects of self-knowledge. Another problem with the excuse of dynamism is more philosophically significant. It treats one's changeability as an issue separate from one's self-knowledge. It assumes that self-knowledge only passively records who a person is, and is therefore at the mercy of one's changes. This view forecloses the possibility that knowing oneself means, or involves, making oneself less changeable and more stable, less frenetic and more deliberate, less will o' the wisp and more well founded. Griswold seems to accept that the stable person could, on account of her stability, come to have self-knowledge; he does not consider whether the self-knowing person could, on account of her self-knowing, become stable.

Griswold's second explanation for Socrates' inability to know himself depends on assuming that the soul is "both simple and complex."[10] It is difficult to know what this means in the case of soul. Griswold defines complexity, perhaps contradictorily, both as the "absence of pattern, structure, shape, and stability" (40) and as "having an articulated structure" (42). Simplicity, in additional presumably to being the opposite of "complexity" – on the one hand, having pattern, on the other hand, lacking articulated structure – is "liv[ing] in harmony with the divine" (41) but also "undiluted sophrosyne," "lack[ing] the eros and dialectically generated knowledge of ignorance characteristic of the philosopher" (41). This might be an intractable explanation. Still, there may be some intuitive grounds for Griswold's pairing. Socrates later refers to the importance for rhetoricians in deciding whether the souls of the people in their audience are simple or complex (ἁπλοῦν ἢ πολυειδές), and thus whether they need to deploy simple or complex speeches to convince those people (270d1, 271a6–7, d1–2). Whatever

[10] Griswold 1986: 43. For a similar view see Rapp 2014: 34–35.

the terms mean, then, the question is whether a complexity–simplicity duality could account for Socrates' delay in succeeding at knowing himself. It is hard to see how this would be the case. On the one hand, being both complex and simple could be not merely paradoxical but a complete contradiction, and probably it is impossible to know a contradiction. But then it is probably impossible, too, to *be* a complete contradiction. More likely, this duality would amount to a person being simple in one guise, complex in another guise. But in this case, self-knowledge just involves knowing oneself under two guises, and this double-vision does not seem so onerous. I rather think likeliest, though, that Griswold's claim reduces to the claim that Socrates, seen pessimistically, is somewhat complex, and seen optimistically, is somewhat simple. But then Socrates is between utmost complexity and utmost simplicity. It might appear that either of the extremes would be the more difficult to know – in the first case, there being too much to grab onto, in the second case, not enough – and the middle point the easier to know. One's mild complexity would not be, in principle, impossible to know.

The third explanation for Socrates' inability, that we cannot know ourselves perfectly, is ambiguous. Griswold could be saying that self-knowledge as such is impossible. This returns us to the odd assumption that Socrates would venture to pursue the unattainable. More charitably, Griswold could be saying that we can know ourselves to a large extent, but not all the way. In this case, however, Socrates would not be trying to get perfect self-knowledge; he would just be trying to get more self-knowledge than he already has. Socrates means, when he says that he is as yet unable to know himself, that he is as yet unable to know himself as much as he could, just short of perfectly. This seems fairly plausible. But this does not explain Socrates' failure to know himself as much as he can (short of perfectly); it simply states it. So I think that Griswold's explanations do not suffice. I propose two others.

One possibility is that Socrates has heretofore lacked the right conversational partner. Our analysis of both the *Charmides* and *Alcibiades* claimed that the proper kind of conversation is the best route to self-knowledge. The *Phaedrus*' Palinode suggests that self-understanding and self-improvement are motivated by a beautiful object of love. Upon seeing a beautiful boy (251a2–3, d7, 252a2) with a sympathetic disposition (252d6), the lover aims to make the boy as much like the god that they both follow (252d6–e5). Their shared god represents the ideals which they by their nature both seek – for example, in the case of Zeus, the practice of philosophy and leadership. But the lover himself may not have yet completely imitated his god (252d2), and so to help his beloved do so, he must himself hurry up in his preparations.

So if they [i.e. lovers] have not previously set foot in this way [*sc.* of becoming like their god], they undertake it now, both learning from wherever they can and finding out for themselves; and as they follow the scent from within themselves to the discovery (ἰχνεύοντες δὲ παρ' ἑαυτῶν ἀνευρίσκειν) of the nature of their own god, they find the means to it through the compulsion on them to gaze intensely on the god (πρὸς τὸν θεὸν βλέπειν), and grasping him through memory, and possessed by him, they take their habits and ways from him … and … they count their beloved responsible for these very things. (252e5–253a5, tr. Rowe 1986)

The narrator of the Palinode says that attraction to the boy's beauty leads the lover to want to help the boy become as fitting to his best nature as possible. This leads him to want to know more precisely about his own nature. This self-knowledge amounts to a recognition of his ideal and an adoption of the ways of life and actions suitable to those ideals. The boy in his beauty and imperfection is responsible for his self-constitution to the extent that the boy provides a great and continued enticement to do right by him. This is an excellent story about the value of love to both the beloved and the lover. It makes the reasonable assumption that we come to know ourselves in order to know our ideals, and know our ideals so that we may pass them on to those for whom we most intensely care. We pass on those ideals through "persuading and training" (πείθοντες καὶ ῥυθμίζοντες, 253b6), and for some ideals this would mean through conversation. The words persuade, and the exchanges cultivate the habit for future conversations.

For all the verisimilitude of this account, I suspect that Socrates does not mean to say that he is lacking the right beloved and conversational partner. It seems clear that he already feels confident about the god he pursues, and thus what most of his ideals are. It seems unlikely that he is seeking Phaedrus as that one perfect and beautiful partner. Phaedrus has aged out of the appropriate cohort, and though Phaedrus is surely not as dull as some readers take him to be, he is not the most sympathetic of all Socrates' friends. None of this means that Socrates does not care deeply for Phaedrus, that he does not aim to persuade and train Phaedrus in the way of their shared god of philosophy and leadership, and that his interest in Phaedrus does not encourage him to improve himself. On the contrary, it means that Socrates needs not the one perfect partner but a continuous run of them. This fact suggests a truer explanation for Socrates' inability.

Self-knowledge, Socrates seems to be saying, takes an entire life. This sounds trite but requires a view of self-knowledge distinct from the observatory or investigative models assumed by many readers. Self-knowledge would take an entire life if it means striving for ever-closer approximations to the divine model as human nature allows. Socrates closes his conversation with Phaedrus with a prayer that he may become beautiful inside (τἄνδοθεν) and that what is inside may befit what is outside (ἔξωθεν δὲ ὅσα ἔχω, τοῖς ἐντὸς εἶναί ποι φίλια, 279b9–c1).[11] Perfecting the match between facts and norms, reality and ideals, takes untold conversations, tests, recollections, critiques, striving, and straining. Socrates still qualifies his understanding of so much that would be best to know, emulate, and follow: the nature of the soul, of dialectic, of proper speech. The Palinode tells of the laborious recovery of knowledge; Socrates hints at the laborious recovery of self-knowledge.

Of course, Socrates has not expressly stated that the self-knowledge he has yet to be able to attain is acknowledging and committing oneself to one's (divine) ideals. The course of the dialogue suggests that this is what he means, but it is worth making clear just what he has established. By early in the dialogue he has made only several points. First, it takes a lot of time to get self-knowledge, on the scale of the overwork-inducing myth-rectification to which he compares it. Even the full-time philosophical conversations to which Socrates appears to have been able to dedicate many decades of his life have not gotten him it all. That it should be difficult is confirmed by the fact that it was inscribed at Delphi; were it easy, it might instead go without saying. Second, self-knowledge involves investigating himself (σκοπεῖν ... ἐμαυτόν) rather than foreign things (τὰ ἀλλότρια, 230a1, 3). He does not say internal rather than external things, or soul-related rather than non-soul-related things. This suggests that self-knowledge concerns itself not with whatever is inside one's mind but with whatever is

[11] On this prayer see Clay 1979.

most characteristic or determinative of oneself, normatively so defined. Inside one's mind could be one's beliefs that one happens to accept on the basis of convention, like the Athenian myths Socrates says he accepts (πειθόμενος δὲ τῷ νομιζομένῳ περὶ αὐτῶν, 230a2). These are foreign things, despite their location. What by contrast is determinative of himself is, for example, his commitment to obedience to the Delphic inscription. Socrates makes a third point about self-knowledge. He says he investigates how he contrasts with Typhon. This third point deserves its own discussion.

Typhon

Socrates enters into his remarks about self-knowledge in response to Phaedrus' question, whether he takes as factual the mythic story of Boreas. Socrates does not say, but admits that some people do not take it as factual. Judging that story and others – for example, about centaurs, the Chimera, gorgons, and Pegasus (229d5–7) – to be false, they nevertheless hope to explain those stories' circulation in popular culture. They conjecture an account that could plausibly (κατὰ τὸ εἰκός, 229e2) lead to the admittedly confused report. Presumably because these stories are numerous, and because an investigator would have to distinguish between competing plausible accounts, this work of myth-rectification takes much time. Dismissing this activity as overwhelming does not mean, however, that mythic stories of beasts have no importance to Socrates, or that some are not more fecund than others. Typhon, for example, serves Socrates' investigative purposes well. He investigates (σκοπῶ)

> whether I happen to be some sort of beast more complicated and inflamed than Typhon (εἴτε τι θηρίον ὂν τυγχάνω Τυφῶνος πολυπλοκώτερον καὶ μᾶλλον ἐπιτεθυμμένον), or whether I am a gentler and simpler animal, sharing by nature in some divine and unconceited portion (εἴτε ἡμερώτερόν τε καὶ ἁπλούστερον ζῷον, θείας τινὸς καὶ ἀτύφου μοίρας φύσει μετέχον). (*Phdr.* 230a3–6)

Socrates does not want to know whether he is like Typhon or not, but in what way he differs. This raises a range of questions. Why does Socrates pick out Typhon in particular? Why does he treat seeking self-knowledge as deciding in which way he differs from Typhon? And what does this mean for Socratic self-knowledge?

Typhon is hundred-headed and morphologically complicated, with human and animal qualities.[12] He speaks in animal and human voices. He fathered Gorgon and Chimera, the latter slain by Pegasus, all creatures just mentioned by Socrates.[13] He may also have fathered the Sphinx, who asked the riddle of man.[14] As we have seen in our study of the *Prometheus Bound* in the Introduction, Typhon thought himself better than men and gods, and was the last to try to defeat Zeus. When he failed, and was punished, he never changed. Zeus imprisoned him in a mountain, but Typhon kept emitting evil breezes. We might conclude from the traits given to Typhon by Greek mythology that being like him would preempt the transformative possibility of self-knowledge. Typhon would get no benefit from the Delphic inscription's charge. He is too hubristic, too complex, and too stubborn to improve himself.[15] Typhon lacks calmness, Socrates says, and for Socrates it is the calmer character (ἡμερώτερον, 230a5) who gets self-knowledge.[16] Socrates' final speech of the *Theaetetus* summarizes his hoped-for effect, what he says exhausts the power of his art, on the young prodigy: by not believing he knows what he does not in fact know (οὐκ οἰόμενος εἰδέναι ἃ μὴ οἶσθα), Theaetetus will become "gentler" and *sôphrôn* (ἡμερώτερος σωφρόνως, *Tht.* 210c3). Socrates links self-knowledge and calmness together and to his general goal of making the young as good as can be (210d1–2).[17] Likewise, in the *Gorgias*, Socrates says that good statesmen, among whom he includes himself, are to make men more gentle (516b2). He then quotes Homer

[12] On Typhon, see Hesiod *Theogony* 820–868, Pindar *Pythian* 1.15–28, Apollodorus *Library* 1.6.3, and among contemporary scholars, Too 1998; Clay 2003: 25–27; Goslin 2010; Ogden 2013: 69–79. Blakely 2009 ad F 61 has an extensive bibliography.

[13] Hesiod *Theogony* 310–320. The Chimera is mentioned at *Rep.* 588c3, just before Socrates' image of the tripartite beast. See Hunter 2012: 79–86, on the relation between Plato's image of Typhon and his other monster imagery.

[14] Apollodorus *Library* 3.5.8, in contrast to Hesiod *Theogony* 326.

[15] Cf. Griswold 1986: 40–41; Long 2001: 30, associates "modeling oneself on a peaceful divinity and not on Typhon" with "the ideas of autonomy, self-control, [and] ruling oneself."

[16] Compare Verdenius 1955: 269.

[17] Earlier in the *Theaetetus* Socrates links self-knowledge, care for others, and thinking of the kind of beast one is. In the "Digression," the notably unsocratic "philosopher" asks the abstract question, "What is man?" (τέ δέ ποτ ἐστὶν ἄνθρωπος, 174b4), but does not know what he does not know (οὐδ ὅτι οὐκ οἶδεν, οἶδεν, 173d9–e1), does not see how his neighbor acts (174b2), and does not even know whether he himself is a human or some kind of beast (εἰ ἄνθρωπος ἐστιν ἤ τι ἄλλο θρέμμα, b3–4). This Theodorus-approved philosopher

as saying that "the just are gentle" (οἵ γε δίκαιοι ἥμεροι, 516c2).[18] Thus in hoping that he is calmer than Typhon, Socrates is hoping that he might be in a position to become a better person.

Typhon – or rather, the same monster under the guise of Typho – is mentioned in our earliest extant piece of Socratic literature, Aristophanes' *Clouds*. As Socrates introduces the Cloud chorus, Strepsiades provides a myth-rectifying interpretation, calling the clouds "mist and dew," but Socrates resists, saying that they serve as the muses of intellectuals (323–334). Strepsiades finds this plausible on the grounds of famous lyrics that vivify storm-clouds, including "plaits of hundred-headed Typho" (πλοκάμους θ' ἑκατογκεφάλα Τυφῳ, 336). This lyric quotation leaves ambiguous whether Strepsiades takes Typho as a natural storm force or as a divine agent. As it turns out, the Clouds chorus takes on the shape of the aspects most characteristic of their viewers; they provide a sort of reflection of their viewer's self (343–355).[19] Typho, a sort of storm cloud, is thus related to the function of manifesting the visible image of someone's self, thereby guiding that person to self-knowledge. Plato's description of Typhon as "complicated, many plaited" (the positive form of πολυπλοκώτερον) likely alludes to Aristophanes' description of him as "plaited" (πλοκάμους). Socrates' likeness to Typho(n) in this context suggests his likeness to an implacable wind, storm, or cloud, on the one hand, and to a self-knowledge-assisting nurturer of intellectuals, on the other hand. That is, Aristophanes' Socratic Typho already manifests the ambivalence between natural force and helpful agent.

Typhon thus stands for an intractability that is anathema to self-knowledge, and in the Aristophanic context, for the ambiguity between irrational force and human agency. Other readers have noted

lacks self-knowledge, is presumably unconcerned with his companions (τοῖς συνοῦσι, 210c3), and would not know how he compares to a beast like Typhon. On the point of the Digression see Peterson 2011: 59–89.

18 There is more evidence elsewhere linking gentleness to self-improvement. Arguing that everyone thinks virtue is teachable, Protagoras says that musical education is about making children gentler, more rhythmic, and more harmonious (*Prot.* 326b3); all of human life requires these traits. The Eleatic Visitor says that belief in Forms makes one more gentle (*Soph.* 246c9). The Athenian Visitor says that the job of the legislator is to make his listeners gentler and more disposed to listen; this makes them easier to teach, and more able to attain moral excellence (*Laws* 718d4, cf. 766a3).

19 See Moore 2015b.

the similarity between this "mythic mongrel" and the many-headed beast of a soul at *Republic* 588.[20] This seems to prepare for the multipart soul in the *Phaedrus*' Palinode. It might even point at the unruly, satyric, even Socratic black horse of that chariot-team image.[21] The Palinode has the philosophers following Zeus; likeness to Typhon would be an easy way to express absence from Zeus' train, and thus the impiety Socrates worries he might sometimes exhibit (242d7). In general, these readers see Typhon as hubristic and complicated.[22] Socrates' reference is richer than that. Seeking self-knowledge is always promissory. We do not know whether we can actually improve ourselves; we perpetually fear that our self-appraisal is mere spectatorship. We worry we are like the Typhon, a being of overly disparate, overly zealous traits. We always seek out evidence that we can become better than we are, that we are not to be locked in a mountain, spewing horribles, for all eternity.[23]

"As if in a mirror"

In the *Alcibiades*, the image of a mirror solves the problem on which the *Charmides* conversation foundered. A person is too close to himself to know himself directly; crammed, he cannot grow in rationality and power. The solution comes in the form of a friend: a second person provides the crucial reflection at a distance. In the *Phaedrus*, the image of a mirror solves a similar problem. A beautiful young man is too close to himself to see himself directly, and thereby to grow in remembrance of the Form of Beauty; another person provides the crucial reflection at a distance. I quote the passage again:

[20] Griswold 1986: 39; Rowe 1986: 140; Ferrari 1987: 12.

[21] Belfiore 2006, noting that in the Palinode the black horse is randomly put together (εἰκῇ συμπεφορημένος) and spews angry abuse (ἐλοιδόρησεν ὀργῇ).

[22] See also De Vries 1969: 51–52; Yunis 2011: 94; Bradley 2012: 38, 48–54, 95–96; Ryan 2012: 102; Werner 2012: 36–43; Rapp 2014: 32–35. On the history of *tuphos* as meaning "hubristic," see Long 1978: 74; Decleva Caizzi 1980.

[23] I conjecture a connection in the Athenian mind between Typhon and the *gnôthi sauton*. The Temple of Apollo at Delphi included a Gigantomachy, with centaurs, gorgons, Chimera, and Pegasus, according to Euripides *Ion* 184–218; cf. Rosivach 1977; Zacharia 2003: 14–20. These battles could have included or implied the battle between Typhon and Zeus. Since the Temple of Apollo at some point became associated with an inscription, the "Know yourself," the Typhon-pointing battle-scene and the saying could have become linked.

Then it is that the springs of that stream which Zeus as lover of Ganymede named "desire" flow in abundance upon the lover, some sinking within him, and some flowing off outside him as he brims over; and as a breath of wind or an echo rebounds from smooth hard surfaces and returns to the source from which it issued, so the stream of beauty passes back into its possessor through his eyes, which is its natural route to the soul; arriving there and setting him all of a flutter, it waters the passages of the features and causes the wings to grow, and fills the soul of the loved one in his turn with love. So he is in love, but with what, he is perplexed; and he neither knows what has happened to him, nor can he even say what it is, but like a man who has caught an eye-disease from someone he can give no account of it, and is unaware that he is seeing himself in his lover as if in a mirror. (255c1–d6, tr. Rowe 1986)

Howsoever bizarre are this passage's fluid dynamics, we should judge as sound the idea underlying the account of the beloved's falling in love. The pleasure and inspiration that the lover feels, at the sight of his beloved, animate his face, his eyes, his step. This vivacity in turn enlivens the beloved who looks at the lover. The beloved comes to think, "How odd that my lover, older person that he is, looks wonderful, and really quite attractive, all of a sudden; I can't understand why." He attaches tender feelings to his lover, feelings that he might not otherwise have directed at him, and with this sentimental education, the beloved stands to gain in education, philosophical practice, and successful emulation of his and his lover's shared god.

This mirror of beauty has the same benefit as the *Alcibiades*' mirror of reasoning. But Socrates' description of the phenomenology of seeing one's beauty in another picks out something his description of knowing oneself in another does not. The description here repeatedly notes the beloved's ignorance. He does not know what he loves; he does not know what has happened to him; he cannot say what he is experiencing; he cannot account for the source of his experience; he does not know that the beauty he sees is his own. The argument of the Palinode treats this ignorance as salutary. Because of it, the beloved does not fall into isolating narcissism or cynical dismissal. His confusion lets him stay by his lover and, with a good lover, be drawn into a well-ordered life and the practice of philosophy (256a7). This ignorance is not wholly unexpected; nor is it wholly an ignorance of one's peculiar self. It is true that the beloved does not realize that the loveliness of his lover merely reflects back his own loveliness.

But his lover reflects his beauty back to him only because his lover has a sensitivity for beauty, and is in the position to be reminded of the Form of Beauty. The lover has the traits necessary for reflectivity. Also, it is not the idiosyncratic image of some individual person's beauty that by itself provides improvement. The universal Form of Beauty, not some particular instantiation of it, has the causal power. So while the beautiful boy's peculiar beauty contributes to his own activation, it does so only by providing access to the non-peculiar force of Beauty itself. The young beloved could hardly be expected to understand this; presumably the lover himself would not understand it without the sort of explanation Socrates provides for Phaedrus in the Palinode.

Indeed, the Palinode's mirror-imagery suggests not just the route from non-love to love. It suggests a route from ignorance to non-ignorance. Presumably the life of philosophy and conversation to which the lover draws his beloved (cf. 257b6) would involve talking about the nature of falling in love – talking, that is, about what the Palinode describes. The beloved could be expected to learn eventually what happened, how his relationship with his lover first deepened when he responded to his own beauty.

Socrates does not discuss failing to recognize oneself when he talks about mirrors and self-knowledge in the *Alcibiades*. But he leaves open the possibility. This passage in the *Phaedrus* encourages reconsidering the *Alcibiades* passage. An eye would need to see itself only if it did not yet know what it looked like. Just so, a person would need to know himself only if he did not yet know himself. So "know yourself" applies to the self-ignorant. Were the eye looking at itself in a mirror never to have seen itself before, it would have to seek itself out. It would not know what on the reflective surface – various facial features, the face itself, the body, background objects – corresponds to itself. The process of seeing itself would be protracted, enabled not simply by facing the correct surface but by figuring out what counts as itself. For a period of time it would be *able* to see itself but not yet see itself, and for another period of time it would actually be *seeing* itself but not realizing that it is seeing itself: it would not recognize itself, or be able to acknowledge itself.

The same would hold for knowing yourself in the soul of another. It would not be an instantaneous success. A conversation with another "reflective" person would not guarantee self-recognition or acknowledgment. There would be a span of time during which you would listen to your interlocutor and get lost in his remarks and interpretations. There would be another span of time during which you would be hearing reflections of your own views but would be failing to recognize them as yours.[24] You might have an odd sensation of critical success or conceptual clarification, without observing that the successful criticism is of your own theories, or that your interlocutor helped clarify concepts that you yourself had garbled. So self-recognition and self-knowledge, even with a partner, would be an accomplishment, a figuring-out.

Indeed, a person's self-recognition differs from an eye's or face's self-seeing in a way that makes the former – self-recognition – an even larger accomplishment. The eye exists in a face, with a color and texture perceptually different from surrounding skin. It is still in some respect a decision to call the eye only that which is in the orb, even though it could not see itself without the surrounding musculature and optical nerves and brain; these other parts could be considered aspects of the eye. But the decision is not so difficult or controversial. By contrast, the self one recognizes does not cleave so readily from other parts of one's person. What counts as one's most authoritative elements, or as properly one's own – as opposed to what is merely imitated from others ("someone else's lines"), or a conditioned response, or unconscious psychic forces – is the result of careful and hard-won judgment. So the process of self-recognition takes more than finding oneself in the murk of background information or the reflective surface itself; it takes determining what should be differentiated from everything else one learns while talking and acting before someone else's reflective soul. Thus the Palinode's image of the bewildered beloved, excited by beauty and open to emotional connection, but baffled at the source or reason for this excitement and openness, is an image particularly apt for self-knowledge. In conversation we may be excited by the clarity and reasonableness of the ideas discussed, and feel open to deeper or more vulnerable further exchange, but be unable to explain the charm and refreshment, or the authenticity or pressure, of that exchange. We may feel at most some resonance or echo of a hard-to-reclaim past.

24 The Platonic *Clitophon* describes a man who attributes to Socrates views that would be more properly attributed to himself; see Moore 2012a.

Mania and sôphrosunê

In the *Charmides* and *Alcibiades*, Critias and Socrates relate *sôphrosunê* directly to self-knowledge; so too does the *Rival Lovers*, as we will see later. Other dialogues present both concepts in the highest lights. But the *Phaedrus* appears to resist the equation and to question the value of *sôphrosunê*. It looks instead to vaunt *mania*, an inspired and non-rational *erôs*, as a route to blessedness, philosophy, social companionship, and education. Were this really the source of the greatest goods, then self-knowledge, to the extent it is like or coincides with *sôphrosunê*, would be limited in value, and while perhaps a partial avenue to self-improvement, would have value only as a partner with *mania*.

Not all of the *Phaedrus* so minimizes the importance of *sôphrosunê*. In Lysias' speech, the admirable non-lover is imagined to be *sôphrôn* (231d3) and self-mastering (231d4, 233c2), and love is imagined as the dubious and trying opposite. The non-lover remains cognizant of his situation, and preserves his stability in contrast to the lover's erratic changes of mind. Socrates' first speech, matching Lysias', makes the same connection between *sôphrosunê* and acting well (241a3–4).

But the Palinode opens with the claim that *mania*, not *sôphrosunê*, brings the greatest goods (244a5–7). In prophesy, for example, *mania* brings great good but the *sôphrônes* bring little or nothing (244a8–b5). Purification of ancient curses depends on *mania* (244d5–245a1). Poetry is worse when composed by the *sôphrôn* than by the manic (245a1–8). These three instances prepare the argument that *sôphrosunê* should not, in general, be taken as better than *mania* (245b1–c1). The Palinode returns from the general claim to a specific one. The primary benefit of manic love is a discovery and then emulation of one's sympathetic god (252d1–253c5), and to do this in tandem with one's beloved. Then,

> if the better elements of their minds (τὰ βελτίω τῆς διανοίας) get the upper hand by drawing them to a well-ordered life (τεταγμένην τε δίαιταν), and to philosophy, they pass their life here in blessedness and harmony, masters of themselves and orderly in their behavior (ἐγκρατεῖς αὑτῶν καὶ κόσμιοι ὄντες), having enslaved that part through which evil attempted to enter the soul, and freed that part through which goodness enters it. (256a7–b3, tr. Rowe 1986)

The *mania* of love (256d5–6) thus allows the greatest happiness and best travel through this world. As the Palinode appears to argue, it is *mania* that conduces to leaving self-ignorance, and by implication, not *sôphrosunê*.

It could be thought that Plato's thinking about *sôphrosunê* has developed from the other dialogues to this one, but besides being generally improbable, this thought would depend on controversial views about chronology.[25] More than that, it would assume that Socrates' remarks, whatever the rhetorical and dialectical situation in which he says them, reflect Plato's present views. It could instead be thought that, while *mania* and *sôphrosunê* may produce the same benefits, they operate in distinct contexts. Perhaps only *mania*, or *erôs*, promotes the following of ideals, or the improvement of the younger generation; perhaps it has more motive power than *sôphrosunê* does. Yet this does not account for the explicit derogation of *sôphrosunê* in these passages, and if the benefits are the same, then the Palinode should hardly contrast *sôphrosunê* and *mania*.

We must remember that Socrates' Palinode has a persuasive function, as do his other arguments in the dialogue.[26] As persuasive, the statements in the Palinode need not hew to Socrates' beliefs, or use only valid reasoning. Dominic Scott has shown the questionable moves in this passage.[27] The Palinode never argues that the philosopher actually depends on *mania* and on foregoing rationality. Instead it conflates and assimilates three traits to *mania* that merely resemble *mania*. First, the philosopher is eccentric, unfamiliar, and eager, and so appears manic to those untrained in philosophy (249d2–e4, 252a2–6). His apparent *mania* might just as well be a higher form of rational coherence and self-mastery. Second, the philosopher is infused with the divine, but only in that he reasons about the immutable forms – justice and so forth – and these are putatively divine (247c6–e4, 248b6–7, 249b6–c6, 249e5). He is enthusiastic in being ideally rational, and this is the opposite of being out of his mind. Finally, the philosopher starts out disoriented and baffled, but as he learns what he is doing, as he gets past the startling initiation to beauty and the eternal verities,

[25] Yunis 2011: 22–25, argues for a date of composition between 370 and 350, and at least after 380, when Lysias dies. This seems safer than, e.g., Usacheva 2010, who argues for a first draft in 390 and a second draft late in Plato's career. Rowe 1986: 14, observes the challenge in dating the dialogue but goes on to relate it chronologically to many different dialogues.

[26] See Moore 2013b, 2013c, 2014a.

[27] Scott 2011.

he loses that disorientation (250a6–b1, 251d8–e1). *Mania* here tracks the *aporia* or wonder that prompts rational investigation and reinvestigation. The Palinode thus substantiates no claims about the value or disvalue of *sôphrosunê*, for it aims to convince Phaedrus to accept the value of love.

A related explanation, also attentive to the rhetoricality of the speeches in the *Phaedrus*, relies on the observation that among the eternal verities sought, as the Palinode presents it, is *sôphrosunê* itself (247d6, 250b2, 254b7). Knowledge of true *sôphrosunê* could still have wonderful powers, perhaps the integration of the multiple elements of the soul. The *sôphrosunê* lauded by Lysias, and thus disparaged by the Palinode, may be a vulgar and pleasure-indexed disposition. In the *Phaedo*, for example, Socrates defines the commonplace *sôphrosunê* as the ability not to be excited by desire (68c8–10; cf. *Symp.* 196c4–5). Vulgar *sôphrosunê* is a kind of calmness before and insensitivity to the erotic and ethical demands in life, for the sake of a moderated flow of pleasures. It masters one's desires but does not, it would seem, know what is best. True *sôphrosunê* promotes excellent ordering within the soul.

A parallel practice

I return to Socrates' claim about his inability yet to know himself.[28] Three things are strange about it. First, Socrates says neither what self he wants to know, nor how he tries to know it. Does he want to know his concrete individuality, or instead a set of abstract truths about humans or souls in general, or indeed nothing about selves at all?[29] Does the process take introspection, or reflection, or conversation, and does he seek something already present within, or must he transform himself and seek something new? Second, this remark about knowing himself comes amid talk about myth-rectification, not, as in

[28] A version of this section has been published as "How to 'Know Thyself' in Plato's *Phaedrus*," *Apeiron* 47:3 (2014), 390–418.

[29] Griswold 1986: 43, thinks it is the individual; Yunis 2011 ad 229e5, thinks it is the human generally; Rowe 1986 ad 230a3–6 thinks it is both, seen from the Socratic and Platonic perspectives respectively; both Nichols 1998: 94–101, and Nicholson 1999: 22–23, are ambiguous between Socrates' own soul and human soul in general; Ferrari 1987: 11–12, says that it is "the human and especially the philosophical soul" – that is, "general truths about [one's] human nature" – but, also, "what it is to live the good life."

the *Alcibiades* or, as we will see, in the *Memorabilia*, in the process of examining his interlocutors' failure to know about justice, goodness, and their desires. Does this mean that the remark about self-knowledge is of minor importance relative to that of myth-rectification, a perhaps newly dangerous pastime? Or, by contrast, does Socrates think that a person should value myths only when using them to investigate his own nature? Or is the relation something else entirely? Third, the discussion of myth-rectification, so early in the dialogue, is much more detailed (229b4–229e4, 26 OCT lines) than his remarks about self-knowledge (229e5–6, 230a3–6, 6 OCT lines), an odd imbalance if the talk about myth-rectification provides just a warning against joining in some cultural fad.

I hope to address these three strange elements together. I argue that Socrates juxtaposes these two issues – myth-rectification and knowing oneself – to recommend taking the former as a model for the latter. The long discussion of myth-rectification shows what getting self-knowledge might be like. Dealing with myths of the sort we will come to see are interesting to Socrates, those concerned with civic geography and heroic lineages, involves piecemeal efforts and the acknowledgment of one's civic commitments to the history, identity, and alliances of one's city. Becoming able to know oneself in the way interesting to Socrates also involves piecemeal rectification and acknowledgment of one's commitments, here to what is true about living well and worthy of pursuit. This latter work of rectification and acknowledgment requires knowing both about human nature generally and about one's current condition and aspirations specifically. Knowing oneself thus depends not just on epistemological considerations, about what one can know about souls and characters, nor on metaphysical considerations, about the nature and structure of persons, but on practical ones as well, about how one can make oneself a better person, and individual ones, about one's particular hopes and dreams for oneself.

This reading of Socrates' interpretation of the Delphic inscription treats self-knowledge as practically oriented toward self-improvement and as modeled by the process of myth-rectification. It depends on two subordinate interpretative claims. First, Socrates says that myth-rectification (ἐπανορθοῦσθαι, 229d6) is laborious because it has to take the stories one by one (ἀνάγκη, 229d5 … ἕκαστον, 230e6). He does not explain why this is necessary. The nature of the task gives the reason. Myth-rectification would be easier if every historical story of the mythic type – that is, the fictitious or erroneous type – could be dismissed at once. But myth-rectification starts from the premise that Greek history does not distinguish sharply between the human and the legendary past, between the age of heroes and the age of monsters, and so each story must be assessed in turn. Myth-rectification also assumes that repair, not just rejection, is the goal, and since different stories have gone wrong in different ways, each needs its own correction. As a model for self-knowledge, this gives a further explanation for Socrates' inability yet to know himself, despite having surely tried for a long time. Self-knowledge is not merely introspecting or having true beliefs about the contents of one's consciousness. It is judging which of one's commitments are worthiest of acknowledgment, and making those, rather than others, the commitments on which one acts. This takes a long time: in part because one's dubious commitments are not so marked and therefore one has to deal with them in turn, and in part because the self-knower aims to commit himself to goodness, not just reject false beliefs.

The second subordinate interpretative claim explains Socrates' remark that myth-rectifiers bring the stories in line with the plausible (προσβιβᾷ κατὰ τὸ εἰκός, 229e6). Because Socrates later expresses skepticism about the rhetorician's confidence in plausibility-arguments (272d7–273d6), he may seem to reject myth-rectification because it too relies on plausibility. But he in fact does not say this. He instead says only that having to deal with each story one by one makes rectification take too long. The reliance on plausibility in fact cannot be the problem, since what is plausible is simply what seems true to a person. A problem arises only if one thinks one can pursue the plausible without at the same time pursuing the truth; this is Socrates' criticism of Tisias, but not of the myth-rectifiers. Just so, when a person audits his own beliefs, he aims to make them plausible – true from his perspective – because this is the only way to bring them closer to the truth.

The second half of this chapter begins with a closer reading of 229b4–230a6 than provided above, and then shows that Socrates presents the discussion of myth-rectification as a model for self-knowledge. Once we explain why myth-rectifiers must go myth by myth, we can see why becoming able to know oneself takes so long. We can also judge the significance of myth-rectification's proceeding in terms of plausibility.

Myth-rectification and self-knowledge

Socrates' claim about self-knowledge is intertwined with his remarks about myth-rectification. Socrates and Phaedrus have been looking for a place from which Phaedrus could recite Lysias' speech. They turn toward the river outside Athens' walls.

Phaedrus: Tell me, Socrates, is it not here from where, from the Ilissus, Boreas is said to have seized Oreithuia?

Socrates: So it's said.

Phaedrus: So was it from here? At least the rivulets appear charming and pure and clear, and just right for girls to play beside.

Socrates: No, but from down about two or three stades, where we cross over to the sanctuary in Agra. And somewhere there is the altar of Boreas itself.

Phaedrus: I haven't really noticed. But tell me, by god, Socrates, are you persuaded that this story is true? (229b4–c5)

This reference to the Boreas story is hardly mere trivia. Athens took Boreas as a favorite son-in-law. Though he abducted Oreithuia – perhaps on procession to the Acropolis – he also married her, and then twice destroyed the Persian fleet.[30] The Athenians commissioned Simonides to celebrate the second defeat, and the song was sung every year at the Festival of Athena to invoke the winds to accompany the Panathenaic ship to the Acropolis.[31] Both Aeschylus and Sophocles wrote plays about Oreithuia and the Boreads.[32] Vase-painters decorated dozens of pots with surprisingly sedate scenes of the abduction.[33] References to Boreas also had, popularly, an erotic dimension.[34] Ibycus likens *erôs* to mania and to Thracian Boreas, a parching lightning rushing from Aphrodite.[35] And just as Ibycus contrasts the turmoil of love with the calm garden of the maidens, in Hesiod's contemplation on Winter, harsh Boreas is said to violate everything except the virginal maidens warm by their mothers' sides.[36] Given Phaedrus' praise

[30] Acusilaus fr. 30 Jacoby; Herodotus 6.44, 7.189; Pausanias 1.19.6.

[31] Simonides fr. 534 Page; Munn 2000: 26, 30–31.

[32] Aeschylus fr. 281 Radt; Sophocles fr. 956 Radt (found in Strabo 7.3.1, who cites this section of the *Phaedrus* in its connection), *Antigone* 981–986.

[33] Agard 1966.

[34] Kaempf-Dimitriadou 1979; Keuls 1993: 52.

[35] Ibycus 286 Page.

[36] Hesiod *Works and Days* 519–523.

of the bucolic rivulets and Socrates' song about the grove (230b2–c5), the figure of Boreas is doubly well suited for the context. His being depicted as a winged horse,[37] and contrasted with Typhoeus,[38] makes him even more deeply relevant to the dialogue.

Given the connection of Boreas to talk about Athens and love, key themes in the *Phaedrus*,[39] Phaedrus' ignorance about him is remarkable. Why does Phaedrus ask now about him? Has recent political discussion activated his curiosity?[40] Does he have an antiquarian interest in stories about the gods, and has a new path occasioned the question?[41] And what does his question reveal about him? Does his concern for appearance and aptness (φαίνεται, ἐπιτήδεια, 229b8) show his preference for plausibility over truth (cf. τὸ εἰκός, 229e6)?[42] The dialogue does not develop any of these possibilities. It leaves us to infer only two concrete facts from Phaedrus' questions. First, his questions express his diffidence about his own powers of examination. He relies on someone else for a view rather than resolving to think about it himself. Second, he wants to know not the explanation but the result alone. He wants Socrates to report his belief about the Boreas story, this matter of significance to Athens, rather than account for the plausible and implausible features of the story.

Socrates' response shows that he thinks Phaedrus wanted to hear a simple report, and that he was wrong to want this. He does this by explicitly withholding any such report. Socrates sets out instead the method of the *sophoi*, the intellectuals he later calls myth-rectifiers.

If I weren't convinced [*sc.* that the story about Boreas is true] – as the intellectuals aren't – I wouldn't be out of the ordinary; I'd make the sophisticated claim that a Borean gale, while Oreithuia was playing with Pharmaceia, came down off the nearby rocks and thrust her off, and that it was by coming to her end in this way that it came to be said that she had been seized by

[37] Boreas as a horse: Homer *Iliad* 20.220.

[38] Hesiod, noting the good services Boreas and his brothers provide (*Theogony* 378–379), contrasts his usefulness (θνητοῖς μέγ ὄνειαρ, 871) with the painful random gales caused by Typhoeus (869–874).

[39] Athens: 227a1–b5, c9–d2, 230d3–e1, 243c2–d3, 257c4–258c10, 278e4–279c8; love: 227c5 and *passim*.

[40] Thucydides 2.29 suggests that considerations about allegiances with Thrace brought up discussion of relevant myths.

[41] Yunis 2011 ad 229b4–5.

[42] Ferrari 1987: 4, 9–12.

Boreas – or from the Areopagus, for that story too is told, that from there and not from around here she was seized. (229c6–d2)

Socrates says that some people are not persuaded by the Boreas story. He then reflects on the kind of examination that follows such an episode of skepticism. Such examination tries to explain why other people *are* persuaded by the story. It assumes that a central fact is right: Oreithuia really was taken, and Boreas was responsible. It tries simply to explain that fact in a more plausible way. Boreas the north wind is a phenomenon one might regularly experience, and so it could plausibly explain Oreithuia's being seized; Boreas the monster is not, and so it could not plausibly explain it. What then explains why people ever told the myth? Socrates' implication is that some people must have had a misunderstanding, misheard someone else, or made another sort of mistake, and they reported what they thought they heard to be so. Socrates says that there is another version of the myth. All historical narratives are susceptible to some uncertainties.

We do not know whether Socrates invented this rectification, or whether he had similar rectifications to draw from.[43] It appears not to matter. Socrates continues to a more important point, that coming up with such plausible stories is not for him.

But I, Phaedrus, while I find these sorts of things charming (χαρίεντα) in other ways, I find the man responsible for them to have too much cleverness and labor and to be not altogether fortunate, if only because for him it is necessary (ἀνάγκη) afterwards to rectify also the form of the Hippocentaurs, and again that of the Chimera, and then a mob flows of such Gorgons and Pegaguses and masses of other intractable, strange, and extraordinary natures (ἀμηχάνων πλήθη τε καὶ ἀτοπίαι τερατολόγων τινῶν φύσεων). If someone isn't convinced (ἀπιστῶν) by these things he will bring each in line with what is plausible, using some rustic kind of wisdom, and he will need much leisure. (229d2–e4)

[43] Approximately these two versions of the myth are attributed to Acusilaus frr. 30–31 Jacoby. Palaephatus' *Peri Apistôn* 22 says that Boreas was a man, not a wind; Heraclitus the Paradoxographer's *Peri Apistôn* 28 emphasizes that he was a king. Yunis 2011 ad 229c5 claims that Socrates' rectification "is an obvious one"; it would take no great originality to invent it. All the same, Socrates is highly competent at making difficult things look easy; consider his two speeches in this dialogue.

Socrates gives a single reason for disapproving of the life of the myth-rectifying intellectual. He cannot stop at a single rectification. He would be forced to confront an unending stream of mythical beings. The necessity of continued rectification would use up all one's time. Socrates does not express doubt about the success of such rectifications. His charge is that this unavoidable burden is simply too laborious. He has something more pressing to do.

> But for these things I have no leisure at all. The cause of it, my friend, is the following. I am not yet capable, in line with the Delphic inscription, to know myself. Indeed it appears laughable to me, being still ignorant about this, to look into alien things. So giving leave to these things, being persuaded by what's conventional about them, I look, as I just said, not into them but into myself, whether I happen to be some kind of beast more twisted and furious than Typhon, or a gentler and simpler living creature, sharing in some divine and un-puffed-up portion by nature. (229e4–230a6)

The myths and their rectification may be interesting or politically relevant, but Socrates judges the myths alien, outside the scope of his urgent focus on himself. This judgment leaves him to accept those myths as his culture presents them to him; he believes what is conventionally thought about them. By contrast, he investigates himself. We will discover what Socrates' self-investigation involves, rather than simply assuming what it is, by looking to what the myth-rectifiers' investigation involves. If the comparison is complete, we will see that, just as the intellectuals do not simply accept what they first thought about the myths, Socrates does not simply accept what he first thought about himself. He must determine which of his ideas, assumptions, and commitments he finds unpersuasive and then try to give them a better account. It is a matter of querying oneself and making oneself acceptable to oneself. Socratic dialectic, done socially or privately, is probably his means. As is clear from the dialogues, this process takes all one's time.

Two analogical practices

The narrative of the passage brings into parallel myth-rectification and knowing oneself. In particular, the language with which Socrates describes myth-rectification is the language of self-knowledge and improvement he uses elsewhere.

Both practices share the language of searching. Being ignorant about himself, Socrates says, it would be laughable "to look into alien things" (τὰ ἀλλότρια σκοπεῖν, 230a1). A sentence later, Socrates says of himself, "I look into not *those* things, but into myself" (σκοπῶ οὐ ταῦτα ἀλλ' ἐμαυτόν, 230a3). In both places, the verb σκοπεῖν ("look into," "investigate") is taken as the appropriate one for both activities. The work done on implausible myths is in other authors described as "inquiring into,"[44] "deconstructing,"[45] "curing,"[46] "treatment,"[47] or "revealing as believable."[48] That σκοπεῖν is Socrates' choice here recalls his constant reference to dialectical examination as σκοπεῖν. Plato uses the word hundreds of times. Just in the *Phaedrus*, Socrates speaks about investigating Phaedrus' beliefs that came from wise people (260a9, cf. 260a6); whether their account accords with Hippocrates' (270c7); whether Lysias' speech is structured like an organism (264c7); what the powers are of anything one investigates (270d3); and how to prepare a good speech (259e1). The Palinode narrator also says that the followers of Zeus "look into" whether their beloveds are predisposed toward philosophy, and then help them become more philosophical (252e2). Speaking of myth-rectification as a process of σκοπεῖν, then, assimilates it to more familiar Socratic practices.

The other word Socrates uses to describe myth-work is ἐπανορθοῦσθαι (229d6). All ancient authors use it with positive inflection, meaning to "rectify" or "restore" some situation to a good state.[49] The earliest extant usage is from Thucydides, at the climax of Nicias' speech; the general tells the Athenians to bring themselves back up from their low point (7.77.7.6). Aristophanes uses it in the context of fixing up a mess (*Lys.* 528), and Xenophon paraphrases Socrates as saying that friends help each other when they "fall down" (σφαλλόμενους, *Mem.* 2.4.7.1). In the *Laws* and the *Republic* Plato uses the term in constitutional

44 ἱστορήσας, Palaephatus 269.9.

45 ἀνασκευή, Heraclitus Paradoxographer, epigraph.

46 θεραπεία, *ibid.*

47 ἀντιφάρμακον, Heraclitus *Homeric Allegories* 22.1; on these last three terms, see Stern 2003: 62–64.

48 ἐμφῆναι πίστιν, Eustathius 1504.55 Stallbaum.

49 Thompson 1868 gives a proper translation but sees the wrong object when he says that "the office of the mythologer is humorously said to be to 'rectify' or 'integrate' by restoring to their proper shape the monsters he has to do with"; as I show below, rectification applies especially to speeches, reports, and norms.

contexts, referring to the actions of legislators in maintaining the quality of a legal system.[50] More frequently he uses it in conversational and investigative contexts, to refer to making arguments more consistent, articulated, responsive, adequate, or true.[51] People should help each other give the best argument possible (*Tht.* 167e7); the young can correct the errors of their negligent elders (*Grg.* 461c7; *Tht.* 143a4); and analyses may be improved upon further reflection (*La.* 200b4).[52] Socrates' efforts to make Simonides consistent, in his poem about becoming and being good, by distinguishing key psychological words, are twice called ἐπανόρθωμα (*Prot.* 340a8, d7).[53] This means that, for Plato, the term is connected with Socrates' central practical-analytical activity, improving the way one thinks, especially in dialectical settings. (Even the legal cases have this sense of intellectual and moral improvement.) If Socrates says he always seeks self-knowledge, but we also know him to do this mostly through conversations in which he is constantly correcting and being corrected, then readers would take ἐπανορθοῦσθαι to be a term appropriate both for myth-correction and self-correction. This cross-over terminology would suggest shared processes.

The same can be said for the way by which the myth-rectifiers do their work, "using some kind of rustic wisdom" (ἅτε ἀγροίκῳ τινὶ σοφίᾳ χρώμενος, 229e7). It is not immediately clear what this is supposed to mean, even if we note a joke on the wild beasts that get rectified and on Phaedrus' and Socrates' journey beyond the city walls. Perhaps the most we can say is that Socrates means that the myth-rectifiers must speak bluntly, even cynically, puncturing traditional pieties and accusing their predecessors of confusion.[54] This may not, of course, be the way the myth-rectifiers refer to themselves; it is Socrates' own understanding of their practice. What is notable is that in the Socratic

[50] *Laws* 644b3, 653d4, 769c2, d7, e8, 772b3, c3, 781b4, 951c2, 957b2; *Rep.* 361a2, b2, 425a5, e6, 426e6.

[51] *Symp.* 180d2; *Grg.* 462a2; *Ep. II* 311d4, d7; *Rep.* 604d1; *Euthyp.* 9d2; *St.* 276e6; *Prot.* 340d8.

[52] The frequent uses by Isocrates and Isaeus are consistent with these other early fourth-century uses.

[53] Socrates uses this noun to refer to attempts to improve the definition of knowledge at *Tht.* 183a2.

[54] Cf. *Euthyd.* 283e2, 284e9, where Dionysodorus is accused of speaking rustically in saying that some people – unbeknownst to them – want their friends to die.

conversations written by Plato, the adjective ἀγροῖκος almost always refers to speaking what one takes to be true irrespective of social niceties and conventional morality. Socrates apologizes for his "crudeness" in saying that death matters not at all to him (*Apol.* 32d3); that the argument against doing injustice has never been contravened (*Grg.* 509a1); and that he would like to ask more questions redeeming the usefulness of philosophy (*Eras.* 136e5). So-called rustic speak contrasts with polite silence.[55] Socrates' efforts of self- and other-examination has always been found uncultured and direct (*Apol.* 17c9–d1), as speaking without urbane restraint (cf. *Phdr.* 269b1). He refers to his urgent request to know the difference between knowledge and wisdom, to get a conversation going, as being "rustic" and due to a "love of language" (ἐγὼ ὑπὸ φιλολογίας ἀγροικίζομαι, προθυμούμενος ἡμᾶς ποιῆσαι διαλέγεσθαι, *Tht.* 146a5–8).[56] Saying that the myth-rectifier uses some sort of rustic wisdom would then put one in mind of the unimpeded register of the Socratic search for true and good commitments.

The myth-rectifier works on those stories that are unconvincing (ἀπιστοίην, 229c6; ἀπιστῶν, e2). Socrates regularly introduces his own investigations with the same terminology. Socrates' most famous investigation into knowledge begins with his saying that we distrust what people say when we learn that they are not expert (*Tht.* 144e6). Socrates admits that he doubted, before Protagoras' big speech, that virtue could be taught; while he doubts it less now, he has just a small question to ask (*Prot.* 319b1). In the reverse direction, what he once found certain before talking to Hippias, a man famed for wisdom, he now might doubt, if Hippias does not agree (*HM* 300c10). Just

[55] *Grg.* 462e6: Socrates hesitates to say what he really thinks of rhetoric, "if it's so rude to speak the truth" (μὴ ἀγροικότερον ᾖ τὸ αληθὲς ειπεῖν), but does so anyway; he seems to be echoing Polus' complaint that Socrates' commitment to consistency is a sign of "crudeness" (461c5). *Phdr.* 260d3: Socrates wonders whether their argument against rhetoric – an ignorant speaker can bring his city to ridicule or harm if it too is ignorant – has been spoken too crudely. *Critias* 107a3: Critias recognizes it is somewhat crude to beg his listeners' indulgence for his coming speech, but he has good reasons to need it. *Rep.* 361e1: Glaucon apologizes for lauding the value of injustice, excusing his crude speech by saying that this is what others say. *Grg.* 486c2: Polus excuses himself for speaking so bluntly about the powers of tyrant (it is this speech to which Socrates alludes when he excuses himself for speaking bluntly at 509a1). Cf. Isocrates 5.82; Michelini 1998.

[56] This is the only extant use of the verb through the third century, giving reason to think that this ethical application of "rustic" is special to Socrates.

before the heart of his inquiry into language in the *Cratylus*, Socrates says that he has expressed what he thinks is right, but admits that it is not set in stone. Since his interlocutors have already done more investigation, he anticipates having his views revised by them; he even hopes to become their students. Once Cratylus says that he agrees with Socrates, Socrates says that he has long been amazed – and doubtful (ἀπιστῶ) – about his own wisdom. One must always return to a topic, reviewing and reassessing it (*Crat.* 428d2). In many other dialogues, the central puzzle about wisdom, virtue, or soul is introduced with the verb ἀπιστῶ.[57]

Finally, Socrates says that both myth-rectification and knowing oneself require leisure (σχολή, 229e3, e4). Leisure is the time for building virtue.[58] This point has just been thematized at the beginning of the dialogue.[59] Phaedrus asks whether Socrates has time (σχολή, 227b8) to hear about his morning with Lysias; Socrates responds with a quotation from Pindar about valuing speech-activities over other less-beneficial business (ἀσχολίας, 229b9–10).[60]

Besides sharing language, the two connected passages in the *Phaedrus* share a concern for mythic stories. Naturally this is so in the case of the myth-rectifiers. Their work begins only upon realizing that

[57] Socrates doubts that virtue is knowledge; he has reasons to think it is not, and this issue is of central importance to the question whether virtue is teachable (*Men.* 89d2, 6). He is doubtful whether Euthydemus and Dionysodorus can really teach virtue more efficiently than anybody else (*Euthyd.* 274a4). He is also incredulous whether he really does have knowledge at all times, per Euthydemus' contention; and he would like nothing better than to be refuted on these points, since he would then know about his wisdom (295a2). Wondering whether knowledge could know itself, and finding that some powers cannot be reflexive, Socrates notes that for the powers they doubted could be reflexive, they can still hope a great man will intervene and explain (*Chrm.* 168e4). It is not easy to doubt (*Rep.* 331e5) Simonides' definition of justice, because the poet is wise and godlike; nevertheless, Socrates does, and this instigates the remainder of the dialogue. After the final argument for immortality, Simmias says that he does not doubt anything (*Phdo.* 107a9), but really, because of the importance of the discussion, and his scorn for human weakness, he does actually have some private misgivings. Socrates says that Simmias is right to say this, and says that they should investigate them more and more clearly. Socrates then recapitulates and says that the soul requires life-long care, if it is indeed immortal. See also *Phdo.* 77a9, 87a8.

[58] Cf. Anastasiadis 2004.

[59] Cf. Burger 1980: 9–10, 127n4; Rowe 1986 ad loc.; Griswold 1986: 250n11; Ferrari 1987: 15; White 1993: 12; Yunis 2011: 87.

[60] On this exchange see Moore 2014b.

they are not persuaded by a story. But Socrates also treats myths as the starting-point for some of his own investigations. The way he introduces the Typhon image is so unexpected, so rhetorically wrought, so full of puns, so poignantly connected to his range of abstract interests, and then so explicitly interrupted (230c6), that the reader cannot avoid seeing the mythic status as salient.[61] Typhon was already prefigured by the mention of Boreas, to whom Hesiod explicitly links him. As mentioned above, Socrates' inquiry into Typhon must be prefatory to a complete investigation of himself. At this point he is asking only about his most basic contrasts with Typhon. Both the myth-rectifiers and Socrates begin with an uncertainty about their relations to mythic beings.

Plato also unifies the two practices by linking their discussion dramatically. The discussions are intertwined during Socrates' and Phaedrus' walk seeking a good place to read Lysias' speech. They have just foregone a display of Phaedrus' memory, and they are preparing to contemplate the value of Lysias' paradoxical speech on love. That means they are here reflecting on set speeches. Since both rectifying myths and trying to know oneself are related to set speeches – the one used for making speeches better, the other for making better speeches – they are related to one another.

The relation between the two practices is most powerfully shown by the fact that Socrates' discussion of neither makes sense in the dialogue on its own. On the one hand, the myth-rectification discussion is too long and has too much detail for it to exist simply for Socrates to reject it. Socrates is the one to have introduced it, in response to Phaedrus' theoretically naïve question, and he is the one to have given it its complete development. Instead of providing all the detail he does, Socrates could simply have said that he lacks time for thinking about the truth of myths because he spends all his time thinking about himself. Or he could have said that he does not believe gods do bad things; Boreas is a god; and the myth about Boreas is that he did something bad.[62] Socrates would not need to have given an example of myth-rectification, nor listed the reasons for finding myth-rectifiers unfortunate men, nor enumerated the range of monsters they need to deal with, nor reiterated

[61] On the literary structure, see Yunis 2011 ad loc. and Hunter 2012: 83–86. See Werner 2012 and Moore 2013d on the role of myth generally in the *Phaedrus*.

[62] I thank Elizabeth Belfiore for this idea.

exactly what the rectifiers do ("bring things in line with the probable," etc.). At no later point in the *Phaedrus* does myth-rectification again arise (Phaedrus merely says that Socrates has invented the Theuth myth, 275b4), and at no earlier point did Phaedrus express any interest in myth-rectification or related processes. This discussion occurs in the very pregnant early pages of the dialogue. It would be foolish to dismiss the remarks as a Platonic aside, a score-settling against annoying intellectuals,[63] given that this ignores the much-vaunted rule that literary works must be fully integrated (264b3–e2). It would be better to find the reasons Socrates would have for setting out the practice of myth-rectification in such detail. Since this dialogue is otherwise full of paradigm production, it is reasonable to suppose that this section also serves as a paradigm for some harder-to-grasp practice.[64] In this way, the *Phaedrus* does with the model of myth-rectification what the *Alcibiades* does with the self-seeing eyes, the *Clouds* with *mania*-reflecting meteorology, and, as we will see later, *Memorabilia* 4.2 with horse-buying.

Whereas the myth-rectification discussion seems oddly long, the self-knowledge discussion seems oddly short. What is the self – in contrast to foreign things – that the Delphic inscription commands one to know, what abilities constitute such knowing, what is the epistemology of this knowing, what are the conditions of its satisfaction, what causes the process to have taken so long and to continue to take so long, and in what part of Socrates' depicted practices, if any, is he seeking to know himself?

The necessity of continuous myth-rectification

Socrates could have said that he has no time for myth-rectification on a number of grounds: it aims not for truth but for plausibility; it is reductionistic about mythology and culture; it assumes that the world has always been the same way; or it is needlessly impious. But he does not make these criticisms.[65] He cites a different problem. Myth-rectification, as a practice, simply takes too long given his other

[63] A possibility suggested though not defended by Rowe 1986 ad 229c6.

[64] 246a5, 263a6–b1, 264c7–e2, 265e3, 270b1, etc.

[65] This view contrasts with Werner 2012: 30–38, who argues that Socrates charges against the method that it cannot distinguish between possible

obligation, coming to know himself. But it is puzzling why it must take so long. Socrates states that the myth-rectifier must confront and deal with monster after monster, but he does not reveal the source of this necessity. Most commentators take little note of this issue.[66] But the necessity is what causes the problem; if one could meaningfully rectify only a few myths, then doing so would not get in the way of striving for self-knowledge.

Socrates appears not to be thinking about *sophoi* who, as part of whatever other pursuits they have, merely rectify a story here or there. He calls the relevant people excessively clever, put-upon, and not altogether fortunate (229d4), and he explains this by saying that once they correct the Boreas story they must set aright an unending mass of other creatures. He must then be thinking about a class of people for whom such rectification is a central part of their work. Who would fit this description?

By the early fifth century the logographer and mythographer Acusilaus recorded two distinct histories of Boreas' abduction of Oreithuia (frr. 30, 31 Jacoby), which were presumably set into a genealogy of Athenian and Thracian personages.[67] Herodotus, at least half a century later, tells of Boreas' relevance to the Athenian success in the Persian War. A great boreal wind (βορέης ἄνεμος μέγας, 6.44) crushed the Persians rounding Athos in 492. Twelve years later, when

interpretations. Hackforth 1952: 26, thinks that Socrates' charges are really just apotreptic, dissuading Phaedrus from querying Socrates' coming inspiration by local deities, e.g., at 238d1. Verdenius 1955: 268, says that the method fails for not being directed by self-examination, but this argument seems misplaced, since it is hard to see how investigating the truth of the Boreas story could involve self-examination.

66 Of those who do, Verdenius 1955: 268, says "the art of allegorical interpretation is still in its infancy, so that it works slowly and laboriously"; Griswold 1986: 37, that "the throng of mythic figures is gigantic"; Ferrari 1987: 11, that they are "mere antiquarians, for whom completeness" is key, and that they have "no better reason [to address these stories] than that their stories are bruited about"; Nichols 1998: 94, that "once begun, there is no end to it … something in human beings … forever produces such tales"; Nicholson 1999: 20–21, that "*mythologêmata* constitute a system"; Yunis 2011 that the stuff is tedious and there is always more material; Werner 2012: 31–33, that "it would be inconsistent with [the] supposedly 'rational' intent to allegorize one myth … but not others," and that "the interconnected nature of Greek mythology … [makes impossible the] selective application of the allegorical method."

67 At *Symp.* 178b9, Phaedrus says Acusilaus gives a convincing corroboration of Hesiodic genealogy.

the Athenians saw a storm approaching the Persian fleet, they sacrificed to Boreas for luck again. As Herodotus writes,

> there is a story that the Athenians had called upon Boreas to help them, in consequence of another oracle, by which they were advised to "ask the assistance of their son-in-law." Boreas, according to the Greek account, married a woman of Attica, Erechtheus' daughter Orithyia, and in consequence of this marriage the Athenians, so the tale goes, supposed Boreas to be their son-in-law. (7.189, tr. de Sélincourt 1996)

Herodotus expresses his skepticism about the myth: "I cannot say if this was really the reason why the fleet was caught at anchor … but the Athenians are quite positive about it: Boreas, they maintain, had helped them before, and it was Boreas who was responsible for what occurred on this occasion too." People thought that the storm ended only after sacrifices and charms set on the wind, but Herodotus notes that "it may be that the wind just dropped naturally" (7.191). This is merely one instance of Herodotus' myth-rectifying stance.[68] Though Thucydides does not mention Boreas, he does rectify Thracian mythology, presumably in response to political questions about Athenian alliance at the start of the Peloponnesian war (2.29).[69] Boreas would be a central figure in Athenian-Thracian politics, and that Plato knew about such politics is clear from his attention to the Bendis festival in the *Republic*.[70]

This evidence from three historians suggests that the *sophoi* Socrates mentions were those concerned about local histories, likely for political or more generally national purposes.[71] They were probably not

[68] See Rose 1940; Cook 1976; Stern 1989 and 1996: 12–13; and Gehrke 2011: 41–42, 45, for examples. See Cohen 2000: 383 for more on this particular story.

[69] Cf. Hornblower 1997 ad loc.; Lattimore 1998 ad loc., calling this "probably the most unusual digression in Thucydides."

[70] Cf. Cohen 2000: 364–389, on these relations more generally, and Steinbock 2012 for a recent example of the study of mythic history in political deliberation (on Athenian thought about Thebes).

[71] Morgan 2000: 65–66; Stern 2003: 55–56; Gehrke 2011. We need not suppose that Plato refers to particular men. Rowe's 1986 "rationalists" is simply too broad (and not much of a class against which to cut). Yunis 2011, following Ferrari 1987: 234–235, writes that "rationalizing and allegorical interpretations with the aim of removing supernatural and morally objectionable actions on the part of gods became a trend among

mere allegorists, who assumed that earlier poets disguised metaphysical doctrine in narrative language.[72] Socrates' era abounded in atthidographers and other researchers into geographical history.[73] The most detail about myth-rectification comes from the fourth century, and funeral orations in particular. The "Funeral Oration" from Phaedrus' erstwhile teacher Lysias establishes a plausible legendary history of Athens only having first excised its incredible elements (2.3–20). The Amazonian marvel is explained (3–6), and Heracles' deeds are mentioned as models of courage but not themselves enumerated (11, 16). Demosthenes' "Funeral Oration" gives a similarly purified legendary history (60.5–9), dwells mainly on the moral of important myths (27–31), and even engages in explicit rationalization: "the Cecropidae knew their founder was said to be part dragon and part man, only because he resembled a man in intelligence and a dragon in strength (30, tr. Worthington 2006). Hyperides (6.7), the *Menexenus*'s Socrates (239b), and Thucydides' Pericles (2.36) each observe the importance of giving a sterling genealogy, but then pass over it, drawing out the moral tone without having to worry about explaining away implausibilities.[74]

We can be sure speakers used myth-rectification regularly; from the fourth century we have a compendium of such work, the "On Unbelievable Things" by Palaephatus. In it, as in similar works, we find rectifications of Boreas, centaurs, and Chimera (the creatures mentioned by Socrates).[75] By looking at many of these stories, and reading Palaephatus' short preface, we can understand the purpose of myth-rectification. Palaephatus wants to encourage belief in the

natural scientists, sophists, historians, and literary men of the fifth and fourth centuries"; this is right but it is worth thinking about their goals.

72 Thompson 1868; Hackforth 1952; Verdenius 1955; De Vries 1969; and Werner 2012 all think the *sophoi* are allegorists like Metrodorus – who revealed the metaphysical content in poetry hidden behind narrative – without sufficient argument. The difference between allegorical interpretation of poetry and "rationalization" or naturalistic myth-rectification, which they appear to conflate, is made clear by Morgan 2000: 62–67.

73 Pearson 1939; Stern 1996: 10–16; Lenfant 1999: 206–213.

74 See Loraux 2006 for the civic effect of epitaphic genealogy.

75 See generally Stern 1996, 25; centaurs: Palaephatus 1, Heraclitus Paradoxographer 5; cf. Xenophon *Cyropedia* 4.3.18–22; Chimera: Palaephatus 28, Heraclitus Paradoxographer 15, Plutarch *Moralia* 248c, Strabo 14.3.5, Servius on *Aeneid* 6.288; Boreas: Palaephatus 22, Heraclitus Paradoxographer 28, Apollonius Rhodius 1.211–218.

legendary heroes by clearing away the improbable accretions to their stories. He does so guided by two goals: to find nature constant, and to save the appearances. What we see now is what we would have seen in the past; and the stories told now must have some basis in somebody's actual experience. Despite these two principles, Palaephatus was not atheistic; he did not rationalize away the stories of the gods of the Pantheon. He largely restricted his scope to human history.[76]

Historians want to provide a complete account of a city, region, or people. Because their work requires them to consider and take seriously certain aspects of the otherwise legendary Hellenic past, rectifying one item – a hero or a lawmaker, for example – compels them to rectify all the dubious material connected to him, which in turn rests on material subject to further rectification. A proper laudation of one's founding fathers, for example, requires that those fathers be plausible, their actions be plausible, and the obstacles they overcame be plausible. Deliberators in a political debate will have similar requirements, if they appeal to historical precedent. Wanting to legitimate their historical claims, they will have first to insulate their evidence against charges of implausibility. For either history or politics, then, myth-rectification is an all-or-nothing affair. The goal of either pursuit need not be the wholesale disenchantment of nature itself. Given the connectedness of historical explanation, however, whatever good is sought requires a rational account that ramifies far through time and space.

The comprehensiveness of the myth-rectifying project does not itself explain its oppressive demands on one's time. After all, it seems one could simply deny the existence of all mythological beings, or dismiss them from any chains of historical causality. Rather than being confronted with one weird hybrid after another, one should seem to be able to allow oneself only the naturalistic, the physical, the plausible. Were this possible, Socrates would be wrong to pity the practitioner. Rather than being put-upon, the practitioner could, at a wave, dismiss the madding crowd and live a life in accordance with natural plausibility.

Such an all-at-once dismissal is appealing, but at the same time it is impossible. Socrates is not wrong to pity the practitioner. Socrates says that the myth-rectifier must go step by step. Two explanations for this

[76] Stern 1996: 9–25.

necessity present themselves. The weaker, psychological explanation is that our individual concrete beliefs about weird creatures are so deeply entrenched that a high-level, abstract dubiety about them is not enough to extricate or negate those particular beliefs. We can resolve to refuse to accept the reality of any mythic creatures, but when it comes to thinking about them in actual circumstances, the pull of our commitment to their existence trumps our universal dismissal. Phaedrus' request to hear examples to bolster his perhaps weak acceptance of a general claim is consistent with this explanation (262c9).

The stronger, epistemological reason for our being unable to dismiss all mythic creatures at once is that we can form no such concept – "mythic creatures" – all of whose members we can then dismiss on contact. A precondition to an all-at-once doubt is being able to identify a corpus of implausible beasts. Mindful of nature's constant path, we might believe that we can ascertain instantly those beings that swerve from it. But this is impossible. A mythic story presents itself as true, internally coherent, and fitting within its context. There is no immediate marker that distinguishes, for example, a centaur from Achilles' horse in terms of plausibility.[77] The only way to determine the implausibility of a myth is to think about the details of the myth itself. A further obstacle to all-at-once dismissal is that the mass of monsters is so large that, considered as a mass, it might even seem plausible; land-animals with wings, for example, come to seem a regular occurrence, and it becomes hard to believe that so many people could be so wrong about such a large part of human experience. All the same, each story alone, inspected closely against our experience of the world, may be wholly implausible. Further, true history is instructive and entertaining largely because it involves the unexpected and the novel. Neither unexpectedness nor novelty, therefore, could be used as a criterion for dismissing stories as implausible. In writing local history, then, one can at best confront the stories as one meets them, and deal with them as rigorously as possible. Because even the most rational person cannot form a concept of dismissible stories independent from a judgment of those individual stories, the historian, in practicing his

[77] Contra Nicholson 1999: 16, who thinks that Phaedrus' calling the Boreas story a *mythologêma* means that "if this myth should not be true, it is … because of something about the whole class of myths." But the fact that some story is *called* a *mythologêma* is no evidence that the story is in fact fictitious and immediately dismissible; whether the story can be sustained in the light of scrutiny is what the historians investigate.

demythologizing trade, must deal with each (relevant) story on its own. This is why Socrates pities the professional myth-rectifier. Greek culture contains so much that is implausible, one will hardly ever get a chance to stop saying what is plausible.

Knowing oneself as putting oneself in line with what is plausible

Socrates could have said that the most bizarre Greek myths do not convince him, but since he is not working out Attic history, he does not need to assess each story for its plausibility, and he does not need to rectify the ones he disbelieves. Instead, he says only that he ignores this sort of thing (ὅθεν δὴ χαίρειν ἐάσας ταῦτα [*sc.* τὰ ἀλλότρια], 230a1–2), and (presumably if pressed or obligated to perform in civic ritual) accepts whatever others believe (τῷ νομιζομένῳ, 230a2). He does not ignore the rectifiability of mythic stories out of a lack of interest or ability; he admits that there are charms to engaging in myth-rectification (229d3), and he shows he can rectify the Boreas myth. He ignores them out of a lack of time. He must investigate himself, leaving investigation of "foreign" matters aside.

Socrates says that he is not able yet to know himself, and that he investigates himself. Generations of readers have taken Socrates' "myself" quite generically, as referring to the nature of humans, or of ensouled beings, or his immaterial soul.[78] But those who interpret Socrates' repeated mention of himself (ἐμαυτόν, 229e6, 230a3; τοῦτο, 230a1) as a mention of a generic object lack grounds for restricting his meaning in that way, given Socrates' attention to one's personality and to personal responsibility.

I argued above that Plato wove together Socrates' remarks about myth-rectifiers and self-knowledge so as to encourage interpreting the latter on the basis of the former. This means that Socrates' inability yet to know himself is somehow similar to the myth-rectifier's inability yet to put all the myths in line with plausibility. It also means that the structure and goal of his self-investigation are somehow similar to the myth-rectifier's project.

The myth-rectifier comes to find a certain one of his beliefs implausible, and takes commitment to it contrary to his ultimate

[78] Rowe 1986: 140–141 and Yunis 2011: 94 assume this without argument.

goals: understanding his city, praising his heroes, arguing for a military alliance. Rather than simply negate the belief, he aims to repair it, discovering what is most likely true. Just so, as we will see, the person seeking self-knowledge comes to find certain of his beliefs implausible, and takes commitment to them contrary to his ultimate goals of living well. Rather than simply negate the troubling beliefs, he aims to repair them, discovering what is most likely true. The historian cannot know what is absolutely true: he deals with the unrecoverable past; thus he deals in plausibility. The seeker of self-knowledge cannot know what is absolutely true, either: he is a limited mortal and can test his beliefs only against his other beliefs, his experiences, his tentative abstractions, and his intuitions; thus he too deals in plausibility and the recognition that one can provide no account that is not itself open to further critique (cf. *Tht.* 210b1). The historian assesses and reconstructs his beliefs one at a time, having neither a rubric against which to judge stories dubious all at once nor a structure into which to rebuild those dubious stories all at once. The seeker of self-knowledge cannot tell himself to disbelieve everything that does not accord with justice, or the good, or the true – these are, after all, just what he admits he does not yet know – and so he too must go one belief, one commitment, one desire at a time, inspecting each for its plausibility and coherence with his other views. If the *sophoi* are historians, the myth-rectifiers want to know about *their* country, *their* political past, *their* heroes. Their concern with local myths is not a concern with the nature of history as such; indeed, the implausibility of those myths depends on a preexisting attitude toward history (that it is constant, coherent, law-bound, etc.). The seeker of self-knowledge, too, wants to know about himself. But his concern with himself is not a concern for the nature of a self as such, as some entity distinct from the person engaged in knowing, except to the extent that knowing about selves (as intelligible, mutable, improvable) gives one confidence that self-knowledge is even possible, and provides the ideal to which one might be committed. The historian's task feels never-ending because the mistakes people have made in trying to understand their past are innumerable, and some of the most significant moments in the past are hard to make sense of. The seeker of self-knowledge can never stop either, given the depths of human ignorance and the difficulty of comprehending one's goals.

If this account is cogent, we can give more precise answers to the questions motivating this inquiry: what is the "myself" that Socrates investigates; what is the epistemic goal of knowing (γνῶναι) or investigating (σκοπῶ) oneself; what precisely makes coming upon the ability to know oneself take so long; and in what way could "plausibility" be a worthy goal for the seeker of self-knowledge?

Socrates refers to himself in a colloquial way, not with theoretical rigor. There is no reason to think he refers here to the soul as a metaphysical item or to its immateriality or immortality. The narrator of the palinode, of course, talks about the soul, but little can be drawn from this to apply to the passage at 229c–230a. The immortality argument – which is of questionable validity – is about soul in general, not explicitly about distinct, personalized souls.[79] Not only is the immortality argument about soul in general, it finds that soul is self-moving and immortal. It seems unlikely that Socrates would want to know only this about himself; and since Socrates says he cannot yet know himself, something the knowledge of which his speech pretends to demonstrate twenty minutes later cannot be that thing. Anyway, Socrates has implied that knowing himself is an ability; the argument about the immortality of soul is something to be familiar with, not something to be able to do. These reasons show that the austere and impersonal soul of the immortality argument is not the direct referent of the ἐμαυτόν.

The images of souls in the chariot-story are more the sort that Socrates means. These souls are individual (246b1, 248a1); they follow the gods most related to their private characters (250b7–8); they have different jobs (248d3–e3); they have a range of experiences, goals, and achievements (249c1–4, 250a1–4). They are not merely identical metaphysical structures of reason, spirit, and appetite; they are unique, temporally extended, modifiable, self-aware, indeed self-modifying entities. Of course this is an image, not meant to present more than the kinds of experiences souls might undergo in pursuit of the goals they have. But if being a soul is most importantly an experience and a striving, rather than a metaphysical structure, then the winged horse-drawn manned chariot is a very apt image.

If one's nature can in some respects be imagined through a story about a particular charioteer, and thus as a tale of striving, frustration, correction, and increased success, then knowing oneself can be taken as coming to appreciate oneself as this sort of soul. But investigating

[79] Moore 2014a.

oneself is not, therefore, knowing that the soul is the sort of thing Socrates describes in the Palinode. That would be "investigating what people are like." Investigating oneself should be about oneself. And a person is not a generic image. It is not a charioteer. It is not some entity for which the charioteer stands.

Socrates says he does not look into foreign things. These foreign things are not, in some sense, literally foreign; they are his own beliefs, as it were about Attic geography and history. They must be foreign to the extent they do not, for him, appear to play an important role in helping him live well. (Perhaps they are central for some other people.) Socrates does not enumerate the sorts of beliefs that contribute most importantly to the way he lives. Throughout the dialogue, however, he expresses concern about a range of beliefs: for example, to whom should favors of love go (227c9–d1); what honors or scandalizes the gods (242b8–243b7); how a free citizen would act (243c3–d1); what encourages the continuation of philosophical conversation (258e6–259d8); and who is willing and able to teach (230d3–5). Socrates is obviously not interested simply in the abstract question about the nature of man. He is instead interested in the beliefs, desires, and other commitments he has, knowing which ones are important, and determining how well his actions conform with his ideals.

If we take Socrates to be, in a central way, his most significant beliefs and desires, then to recognize and investigate oneself is to recognize and investigate those commitments. What does doing this amount to? It could seem that it is simply to discern those commitments.[80] This may be an adequately challenging task, given that we are changing and complex beings. But if they are really commitments, norms we hope to live up to, we would not want merely to discern them. We would want to learn whether we are meeting them and what meeting them fully would amount to. If we are not, it might not be unreasonable to say that in some respect we fail to know ourselves. For if we knew them, we would be following them. Knowing about justice should lead one to being just; not being just implies not adequately knowing justice. Naturally, this is the central Socratic paradox. The commitments on which we do not act must be not adequately vivid, not

[80] Thompson 1868: 8: "the self-knowledge of Socrates consisted in the rigorous examination of the *notions* of his own mind rather than of its operations and faculties, and chiefly of those notions which relate to moral distinctions."

adequately known. We believe that we should act in various ways; but these beliefs do not always guide our behavior. We are not competent actors of our normatively constructed part. As the amateur compared to the expert, our beliefs about correct technical performance direct us only infrequently, or accidentally. Knowing our commitments, then, is having them attain the status of knowledge. And thus becoming able to know oneself is bringing one's most important commitments into an active, vivid, dominant status.[81]

Acting in accordance with one's central commitments takes one's entire life, as I have suggested above. This is not because our commitments are always changing; in fact our best commitments may not change. One problem is that some may conflict. We may not discover this conflict for a long time; and then we may not be able to readily determine which commitment deserves priority. Another problem is that our habits, impressions, and physical desires may draw us away from discharging the obligations that our commitments create. Since we cannot extirpate all habits, impressions, or physical desires from ourselves, our actions will always skew from our commitments. This would be so even for Socrates. His taste for competition with Lysias seems to have drawn him away from his commitment only to praise the gods (243a1–2). He can know himself – recognize himself, per the Delphic inscription – only progressively: seeking out potential conflicts, determining which commitments to retain, identifying divergence from ideal action, and attempting to eliminate such irrational behavior.

One might think that Socrates could simply adopt and commit himself to the abstract norms he seems to endorse: do no harm, care for justice, love wisdom. But Socrates remains human, and so the psychological force of appetite, self-image, and limited memory prevents his perfect adherence to those norms. There is also the epistemological problem discussed above. It will not be instantly clear what action is the harm-free one, or the one that cares for justice, or the one that advances wisdom. The cases are not self-evident. They take prolonged examination.

The myth-rectifiers had to investigate and reconstruct individual myths because no general criteria would explain away their "mythological"

[81] This is the view of Aristotle *EN* 1109b2–8: we investigate (σκοπεῖν) the problems to which we are most prone (εὐκατάφοροί), and then we pull ourselves in the opposite direction (εἰς τοὐναντίον δ' ἑαυτοὺς ἀφέλκειν). He compares this process to the carpenter straightening bent timber (τὰ διεστραμμένα τῶν ξύλων ὀρθοῦντες ποιοῦσιν).

beliefs while preserving their "plausible" beliefs. The same reasoning would explain why it takes so long to come to be able to know oneself. A person has many beliefs that are relevant to the way he lives. The ones that seem dubious must undergo assessment. Phaedrus worries that all composition is bad (257d6). Is this so? No; he is right that some writing is bad, but not all of it. The more important thing is composing in a fine way and having the correct attitude toward one's compositions. Phaedrus thinks Lysias can serve as a mentor (228a1–4). Is this so? No; he is right that Lysias has impressive talent, but Lysias does not think about the true value of the things about which he writes. The more important thing is spending time with a person who challenges you. Socrates leads Phaedrus to find his beliefs less than convincing, and then to rectify them. This is a long process, one they have barely begun.

The myth-rectifiers bring their beliefs in line with the plausible (κατὰ τὸ εἰκός). On the analogy proposed here, so do those seeking self-knowledge. This does not reduce the analogy to absurdity, as is commonly thought. The person seeking self-knowledge wants to bring his beliefs in line with what is actual and true. Unfortunately, he can rely only on himself and his conversational partners, and even then he must rely on himself when deciding what to accept from his conversational partners. So he must rely on what appears to himself so. The plausible what appears so to him – is his only standard for judgment.[82]

Harvey Yunis claims that "the probable (τὸ εἰκός), which figures in the critique of sophistic rhetoric (259e7–260a1, 272d2–274a5), is what the masses believe (273a7–b2). Insofar as the probable is the norm for which mythical interpretation strives, mythical interpretation is doomed to be a vain, unproductive pursuit."[83] But this is a misleading report and therefore a mistaken conclusion.[84] Phaedrus says he has heard that oratory requires knowing what persuades people rather than what is objectively true (259e7–260a4). Phaedrus does

[82] Cf. Hecataeus, fr. 1, 7 Jacoby: "The following matters I write as it seems true (δοκεῖ ἀληθέα) to me: for the stories (λόγοι) of the Greeks are many and absurd, as it seems (φαίνονται) to me." Hecataeus is trying his best to put the stories in line with the truth, and thereby with plausibility from his perspective. That Xenophanes shares this epistemological modesty, see Bryan 2012: 6–57.

[83] Yunis 2011 ad 229e1–2. Ferrari 1987: 11, is less critical, but says that the myth-rectifier's "ostensible search for the truth behind the tales will degenerate into speculation on the tales as hearsay."

[84] But it is common; even Bryan 2012: 128, who shows how epistemically respectable *to eikos* can be, simply assumes that the *Phaedrus* criticizes *to*

not use εἰκός-family words here. Socrates responds to Phaedrus' belief in two parts (260b1–d2; 261e6–262c4), but never denies that one needs to know what one's audience believes. He argues only that, to the extent that one wants to avoid unintended harms and to be as persuasive as possible, one should also pursue knowledge. Later in the dialogue, Socrates recapitulates his claim against a focus on what is "persuasive" (πιθανοῦ, 272d8) alone. In consideration for what people tend to believe, Socrates says, an orator sometimes emphasizes the plausible (τὰ εἰκότα, 272e3; τὸ εἰκός, 272e4, 273b1). This may often involve not saying what is true (πολλὰ εἰπόντα χαίρειν τῷ ἀληθεῖ, 272e5). The advocates in the case between a weak brave man and a strong coward will lie, appealing to what usually happens, since an audience with no other evidence will have to rely on plausibility (273b4–c4). Socrates takes no issue with this maneuver as such. He instead says that a properly technical pursuit of rhetoric – as an overall discipline – will not forget to seek the truth too. After all, what is plausible (τὸ εἰκός, 273d3) to people depends on, by being very similar to (δι ὁμοιότητα, 273d4), what actually is true (τοῦ ἀληθοῦς τυγχάνει, 273d4). Socrates does not present *to eikos* as contrary to truth; he allows that it is compatible with, and connected to, the truth. *To eikos* differs from the truth in being the thing that people accept *as* true. Because Socrates has been talking about public speech, he is treating audiences without further specification; but he necessarily implies that the content of *to eikos* will differ depending on the audience. Elsewhere in Plato *to eikos* is not contrasted with the truth. Timaeus, speaking affirmatively, says that "from everything we have said about the kinds, this is what would be most in accordance with what is likely" (*Tim.* 56c8–d1).[85]

The myth-rectifiers are not saying that they are putting stories in line with the probable in contrast to putting them in line with the truth. Socrates does not say that he puts himself in line with the truth. Neither even *could* put their focal material in line with some external objective standard that did not itself seem true to them. Both practitioners aim to make their beliefs cohere better with their other beliefs.

eikos as such; and Ferrari 1987: 11, refers to "merely 'plausible' speculations ... [the] ostensible search for the truth behind the tales will degenerate into speculation on the tales as hearsay."

85 Citation and translation from Bryan 2012: 157.

Not to accept this is to ignore the private arena of self-understanding. It is the plausible (which is connected to truth), rather than the given (connected to tradition), or the desirable (connected to pleasure), that must guide a person's search for self-knowledge.

Conclusion

Consistency with other parts of the dialogue

We have already seen that this picture of self-knowledge is depicted in the Palinode. Socrates' prayer that Phaedrus give himself to love and philosophical talk (257b5–6), the latter strikingly depicted in the myth of the cicadas (258d7–259d9), strengthens it. The dialogue's closing prayer reiterates the lesson about self-knowing as working to become better and to know the good. "Grant to me to become fine within," Socrates says, "and that what I have on the outside befits what I have on the inside; and that I consider the wise man to be rich; and that I have no more gold than a temperate man could carry or manage" (279b8–c3). Socrates' final concern, the one for which he wants the gods' help and Phaedrus' agreement, is not about getting any information about himself. He does not ask for knowledge about human nature. It is to become well ordered in all respects. He desires to follow the wise and the temperate, those who embody the most goodness. That he prays to the god, and puts his desires in the optative, means that he knows this goal will be hard or impossible ever to reach completely. He may not ever be able to obey the Delphic inscription perfectly. But his faith shows he means always to work hard on himself, in conversation with others (cf. *Alc.* 132c5–135e10), seeking the good (cf. *Chrm.* 174b10–176a7), to do so.

Of course, Socrates in the *Phaedrus* talks about helping people know themselves more than he talks about knowing himself. In particular, he says, in a roundabout fashion, that he will examine Phaedrus himself. It is worth seeing how this is so, since the dialogue's element of examination is rarely noticed. After the dialogue's first back-and-forth argument, Socrates asks: "What is the way to write finely or not finely?" He continues: "Do we need, Phaedrus, to examine (ἐξετάσαι) Lysias about this, and anyone else (ἄλλον) who has so far written anything or will write anything, whether a political writing or an ordinary one (ἰδιωτικόν), whether in meter as a poet or without meter as an ordinary person (ἰδιώτης)?" (258d7–11).[86] Phaedrus' tutelage from, reverence for, and desire to emulate the writer Lysias, his self-description as an ordinary person with respect to writings (ἰδιώτην, 228a2, cf. 236d5), and the frequent linking of speechwriting to speechmaking together make it clear that the speech-loving Phaedrus is a prospective writer and thus one of the people who must be examined.[87] As the only prospective writer present, this examination must fall on him.[88] The first half of the *Phaedrus* would be an unsurprising entry to this examination: it would bring Phaedrus to realize that speeches vary widely in quality, even speeches he at first loved and found exceedingly fine, and thus that he needs to work on his presently inadequately sensitive judgment.[89] Phaedrus expresses eagerness to examine the nature of fine speaking and writing, the activities he is studying, and thus what he would like to constitute himself. That Socrates immediately digresses to the story of the cicadas (258e7–259d10) before entering that examination gives further evidence that Socrates means to be revealing Phaedrus to himself and themselves. The story gives reasons to an already eager-for-talking Phaedrus to keep talking (259d6); doing so makes sense only if Socrates needs to preempt any future slackening once Phaedrus realizes the examination concerns himself and so will not be easy.

When Phaedrus reports that he believes writing and speaking finely take only knowledge of what seems to one's audience to be the case (259e1–260a4), Socrates says that Phaedrus' report must have come from some wise people, and goes on to say that they have reason to look into what the wise say (σκοπεῖν, 260a5–7).[90] Though Socrates

86 A similar list of people arises at 277d6–7 and 278c1–4.

87 Cf. Moore 2012b for the argument that Socrates conflates writing and speaking insofar as both rely on composition.

88 Lysias as writer: 228a2, 257c7, 279a; linking of writing and speaking: 258d4–5, 259e, 261b4, 271c4, 272b1; speech-loving Phaedrus: 228a4, a5–c1, e4, 234c6–d6, 242a7–b4. Added evidence is that as soon as Phaedrus agrees that they should engage in examination, Socrates says that they have the leisure for it (σχολή, 258e6); this appeal to leisure indicates a time for examination and the development of virtue (e.g., *Tht.* 172c, d). Perhaps Socrates, too, is to be examined, but he denies the ability to write (235c8).

89 A parallel case might be Socrates' extended and variegated examination of Agathon in the *Symposium* about love, given the tragedian's commitment to and confidence in writing about love in his plays. That Socrates must provide Phaedrus with a range of spoken artifacts to effect his examination may explain the "unity" of the dialogue.

90 Phaedrus studied Lysias' speech upon his departure from Lysias (ἐπεσκόπει, 228b2, cf. 272b7).

is saying that even what the wise say must be determined to be nonsense or not (cf. 235c3 with 242c4–244a3),[91] since Phaedrus accepts it, the examination of the wise becomes the examination of Phaedrus. Phaedrus' later interest in the challenge the *logoi* make against the Skill of Speech causes him to ask Socrates to examine them (ἐξέταζε, 261a2). But of course Phaedrus becomes the recipient of their questions and so the examination is turned against him.[92] By dialogue's end, the examination of Phaedrus has led the man to decide to abandon Lysias' tutelage, to esteem philosophy, and to join Socrates in friendship and the pursuit of wisdom. If what Socrates thinks is important – trying to know himself – is what he thinks is important for his friends, then Socrates is trying to get Phaedrus to achieve self-knowledge. But Socrates does not simply teach Phaedrus the nature of man or the nature of soul. He specifically disclaims being able to say anything precise about these matters (246a4–6, 271c6–8). Seeing that Socrates means to examine Phaedrus' view about good speech and writing, we can infer that self-knowledge for Phaedrus means understanding his attitude toward rhetoric, and understanding that attitude means coming to change it for the better. It involves knowing what is good and what is better. Self-knowledge is self-rectification.[93]

Consistency with other Socratic literature

The Socratic project announced in the *Phaedrus* is contiguous with the Socratic project encountered elsewhere: eliminating inconsistencies in one's beliefs, caring for one's soul, engaging in rigorous and helpful conversation, and avoiding wrongdoing. The reason Socrates cannot

91 For more on these wise people, see Rowe 1986 ad 235c3. Socrates is modeling, and presumably recommending, openness to being refuted (εξελέγξουσι, 235b6).

92 Cf. Moore 2013c.

93 Burnyeat 1977: 12, in the context of the *Theaetetus*, describes self-knowledge in a similar way: it is not merely discerning one's private belief or articulating a theoretical framework (either of which he would call "to have formulated a proposition in words") but having "thought through its implications in a systematic way, confronting it with other relevant beliefs and considering whether these require it to be withdrawn or revised." This evaluative effort, which Burnyeat says is also "a vital force in the process itself … sustained by the pupil's growing awareness of his own cognitive resources, their strengths and their limitations," is, as is clear from the structure of the *Theaetetus*' argument, something that takes awareness simultaneously of one's current commitments and of one's norms governing and limiting those commitments.

yet know himself is the same reason he cannot yet have any knowledge. Coming to have fully consistent beliefs, adhering to each of the beliefs and desires to which one has committed oneself, and developing a perfect soul all simply take too much time, perhaps more time than humans have allotted to them. We must be proud to learn that we do not know what we thought we knew, and that we can recognize the errors we did not realize we were making.

We have most recently seen the central role the *Alcibiades* and *Phaedrus* each play in setting out Socratic self-knowledge. The *Alcibiades* shows the Delphic inscription in three distinct lights. The inscription urges that one clarify one's commitments, consider oneself a unified point of responsibility, and engage in rational conversations with good conversational partners: in general, what Socrates himself urges. The *Phaedrus* shows Socrates describing his search for self-knowledge as avoiding shortcuts. He cannot simply tell himself that he stands for justice, love, and philosophy; he must work through each belief and desire he has to see whether they conform to the principles he takes most seriously.

5 Philebus: *pleasure and unification*

Pictures of useless and useful self-knowledge in three dialogues

Both the *Charmides* and the *Alcibiades*, as we have read them, warn against picturing self-knowledge as too tightly reflexive or austerely defined, as a knowledge either purified of all objective content or a self stripped of its particular constituting qualities. The conversation in the *Charmides* foundered on the image of a knowledge torn away from any person knowing and any topic known, engrossed in itself. In the course of Socrates and Critias' conversation, the focus of self-knowledge slipped away from its appropriate intentional object, "myself," and landed right back where it started, on "itself." This knowledge of nothing except knowledge and ignorance, as Socrates put it, seemed unlikely to exist. More importantly, even were it somehow possible, it looked incapable of doing any good. Its pursuit would be nugatory, yielding its possessor no happiness. The highly reflexive self-knowledge would float impressively but disconnected above the scrum of the familiar sorts of knowledge – medicine, construction, etc. – and thereby float too high up, since success in life seemed to come through competence only in those specific and concrete fields. This picture of self-knowledge bleached the Delphic "Know yourself" of any of the value a Greek might expect from it. Just as the dialogue diagnoses that dead-end picture of self-knowledge, it suggests a better picture. The object of "knowing oneself" could be, remarkably enough, "what is good." This is a remarkable object, because "myself" and "what is good" seem distinct. But they seem distinct, again, only on a specific picture of the self, as some value-neutral structure that contains appraisals of value rather than as constituted by those value-judgments themselves. The value-neutral picture is not necessary. The arguments and drama of the *Charmides* suggest thinking of the self as the set or construction or network of one's value-judgments, one's normative commitments. Thus coming to know oneself means coming to know one's normative commitments, what one takes as right to believe, good to desire, or admirable to imitate. Knowing what is good is knowing oneself, then, in the following way. Knowing what one *takes* to be good, which is what one will start with, will be a sort of knowing one's commitments; but since one's commitments can change, one's self-knowledge will be unstable. But with enough testing, refinement, and verification of one's beliefs about what is good, those beliefs come to count as knowledge, and one will have self-knowledge properly so-called. So conversation about what is good leads one to increasingly true and stable beliefs about what is good, and such beliefs constitute oneself as a self. This is a good state of affairs, because then one will have true beliefs and good desires and admirable ideals to emulate. And thus self-knowledge seen as something more than a unique instance of reflexivity becomes both possible and a most helpful thing.

We learned a similar lesson from the *Alcibiades*. Socrates likens knowing oneself to an eye seeing itself in a reflective surface, and this seems reasonable; we recognize ourselves through the mediation of something facing us. He tightens the analogy: an eye sees itself best in the most reflective surface, which is the sensorily active part of another person's eye – their pupil – and thereby, it would seem, would be most interested in seeing its own pupil (which is perfectly clear and black, like everyone's). Thus a person knows himself in another's most reflective part, which is the epistemically active part of their soul – their capacity for reason – and thereby, it would seem, would be most interested in seeing his own capacity for reason. And this capacity for reason, likened to god and the divine, would seem something perfectly regular and logically crisp, just as everyone's is. Self-knowledge, then, even if mediated by another person, seems to culminate in knowing, not one's idiosyncratic self, but the purified capacity for knowledge. Socrates had told Alcibiades that his desire for public service required self-knowledge as a precondition, but this picture of self-knowledge does not readily deliver the goods. There is a long step from knowing the ideal of rationality to leading a city well. Once again, however, the presumed length of this step is factitious, coming from an arbitrary picture of selfhood. From Socrates' analogy we tend to assume that he identifies the self with pure reason, or the capacity for knowledge, and excludes any objects of thought or knowledge, treating such objects as external to the capacity, or idiosyncrasies purged in the vision of the ideal. We do not need to assume this. Socrates' identification of self-knowledge with *sôphrosunê* explains. *Sôphrosunê* makes sense only for a person with diverse desires and beliefs, ones that need winnowing and integration. This means that self-knowledge winnows and integrates one's beliefs and desires. Thus the recognition of one's rationality seems to mean a recognition of the possibility of winnowing and integrating. In other words, selfhood is the making of authoritative and reasonable judgments about one's beliefs and desires.

The *Philebus* shares with the *Charmides* and *Alcibiades* this attention to the limitations of reason distilled from the life of practical choices. The conversation in the *Philebus* comes in its first ten pages to an acceptance that the life of reason does not suffice for a choiceworthy human life. Reason uncut might satisfy a god; but humans are not gods. Humans would choose only a life that included pleasure. But accepting the insufficiency of reason and the necessity of pleasure does not alone help a person realize the choiceworthy life. The *Philebus* entertains a grander pair of questions. Socrates and Protarchus pursue, in general, the role reason plays in the choiceworthy human life, and in particular the way reason incorporates pleasure, which by itself hardly makes a life worth living, into that choiceworthy life.

In this chapter I draw attention in a way unfamiliar to *Philebus* scholarship to the way Socrates in this dialogue treats self-knowledge and self-constitution as crucial to understanding the role reason, and through reason, pleasure, contribute to the good life. This scholarly silence heretofore about self-knowledge in the dialogue might not be altogether surprising. The epistemic or cognitive attitude Socrates emphasizes most is "reason" (φρονήσις). He does not define reason, instead pairing it with "understanding" (νοῦς) or linking it with a longer list of generally epistemic or cognitive functions, including "remembering" (μεμνῆσθαι), "correct opinion" (δόξαν ὀρθήν), "true calculation" (ἀληθεῖς λογισμούς), and their unnamed kin (11b4–c3). He contrasts it with "pleasure" (ἡδονή) and the other positive, pleasurable feelings, including "rejoicing" (τὸ χαίρειν) and "delight" (τέρψιν), and their unnamed kin.[1] Self-knowledge is defined by its object; and yet in the dialogue's first half, Socrates never distinguishes epistemic attitudes

[1] This list of states or dispositions of souls (ἕξιν ψυχῆς καὶ διάθεσιν, 11d4) is recapitulated at 19c8–d6. In the *Protagoras* Socrates says that Prodicus distinguishes between these types of pleasure, but that those distinctions are irrelevant to his current purpose.

by object. In the dialogue's second half, Socrates ranks types of knowledge (ἐπιστήμη) by appeal to their object, where knowledge of eternal and immutable abstractions ranks higher than that of human items (61d7–62d2), but even this scale simply orders instances of knowledge by the degree to which they could be true (61e3). Nowhere in this discussion is the self, or oneself, mentioned. Because the dialogue begins in a contest between the pure hedonist and the pure intellectualist, a moderating compromise seems to provide the solution: the happy life has secured the right mixture or blend of reason and pleasure. The focus on the blend, and its connection to limit and the unlimited, steals attention away from the nature of this reasoning. Even more intriguing is Socrates' overwhelming curiosity about false pleasures, the constituents in an universal ontology, and the recipe for the perfect mixture.

But there are several reasons for supposing that the *Philebus* might aim to encourage thinking deeply about self-knowledge. First, Socrates associates reasoning with knowing one's pleasures in a way that makes them one's own (cf. 63c1–3). Reason allows the very experiences productive of pleasure to become pleasurable for the person who knows them. Reason *realizes* pleasure: it recognizes an experience as a pleasurable one, and it recognizes the pleasure as mine, and thus worthy of my choice. This knowledge both concerns aspects of oneself, one's pleasures, and generates that self, a subject that has pleasurable feelings; it is self-knowledge from the perspective both of intentionality and of self-constitution. Second, early in the dialogue Protarchus says that next best to being wise and knowing everything – perhaps an impossible condition, and one hardly lauded later in the conversation – is not being mistaken about oneself (19c1–3). In a dialogue about the ranking of lives, we see that the self-knowing life is among the best. Third, Socrates brings up the Delphic *gnôthi sauton* as he concludes his analysis of the mixed pleasures (48c8–10). Though ostensibly about the experience of comic theater, and divided into knowledge of one's money, of one's looks, and of one's virtue, the reference proves to have a much broader relevance. Socrates says that what holds for the stage holds also for life (50b1–4), and what holds for comic malice holds also for all other emotions (50b7–d6). So he indirectly links the failure to know oneself, and self-knowledge, to all emotional, and apparently all ethical, experience. In fact, comedy appears to point out our normative expectations for others: that people are risible, even worthy of our scorn, unless they know themselves. Self-knowledge provides a necessary standard for our judgment of someone's having dignity. The honorific "selfhood" is achieved only through self-knowledge.

This chapter argues that the idea of self-knowledge clarifies the interlocutors' conversation about the joint necessity of reason and pleasure for happiness. It shows the direct relation Socrates helps draw between the *gnôthi sauton* and the analysis of the good life. Even in one of Plato's most erudite works, Socrates spins his usual concern for self-knowledge into questions about being a happy person.[2]

A prelude about reflexivity and pleasure

A first clue that reflexivity and selfhood will matter to the analysis of reason and pleasure comes early in the dialogue, when Socrates claims that pleasure differs in kind (ποικίλον, 12c4; μορφάς ... παντοίας, c7), and presents an argument that this is so. Everyone agrees, he says, that the undisciplined human (τὸν ἀκολασταίνοντα ἄνθρωπον) and the thoughtless person (τὸν ἀνοηταίνοντα) experience pleasure. He does not say what they find pleasure in. It must be obvious. The undisciplined person surely enjoys drink and food and sex. The thoughtless person is "filled with thoughtless beliefs and hopes" (ἀνοήτων δοξῶν καὶ ἐλπίδων μεστόν, 12d3), and so his pleasure is surely in the (unsubstantiated) expectation of great success. Later in the conversation Socrates spells out the dynamics of that expectation. Inside a person with hope, "there are painted images, and someone often sees there being bounteous gold for himself and, with this, great pleasure. Moreover, this man sees himself, with respect to this inner painting, being beside himself in exceeding gladness" (40a9–12). So the thoughtless person gets pleasure from believing in the content of his idle daydreams. But it is probably not simply because it is obvious that Socrates omits reference to the source of pleasures for undisciplined and thoughtless people. Their particular sources of pleasure are not in fact important. What is important is that their lives are oriented to, or explained by, their pleasure-seeking or pleasure-imagining. They have the names they

2 See Frede 2000 on Socrates' performance in the dialogue, and his efforts to help Protarchus come to self-understanding; Meinwald 2008: 487 has a more pessimistic view of Protarchus and the dramatic content of the dialogue, and surmises that the dialogue is "imagining how Socrates lives on in 'Platonic heaven.' "

do because of their rambunctious pleasure-taking. Indeed, Socrates classes whatever pleasures they pursue into a single category, to be contrasted with something else.

For the comparison case, Socrates brings up the pleasures of the disciplined or soundminded person (τὸν σωφρονοῦντα) and the thoughtful person (τὸν φρονοῦντα). Perhaps it is surprising that these people experience pleasure; the exercise of virtue and mind might not appear to yield pleasure. Accordingly, Socrates specifies what they take pleasure in. For the *sôphrôn* person, it is his exercise of discipline itself (αὐτῷ τῷ σωφρονεῖν); for the thoughtful person, it is his thinking itself (αὐτῷ τῷ φρονεῖν, 12d1–4). These men take pleasure in their very way of being. But in what respect are these pleasures categorically different from those of the undisciplined and thoughtless men? For all of them, their respective pleasures are related to their particular character-traits. So the distinction must be in something else.

In one sense, the distinction is simple. As Socrates claims a few moments later, some pleasures are bad, and others are good (13b1). By itself, however, this begs the question against the hedonist (as Protarchus remarks, 13b6–c2); it fails to clarify Socrates' reason for describing the pleasures of the *sôphrônes* and thoughtful men as their own virtuous activity;[3] and it does not specify what underlies the goodness or badness of pleasures. The examples need further explanation. We can canvass several possibilities.

Naturally, good pleasures but not bad pleasures might be those felt by good people. It is possible that good people would be able, or would choose, to get pleasure only from good sources. But this does not explain what makes those sources good other than they are chosen (the *Euthyphro* problem). Nor does it explain Socrates' specification that *sôphrônes* and thoughtful people get pleasure from the exercise of their virtues. Dialectically it fails, too, since against the hedonist the argument would hold little appeal. For the hedonist, a person's goodness would have to depend, somehow, on the amount of pleasure they experience. We would have to believe that the more pleasure a person feels, the better the individual pleasures they have are. Perhaps this argument about connoisseurship might be defended. But it would be harder to see that a person would count as bad because he had heretofore experienced few pleasures.

[3] Contra Frede 1993: 3n3 and 44n1.

Responding to the examples might suggest that the good pleasures have internal objects. The *sôphrôn* person's pleasure comes from his own *sôphrosunê*. An internal object of pleasure has the advantage of enduring presence and proximity, and thus reliable access. Its form and intensity might seem to be under increased control, too. Yet the criterion of internality is inadequate. The undisciplined man presumably takes pleasure at satisfying his hunger or lust; and both these replenishments happen within his body. Even "calming an itch by scratching it" (τὰς τῆς ψώρας ἰάσεις τῷ τρίβειν, 46a8), as dermal, is essentially internal. The foolishly hopeful man has his source of pleasure internal to himself as well, in his complex imaginative projections.

This latter observation, about imagination, mostly undermines another idea as well, that good pleasure comes through reasoning (being soundminded, being thoughtful) rather than by means of something physical or some possession. But this focus on reasoning suggests something familiar from the *Alcibiades*. Perhaps good pleasure is somehow specially from *oneself*. The *sôphrôn* person gets pleasure from his being *sôphrôn*, something constitutive about himself. So too with the thoughtful person, whose very organizing principle generates pleasure. This differs from the undisciplined or thoughtless person, who does not get pleasure from his lack of discipline or lack of thought (this would be a sort of perverse narcissism) but from something else. But this line of reasoning has its own challenges. It is hard to know exactly pleasure's precise relationship to selfhood in the cases of the good pleasure. It could be that the pleasure comes from the fact that one *is* a self, or it could be that the pleasure comes from whatever contributes to selfhood. The bad pleasures might somehow come from something other than one's self, or from whatever contributes to the dissolution of selfhood. There might be significance in the alpha-privative states of being *akolastôn* and *anoêtôn*. The lack of discipline and lack of thought would mean a lack of a well-defined or relevant self.

Despite these challenges, three times much later in the conversation Socrates distinguishes good from bad pleasures in a way suggestive of this view. After addressing false pleasures, Socrates observes that those who live not in soundmindness but in excess (ἐν ὕβρει) experience intense and powerful pleasures (45d3–4). Protarchus agrees and adds that the *sôphrônes* are obedient to the saying "nothing too much" (ὁ παροιμιαζόμενος ... ὁ τὸ μηδὲν ἄγαν παρακελευόμενος, ᾧ πείθονται, e1–2), whereas for "the unreasoning and excessive" (τὸ τῶν ἀφρόνων τε καὶ ὑβριστῶν), their intense pleasures bring them to madness and crazy shouting (μέχρι μανίας ἡ σφοδρὰ ἡδονὴ κατέχουσα περιβοήτους ἀπεργάζεται, e2–4). Protarchus is here describing a reactive individual who lacks a stable core and who fails to engage in deliberate action.

Socrates goes on to say that this latter (reactive) person has a "mixed" experience, of pleasure and pain (46a12). This affectively impure experience seems at first to have little to do with selfhood and unity. But as Socrates proceeds in his discussion, we see the connection again between pleasure and self-constitution. He reiterates that a bad pleasure causes such distortions of people's bodies that in the end it "practically concusses them and makes them shout thoughtlessly" (πᾶσαν ἔκπληξιν καὶ βοὰς μετὰ ἀφροσύνης ἐνεργάζεται, 47a8–9). Again, like *mania*, this *ekplaxis* is a metaphor of being knocked from one's presence of mind; this is reinforced by the language of thoughtless yelling, words disconnected from any deliberation or intention. In Socrates' much later summary of their discussion, he brings together these considerations. The most intense and thus presumably the worst pleasures "agitate the souls in which they reside through madness, and they may not even allow them to develop … and they induce forgetfulness through neglect" (τὰς ψυχὰς ἐν αἷς οἰκοῦμεν ταράττουσαι διὰ μανίας ἡδονάς, καὶ γίγνεσθαί τε ἡμᾶς τὴν ἀρχὴν οὐκ ἐῶσι … δι' ἀμέλειαν λήθην ἐμποιοῦσαι, 63d5–e2). By contrast, the good pleasures blend so well with reason – this mixture has so little factionalizing (ἀστασιαστοτάτην) – that it becomes possible "at some point to strive to discern in [that mixture] what in man and in the world is by nature good, and to presage its very form" (ἐν ταύτῃ μαθεῖν πειρᾶσθαι τί ποτε ἔν τ' ἀνθρώπῳ καὶ τῷ παντὶ πέφυκεν ἀγαθὸν καὶ τίνα ἰδέαν αὐτὴν εἶναί ποτε μαντευτέον, 64a1–3). Bad pleasures are those that wrench or shake one from one's comportment and presence of self; they inhibit the maturation of one's soul; they cause ignorance; and they obscure from view what is good. By contrast, good pleasures participate in a stable and unified constitution. This constitution is apparently organized to reveal what is good. This sounds very much like the *Charmides* and the *Alcibiades*, where selfhood is a normative structure, oriented by and toward the good. A bad pleasure has pain mixed in. But this is not the most important point. A bad pleasure prevents stable self-constitution determined by what is best.

This reasoning gives a good reason for supposing that the *sôphrôn* person's pleasure is good. Practically by definition, *sôphrôsunê* does not put one out of oneself, does not incite mania, does not inhibit psychic development, and does not obscure the nature of the good. The same would go for thoughtfulness. In fact, *sôphrôsunê* and thoughtfulness could epitomize the good pleasures, pleasures unmixed with pain and conducive to self-organization. Socrates notes late in his conversation that the true and pure pleasures include "being *sôphrôn* and following virtue everywhere as one follows (συνακολουθοῦσι) a god" (63e4–6), that is, being good.

Socrates' argument here depends only on the claim that the pleasure of the *sôphrôn* person – namely, the pleasure in his *sôphrôsunê* itself – is good, whereas other pleasures are not good, or anyway, are different. His argument does not make clear how he imagines the *sôphrôn* person getting pleasure from his own virtue, or in other words, what self-knowledge the *sôphrôn* person deploys for this purpose. There look to be two similar possibilities. The *sôphrôn* person might take cognizance of his own virtue, as Socrates pretends to want Charmides to, and in judging it good, get pleasure. But he might also turn his attention outward, to his actions, and judging them good, get pleasure from them. Probably, of course, these routes cannot be differentiated materially. One judges one's virtue by judging how one acts. It takes knowing what is good, and what one does.

It is worth noting, in closing here, that the passage appears to show that pleasure can come from thoughtfulness or virtue. This suggests that while the life of reason without pleasure is not choiceworthy, in fact the life of reason may suffice for a life with pleasure too.

Debaters' puzzles about unity and selfhood

Protarchus agrees to allow diversity among the kinds of pleasure, at the price of Socrates' concession that the kinds of cognition also differ (14a6–b7). Before proceeding to get clear about the nature of pleasure, Socrates urges them to get clear about the nature of unity and multitude, if indeed both pleasures and cognition have different species within their respective genres. But clarity about unity and difference is difficult; the terrain is susceptible to captious debate about pseudo-puzzles. Protarchus reveals his awareness of such debate. His first example concerns the identification of selfhood: "Someone might say that I, Protarchus, having become one by nature, am in turn many 'I's and even opposites to them – that someone assigning the large and small, the heavy and light, to the same thing" (14c11–d3). Such absurdities show the folly of determining selfhood by appeal to relative properties (larger than her, smaller than him; heavier than a mouse, lighter than a tree). Even appeal to composites has its risks, as Socrates points out: "Someone, having distinguished by speech the parts and the limbs of each person, and having gained agreement that all these things are that unity, might refute you, laughing that he has thoroughly forced you to proclaim absurdities, both the one being many and unbounded, and the many being one alone" (14d8–e4). A particular self proves disjoint, and distinct parts lose their individuality. As it turns out, the absurdities of relative or composite properties arise only with physical bodies – that is, things that grow or decay. The puzzles concerning universals have more value; presumably they are about species and genera. Socrates illustrates this first with the puzzle that comes "when someone tries his hand at assigning 'human being' as one" (15a4–5). This introduces a discussion of parts and wholes, division and collection, especially in the context of language. But it is clear that such discussion is at least in part motivated or made familiar by questions of our nature as human beings and the possibility of self-constitution. Later in the dialogue Socrates' example about uncertain perception concerns the recognition of a man as a man, and not as a statue (38c5–d10). In both cases – what people debate about, and what people mistake for something else – Socrates reminds us that we want to know about selves, and that many of the other questions epistemology and metaphysics take up spin off from this curiosity.

Other dialogues also treat much of philosophy as underwritten by a curiosity about selfhood and unity. In the *Parmenides*, for example, Socrates asks whether he is both one and many (129a2, c3–d2) and whether there is "form" of the human (130c1); Parmenides notes that the youthful Socrates seems more concerned with questions of human value (beauty, justice, goodness) than dialectical training (130c6–d8). In the *Theaetetus*, as Socrates asks about recognition and knowledge, he continually uses examples of self-identity (155b, 159b–160b) and recognition of others (144c4, 209a2–c7). The *Phaedo* seems to show a biographical development in Socrates' questions about humans, from biological composites to unified selves. Earliest in his career he asked whether perception, cognition, and knowledge come from the brain

(96b4–9); then he wondered about the identity of a person through bodily growth (96c7–e4); then about his being in one place rather than another (98c4–99a4); and last about the single soul.[4]

But in the *Philebus*, before Socrates goes far into mereology, he notes that such puzzles, which come about through the flexibility of language, affect their promulgators first and most powerfully (εἰς ἀπορίαν αὐτον μὲν πρῶτον καὶ μάλιστα καταβάλλων, 15e4). These people think the puzzles are a "treasury of wisdom" and make them "divinely enthusiastic with pleasure" (e1). To the extent that these puzzles are about selfhood (they are also about animals and virtue terms; perhaps these puzzles too are relevant to selfhood), the puzzlers puzzle themselves about selfhood; to the extent thinking about selves requires, involves, or results in thinking about oneself, the puzzlers puzzle themselves about themselves. In aiming to know better what to say about the puzzles, they aim to know themselves better.

The conversation heads off into talk about the Promethean method of generic division, which gives to us "searching and learning and teaching each other" (16e3–4). Socrates' favor toward this method has two implications. First, we are to gain understanding of something, a letter, for example, by investigating the relations it has with its neighbors, in this case the rest of the alphabet. Understanding is not perceptual but somehow practical and contextual, dependent on the examination of similar and different things. Second, the Promethean method is to be fundamentally social, or conversational, used in co-investigations and the passing on of the acquired insight. These two implications make the Promethean method seem rather like Socrates' wonted dialectical procedure itself.[5] Socrates, as Plato regularly depicts him, asks about the relations between virtue terms, for example (in the *Protagoras*), or between virtue terms and behavior terms (in the *Charmides*), and he does so in coordinated searches with others. And just as Socrates elsewhere advertises his activity as promoting the greatest benefit, in the *Philebus* he says that his Promethean method has a direct relation to our wellbeing: "without being able to do this in terms of every unity and likeness and identity ... not one of us would ever come to be anything worthy of anything" (19b5–8). Talking and investigating, and thus thinking, about whatever it is for something to be a self, has

[4] See Davis 1980; Zuckert 1998: 882–886, and 2004: 192–210; Roochnik 2002.
[5] Cf. Thomas 2006.

foundational value in seeking the happy life. It would not be surprising, then, if the Promethean method were, like Socrates' normal procedure, organized toward establishing true propositions but, in effect, worried most to highlight conceits of knowledge and to establish principles of self-constitution.

Though the conversation soon takes a metaphysical turn, setting out four basic cosmological elements,[6] the dialogue's first quarter reminds us that intellectual conversations and debates often care most about the nature of the self; that these discussions have a self-applied aporetic effect; and that skill in these discussions about the self benefits oneself in a most fundamental way. These notices about the self and the self's attitude to itself gain thematic weight once Socrates talks explicitly, in two crucial scenes, about knowing one's pleasures and knowing one's self.

Realizing one's pleasures

Protarchus doubts that employing the Promethean method will resolve the conversation's starting issue, whether one should prefer the life of pleasure or the life of reason. He asks that Socrates either defend this method more concretely, or seek another route to resolution (19c1–20a10). Socrates chooses the latter. To verify what he treats as a dream telling him that neither life is preferable, he proposes looking at the lives on their own.[7] By defining the good – as perfect, sufficient, and uniquely desirable (20d1–d8) – the interlocutors may see whether any particular life shares all those traits and thus qualifies as good.

Socrates and Protarchus begin by positing a life of "enjoying all the greatest pleasures." This life would have "no need of anything else," in particular no "thinking, understanding, or calculating" (21a8–14, recapitulated at 60c–e). By hypothesis, it would be perfect, lacking in nothing; sufficient, having all one needs for happiness; and desirable,

[6] Cooper 1977 argues that Socrates' four-fold ontology does allow a straightforward analysis of the good life; the better the knowledge, the more rationally or systematically "bounded" it is. One might infer from Cooper's analysis that getting self-knowledge requires purifying, stabilizing, and expanding one's range of knowledge.

[7] In both the *Charmides* (173a7) and the *Theaetetus* (201d8), Socrates introduces key considerations about the nature or value of knowledge by appeal to a dream of his.

being purely pleasurable (21b2–5). In the face of Protarchus' reasoning, Socrates produces a stunning argument. He undermines all three criteria of goodness simultaneously. He does so by destroying Protarchus' most basic assumption: that pleasure, by itself, has any positive value whatsoever. The life solely of pleasure lacks everything, does not have all one needs, and is in no respect desirable in itself. Therefore it is not good. Socrates' argument is, in essence, that without reason, pleasure has nothing to lodge in, and so would not be *my* pleasure. It would not be part of *my* life, and thus it would not make my life choiceworthy. Reason is what makes pleasure one's own.

Socrates starts his argument from the assumption that this maximally pleasurable life lacks mind, memory, knowledge, and true belief (νοῦν … μνήμην … ἐπιστήμην … δόξαν … ἀληθῆ, 21b6–7). He develops the argument in four parts, showing that without these, Protarchus cannot say he would find this life choiceworthy (αἱρετός, 21d3). It is uncertain whether Protarchus finds each loss sufficient to topple his confidence, or only the entirety of them, but it does seem that he finds each troubling. More interesting than the power of Socrates' series of arguments, though, is the shape of the self it traces. The benefits provided by the four cognitive faculties that Socrates discusses reveal the appropriative, temporal, judgmental, and practical aspects that constitute a person.

Not every reader has found Socrates' argument so gratifying or informative. John Cooper says it presents "a very circumscribed conception of what knowledge is. Clearly, [Protarchus] sees that it is an indispensable good thing to understand one's present, past, and future conditions of life, but no doubt he envisages in this nothing beyond some rather simple egocentric self-knowledge."[8] Daniel Russell reduces its value further, claiming that "intellect enables one to remember past pleasures and to plan for future ones."[9] I aim to show, by contrast, that Socrates relies on a rich, normative view of self-knowledge and self-directed cognition in his argument for the necessity of reason in the choiceworthy life.[10]

8 Cooper 1977: 718–719. Harte 2014: 6, 10, also identifies only three consequences, ignoring "true belief" (δόξα).

9 Russell 2005: 168–169. Hampton 1990: 39, claims this passage proves nothing except "that Protarchus would prefer a life that includes both pleasure and knowledge to one that consisted exclusively of one or the other."

10 Good general accounts of the argument's purpose and Protarchus' reaction to it, with little detailed attention to the cognitive functions, may be found in Gosling 1975: 181–184; Benardete 1993: 130–133; Evans 2007: 343–351.

Phronêsis *and acknowledgment*

Socrates starts with what has become the scholarship's most controversial sub-argument, that *phronêsis* allows you to recognize whether you are being pleased.

> Were you void of all *phronêsis*, you would necessarily not recognize whether you were being pleased or not being pleased (εἰ χαίρεις ἢ μὴ χαίρεις, ἀνάγκη … σε ἀγνοεῖν, κενόν γε ὄντα πάσης φρονήσεως). (21b7–9)

The scholarly controversy arises from the implication that a person must recognize her pleasure for it to make her life good. While controversial, it is also the sub-argument most explicitly connected to self-knowledge. Without *phronêsis* you would be ignorant (ἀγνοεῖν) of your most basic experiences; this is the opposite of recognizing or knowing them (γιγνώσκειν). *Gignôskein* is a significant verb, not to be treated here as "note" or "observe that." It is used early in the dialogue, when Philebus says to Protarchus that while he himself already prefers the life of pleasure, "you will yourself have to recognize" which life is best (σύ … αὐτὸς γνώσῃ, 12a8). The verb also constitutes half the Delphic command, which arises later in the dialogue, in Socrates' discussion of comedy, in both positive and negative forms (48c10, d2, d8). At that later point, Socrates notes three kinds of types of self-ignorance that we see often enough and find ridiculous: ignorance of one's wealth, of one's strength and looks, and of one's virtue. He does not mention ignorance of one's pleasures. Either he believes that few people fail to recognize their pleasures, or that they do, but that this case is not essential for his analysis of comedy. This matter will arise again in the next section.

Socrates seems to be saying that if you did not recognize your pleasure, your pleasure would not do you any good. But this goes against the intuition that the experience of pleasure is cognitively unmediated, and further, that when it is mediated, it is flattened or restrained. Indeed, this is not only an intuition; it is the foundational principle of pure hedonism, which is that pleasure alone suffices for the good life. As Socrates and Protarchus repeatedly assert, by hypothesis they are assessing what is already the most pleasant life. It is easy to accept that, in some cases, recognition that one is pleased could cause the additional pleasure of pride ("I'm such a fun-loving person!") or relief ("At long last, pleasure!"). But these instances of pleasure would be like minor editorializing comments on the more substantive first-order pleasure.

Yet Socrates argues the case, and Protarchus cannot deny it. G.E. Moore cites the passage as a particularly clear argument against hedonism.[11] Moore does not say, however, exactly what he takes the argument to be, and readers have struggled to give it plausibility. In a defense of Moore and Socrates, Dorothea Frede rejects the hedonist's charge "that it is unfair of Socrates to abstract all awareness from pleasure, as if even bare awareness of pleasure had to be a kind of intellectual activity." She says that "any self-respecting hedonist would want more than the bare recognition of pleasant feelings at the moment they happen. If there is to be anything worth calling a *human life*, there has to be memory of past pleasures and full comprehension of present and possible future ones."[12] But Frede's argument in effect concedes the objection! She does not explain how "bare awareness" or "bare recognition" of pleasure needs intellectual capacity, and seems to think that a person could actually find bare pleasure at least somewhat desirable. J.C.B. Gosling, who also seems to accept Socrates' point, gives it an austerely intellectualized reading: "Plato means that an animal, lacking the power of conceptual judgment, cannot recognize the truth or falsity of 'I am enjoying myself,' since it is incapable of justified true judgment and so of knowledge."[13] It is unclear what such conceptual recognition achieves. Verity Harte adamantly rejects Socrates' argumentative maneuver, observing that by hypothesis this life already contains the greatest pleasures (σὺ ζῆν τὸν βίον ἅπαντα ἡδόμενος ἡδονὰς τὰς μεγίστας, 21a8–9, cf. b3–4), and so reason could not increase those pleasures.[14] For all this, it would be odd for Socrates to begin with the least likely or the weakest argument. What then could Socrates mean?

We might first ask what it means to recognize your being pleased, and why, absent any *phronêsis* whatsoever, Socrates claims that this recognition would be impossible. There seem to be two possibilities.

11 Moore 1903: §52.

12 Frede 1993: xxxii. Harte 2014: 12, believes similarly that the emphasis is on our expectation of psychological continuity in a human life.

13 Gosling 1975: 88. At 183, Gosling adds that recognizing one's pleasures "could be seen as adding to one's pleasures," but he does not explain whether this means creating additional pleasure or simply making unrecognized pleasure count as recognized pleasure.

14 Harte 2014: 9–11.

You might not recognize *that* this experience of being pleased is happening (rather than nothing at all). Alternatively, you might not recognize that this experience is happening *to you* (rather than to somebody else or nobody in particular). Perhaps most readers have assumed Socrates means the first possibility, and is saying that it is the *recognition* that being pleased is happening that provides the value, not the being pleased itself. Critics of this view wonder why being pleased itself does not suffice. After all, Socrates has already granted maximal pleasure. Not so many readers have assumed that Socrates means the second possibility, and is saying that the recognition that *you* are experiencing the pleasure provides the value. But this seems a plausible interpretation of Socrates' remark, and it may even be a good argument.

There is a provocative linguistic reason for entertaining the second possibility. When Socrates identifies what it is that *phronêsis* allows one to recognize, "whether you were being pleased or not being pleased" (εἰ χαίρεις ἢ μὴ χαίρεις), he uses the second-person singular rather than the articular infinitive (e.g., εἰ ἔστιν τὸ χαίρειν ἢ τὸ μὴ χαίρειν). This suggests that the person with *phronêsis* recognizes whether *he* or *she* is being pleased, rather than simply whether there is pleasure. As it happens, Socrates' use of the finite verb may account for some of the interpretative difficulties in the first place. It seems to assert that you are already experiencing pleasure; what could you need to recognize on top of that? But it is probably not asserting that. Socrates may very well be saying instead that your recognition of something being pleasing is what accounts for it pleasing *you*. In other words, we cannot rightly say that *you* are being pleased (χαίρεις) until you have a moment of recognition. An alternative formulation, along the same lines, is that Socrates could be saying that though there is some experience called χαίρεις, this experience is not valuable, is not pleasurable in the way a hedonist enjoys, until it is recognized. There is a neutral process called χαίρειν, this view supposes, that happens whether or not you notice it; but it is not enjoyable or valuable or properly pleasant until it is recognized.

In either case, Socrates claims that χαίρειν is desirable and choiceworthy only if you recognize that it is *you* experiencing the pleasure, or if you *recognize* that you are experiencing the pleasure. Somehow pleasure without proper mooring or acknowledgment does not contribute to the life the hedonist finds choiceworthy. The mere fact that pleasure happens in the body – surely where pleasure resides – does not make that pleasure valuable. We see the truth of this on a small scale later in the dialogue. Socrates says that some of the experiences each of us has "stop before getting all the way to the soul, leaving it unaffected" (πρὶν ἐπὶ τὴν ψυχὴν διεξελθεῖν ἀπαθῆ ἐκείνην ἐάσαντα, 33d2–4). These bodily events, even if they have restorative or dissolutive properties – the material causes for pleasure and pain – have no psychic component; they are "missed" (λανθάνειν, 33d9) and "not perceived" (ἀναισθησίαν, 34a1). So while these events are located in our body, we do not recognize them and so do not care about them. We might assume this holds on a large scale as well. The body may undergo important instances of refilling (πληρῶσις, 31e8, 51b6, etc.), but unless they are recognized as one's own instances of refilling, they will not be registered as pleasures, and they will not be desirable. This argument assumes a contrast between self (or soul) and body, where the self is that which chooses, recognizes, and evaluates. But since the hedonist agrees to a debate about the most choiceworthy life – Philebus tells Protarchus to recognize, by himself, the best one – he must accept that there is the self, not merely a body, that can engage in debate, and thereby evaluates, recognizes, and chooses.

So far we have seen that Socrates is saying that *phronêsis* allows one to recognize that one's pleasure is one's own, is part of one's own life, and therefore contributes to that life's choiceworthiness. Without that recognition of ownership, the replenishment, even the pleasure itself, would float free, perhaps located in one's body but not of any more significance than any other natural process in one's body. It would not make one's *life* choiceworthy.

In fact, when Socrates talks later in the dialogue about the failure to obey the Delphic precept in people who fail to recognize the magnitude of their true wealth, we get a good example of his reasoning – and some clues about readers' misunderstanding of this passage. The existence of one's wealth appears to depend on nothing but the sheer fact of its existence. Misidentification of its size, even wholesale ignorance of its existence, neither lessens nor obliterates it. This is why people can be self-ignorant about their wealth. Yet self ignorance about one's wealth is bad not merely because it leads to misreports. It prevents the wealth one actually but unknowingly has from contributing to a choiceworthy life (20d7–10, 20e6–21a2). We can spend our money – and thus have wealth – only when we know about it.

An unacknowledged inheritance provides no windfall, and overestimating one's capital leads rapidly to debt. Wealth removes barriers to action, but deciding to act requires knowing of those barrier-free circumstances. The fact that objective transferrable items underwrite any instance of wealth is irrelevant to the existence of a choiceworthy life; they are just so many impersonal items until they are acknowledged as one's own. The case holds even for strength, another of Socrates' examples of the personal accouterment that self-ignorant people misjudge. Good bodily fortune opens avenues for athletic achievement; but only when one knows one has it does it contribute materially to the pursuit of such achievement. In such case, too, we may locate some undergirding objective reality, such as muscle mass, but this does not count as strength until it is made one's own. It is made one's own only with acknowledgment of it.[15]

One might feel resistance to assimilating the case of pleasure to the case of wealth, or even to the case of strength. Using one's wealth and strength is separate from possessing them. Money sits there until deployed for a desired purchase; one strength resides in one's muscles until a desired task calls for them. Using pleasure, by contrast, does not seem separate from possessing it. Its use – its experience – seems an internal, immediate, and necessary effect of possessing it. Granted, one does not always bask in one's pleasure or turn one's attention wholly to it. Still, it seems unavoidably pleasant and desirable. Another way of putting this is as an asymmetry in appearance–reality distinctions. The reality of my wealth may not match the amount I acknowledge. Or my extreme modesty may blind me to my considerable brawn. But pleasure does not cleave easily into appearance and reality. How often do we countenance unfelt pleasures, or pains we are unaware of?

The failure to fit pleasure to the wealth model misunderstands both wealth and pleasure. Wealth does not have, so we have argued, an impersonal existence, even if one's moveable and real property have, as material entities, objective reality. Such things do not exist *as wealth* unless they are acknowledged as one's own. An error about one's wealth comes not from mistaking appearance for reality, but in attributing more or less power to oneself than the circumstances would allow. Since wealth has no clear appearance–reality distinction, pleasure does not differ from it in that way. The sense that *something*

[15] Burnyeat 2003 explains how, for Socrates, something's being good for you requires knowing you have it.

provides the acknowledgment-independent ground for wealth may still remain. From this perspective, however, pleasure remains in step. For it also has some underlying objective reality. Something about me – my body or soul – undergoes some process that undergirds pleasure in the same way that objective transferrable items undergird wealth. The refilling is the objective reality undergirding pleasure. But refilling is hardly choiceworthy in itself; coins secretly dropped beneath a sofa are hardly choiceworthy either. But the *acknowledgment* of refilling as *one's own* is desirable just as the acknowledgment of objective transferrable items is desirable.

Neither Socrates nor either of his interlocutors ever define *phronêsis*. In this dialogue, it usually signifies the life that contrasts with that of pleasure.[16] It is sometimes paired with *nous*,[17] and occasionally clumped with three or four other cognitive activities.[18] It is never directly related to *sophia* or to *epistêmê*. In the *Apology*, Socrates treats *phronêsis* as the wisdom suitable for living well (29e1). Here, it is the recognition of what is one's own; indeed, it may even be the deliberation about what is one's own. Thus while *phronêsis* counts as an awareness, for example of the experience of *chairein*, it is not merely redundant oversight of first-order human events. This awareness is what allows such events to matter, by incorporating them into one's life.[19] So without *phronêsis*, Socrates says here, it is impossible to acknowledge anything as one's own, and thus as contributing to one's good, making one's life more livable.[20]

[16] As noun: 12a1, 12a3, 18e3, 19b4, 20b7, 20e2, 20e4, 20e5, 27c5, 27d2, 59d10, 60b4, 60c8, 60e2, 60e3, 60e4, 60e5, 61c6, 61d1, 63a9, 63b4, 63c5, 63c7, 65a8, 65d5; as verb: 11d9, 12a3, 12d4, 33a8, 55a7, 60c8, 61d1, 63a9, 63b4.

[17] As noun: 22a3, 28d8 (governors of the universe), 58d7 (source of purest dialectic), 59d1 (names of highest honor), 65e4 (both beautiful), 66b6 (third-place life); as verb: 33b4.

[18] As noun: 13e4, 21d9, 28a4, 60e3; as verb: 11b7, 21a14.

[19] Kolb 1983: 502–505, gives a powerful argument for the same conclusion, that knowledge allows pleasure to be part of one's own life; he does so from the perspective of challenging readers who take Plato for an ontological and psychological atomist. Gadamer 1991: 126–128, argues similarly that pleasures begin as "present-at-hand" just as all other objects in the environment do, and become "mine" only when possessed in the human way: by knowledge. Veith 2013 argues that at least in Aristotle, *phronêsis* has self-knowledge as part of itself.

[20] Some recent accounts of pleasure in the *Philebus* do not account for Protarchus' belief that an unacknowledged pleasure provides no good. Tuozzo

Memory and time

As we have seen, readers of the *Philebus* have had a hard time accepting Socrates' first claim, about *phronêsis*; but most take his second claim, about memory, to be reasonable.

> Likewise, not possessing memory, you could neither remember that you ever were being pleased, nor retain any memory whatsoever of the pleasure that would at that moment be befalling you (ὡσαύτως μνήμην μὴ κεκτημένον ἀνάγκη δήπου μηδ' ὅτι ποτὲ ἔχαιρες μεμνῆσθαι, τῆς τ' ἐν τῷ παραχρῆμα ἡδονῆς προσπιπτούσης μηδ' ἡντινοῦν μνήμην ὑπομένειν). (21c1–4)

Much better than pleasure at the moment alone, so the usual argument goes, would be pleasure at the moment plus the memory of all one's previous pleasures, and the ability to build up sequences of memories for the future. Yet Socrates' position here is more complex than it first appears – it is in two arguments – and it reveals something crucial for the self-constituting quality of self-knowledge.

The first argument is that without the cognitive faculty of memory, what Socrates calls "a preservation of perception" (σωτηρίαν αἰσθήσεως, 34a10), you would remember no past instances of pleasure. That would prevent basking in one's past pleasures, either individually or in their accumulation. But I am not sure that this is Socrates' main point. The lack of memory would prevent a person from appreciating the good accruing to her entire life; and this would prevent her from judging that life to be most choiceworthy. After all, the hedonist must accept that many moments will be devoid of pleasure (he agreed to the life with the most pleasure, not the life with evenly distributed pleasure), but think that his prior accumulation of pleasure justifies his preference for the hedonist life. Otherwise, hedonism would be an appealing theory only at those moments when a person was feeling pleasure. This means that the hedonist life would be choiceworthy only sporadically, which is to say, not always, and perhaps not generally. The hedonist might think that he could simply choose the life he knew to be full of the most pleasures, but within that life, unless he

1996: 497, plausibly unifies physical and mental pleasures by saying that both are "conscious psychic process[es] caused either by the reality of the restoration of a bodily or psychic harmony, or by entertaining the image of such a restoration," but he does not explain how these psychic processes are related to evaluative, good-sensitive types of thought.

had memory, he could not remember, at times of non-pleasure, that his life was the one with overall the most pleasure.

Socrates' second argument has two distinct interpretations, depending on our understanding of memory (μνήμην) as short- or long-term. If Socrates refers to long-term memory, then his second argument perfectly mirrors the first argument. Just as you must be able to remember what happened in the past – if you want a store of pleasures, either to re-experience or to consolidate as a choiceworthy life – you must also be able to store memories for the future. Recall and storage are at least conceptually separate cognitive functions; the loss of either, in an ongoing life, would minimize the putative value of the life solely of pleasure.

If, however, Socrates refers to short-term memory in this second argument, he would be making a separate and perhaps more profound claim. All pleasurable experiences beyond luxuriating in the sunshine or drinking some cool water – thrills of the moment – require the capacity to unify temporally extended objects of perception. Speech, music, action: instances of none of these could be understood or experienced instantaneously, at a single slice of time. Their constitutive sounds or sights would slip through your mind, not to be assembled with the earlier and later sounds or sights, and thus not to be comprehended as the source of pleasure they can be. So memory is required not just for accumulating past or future pleasures into a well-inventoried life; it is required for all but the most evanescent experiences. The life of the greatest pleasures would have a low ceiling, for it would be only the instantaneous experiences.

Later in the dialogue Socrates gives yet another argument for the importance of memory to pleasure. Desire is painful to the extent we recognize a lack. But it is also pleasurable to the extent we remember, and therefore anticipate or hope for, the experience of satisfying that desire (35a6–c14).[21] Since desire motivates every decision, desire is widespread, and so too the pleasure concomitant to it. Socrates' image of the soul as a book (38e12) and his claim that we are, through our entire life, always full of hopes (39e5–6) vivify the sense that each person is unified as an individual across time by memory. Indeed, our higher-level desires – those that organize large segments of our lives, and that give our lives their distinctive direction and autonomy – require

[21] Cf. Tuozzo 1996: 508–510, 513.

elaborated plans for their satisfaction.[22] Constructing and following these plans require memory. While the hedonist may think he wants simply to experience the moment, the truth is that living in the moment without planning one's life would yield little pleasure, perhaps even less pleasure than pain. So even the hedonist should want to live a life of agency and planning, and this requires memory.

There is implicitly in the *Philebus* even a dialectical argument for the importance of memory to the choiceworthy life. Memory is necessary for conversation – as is indicated by the fact that this dialogue starts with the interlocutors in the midst of a conversation, and Protarchus' frequent forgetfulness about their position – and conversation is necessary to support the hedonist's claim. (Conversation is also an important source of pleasure and the discovery of new ways to get pleasure.)

All readers of Socratic literature know the importance to Socrates of memory. The *Clouds* and the *Phaedrus* give special attention to it.[23] We can now see more sharply its importance to human life. Memory allows us to take a perspective on our life *as* a unified life, and thus to decide on its choiceworthiness. It allows our life to grow as our life goes on. It allows the enjoyment of temporally extended phenomena. It underlies the hopefulness of desire and thus motivates all our actions. It allows rational planning and the constitution of a life, an ongoing self, to enjoy. And it allows the kind of conversation and debate necessary for demonstrating memory's importance to others and to ourselves. Self-knowledge draws on, to critique and commit to, our experiences, our beliefs, and our desires; memory underlies all of these.

True belief and choice-making

Socrates has now accounted for the importance of *phronêsis* and memory to the choiceworthy life. Both had extraordinary reach and depth; both look necessary for the most significant elements of life: its structure, its unity, its self-awareness, and self-possession. Yet he has so far given only half his statement. He now turns to "true belief" (δόξα … ἀληθῆ):

[22] See Bratman 2000; Frankfurt 2006: 10–20.

[23] *Clouds*: 21–22, 129, 242, 483–485, 629–631, 785, 855; *Phaedrus*: see Moore 2013c.

If one didn't possess true belief, one would have no belief about being pleased while being pleased (δόξαν ... μὴ κεκτημένον ἀληθῆ μὴ δοξάζειν χαίρειν χαίροντα). (21c4–5)

Somehow a belief about a pleasure must differ from a recognition of it (as one's own) and from a memory of it. Socrates says that beliefs come from memories and perceptions (ἐκ μνήμης τε καὶ αἰσθήσεως δόξα, 38d12; cf. *Chrm.* 158e7–159a7). The beliefs themselves appear to concern, in the case of pleasures, their size and intensity (37d9–10), probably their object (37e5), and at what moments they occur (39c10–11). They even concern whether you are in reality feeling pleasure rather than merely experiencing it in a dream, in one's overheated imagination, in madness, or in delusion (36e58). But in general, true belief articulates certain facts about experiences, and allows measurement, comparison, explanation, and inference (42b2–6). The thoughts that some pleasure is stronger than another, or has a finer texture, or shows up erratically, depend on the faculty of opinion.

The hedonist probably does not disdain false beliefs as such; truth is not itself good for him. But given that he takes pleasure as the good (11b4), he has reason to seek what is true to the extent it conduces to pleasure or the avoidance of pain. True beliefs about the pleasures available to you allow you to choose between different available actions. They facilitate coherent decision-making. Without true belief, you might keep doing whatever you believe produces pleasure, even if you are wrong, or the pleasure is paltry compared to the pleasure that alternative actions would realize. As Socrates argues in the *Protagoras*, failure to judge correctly the magnitude of one's candidate pleasures is a primary source of badness in a person's life. We might call "true belief" the present-oriented cognitive attitude in parallel with "memory" as the past-oriented cognitive attitude, though in both cases these temporal categories are impoverished. Memory is useful both at the present moment and for one's future actions. True belief is important for future activities, and assesses not just one's present experiences but also those from the past. The life of greatest pleasures without good judgment (true belief) about one's pleasures could at best be the outcome of extraordinary luck, always appearing to risk downturn, and out of one's control and understanding.

We turn now to Socrates' final cognitive attitude, a genuinely future-oriented one.

Calculation and the future

The final argument for the importance of reason to the choiceworthy life is concerned with forecasting and prediction.

> And lacking in calculation, it's not possible to calculate for the later time that you will be pleased (λογισμοῦ δὲ στερόμενον μηδ' εἰς τὸν ἔπειτα χρόνον ὡς χαιρήσεις δυνατὸν εἶναι λογίζεσθαι). (21c5–6)

True beliefs allow a person to make good decisions. Calculation goes from a current true belief to a new true belief, following regularities in the world, and thus it allows a person to make additional good decisions. Calculation concerns future moments because it allows one to determine likely outcomes (cf. 52a8–b1). Such calculation is not of minor importance. Socrates says that "if someone were to remove counting, measuring, and weighing from every skill, the remainder would be worthless" (55e1–3). It is hard to imagine having a good *life* that lacked control over one's actions to come, that had to deal solely with the immediate present. Any choiceworthy life is unified – in this case by calculation – by care for oneself and preparation for situations that unfold over time.

The human life with pleasure

Socrates closes the argument by saying that a life without reason would not be a human life but rather the life of some jellyfish or bivalve (21c6–8).[24] His argument is that without knowing, remembering, judging, and calculating one's experiences, pleasures move through the organism without becoming one's own or becoming valuable, and without helping constitute a choiceworthy life. A reflexive attitude toward one's pleasures is needed; and the different modes of reflexivity, called by the names of the different cognitive attitudes, contribute to a life in a complicated, temporally extended world. They are responsible for one's constitution as a unified and good-seeking person.

What ensues is an agreement by Protarchus and Socrates that just as the life solely of pleasure could hardly be choiceworthy, nobody would

[24] Later he wonders whether all animals, bovine and equine included, might advocate following pleasure: 67b1–2.

choose the life solely of reason (21d9–e4). At this point, our interlocutors do not really explain their reason for taking the insensate life (τὸ παράπαν ἀπαθής, 21e2) to be absolutely unappealing. The idea is connected to the fact that humans are not gods (22c5–6, 32e5–33c1). It must be that pleasure is unavoidably choiceworthy, and indeed pleasure may be what makes reason itself choiceworthy. A human life without pleasure, just as a human life without consciousness, simply makes no sense as a human life; it would never be chosen over a life of pleasure.

Comedy and self-ignorance

As we have seen in the previous sections of this chapter, the *Philebus* looks to be especially concerned with self-knowledge. Yet Socrates refers to the *gnôthi sauton* (48c10) only once, as he tries to convince Protarchus that some pleasures are ineluctably mixed with pains. The pleasure of comedy provides Socrates with a limit case for this: the mixture is so subtle that Protarchus has never registered or noticed the pain (48a8–b6, 50c10–d6). Because he cannot point to it, Socrates must give an argument. In fact, he does so twice (48b7–49c5, 49c8–50a10). I present it here as a single argument. The Delphic precept arises as the injunction that the ridiculous person most fails to obey.

1. All our laughter (γελῶμεν) is pleasurable (χαίρομεν) (49e9–50a1).
2. But the laughter of comedy is at the ridiculous (γελοίοις) (49b7–8).
3. The ridiculous is self-ignorance (ἄγνοια) too weak to avenge itself (49b6–8, c4–5).
4. Ignorance is a bad (κακόν) state (48c2, 49a4–5).
5. So the ridiculous is a bad state (48c6–7).
6. But the ridiculous people of comedy are not enemies (49d6–7, d11–e4, 50a2–3).
7. It is unjust to be pleased at the bad state of non-enemies (49d1).
8. This unjust pleasure comes from malice (φθόνος) (48b11–12).
9. Malice is painful (47e2–3, 48b8–9, 49d1, 50a6–7).
10. So the malicious laughter of comedy mixes pleasure and pain (50a5–9).

Socrates argues that while we enjoy laughing at those who fail to know themselves, because they are not our enemies we act badly in laughing at them, and in acting badly, we cause ourselves pain. Thus this seemingly pure pleasure, laughing in comedy, is actually mixed, and as much as this is so for the theater, so much is it for life (50b1–4).

This argument has a certain plausibility, especially in its observation that we enjoy our laughter when we laugh safely, and that people's self-ignorance is a cause for great amusement (cf. Soph. *Ajax* 65–67).[25] But it also prompts an urgent question. Why is self-ignorance ridiculous and pleasing but not other sorts of ignorance, and why does Socrates divide self-ignorance into three sub-types?[26] The answer to this question will give an excellent view on the meaning of self-knowledge in this dialogue.

Socrates constructs his theory of comic malice with remarkable precision. He selects ignorance from among many other grounds for foolish behavior. Protarchus had recently mentioned another Delphic encouragement, "Nothing in excess" (τὸ μηδέν ἀγὰν παρακελευόμενος, 45e1); excessiveness would be a likely candidate for comedy. But Socrates does not aim to explain all pleasure or even all humor in comedy; he means only to explain malicious laughter. The malicious laughter he cares about takes as its object not just any ignorance (ἄγνοια, ἀβελτέραν, 48c2), but that ignorance interdicted by the Delphic saying, ignorance about oneself.[27] Because malice requires an observation of someone's faults (κακοῖς, 48b11) where such an observation causes pleasure, these instances of self-ignorance must be either rather worse or rather more pleasure-inducing than other kinds of ignorance, or both.

We might consider ignorance of matters other than oneself to be disappointing, but we hardly call it bad. It would be a great thing to know everything (19c1–2), but it is not to be expected. Indeed, society is so arranged to take this into account. One person knows one thing, another person another. As long as you can find who knows

[25] The account of comedy at *Rep.* 606b2–10 does not link the laughable with the ignorant; this suggests that Socrates has a special reason for focusing on ignorance here.

[26] It also prompts other urgent questions not yet adequately addressed in the literature but tangential to the discussion here: (i) Why does Socrates consider the self-ignorant people in comedies "not enemies"? (ii) Why is malice painful? (iii) How does what holds for the comic theater hold also for life, given that one context is fiction, the other reality? (iv) Why really does Socrates digress for two pages to show that even comic pleasure is mixed?

[27] Tulli 2010 sees a reference to Aristophanes' *Clouds*; cf. Strauss 1966: 5; Benardete 1993: 207–208.

what you do not know, then ignorance about something – the Persian language, for example, or shoe-making – yields no great harm to oneself. What we would call bad is the kind of ignorance that prevents relying on others who know. This is ignorance about your ignorance. Self-ignorance, thinking you can do what you cannot do, or thinking you cannot do what you can in fact do, can lead to harm.

Socrates does not say that just any sort of self-ignorance is what is bad. He says it is disobedience to the Delphic injunction, and that there are necessarily (ἀνάγκη) three ways to be ignorant of oneself (48d8–9). The first, in terms of "useful items" (χρήματα), is believing (δοξάζειν) oneself to be richer (πλουσιώτερον) than one is in reality (48e1–2). The second, a more common malady or object of ridicule, involves believing oneself to be brawnier and handsomer (μείζους καὶ καλλίους) and more superior in body (τὸ σῶμα ... διαφερόντως) than one truly is (48e4–6). The third – and by far the most widespread, he notes – is believing oneself to be rather more virtuous (ἀρετῇ), and indeed rather wiser (σοφίας), than the facts allow (48e8–49a1). Ignorance here, Socrates says, leads one to be quarrelsome (ἐρίδων) and conceited (δοξοσοφίας ... ψευδοῦς, 49a2).

This list more than accounts for ignorance about the skills one knows, which Socrates would include in "wisdom." This triad of, first, the tools adjunct to one's person, second, the strength and social appeal thanks to one's body, and third, the perfection of one's virtue and wisdom corresponds exactly to the *Alcibiades*' analysis of self-knowledge as concerned with tools, body, and soul (*Alc.* 129c4–130a1).[28] These are the three categories of capacities necessary for autonomous action, action for which an actor may be responsible. So ignorance in any of these categories means *acting* ignorantly. This is bad because acting without knowledge may at worst lead to harm; and at the least, it will make the result of the action dependent on luck, not on intention, and so it makes the action in some respect not the action of the putative actor. Socrates is interpreting the Delphic imperative here as "Know what you are doing." Acting ignorantly is bad.

A person who believes himself richer than he is will act on the assumption that he possesses resources that he cannot in fact deploy. He takes his sphere of influence, and in a sense his identity, to spread more capaciously

[28] Avnon 1995: 307–308, by contrast, claims that these three modes of ignorance represent three modes of self-knowledge, with knowledge of one's virtues both best and most private.

than it does. He has a false view of his range, a false view of what he can do, and thus a false view of himself (as a person with such range and potentiality). A person who believes himself more charming, attractive, or strong than he is will likewise act ludicrously, seeing himself differently from, and better than, the way his audience sees him. Finally, the person who believes himself a better decision-maker, more knowledgeable, or more adaptable and insightful than he is will take on judgments, commitments, and engagements that he will not be able to vindicate.

Were self-ignorance bad but common, its depiction on stage would be boring. Were it extremely bad, it would be piteous. Were it to an onlookers' advantage, the onlookers would feel malicious glee, not malicious laughter.[29] Socrates says onlookers find self-ignorance ridiculous. Though he does not say it, I assume this means that laughing at the self-ignorant involves a kind of incredulity that is resolved into some sort of positive realization. We face someone else's self-ignorance with incredulity because it seems preeminently avoidable: everything to know is *right there*, and so we think, *how could you make that mistake?* Self-ignorance is caused by obsession, wishful thinking, or complacence, and these are removable delusions. The harm of self-ignorance is potentially profound – undermining the most important human actions – and this gives good reason to everyone to try avoiding it. And of course there is an immensely popular saying warning against just this self-ignorance.

Socrates does not account directly for the pleasure derived from seeing people acting without self-knowledge. He seems to believe, at any rate, that the person laughing has a feeling of superiority. This is suggested by the fact that, if this attitude were shown to someone strong, the superior-feeling or -acting person would incur retribution (τιμωρεῖσθαι, 49b7). Other potential causes of pleasure – for example, the relief at thinking that you do not yourself have the self-ignorance on display – would seem not to incur retribution. Or the recognition that while you in fact do have the self-ignorance on display, you are not alone in that benighted state, would seem even less likely to incur retribution. So a laughter that would earn retribution must be one due to revelling in one's own relative self-awareness.[30]

[29] On *phthonos* as malice, see Gadamer 1991: 183–187; Russell 2005: 189–190nn49–51.
[30] Tuozzo 1996: 510–512.

This laughter is not obviously salutary.[31] It seems cruel, taking (even self-directed) pleasure at the poor situation of someone else. In the theatrical context, this cruelty is bad if it habituates a person to cruelty in the real world. Further, the desirability of pleasure reinforces the belief in one's relatively good position with respect to self-knowledge.[32] This is always problematic. This problem may be alleviated by the pedagogically clever playwright who makes the audience see themselves in the comic butt, and go on to discover their own self-ignorance. But this experience of discovery is not itself the source of malicious pleasure.

It is not Socrates' goal here to redeem comic pleasure; in fact, he points to its painful qualities. But he does seem to have the ancillary goal of redeeming self-knowledge. The audience judges the person lacking self-knowledge to fail to live a choiceworthy life, even if blissful idiocy has its occasional appeal. To act on the basis of a remediable misconception, indeed on a misconception it is the human duty to avoid, is not just to act in a questionable way; it is practically a failure to act at all. It is instead to do whatever the prevailing desire or *idée fixe* or impulse causes, and behaviors caused by impulses are not themselves actions. Foregoing self-knowledge, the person foregoes effective assessment of that irrational force, and so he cannot take that force on as his own, and thus as the motivation for his rationally chosen action. This self-ignorant person does not deserve pity, for he could have prevented hindering himself as he did by more rigorously attending to his effects. He has abdicated his humanity and his ability to investigate his capabilities, his will-power, his resources, and his surroundings. It is at this dehumanization, this abandonment of due diligence and personal responsibility, that we laugh.

Socrates thus shows that we understand the comic figure's ridiculously ignoble ignorance by appeal to the fact of our having been charged, as humans, to come to know ourselves. The comic figure fails to do what he thinks he can do, and the audience knows that he could

[31] This is a common worry, and many commentators try to distinguish Socratic laughter from malicious laughter: Wood 2007; McCabe 2010; Austin 2012.

[32] Hampton 1990: 64–67, claims that "the secret pain of comedy is that we perceive that we are really laughing at our own unfortunate self-deceit" that we must discover through our sympathizing with our self-deceiving "friend." This does not square with the text, however, for apparently all malice whatsoever is painful (48b8–9, 50a56), and this pain is connected to its being unjust (49d1).

have avoided that failure if he had chosen not to keep himself delusional. He has lost some selfhood, and thus some of our respect.[33]

Even if we now understand the relationship between the *gnôthi sauton* and comedy, and comedy and mixed pleasures, we may wonder why, in the dialogue about the happy life for humans, "know yourself" comes up, in its connection to Delphi, only here. The most explicit clue comes in Socrates' return from the specific example of comic theater to the broader context. He says that, just as pleasure and pain mix in this way in drama, so too do they in the entire tragedy and comedy of life (50b3). This implies that we do not feel disdain for the self-ignorant only in their fictional representation, but also in the real world. And thus we judge the failure to know oneself to be a primary way to fail at being human. The converse would be that we judge knowing oneself to be central to being human. It is perhaps easier to see this in the controlled setting of the stage, but the lesson is really for us, the spectators.

Self-knowledge, unification, and the choiceworthy life

Socrates concludes the conversation of the *Philebus* with a ranking of life's constituent parts with which Protarchus can agree. First is measure, the measured, the timely, and their like (μέτρον, τὸ μέτριον, καίριον, 66a6–7); second, the well-proportioned, beautiful, perfect, sufficient, and their like (τὸ σύμμετρον, καλὸν, τὸ τέλεον, ἱκανόν, 66b1–2); third, mind and reason (νοῦν, φρόνησιν, 66b5–6); fourth, that which is the soul's own, namely knowledge, skill, and true belief (ἃ τῆς ψυχῆς αὐτῆς ... ἐπιστήμας τε καὶ τέχνας καὶ δόξας ὀρθάς, 66b8–9); and fifth, the painless pleasures that have (also) been called the soul's own, being affixed to knowledge and perception (ἃ ἡδονάς ... ἀλύπους ... ἐπονομάσαντες τῆς ψυχῆς αὐτῆς ἐπιστήμαις ... αἰσθήσεσιν ἑπομένας, 66c4–6). The two best parts appear to refer to unity and unification,[34] which is the nature of selfhood. Mind and reason, the third part, elsewhere called the cause of unification for humans, work through self-knowledge.

[33] Miller 2008 is a fascinating alternative approach to the importance of self-knowledge to the *Philebus*; see also Benardete 1993: 201–208, on the importance of this passage to the dialogue as a whole.

[34] Frede 1993: 81nn2–3, calls the first "limit in all its application," and thus the logical prerequisite for any harmonious mixture, and the second "harmonious mixtures themselves."

The last two parts have been appropriated, by self-knowledge as we have seen earlier in the dialogue, to the soul itself. So all that makes life good – beautiful, proportionate, and true (65a2) – concerns making the self a self. This principle of unification has attracted many previous readers.[35] What the present reading has shown is the frequency and depth with which Socrates identifies the process of unification with self-knowledge.

We can now see the scope of the dialogue in the context of this shared emphasis on self-knowledge and unification in the prosecution of a good life. Eristic debaters entice people into quibbles about the unity of man because their arguments sound like a real debate about the human condition: how might we be individuals, rather than bundles of limbs and desires? Foolish and excessive people, lacking self-knowledge, do not get pleasure from themselves, getting it instead from any old place, and in their manic chasing of ephemera, they belie their lack of unification. Pleasure is a valueless filling up and arranging of body until it is recognized as the attainment of a desirable harmony, one's self-perfection; only at this point is it properly pleasure, and good. We disvalue the failure to know one's own, even aside from the dangerous effects overweening pride can cause. Finally, the only constituents of the good life are those things that are already made ours by being appropriated by the soul to itself. This chapter has argued that such appropriation is the task of self-knowledge, and that *phronêsis*, in this dialogue, names the psychic faculty heading up that task.

[35] E.g., Gadamer 1986; Riegel 2011.

6 *Xenophon's* Memorabilia *4.2: owning yourself*

A reputedly impoverished picture

Xenophon's Socrates seems to give much less thought to the *gnôthi sauton* than Plato's does, referring explicitly to it only once (*Mem.* 4.2.24).[1] His single discussion also seems hardly to make up in philosophical interest what it lacks in quantity; according to many readers, his analysis shows little depth of analysis or exploration. For David Johnson, for example, his argument about self-knowledge "shows no inkling of the complicated problems with the possibility of second-order knowledge that Plato discusses in the *Charmides*." Johnson takes Xenophon's Socrates to espouse a simpler view: it "consists not in knowing that one knows nothing, or in knowing *what* or even *that* one knows, but in knowing what one knows *how to do*."[2] For Xenophon's Socrates, Johnson says, knowing yourself is a matter neither of recognizing your ignorance nor of acknowledging your knowledge, but simply of knowing your powers, a skill of self-assessment or self-inventory.

This chapter argues against this prevailing disappointment with Xenophon's Socrates. That particular Socrates has a notion of self-knowledge much closer to the Platonic Socrates' self-constitution view than Johnson and other recent scholars have assumed. The "know your powers" view frequently attributed to Xenophon's Socrates wrongly takes the initial interpretation by Socrates' interlocutor, Euthydemus, as the view articulated throughout the entire conversation depicted in *Memorabilia* 4.2. While knowing one's powers contributes to knowing oneself, a closer reading of Xenophon shows that it is only part of the story. The fuller story that emerges from the conversation between Socrates and Euthydemus relates

[1] This chapter has been published in a related form as "Self-Knowledge in Xenophon's *Memorabilia* 4.2," *Classical Journal* 110:4 (2015): 397–417.

[2] Johnson 2005: 62, 65.

self-knowledge to self-ownership, knowledge of justice and the good, and conversation. Coming to know oneself means coming to act on the basis of one's knowledge of justice and goodness, and acting on this frees the self from a self-imposed enslavement. Freedom from enslavement means self-possession, the constitution of oneself as a thoughtful and rule-following master of oneself. Xenophon's clever use of characterization and drama, depiction of wide-ranging ethical inquiry, and imagery of a horse-buyer contemplating the purchase of a horse make this work a key text in the Socratic literature about self-knowledge, and thought-provoking in its own right. I begin with a brief summary of *Mem.* 4.2; discuss the popularity of the "know your powers" gloss of "know yourself" and adumbrate some criticisms of that gloss; and then articulate Xenophon's positive picture of self-knowledge. I conclude by discussing Socrates' indirect way of talking about self-knowledge.

A dialogue about self-knowledge

Xenophon wrote *Memorabilia* 4.2 as a unified literary whole that is fitted both within the context of Book 4 and a complete account of a multi-day Socratic interaction.[3] Euthydemus, a young man eager for wisdom and leadership, fails under Socratic examination to distinguish the unjust from the just (*Mem.* 4.2.1–19). He begins to suspect that he might be confused: "I no longer believe in what I answer, for even all the things earlier now seem to be otherwise for me than as I then thought" (19). After another refutation (20–21), he bursts into self-conscious awareness of his trouble (23). He sees himself unable (ὁρωντα ἐμαυτὸν … οὐδὲ … δυνάμενον) to speak well about the most crucial matters, and recognizes no way to change for the better. Socrates responds by extolling the importance of "knowing yourself" (γνῶθι σαυτόν). This ability contributes more than other abilities to personal success, and it helps oneself and others avoid harms (24–29). Euthydemus, persuaded, asks how he might start self-investigation (ἄρξασθαι ἐπισκοπεῖν ἑαυτόν, 30). Socrates answers by asking Euthydemus whether he knows what things are good rather than bad. When Euthydemus claims it would be slavish

[3] Rossetti 2011 treats the passage as a discrete dialogue worthy of the title *Euthydemus*; Morrison 1994 studies Chapters 1 and 2 together as a unified and multi-stage pedagogical seduction.

not to know at least this, and so implies that he does know what is good, Socrates refutes him. Straightaway, Socrates asks about the nature of those whom Euthydemus hopes to lead, and when Euthydemus answers, he refutes him once again. At this point, Xenophon switches from direct narration to capping comment and reports that Euthydemus finally realized his need for Socrates' companionship and so became a regular associate of his (39–40).

This entire conversation provides information about Socrates' understanding of self-knowledge, as I aim to make clear below. I focus first on the usual interpretation of Xenophontic Socratic self-knowledge.

Knowing yourself as knowing your powers

Immediately after asking whether Euthydemus has noticed the "Know yourself" inscribed at the Temple of Apollo at Delphi, Socrates glosses its meaning. He starts by rejecting the seemingly superficial equivalence "Know your name," and continues by comparing knowing oneself with a horse-buyer coming to evaluate the character traits and abilities of a horse he might buy. Euthydemus accepts the comparison and infers that "the one not knowing his powers is ignorant of himself" (ὁ μὴ εἰδὼς τὴν αὑτου δύναμιν ἀγνοεῖν ἑαυτόν, 4.2.25). Knowing one's powers is necessary for self-knowledge. The advice is apt for Euthydemus. He has already revealed himself to know his powers inadequately. He thinks that his book-collecting (1, 8–10) suffices for his aspiration to political wisdom (9, 11). He already believes that he "will excel all others in the power to speak and act" (παντων διοίσειν τῷ δύνασθαι λέγειν καὶ πράττειν, 1). But his conversation with Socrates has shown that Euthydemus has not yet accurately determined whether he has the power to get this political wisdom.

Whereas Euthydemus simply denies you can know yourself without knowing your powers, most recent scholars have assumed that Xenophon's dialogue here defines self-knowledge *as* knowing your powers. I have already quoted Johnson's view, that knowing yourself is "knowing what one knows how to do." We find the same perspective in studies of this passage by John Phillips and Louis-André Dorion.[4] Pierre Courcelle glosses knowing yourself as being able to measure

[4] Phillips 1989: 368; Dorion 2004: 240–251, 2006: 96.

your capacities from a social point of view, and Eliza Wilkins fits it into her category of "γνῶθι σαυτόν as know what you can and cannot do."[5]

These commentators gloss knowing yourself as knowing your powers presumably because Euthydemus' answer tracks Socrates' question, whether the self-investigator will have come to know his own power (ἔγνωκε τὴν αὑτοῦ δύναμιν, 25). Socrates seems even to affirm Euthydemus' answer when he says that those who know themselves discern the powers they have (διαγιγνώσκουσιν ἃ … δύνανται, 26). Xenophon's frequent discussion of powers in this chapter makes talk of them appear especially significant.[6] And in the context of the chapter, the "knowing your powers" view accounts plausibly for the benefit of self-knowledge. If self-knowledge means knowing one's powers, then having self-knowledge would allow a person either to act in accordance with his powers or, should he wish to act differently, to increase his powers.[7] Self-knowledge would serve either restrictively, as a chastening, or positively, as a goad to self-improvement. It would be a prompt to be diffident or to seek personal development. Euthydemus, in his desire for the kingly art, that most excellent skill sought by politicians, estate-managers, and leaders, must see whether he has what it takes. So while these scholars do not always make precise the relationship between self-knowledge and knowing your powers – and perhaps

[5] Wilkins 1917: 23; Courcelle 1974: 19–20. Annas 1985: 121, reads the passage more complexly, as arguing that "those who know themselves know what is suitable (ἐπιτήδειον) for themselves, and discern what they can and cannot do," and thereby obediently fulfill their station and duties. In what is otherwise a close reading of Socrates' rhetorical strategy in *Mem.* 4.2, Rossetti 2011: 76–80, leaves the γνῶθι σαυτόν passage unanalyzed at the level of content, though he speaks to its dramatic function; Morrison 1994: 187, notices it only in passing.

[6] In addition to the instances already cited (Y.2.1, 25, 26): Socrates finding it contradictory that some people think that they become "able" (δυνατοί, δυνατῶν) to play music only with help but that they are "able" (δυνατοί) to speak in the Assembly instinctively and without adequate preparation or training (ἄνευ παρασκευῆς καὶ ἐπιμελείας αὐτόματοι, 6); Euthydemus making his collection of books as complete "as I am able" (8); Euthydemus asserting he "is able" to list what is just (12); Euthydemus saying that the man "able" to err in reading and writing is the most literate (20); Euthydemus complaining that he is "unable" to answer questions he should be able to answer (23); Socrates observing that cities "ignorant of their own power" enter foolish wars (29); also 33, 37. Dorion 2004 discusses the phrase *kata dunamin* throughout the *Memorabilia*, showing its connection to political power and Socratic ethical thought.

[7] Tortzen 2002: 11, glosses this passage: "know your limits, *i.e.*, accept that you are ignorant and try to be wiser."

not all assume an identity between them – they have good reasons for positing an important relationship there.

In fact, while only in *Mem.* 4.2 does Xenophon's Socrates talk about the Delphic inscription, throughout the previous book he repeatedly and usefully corrects his interlocutors' self-understanding about their suitability for their desired goals. For example, Socrates' aspiring cavalry-commander friend fails to recognize that he will have to care for and improve his men's horses and the men themselves; and to be obeyed, he will have to speak well about goodness and have deep knowledge about the most important matters (3.3). In another conversation, Socrates shows Nichomachides that he neglects to consider the skills appropriate to generalship; he should know what he needs and how to get it, as a good businessman does (3.4). Glaucon, who wants to lead the city, ignores how little knowledge he has for that purpose, including the sources of the city's revenue and expense, military and defensive strength, and the productivity of mines and fields. Just as the estate-manager knows his inventory and makes efforts to replenish supplies, the statesman must understand all that about which he might speak and on which he might act (3.6). Charmides, Socrates' next interlocutor, has the reverse problem, having competence enough to lead the city but too much reserve and fear to do so. Socrates tells Charmides that he is ignorant of himself (ἀγνόει σεαυτόν), having failed, like many men, to examine and pay attention to himself (τὸ ἑαυτοὺς ἔξετάζειν ... τὸ σαυτῷ προσέχειν); he must realize that the assembly deserves no fear and that his ability to improve public affairs will benefit even himself (3.7). In these four exchanges, Socrates appears to want his friends to know their powers, and expects that by knowing them, and thus themselves, they will succeed in the lives they desire.

In what follows, I will argue that while "Know your powers" may partially gloss "Know yourself," it is inadequate as a full analysis of the injunction as presented in *Mem.* 4.2. Knowing yourself does involve some amount of self-observation and self-inventory, and close scrutiny of one's strengths and weaknesses. You do not have to be profoundly incurious to overlook certain unpleasant or unfortunate aspects of yourself; surely all humans obscure from themselves their qualities inconsistent with their self-ideal, and so Socrates' advice is perennially valuable. Yet Xenophon gives Socrates a more realistic, complex, and satisfying view of self-knowledge than this.

Problems with the "knowing your powers" view

Socrates' remarks about self-knowledge throughout *Mem.* 4.2 give a positive picture of self-knowledge connected to the concepts of mastery and slavery, knowledge and ignorance of justice and goodness, and conversation with and reciprocal ethical diagnosis of others. But before reconstructing this positive picture, it is worth canvassing the most immediate reasons against taking the "knowing your powers" view as the complete story.

First, if Socrates had wanted Euthydemus simply to know his powers, he could have said "Know your powers." Instead, Socrates cites the Delphic precept "Know yourself," and reiterates the Delphic provenance of that maxim (24).[8] The Delphic maxim does not obviously mean "know your powers," and whether its meaning is confusing, multiple, or indeterminate, Socrates' appeal to it suggests that he is alluding to some deeper meaning linked to its profound position in Greek intellectual, moral, and even spiritual life.

Second, when listing the benefits of self-knowledge, Socrates says that it gives you information about more than yourself. Perhaps paradoxically, by knowing yourself you may know others. Socrates says that it is on account of self-knowledge that people may assess others (διὰ τοῦτο δὲ καί … τοὺς ἄλλους ἀνθρώπους δυνάμενοι δοκιμάζειν, 26), and this assessment is the same action you perform on yourself. It is strained to think that knowing your own powers would allow you thereby to know others' powers. Your own powers appear too narrow an object of knowledge for this broader social outcome.

Third, once Euthydemus accepts the importance of knowing himself, he asks where one ought to begin examining oneself (ὁπόθεν δὲ χρὴ ἄρξασθαι ἐπισκοπεῖν ἑαυτόν, 30). Socrates answers Euthydemus' question by asking his own question in return: "Well then … I suppose you know full well what sorts of things are good, what sorts bad?" (οὐκοῦν … τὰ μὲν ἀγαθὰ καὶ τὰ κακὰ ὁποῖά ἔστι, πάντως που γιγνώσκεις; 31). This suggests that knowing yourself begins in a certain kind of knowing: knowing what is good. And yet knowing your powers does not obviously begin in knowing what is good.

[8] Except in *Apol.* 14, Xenophon's Socrates appeals to Delphi only one other time, in the following chapter on veneration of the gods: the Delphic god says that one pleases the gods by following the law of the state (4.3.16).

Fourth, at the very point Socrates refers to the Delphic maxim, he gives a two-part gloss. Knowing yourself involves, at the same time, both recognizing your power and investigating what sort of a person one is in light of human purposes (ὁ ἑαυτὸν ἐπισκεψάμενος, ὁποῖός ἐστι πρὸς τὴν ἀνθρωπίνην χρείαν, ἔγνωκε τὴν αὑτοῦ δύναμιν, 25). Socrates repeats this doubling in his next speech: those who know themselves know what is valuable to them while they also discern what powers they have (τά τε ἐπιτήδεια ἑαυτοῖς ἴσασι καὶ διαγιγνώσκουσιν ἅ τε δύνανται καὶ ἃ μή, 26). It is not yet clear what this adjunct to knowing your powers is, but it is obviously something more than knowing your powers, and not simply to be assimilated to it.

Together these observations provide reason enough to revisit the view of self-knowledge in *Mem.* 4.2. This revisiting demands a more synoptic perspective on the whole chapter.

Knowing yourself as knowing about justice

We may understand *Mem.* 4.2 better by seeing its position in Book 4. In *Mem.* 4.1.3–4 Xenophon describes Socrates' approach toward those who think their natural abilities suffice for lifelong success. He argues that thoroughbred horses, even those from excellent stock, need improvement (παιδείας). Men too need to gain knowledge of what they have to do (ἃ δεὶ πράττειν); otherwise, they would be out of control, implacable, and useless (δυσκατέκτους, δυσαποτρέπτους, φαυλοτάτους). In *Mem.* 4.1.5, Xenophon describes Socrates' approach toward those who believe their wealth adequate for success. Should they not know the difference between beneficial and harmful things, Socrates argues, they would be fools (ἠλίθιος) and failures.

In *Mem.* 4.2, Xenophon describes a third Socratic approach, this time toward those who consider themselves to have received the best education and who think highly of their wisdom (παιδείας τε τῆς ἀρίστης τετυχηκέναι καὶ μέγα φρονοῦσιν ἐπὶ σοφίᾳ, 1). Euthydemus is one of these men. The formal parallels between this section and the previous two suggests substantive parallels in the lessons. In the first two cases, Socrates recommends an abstract knowledge that also has particular application. Those complaisant about their natural abilities must learn what it is necessary to do in general, and then what they in particular must do. Those complaisant about their wealth must understand distinctions of value, and then what they in particular must choose. Xenophon prepares the reader to think that Socrates will convince

Euthydemus that he needs some abstract knowledge that may at the same time serve his particular uses.

Xenophon's account of Socrates' interaction with Euthydemus starts with a humorous account of his indirection. Socrates learns that Euthydemus collects books of the poets and wise men (4.2.1, 8–9). Euthydemus assumes that those anthologies of wisdom will suffice for his education to statesmanship; he thinks he does not need teachers. Socrates disagrees; he thinks that Euthydemus, like everyone else, needs practical guidance. But this puts Socrates in a bind. He needs to teach Euthydemus, who does not accept the value of teachers, that he needs teachers. So Socrates instead talks to his friends – within Euthydemus' hearing – about the importance of teachers to every other skilled person, and the folly in relying on impulse (ἀπὸ ταὐτομάτου) (4.2.2–6). This sideways introduction works; Euthydemus finally enters the conversation. But his entrance to the conversation does not mean he yet recognizes his mistake. Instead he believes that Socrates has been praising the value of wisdom over money, and thus that he has been affirming Euthydemus' value-judgments (9). At least Euthydemus will now answer Socrates' questions; Socrates asks them with an eye to Euthydemus' pride and continued resistance to the value of teaching (10).

The ensuing ten sections appear to take on the question of justice (11–21). Excellence in the political life that Euthydemus desires requires being just. Euthydemus tries to prove that he already embodies justice by showing that he can list the "works of justice" (δύνωμαι ἐγὼ τὰ τῆς δικαιοσύνης ἔργα ἐξηγήσασθαι, 12). He thinks there is a "learning and knowledge of justice" (20). He believes – though admits he cannot substantiate the claim – that knowing justice makes one just; he would seem also to believe that not knowing justice would mean he is unjust. He soon finds out that justice confuses him more than he anticipated.[9] This has two overlapping consequences. First, Socrates convinces him that this confusion, like any confusion, reveals

[9] Socrates examines Euthydemus' knowledge of justice by sketching a simple chart and having them inscribe the deeds of justice and injustice on either side (13). Euthydemus struggles. First they have to redo everything (διοριοώμεθα πάλιν, 16). Then he has to retract what he has said (μετατίθεμαι τὰ εἰρημένα, 18). After these two revisions Euthydemus starts doubting his answers, observing that the deeds of justice now look different than they did at first (19). Socrates drags him through a trying sequence of questions about intentional and unintentional deception, and the equation of knowing justice with being just. At this point, Euthydemus becomes even more sensitive to his uncertainties: "I seem to myself about even these things not to know what I'm saying" (20).

that "what he thought he knew he does not know" (ἃ ᾤετο εἰδέναι οὐκ οἶδεν, 21). So he comes to know what he does not know, what he is not able to do – in this case, defend his initial ideas about the works of justice; and Euthydemus makes this admission of ignorance explicit (23). Second, the failure to know about justice, just like the failure to know about beauty and goodness, makes him "slavish" (ἀνδραποδώδεις, 22).[10] By lacking knowledge of justice, he lacks self-mastery. These two consequences fit together. Since failing to know oneself involves unknowingly failing to know about justice, and failing to know about justice makes one slavish, failing to know oneself makes one slavish, and unjust.[11] Conversely, not being slavish – embodying self-mastery – involves knowing oneself, by way of consciously knowing about justice.

So far, Socrates has presented several faces of self-knowledge. It is a recognition of what one knows and does not know. This is knowing one's power only in the minimal sense that successfully revealing one's knowledge is an ability. It is also the avoidance of slavishness. This is being in charge of oneself. And it is knowing justice and being just. Knowing justice and being just puts one in charge of oneself; and knowing that one knows justice makes one knowingly master of oneself.

Immediately after Socrates' remarks about Euthydemus' slavish self-ignorance about his ignorance of justice, Socrates asks his questions about the Delphic injunction (24). Socrates seems to treat his discussion of the precept as summarizing, elevating, and elaborating on the previous discussion, which he thus reaffirms to have been about self-knowledge. He shows that Euthydemus' needed attention to justice and his own attitude about his understanding of justice are what the Delphic injunction enjoins. Euthydemus' answer to Socrates' question about his reaction to seeing the injunction – that he thought he

[10] Cf. 4.2.23, where Socrates states that "it is necessary, in every way, thoroughly straining (διατεινομένους), to flee this [i.e., ignorance of the good and just], lest we become slaves."

[11] "But by the gods," he [Euthydemus] says, "Socrates, I really thought I was philosophizing a philosophy, the one through which I thought it best to be educated in the matters appropriate for a man striving (ὀρεγομένῳ) to be a gentleman (καλοκἀγαθίας): but now, how do you imagine I am, spiritless, seeing myself (ὁρῶντα ἐμαυτόν), despite my earlier efforts (προπεπονημένα), not even being able to answer what I'm asked about what it's most necessary to know about, and having no other avenue traveling along which I might become better?" (23)

already knew himself – recapitulates Euthydemus' self-confidence in the earlier sections.

Knowing yourself as coming to own yourself

Socrates immediately glosses the Delphic inscription γνῶθι σαυτόν as "investigating yourself, who you might be" (σαυτὸν ἐπισκοπεῖν, ὅστις εἴης, 24). He does not say that the Delphic inscription picks out subsets of oneself to know; he suggests instead that it counsels figuring out who overall one is. This general knowledge of oneself Euthydemus takes to be the most readily accessible kind of knowledge, perhaps because its object is closer and more familiar than any other. Euthydemus says "hardly would I know anything else, if I didn't know myself" (σχολῇ ... ἂν ἄλλο τι ᾔδειν, εἴ γε μηδ ἐμαυτὸν ἐγίγνωσκον). Socrates parodies Euthydemus' insouciant and reductive view by wondering whether "knowing oneself" really means "knowing one's name" (τοὔνομα τὸ ἑαυτοῦ μόνον οἶδεν). Socrates' joke depends on assuming that one's name is the closest and most easily known aspect of oneself but at the same time the most superficial.[12] But still there is something significant about the joke: one's name identifies not a part of someone but the whole person.

All this is too allusive for Euthydemus, and so Socrates advances to an analogy. He likens the person who aims to know himself to the horse-buyer who desires to know a candidate horse (ὠνούμενοι ... βούλωνται γνῶναι).

> Horse-buyers do not first think they know what they desire to know until they investigate (ἐπισκέψωνται) whether it [a horse] is pliable or stubborn (εὐπειθής ... ἢ δυσπειθής), whether it is strong or weak, whether quick or slow, and as far as everything else about the usefulness (χρείαν) of a horse is concerned, in what way it is serviceable (ἐπιτήδεια) and unserviceable. (25)

It is important that Xenophon specifies a horse-buyer, not a spectator or judge at a horse-show, or a zoologist, or a painter.[13] The significance of

12 See also Plato's *Theaetetus* 203a6–d10, with Roochnik 2002: 45, where Socrates uses his own name as the example of something to know.

13 The Socrates of Plato's *Republic* 333c1 emphasizes the importance of horse-expertise when buying a horse, and at *Apology* 20a6–b2, 25b4–6, he emphasizes the importance for training (see with Lane 2005: 24–25). In the *Phaedrus* Socrates gives buying a horse the central place in his analysis of

horse-buying is clear in Xenophon's *On the Art of Horsemanship*: the horse you buy may determine whether you live or die.

> So to summarize, whichever horse would be sound-footed, gentle, fairly quick, willing and able to undergo toil, and, especially, pliable, this one would, likely enough, be the most painless and safest (σωτηριώτατος) for a rider in wartime. But others, either because of a torpor needing much driving, or because of an excess of spirit needing much coaxing and maintaining, will make the rider's hands full and him spiritless when in danger. (3.12)

Discovering a horse's initially hidden traits proves decisive in assessing its usefulness, and thus in determining whether one should commit oneself to it.

The horse-buyer must have several types of knowledge. He must know, first of all, what makes a horse useful. This is the knowledge of the ideal of a horse, of a horse's function and good state. Xenophon's manuals on horsemanship reflect on this general matter. The horse-buyer must also know how to investigate a horse's abilities. This investigative expertise applies to any horse, but is a practical ability rather than a theoretical discovery. It is concerned with observing, manipulating, and judging individual horses on any occasion. Xenophon's manuals can give some suggestions about this, but would not work as well as an actual teacher. Finally, the horse-buyer must learn the details of the particular horse, in what way it fulfills the various excellences of a horse. This knowledge determines whether to buy a particular horse or not. So knowing a horse well enough to decide whether to attach your life to it requires the ability to discern both the good for horses and the state of a particular horse with respect to it.

Socrates says that the case of knowing the horse one might purchase is analogous to knowing oneself. The analogy suggests at least five important features of self-knowledge: its urgency, its nature as a matter of self-ownership or self-purchase, a technically difficult investigation, a focus on certain qualities, and multiple kinds of knowledge.

Deciding which horse to buy, and thus knowing a horse, has an urgency; the wrong horse could put its buyer in grave danger. Coming

fruitful rhetoric (260b1–c8). See Griffith 2006 for the general importance for the ancient Greeks of thinking about horses.

to know yourself thus also has an urgency. For a soldier, the danger of self-ignorance could be mortal: it could put him in unnecessary risk, or lead him to sacrifice himself for an end he does not actually endorse, or to fail to obey those deserving his obedience. For Euthydemus, an aspiring statesman, the danger may not be to his natural life as such, but to his political success; acting without self-knowledge could cause him social anonymity, or exile, or mediocrity. Or, for Euthydemus or anyone seeking to be a free citizen and a gentleman, self-ignorance puts one into the evil state of slavery, a condition fatal for anyone who desires autonomy. Getting self-knowledge does more than advance a person's self-actualization, as increased literary creativity or athletic prowess may; it has, so this analogy suggests, a much more grave and significant importance.

The horse-buyer seeks to own a horse. Ownership depends on some exchange, but the exchange does not explain the purchase of a particular horse. The specific purchase occurs only once the buyer determines that he wishes to commit himself to some particular horse. This commitment means having identified some horse as the right one and one's exclusive steed. The analogy to self-knowledge may sound forced. It is odd to think of knowing oneself as coming to own or purchase oneself. In the first place, we are already on our own property, as it were. And in the second place, there does not seem much choice; we seem to have only one self to choose from. But the thought of owning oneself is really not so implausible. We already have the notion of disowning parts of ourselves, treating them as foreign, irrelevant, or none of our business. We also have the opposite notion, of recognizing parts of ourselves, treating them as constitutive of or important to who we are. We see Euthydemus disowning certain of his pretentions as foolish and thus no longer part of himself; and we see him eventually owning up to certain aspects of himself, especially the importance of his discipleship to Socrates. The clearest way of seeing the possibility of owning oneself is in the context of slavery. Slaves do not own themselves; they are not responsible for what they do, and do not receive the reward of being who they are. While some slaves are enslaved by slave-owners, Socrates and Euthydemus suggest that others are enslaved by impulse and delusion. The opposite of a slave is a master; one masters oneself only by taking on ownership of oneself.

The good horse-buyer has a skill of assessment. He does not simply look at a horse, or express his feeling about a horse. He uses the series of discrete tests that Xenophon describes, tests that might even strike the amateur as surprising, tedious, or irrelevant. Likewise, knowing oneself takes more skill than knowing one's name, visage, or mood. It may involve a complex of investigations, studies, and tests. The meandering conversation that Socrates instigates between Euthydemus and himself reveals a range of such methods of self-investigation.

One reason for the skillfulness of horse assessment is the specific variety of traits evaluated. For a horse, it is sound-footedness, gentleness, speed, endurance, pliability, energy, and self-control. These traits should not be obscured by one's interest in the horse's coat, lineage, farm, or other less important traits. Human self-knowledge may also concern itself with particular human virtues. If Xenophon implies a close parallel between horse-knowing and self-knowing, then self-knowledge might care about *karteria*, reasonableness, courage, and *sôphrosunê*. Of relatively minor importance are one's name, one's possessions, and even the history of one's education; knowledge of one's virtue is of relatively great importance.

The horse-buyer, as described above, knows not just about some candidate horse, but also how to find out about that horse, and about the ideals of horseness. So too then the self-knower. Knowing *yourself* may seem to have only one object; but it actually requires knowing, in addition to your particular powers, the nature of the good human, and how to measure success against that ideal.

These five parallels between horse-buying and knowing oneself show the ways that knowing oneself could plausibly be likened to coming to own oneself. The most important parallel is that knowing oneself is not a matter of passive observation or inventorying. It is a complex practical decision with deep self-constituting import.

The benefits of self-knowledge and conversation

The next part of Socrates' speech about self-knowledge takes a new tack.[14] It appeals to the "goods" of self-knowledge; Socrates ends up addressing three types of goods. I will speak of the first and third types before proceeding to speak of the second type, the ability to attain the parallel of self-knowledge, a sort of other-knowledge. For each of the

[14] He introduces it with "and isn't this also clear ... ?" (ἐκεῖνο δὲ οὐ φανερον, 26).

three sorts of benefits, Socrates gives two arguments: about the positive consequences of self-knowledge, and about the negative consequences of self-deception (τὸ ἐψεῦσθαι ἑαυτῶν). I start with the positive case.

Socrates recapitulates the two-fold process undergone by those who know themselves (οἱ εἰδότες ἑαυτούς): first, they know something general to all humans, namely what is useful for them (τά ἐπιτήδεια ἑαυτοῖς ἴσασι), and second, they discern (or "recognize completely") what they can do and cannot do (διαγιγνώσκουσιν ἅ τε δύνανται καὶ ἃ μή). This gives them resource and forethought:

> Doing what they understand (ἐπίστανται), they get what they need and they do well; and drawing back (ἀπεχόμενοι) from what they do not understand, they become error-free and get quite free of bad action. (4.2.26)

Knowing oneself, in giving one ownership over oneself, contributes to acting with control. One does only that which one is able to do. One adheres to that which is properly one's own. That which one "stands on," which is one's own, necessarily works in one's favor. Everything else one "stays away from."

Knowing what one *does* is part of knowing oneself. Those who know what they do become well reputed and honored (27). They gain this social credibility all around. Those similar to them can put them to use, presumably in some joint enterprise. Those who somehow miss the mark in their own affairs love them for their advice, their protection, and their support in their own hopes for success. Socrates is saying that self-knowledge has more than a constitutive function, and more than the benefit that comes from improving in what one wants to do. It yields the benefits the *kalos kagathos* seeks: public esteem, helpfulness to his peers, and *noblesse oblige* relative to one's hapless neighbors.[15]

By contrast, neither constitutive nor external goods accrue to those who do not know themselves (27). The situation for them stands exactly opposite to that of the self-knowers. Those who do not know

[15] At *Mem.* 1.6.9 Socrates tells Antiphon that he does not think there is any pleasure so great as "realizing that oneself (ἑαυτόν τε ἡγεῖσθαι) is becoming better and acquiring better friends." At 3.7.9, Socrates tells Charmides that he should focus not just on examining his friends but also himself (ἑαυτοὺς ἐξετάζειν); this will lead best to attending properly to the things of the city, whence both his friends and himself will benefit.

themselves are thoroughly deceived (διεψευσμένοι) about their own powers, about their needs, and about their actions. They miss the good and fall into the bad. Grasping what is actually bad causes them every kind of dishonor (29). Socrates puts the contrast starkly. But his summary of the personal and public consequences of self-knowledge and self-deception does not imply his lack of concern for the central function of self-knowledge. He simply adds to the gravity of the decision to own oneself or not.

Socrates makes a brief but puzzling remark when giving the second benefit of self-knowledge and the second cost of self-deception. He was just talking about the benefits consequent to those knowing themselves doing what they understand. "And on account of this too" (διὰ τοῦτο δὲ καί ...), Socrates says, "they may assess others" (τοὺς ἄλλους ἀνθρώπους δυνάμενοι δοκιμάζειν, 26). He adds yet another item: "and through their engagement (χρείας) with others, they get what is good and guard against the bad." Those lacking self-knowledge, as we have noted, are thoroughly deceived about their own powers; but they are also thoroughly deceived about others' powers and about human affairs more generally (καὶ τἆλλα ἀνθρώπινα πράγματα).

This reveals something crucial about self-knowledge. Knowing yourself is not simply a matter of introspection, remembering your past, or feeling and then cataloguing your desires. The reason is that I cannot introspect another person, or remember her past, or feel her desires. Self-knowledge is not even a behavioristic judgment based on appeal to external criteria. Perhaps we do learn about others by observing their behaviors; we see whether they keep acting whimsically or erratically or impetuously. But much of the material Socrates has attributed to self-knowledge could not be so viewed, for example the good for men or one's powers with respect to justice and goodness. So self-knowledge cannot rely solely on these two spectatorial modes, introspection and observation of behavior. There must be some third mode.

That third mode we see in Xenophon's depiction of Socrates' engagement with Euthydemus. Socrates simultaneously reflects on the good for humans, and determines Euthydemus' powers, in the course of having a characteristic sort of conversation with him. He has investigated the works of justice, and will go on to investigate the infallibly good elements of the happy life. Both he and Euthydemus have discovered unsuccessful views, and have perhaps gotten insight into the more promising directions a future search should take. Because

Socrates can attend to what he knows and does not know, he will not erroneously agree with Euthydemus' unsubstantiated views; this allows him to help Euthydemus identify the places where he has gone wrong. In principle, Euthydemus could do the same for Socrates.

Conversation bridges two people, and in doing so it helps bridge particularity and universality, both of which self-knowledge seeks. To know what generally holds true for people, it is useful to check your potentially partial and self-serving views against those of others. To know what holds true specifically for oneself, one discovers that one's perspective or status is not held or manifested universally. It is also helpful, for learning about one's private views, to have someone ask questions that circumvent one's liability to self-deception. The questioner in a conversation holds the answerer to account: to fail to answer a question is to fail to respect the rights of an interlocutor to have her questions answered. Some people find it easy to lie to themselves, on the thought that it hardly matters whether they do so, and is more pleasant than telling themselves the truth. But many of these people also feel the obligation to speak openly and honestly with those who care about them.

Xenophon's tale of Socrates' conversation with Euthydemus continually reinforces these facts. Without intellectual companionship, people cannot "understand how to judge what it is necessary to do" (κρίνειν οὐκ ἐπισταμένους ἃ δεῖ πράττειν, 4.1.4, cf. 5). Themistocles became great only through some association (διὰ συνουσίαν) with the wise (4.2.2). Others learn their skill only through long tutelage (4–7). Euthydemus, according to Socrates, can make no progress in wisdom simply by collecting and reading books. Xenophon makes clear that Euthydemus did not at first care for conversation: he only gradually grew comfortable with Socrates' way of talking (αὖτον ἑτοιμότερον ὑπομένοντα, 8). Once he does, he answers, and reveals his zeal: he admits to wanting to add to his literary collection (8), thinking Socrates approves of his collecting (9). But he also hesitates in saying what exactly he wants from it (διεσιώπησεν … σκοπῶν, 10). Once Socrates guesses, Euthydemus forcefully (σφοδρα γ') assents (11).

This process of excitement, uncertainty, Socratic input, and then recognition continues through the narrative. Going through the process enough times, Euthydemus finally realizes that his attitude toward himself and his prognosis for his future successes are unsupported by evidence. From his conversation with Socrates, he realizes he has not heretofore taken seriously enough his obligations to himself. This self-realization is essential. Though the process of coming to know himself is the same as the process of coming to know another person, he cannot own another person as he can own himself. Decisions to commit himself to certain courses of action – what self-ownership amounts to – come only from himself.

Knowing yourself as knowing the good

Euthydemus comes to be convinced about the value of knowing himself. He now wants to know how to begin investigating himself (ἐπισκοπεῖν ἑαυτόν); he says he "looks to you [Socrates] if you are willing to go through it" (30). Socrates answers with his own question, as I quoted above: "Well then … I suppose you know full well what sorts of things are good, what sorts bad?" (31). Socrates responds to Euthydemus' question about the start of investigating by seeing whether he knows something already. Were he interested in changing the topic, he could say so. Instead, since much of his discussion with Euthydemus has already concerned self-knowledge and the epistemic prerequisites to it – about knowing whether one knows about justice, the question of intentionality, the issue of slavery and self-mastery, ownership, and the benefits of self-knowledge – Socrates certainly appears to be continuing on this topic.

Euthydemus' answer to Socrates' question shows that the men maintain the topic of self-knowledge. Euthydemus says that if he *didn't* know what is good, he would be "worse than slaves are" (τῶν ἀνδραπόδων φαυλότερος, 31). This echoes exactly the point at 4.2.22 where he admitted that the ignorance of goodness, along with the ignorance of justice and beauty, would be slavish, and that thinking one does know what one does not know would be a failure of self-knowledge. Obviously, then, since knowledge of the good is part of self-knowledge, Socrates' question at 4.2.31 is an answer to Euthydemus' methodological question.

Euthydemus, buoyed by some confidence in this topic, asserts that good things include health, the causes of health, wisdom, and the sources of happiness (31–34). Unfortunately, as with his views of just things, under the pressure of examination he can maintain none of these views. Socrates diagnoses Euthydemus' failure not by appealing to Euthydemus' false beliefs but by observing his epistemic proclivities: "perhaps the reason you did not investigate (ἔσκεψαι) these things is that you intensely believed (τὸ σφόδρα πιστεύειν) that you knew them" (36). Getting self-knowledge requires vigilance about one's habits of self-deception, especially in respect to those fundamental issues that are also the hardest to make sense of. This most fundamental issue is the good for humans. Euthydemus neither knows what is good for humans – and himself – nor, until this point, did he know that he lacked knowledge of those goods. With neither sort of knowledge, he would be unable to act well or revise actions that may be found to have skewed from the proper path. Pursuing self-knowledge appears to include the pursuit of both sorts of knowledge. It may even include a pursuit of further matters: epistemic self-maintenance, for example, and attention to the potentially blinding intensity of one's beliefs. Once Euthydemus has been shown up repeatedly, "he was down on himself, considering himself to be in fact a slave" (καταφρονήσας ἑαυτοῦ καὶ νομίσας τῷ ὄντι ἀνδράποδον εἶναι, 39).

Not only is knowing about goodness part of self-knowledge, mistakenly thinking you know about goodness is a typical failure of self-knowledge. At 4.2.36, Socrates chastises Euthydemus for having been so confident that his beliefs about goodness were instances of knowledge that he never even thought about them. Socrates continues in this section to discover that Euthydemus also fails to know what it is to be a leader of people – the position in society he wishes to occupy – because he does not even know who the people are. He does not know himself *qua* statesman. Put in another way, he does not know the good of the people, or his own good, because he does not know who they are, or who he himself is.

Socratic indirection

I have argued that nearly all of *Mem.* 4.2 concerns self-knowledge, an argument necessary due to the indirect means Socrates uses to make his points. Indeed, when Euthydemus explicitly asks Socrates how to start knowing himself, Socrates does not give him a direct answer. Socrates instead practices indirection, as he did at the beginning of the dialogue.

Were self-knowledge simply the inventorying of one's strengths and weaknesses, we could not easily explain Socrates' omission of a direct statement about the nature of self-knowledge, an omission apparently relatively rare in Xenophon's treatment of his teacher.[16] There would seem to be no harm in helping a person come to know in what dimensions of life he was capable and in what feeble. But in fact teaching a route to self-knowledge could have its risks. Socrates may worry about the following situation: suppose Euthydemus believes that upon following some rules he will have reached his goal. As soon as he learns the guidelines for knowing himself, he may believe he has gone much of the way to attaining self-knowledge. Socrates has reasons for such a worry. He has already diagnosed Euthydemus' susceptibility to premature self-confidence. Euthydemus infers his own wisdom from his possession of books containing the wisdom of Sages. His inference is invalid; Socrates quickly gets him to see that he lacks that wisdom. If Euthydemus leaves the conversation thinking that Socrates told him explicitly how to get self-knowledge, he may believe that as soon as he does what Socrates suggests, he can return to his bid for political leadership. He may observe his strengths and weaknesses, and, on the basis of his putative discoveries, begin to act. He may never think about what Xenophon shows him eventually to conclude (given that Socrates has not propounded an explicit route to self-knowledge): that he is ignorant about goodness (35), about happiness and what to pray for (36), and about whom he intends to rule (36–39); that he is worthless (φαυλότης), ought to be silent, and is almost completely ignorant (39); that he deserves his own scorn and identification with slaves (39); and that he would be respected by nobody unless he were to associate constantly with Socrates (40). If seeking self-knowledge is a commitment to a certain continued self-improving investigation, rather than a report of one's current status (the "knowing one's powers" view), then believing at any time that one had achieved self-knowledge would be self-defeating.

Conclusion

Knowing yourself, for Xenophon's Socrates, includes knowing your powers. This means knowing what you can do. But what you can do

[16] See Morrison 1994 on Socrates' wonted directness. See *Mem.* 4.2.40 on Socrates' later openness with Euthydemus: "And Socrates, since he recognized how things were with him, confounded him minimally, and expounded most simply and clearly what he thought it necessary to know and best to pursue."

includes what you know about. If you do not know about goodness, justice, and beauty, you cannot use these as reasons to act. You instead follow your impulses, suspicions, and self-images as guides for action. These are not really up to you; they are whatever you have absorbed. And so you are enslaved to them. Self-mastery amounts to acting on the basis of what you reflectively believe to be best. Such reflection requires self-knowledge and acknowledgment. Acting on the basis of good reasons can save a person from the risks that error, confusion, and strident self-confidence can lead him to. Thus self-knowledge is a matter of life and death, or at least of good life and bad life.

7 Conclusion: challenges and a defense

The unambiguous benefits of self-knowledge in the *Rival Lovers*

The Platonic *Rival Lovers* depicts Socrates querying a partisan of "philosophy" for a definition of the discipline, and ends with an argument about the benefits of self-knowledge.[1] This argument turns out to be a demonstration that the ability to improve oneself – the core condition of being benefited – is the same as the ability to know oneself. With it Socrates advances the most condensed and direct argument about the value of self-knowledge in the Socratic literature. Socrates treats the acquisition of self-knowledge as constitutive of the development of leadership, self-mastery, morality, and full human usefulness. At the same time, Socrates presents this vision of self-knowledge without its attendant difficulties or paradoxes. He does not explicitly deny the diverse perplexities we have canvassed over the course of this book. But his concern to diagnose the partisan's failure to understand "philosophy," not self-knowledge as such, gives him reason to pass the difficulties over. As a result, this dialogue provides a wholly optimistic synopsis of Socrates' self-constitution theory of self-knowledge.

The *Rival Lovers* opens with Socrates recounting his visit to a school where he sees two teenagers discussing theoretical astronomy with particular zeal (132a1–b3). Socrates approaches their two older lovers and inquires about the value (μέγα τι καὶ καλόν) of their discussion. One scorns it, calling it "prattling and babbling philosophizing" (ἀδολεσχοῦσι … καὶ φλυαροῦσι φιλοσοφοῦντες, 132b8–10). For him, the youths' discussion counts as philosophy, and while he does not say whether he would judge all philosophy worthless, he certainly judges this instance worthless. The other lover interjects. He does not say whether the youths' discussion counts as philosophy, but he takes

[1] On this dialogue, see Evans 1976; Bruell 1987; Peterson 2011: 201–205.

issue with the first lover's judgment of philosophy. He, the second lover, esteems philosophy. He so prizes it that he would doubt the humanity of himself or anyone else if he or they thought philosophy shameful (133b1–6). Socrates asks him the reasons for his great estimation of philosophy. The young man describes philosophy as "admirable" (καλόν); but each time Socrates asks how philosophy is also good (ἀγαθόν) – useful and beneficial – he fails to give a defensible answer. Eventually Socrates decides to help the second lover out, sketching the nature of a practice that would yield something good, not just accumulate hollow honor, and this practice turns out to be knowing oneself.

This sketch proceeds in a way familiar from the *Alcibiades* 133c18–134e6. Socrates works through a sequence of equivalent and entailed sets of skills and moral statuses. He begins with the non-human case. Those who know how to discipline (κολάζειν) horses, dogs, and all other animals turn out to be the same as the people who know how to make those animals better (βελτίσους ποιοῦσιν, 137c1). Thus discipline and improvement, they infer, depend on one and the same skill. Socrates then notes a precondition of this double ability: one disciplines and improves only bad things, and so the skill of discipline and improvement must also be able to distinguish (διαγιγνώσκουσαν) between good and bad instances of a type (137d2). Now he brings the argument from the level of animal husbandry to something closer to home. Just as the coincidence of discipline, improvement, and distinction holds in the case of animals, it holds in the case of humans; and just as it holds for many humans at once, it holds for humans considered individually. In the civic context, we call this skill "legal knowledge" (δικαστική, 137d12) or "justice" (δικαιοσύνη, 137d14). Lacking justice – the triple skill of discipline, improvement, and distinction – would mean lacking knowledge of other people's goodness or badness. Since what holds for many also holds for one, it would mean lacking knowledge of one's own goodness or badness. But being ignorant of one's goodness is being ignorant of oneself (τὸ αὑτον ἀγνοεῖν), and this is failing to be *sôphrôn* (μὴ σωφρονεῖν, 138a5). Consequently, knowing oneself means being *sôphrôn* (τὸ ἑαυτὸν ἄρα γιγνώσκειν ἐστὶ σωφρονεῖν, 138a7). Thus the Delphic inscription, which charges us to know ourselves, charges us to practice *sôphrosunê* and justice (τὸ ἐν Δελφοῖς γράμμα παρακελεύεται, σωφροσύνην ἀσκεῖν καὶ δικαιοσύνην, 138a9–10). In summary, knowing correct discipline coincides with justice, distinguishing one's own and others' goodness (διαγιγνώσκειν καὶ ἑαυτὸν καὶ ἄλλους, 138b2), and *sôphrosunê*. Socrates concludes this sequence of permutations by saying that every type of leader – king, tyrant, statesman, householder, and master – must be a person of *sôphrosunê* and justice (138c7–10). All this goes to show, Socrates says, that the philosopher as defined and praised by the second lover – and not shown to be a leader in any way – proves useless.

Socrates does not explicitly define philosophy as a practice of self-knowledge; but he suggests that one way for philosophy to be useful would be for it to be a practice of self-knowledge. After all, he argues that a practice counts as good when it benefits individuals. But benefiting a person depends on judging that person's level of wellbeing and then working to improve it. These abilities apply impartially to oneself as much as to others. So one's employment of a beneficial practice involves judging one's own level of wellbeing and then working to improve it. This judgment and work are self-knowledge, and they amount to striving, on the basis of adequate judgment, to benefit oneself. At this point Socrates treats his claim as a sensible gloss of the Delphic precept; the second lover accepts this gloss. The precept does not direct humans to quiver before gods or to recognize their mortality. Nor does it direct them to know the structure of their soul or their position in the cosmos. Of course, it does not rule out doing any of these if they would help a person evaluate himself and then improve himself. But those other candidate responses are only contingently demanded, to the extent they contribute to increased justice and *sôphrosunê*. (Finding out whether they do so contribute seems an important task of philosophy, but this dialogue does not get into the matter.) The language of Delphic self-knowledge is the language of civic and personal virtue, not of epistemology and metaphysics.

As we have seen often, and most recently in Chapter 6 on Xenophon, self-knowledge is effected with a double attention, to the ideal and to the actual. Distinguishing between good and bad requires knowing what is good (ideally), and knowing how to identify an (actual) instance of something good. It is also effected with a double judgment, of the theoretical and of the practical. Self-knowledge coincides both with discerning (theoretically) one's level of goodness and with the (practical) application of the skill of discipline or improvement. And again, as we saw throughout the Socratic literature, and most recently in *Memorabilia* 4.2, self-knowledge brings one to the state of composure, autonomy, and efficacy denoted by justice and *sôphrosunê* and practically deployed in statesmanship and other positions of mastery over persons.

The fact that Socrates brings up the Delphic precept in the midst of his argument surely has some rhetorical function. It relates an increasingly abstruse demonstration to something familiar, a piece of culturally inherited wisdom. Socrates does not map out a detailed route to self-knowledge, or warn of its obstacles, or distinguish it from alternative goals. He does not treat knowledge's peculiar epistemic status or selfhood's unifying and normative features. All the same, the reference to the *gnôthi sauton* appears also to have a dialectical function. Socrates does not say that the language of self-knowledge should be abandoned in favor of the clearer ideas of justice and *sôphrosunê*, or the even more everyday concepts of discipline and mastery. He must see some residual analytic value in the concept of knowing oneself. Perhaps its inverse, ignorance of oneself, is especially trenchant; perhaps the notions of justice and *sôphrosunê* become too impersonal too quickly; perhaps we must continually reinforce the sense of responsibility to which the concept of self-knowledge refers. Whatever it is, the Delphic precept remains a most productive way to think about our becoming good and useful adults.

Overturning the *gnôthi sauton* in the *Hipparchus*

The cardinal value of the *gnôthi sauton* for thinking about ourselves does have a critic in the Classical Greek period. This we find in the Platonic *Hipparchus*, another short dialogue with doubtful authorship but likely with an Academic and fourth-century provenance. In this dialogue of conversation surrounding a long central digression, Socrates speaks of the Delphic *gnôthi sauton* expressly in its position as one wise saying among many sayings striving for popularity.

The dialogue begins with Socrates undermining his friend's distaste for the *philokerdês*, the profit-seeker. Since profit is beneficial, they come to agree, the *philokerdês* actually desires the good, and deserves esteem, not opprobrium. The friend, feeling the basis of his moral censure undermined, accuses Socrates of deceptive argumentation (228a8–10). Socrates denounces the accusation, saying that, were he really to be deceiving his friend, "I would act badly, disobeying a good and wise man" (228b1–2). This wise man is Hipparchus, the sixth-century Athenian tyrant. Socrates digresses for a page and a half to justify this attribution of wisdom, and it is here that Socrates mentions the *gnôthi sauton*.

The first part of the digression catalogues Hipparchus' early accomplishments. This "fellow citizen" was the wisest of his brothers (228b4–6). Among the "many and fine works in which he displayed his wisdom," Socrates mentions his introduction of Homer's works and their rhapsodic performance into Athens, and his enticement of the renowned poets Anacreon and Simonides to the city (228b6–c3).[2] "These things he did desiring to educate his citizens, in order to rule over the best possible people, not thinking it appropriate to begrudge wisdom to anybody, given he was a gentleman" (228c4–6). Socrates says that Hipparchus succeeded both in educating the city-dwellers and in making them marvel at his wisdom.

The second part of the digression turns from his education of city-dwellers to the enticement-to-education of those living in the countryside. Hipparchus set up herms – way-point statues – along the routes between rural settlements and the metropolis. Next to the inscription of their location, Hipparchus inscribed maxims encapsulating his wisdom. These were guidelines that he learned from others and discovered by himself, and that he put in the form of poems and exempla. They included "walk with justice in mind" (στεῖχε δίκαια φρονῶν) and "do not deceive a friend" (μὴ φίλον ἐξαπάτα), the latter of which brought the digression to Socrates' mind. Hipparchus set down these sayings for two reasons. First, he did not want his citizens to marvel at (θαυμάζοιεν) the wisdom of the Delphic inscriptions *gnôthi sauton*, *mêden agan*, and similar sayings. He wanted them to judge Hipparchus' sayings as more wise (ῥήματα μᾶλλον σοφὰ ἡγοῖντο). Second, by continually reading these sayings on their travels, the rural folk would develop a taste for his wisdom and come out of the countryside to get educated in the rest of his wisdom (228d1–e7).

Shortly thereafter, Socrates finishes his digression with a sordid account of the envy for wisdom, eventuating in Hipparchus' assassination.

[2] The historical record suggests the poets did come during Hipparchus' rule. There was even a tradition that Anacreon inscribed some herms (*Palatine Anthology* vi 138, 143, 346), but this is doubtful, per Trypanis 1951 and Kantzios 2005. Johnston and Mulroy 2004 describe the ethical implications of herms in the Simonidean context; Ford 2002: 96–112, argues that Simonides was a dissenter about the value of self-memorializing stone inscriptions.

Socrates' digression proves, however, to have little ameliorative effect; his friend says that he still believes Socrates is deceiving him. The two interlocutors backtrack in their argument about profit-seeking. After more circling around, they return to the agreement that the profitable is good (232a3–4).[3]

The course of the refutation reflects, in small form, much of Socratic literature. A once dubious concept, undergoing Socrates' scrutiny, comes out seeming the watchword for the whole Socratic enterprise. Out of "avarice" comes the total "love of the good." The dynamic and meaning of this transformation would repay deep study.[4] The digression in particular is baffling. Its relevance appears to be nothing more than an authoritative source of "do not deceive a friend," and yet the tale goes on much longer than such legitimation would require or even free association would occasion. Its reinterpretation of Hipparchus' reign as enlightened would strike any Athenian as severely heterodox. The otherwise glowing affirmation of Hipparchus becomes unstable when Socrates says the tyrant aimed to subvert the influence of the Delphic wisdom, wisdom throughout Greek literature until this point being treated as unimpeachable, as we have seen.

A consequence of this baffling digression is, among those who strive to take the dialogue seriously, a vast array of interpretations. Allan Bloom takes the tale of Hipparchus to presage the tale of Socrates. Both competed with the Delphic oracle, both died from the envy of democrats who claimed they corrupted their youth, both appeared to pursue the good immoderately, both were connected to herms, both may have taught that the wise should rule. Indeed, Hipparchus' critique of the Delphic wisdom's "know yourself" is a critique of "vulgar moderation," which echoes Socrates' criticism of his friend's distaste for so-called profiteering.[5] To Dale Evans, by contrast, the dialogue gives an ironic, hyperbolic

[3] Zuckert 2009: 26, claims that the refutations "dramatize the way in which Socrates challenges the basis and content of traditional morality."

[4] Guthrie 1986: 389, disagrees, saying "the dialogue is of no great importance," though he observes the paradoxical fact that *Rep.* 9, by contrast, attributes *philokerdês* to the lowest part of the soul, and to the oligarchic character. Thesleff 1982: 375, likewise, does not take the dialogue very seriously, but still waves at an explanation: "the *Republic* is ... implied in [*Hipparchus*'] allusions, and ... the central legend has something (I am not sure what exactly) to do with the murder of Dion in 354 BC."

[5] Bloom 1987: 32–52, who even argues that since Socrates says he is Hipparchus' disciple, Hipparchus must be a *philosophos*, and thus this dialogue is an

defense of the liberal democratic political order. Hipparchus offers wisdom to all; but, in denying the importance of the Delphic injunctions, he has denied the importance of temperance and moderation. Thus society becomes a competition of strength; whoever desires more, and can satisfy his desires, wins. Socrates, for his part, in embellishing his speech, acts like a deceiving sophist, concerned only with the power of his words, greedy for victory.[6] In the same vein, Martin Plax conjectures that Socrates' friend has arrived newly from the countryside and feels that he has been deceived by some *philokerdês* man in the market. Hipparchus introduced the taste for luxury, and thus commercial necessity, and, in turn, overweening desires for profit. "Know thyself" and "nothing in excess" are, for Hipparchus, outdated aristocratic virtues; his new maxims speak to the needs felt by contemporary travelers and traders.[7] A last reader, David Mulroy, takes the *gnôthi sauton* even more seriously. Hipparchus reveals his self-love and immoderation, as he rejects the divine commandment to "be objective about yourself" and avoid "self-infatuation."[8] His herms are "antithetical to self-knowledge" because they are written and *appear* wise rather than engage in dialogical education. The slogan "do not deceive a friend" says too much, opening itself to refutation *à la Republic* Book 1: does it imply that we should deceive *non*-friends?

Each interpretation of the dialogue adduces the *gnôthi sauton* as evidence. This short saying takes on crucial significance. Yet whence the variety in interpretations of the dialogue? It comes, to a significant extent, from the inconsistent variety of interpretations of the precept itself. It is taken to encourage, in turn, "vulgar moderation," "temperance," aristocratic isolation, and objectivity or modesty about

exhortation to philosophy. Zuckert 2009: 29, puts the point more sharply: the dialogue "culminates in an erasure of the distinction between tyrannical and other forms of rule."

6 Evans 1976: 31–61. Evans assumes without argument that *gnôthi sauton* means "temperance." He reads this dialogue as a companion piece to *Minos*, as does Bruell 1999: 3–6; Zuckert 2009: 26–27.

7 Plax 2005. Zuckert 2009: 243n54, claims that Hipparchus understands the *gnôthi sauton* not as an outdated virtue but as a slogan of "popular resistance."

8 Mulroy 2007. Tipton 1998: 210–213 and Samad 2010: 32–33, also hold that Hipparchus is self-deceiving; the latter article argues that the dialogue is about our natural and hard-to-shake conviction that the unlimited love of gain is bad, and reveals this in part through Socrates' use of many invalid arguments. Davis 2006: 556, agrees that Socrates uses invalid arguments, showing that the friend has "moral smugness and intellectual inattentiveness."

oneself. Readers of the *Hipparchus* have not generally justified their interpretation of the saying, despite its large influence on their reading of the dialogue. There are other difficulties with these interpretations. For example, Socrates' so-called "competition with the Delphic oracle," as Bloom puts it, hardly puts him in league with Hipparchus. Socrates' announced bewilderment at hearing the Oracle's proclamation that nobody was wiser than him led him to give a sympathetic interpretation of it, with the outcome that Socrates, as he claims, came to know himself better and to feel impelled to help others know themselves. Hipparchus, by contrast, tried to preempt the Delphic inscription, which, anyway, as we saw in the Introduction, might not always have been the *basso continuo* of the Oracle. On the other hand, when Mulroy advances a rather different argument and calls Hipparchus' precepts "antithetical to self-knowledge," he thereby neuters the *gnôthi sauton* as simply "written."[9] Any proper reading of this dialogue needs, first, a well-grounded reading of the precept; with luck, this book may contribute to that work.

But the purpose of discussing the *Hipparchus* is not to indicate that the dialogue could be better read after having read this book. My real point is simply that the dialogue's Hipparchus has in fact disputed the value of the *gnôthi sauton*. Granted, the dispute could be merely agonistic; the *gnôthi sauton* is the first saying in a canon of Sagely wisdom, and so Hipparchus' victory would launch him into the premier position in Greek intellectual life. But the dispute could also be substantive. Hipparchus could have thought that his precepts had more urgency, impact, or concreteness. (The authors of the dozens of Sage precepts dedicated to Delphi may have thought the same thing.) Both of the Hipparchan inscriptions that Socrates cites – "walk with justice in mind" (στεῖχε δίκαια φρονῶν) and "do not deceive a friend" (μὴ φίλον ἐξαπάτα) – pertain to travelers, trade, and comity among people. They aim to construct a trusting society. Their advice is pretty easy. They are not totally self-explanatory, of course: the scope of justice is debatable, as is the rigor with which one is to bear it in mind; likewise, who counts as a friend, and whether silence can be a form of deception, are open to question. And this is as it should be, if Hipparchus wants his precepts to be propaedeutic, encouraging a fuller in-town education. For all their open-endedness, however, they direct their readers

[9] Mulroy 2007: 128.

more immediately to certain actions than the much less immediately informative "know yourself" or "nothing in excess." Thus to the extent Hipparchus actually has a moralizing mission, as his scheduling of Homeric recitation, installation of poets, and showing off of wisdom suggests, he really thinks his citizens would benefit from these precepts explicitly concerned with justice and friendship. In any event, his citizens would more readily appreciate these precepts and their value, and therefore acknowledge Hipparchus' wisdom and leadership.

The modern Hipparchan attitude toward "knowing yourself"

Diffidence among contemporary philosophers about Socratic self-knowledge, or self-knowledge in the ancient period in general, has some of its source in a feeling of discontinuity of research topic. For those in analytic epistemology, the topic "self-knowledge" means explaining the relationship between knowledge of external objects and knowledge of internal conscious states, where the latter is self-knowledge. These scholars recognize that Socrates does not have this question in mind whenever he speaks of the Delphic inscription. For those in the philosophy of action, issues of agency, rational reflection, and personal maturation have generated such an extensive and elaborated bibliography, especially since the British moralists and Kant, that the Socratic literature looks so technically naïve as not even to be addressing the same definitional or analytic contentions.[10]

By contrast, we could imagine a Hipparchan attitude toward "knowing yourself": that the precept *gnôthi sauton* is sound enough advice but sadly not the best available. The interpretative variety on display among commentators on the *Hipparchus*, and even more broadly among commentators on the Socratic literature, shows that the precept may be simply too indeterminate: too indeterminate for shared discussion about it, for useful distinctions between it and other concepts, for tracing the history of its philosophical deployment and analysis. One man's conceptual fecundity – the breadth of provocative topics evoked by talk of selfhood, knowledge, and reflexivity – is another man's

[10] For a concise history of these issues and the philosophical complexity in the philosophy of action predating Kant, see Darwall 1995: 2–22; Korsgaard 1999 and 2009 are exceptions to the trend of disregarding the ancient material.

conceptual incoherence – a scattershot of ideas linked at best by free association, at worse by historical happenstance. Granted, Greek lore did vaunt the *gnôthi sauton*, and somebody at Delphi did inscribe the precept somewhere there, and some of the most profound literature and philosophy did dwell on its interpretation. Even combining these facts, however, they provide no argument for the value of our own dwelling on them. Even more poignantly, they provide no argument for believing that the ancients themselves ultimately judged it useful to explicate the charge to "know yourself." Aristotle does not analyze the *gnôthi sauton* in his extant works, and as we saw, the Epicureans, Colotes included, had their suspicions about Socrates' proclaimed obedience to it. Even Plato's greatest works, including the *Apology*, the *Symposium*, the *Gorgias*, and the *Republic*, do not cite the *gnôthi sauton*, even if they do broach topics related to self-knowledge. (They could hardly avoid broaching such topics, given self-knowledge's tentacular reach.) They discuss instead the structure of the soul, the principles of psychic motivation, the range of epistemic states, the ideal educational curriculum and institutions, the relation between man and gods, the pull of love, and the importance of critical conversation. This would seem enough; a discussion of the formulation of the *gnôthi sauton* could be, at most, a matter of historical curiosity.

So part of the Hipparchan attitude is that thinking about "knowing yourself" simply slows down thinking about more important topics. These topics may be external to self-knowledge but closely related. They may also be internal – closer specification of the part of the cluster-concept "self" to be known. One might want to know one's beliefs, either what they are, their truth, their source, their relations, or anything else about them. The same could go for one's desires, one's abilities, or one's moods and proclivities. Alternatively, one might want to know that one exists, preparing one to have Marcus Aurelian thoughts about the significance or insignificance of that fact. One might even, perhaps anachronistically, dwell on the outfitting of humankind with self-consciousness or self-awareness, a kind of internalization of the objects of attention. Presumably any of these desires for knowledge would open their own warrens of difficulty, undefined terms, and interrelated programs of research. But they would at least focus on certain of them and send others to the background.

One charm of the study of self-knowledge is its capaciousness, thanks to its surprising connections to becoming good in a human way, pursuing truth through the self-audited use of reason, and making sense of the possibility of norms in a natural world. But this is like saying a charm of one's computer is the access it provides to library collections worldwide. In one sense the computer should impress us; but in another sense the computer is undeserving of our praise; it is the libraries that have earned it. Just so, the questions of human nature – the questions of all of philosophy – are what really interest us, and the *gnôthi sauton* has served us ably if it entices us into those questions, but it has served us in the way an avenue serves us: it is not itself the destination.

An alternative problem arises if self-knowledge reduces to knowledge as such, in the way that self-mastery may reduce to mastery, or self-consciousness to consciousness. It is an interesting conclusion, one whose argument rewards study. The result, however, eliminates any meaningful distinct concept of self-knowledge, and resolves all its problems to the basic problems of epistemology.

There are, finally, two other related Hipparchan worries about "knowing yourself." One is that the assumption of a "selfhood" to be found or posited misleads us into thinking that human life depends on, or seeks the goal of, an essential unity. The other is that the emphasis on self-knowledge and the ideas of rational reflection blind us to the importance of the hidden and irrational aspects of ourselves, the mysterious upwellings perhaps responsible for creativity, idiosyncrasy, motivation, and in general our characteristic actions.[11] Together, these worries are about the utopian ideal of a transparent and coherent personhood activated by true judgments about the world and one's place in it, worries about the validity of the hope for such a life.

Socrates' Hipparchus promulgated new precepts to satisfy his pride, but perhaps also because he thought he had good reason to counter the intellectual gravity ascribed to the *gnôthi sauton*. He did not propose to tear the inscription down, or to proscribe its discussion. He seems instead to have thought that his suggestions were simply better for the Athenians. So too skeptics about the study of self knowledge: they would consider it an interesting, even intriguing pastime, but not the core concern for philosophy as we practice it.

[11] Both Wollheim 1984 and Nussbaum 2001 give putatively psychoanalytic accounts that suggest the importance of recognizing the unconscious.

An apology for Socratic self-knowledge

Philosophy for most of us advances as a series of critical responses and piecemeal proposals to other writers of philosophy. This conversationality, both adversatively and cooperatively engaged, makes philosophy enjoyable, pedagogical, and pertinent. It also constrains the world of topics largely to those active among current practitioners of philosophy. The advantage is a shared familiarity with the argumentative terrain. The disadvantage is that only a historically defined subset of all possible conceptual arrangements gets close attention during any one period. The value of the history of philosophy comes in part in its ability to reintroduce tested ideas into current debates where those ideas might again be fertile.

The criticisms of Socratic self-knowledge adumbrated above – or rather, the possible reasons for hesitating to commit oneself to its study – strike me as largely fair. The concept does not make for a perspicuous research program. It is at once too misleading, too complicated, and too large. Some of my skepticism probably comes out of a personal preference for incremental thinking over large-scale system-building and brute-force reassessment of the central human problems. I am not sure whether this skepticism also comes from a Socratic source, and a feeling that a lot of our time should go toward getting clearer about what we are already trying to say. In any event, I sympathize – if not with many of the particular questions contemporary philosophy of self-knowledge takes on, then at least with the desire to delineate the proper sub-topics of this overwhelming topic.

At the same time, I have written this book in the belief that the Sage precept "Know yourself" addresses all of us with as much urgency, and cogency, as ever. I judge Socrates' life to exemplify the sensitive and serious response to the charge. Socrates presents the *gnôthi sauton* as querying the reader or listener about his degree of being grown up. He observes that adulthood, considered as an honorific, means being able to take responsibility for one's actions, beliefs, and expressed desires. Socrates wants to understand the meaning of that responsibility.

I have my doubts that Socrates heard "know yourself" primarily as "recognize your mortality," though he certainly talked about mortality, as Plato depicts him doing in the *Apology*, *Gorgias*, *Phaedo*, and *Republic*. I also doubt that he heard it primarily as "avoid hubris," though he may have thought more about what this means than just about anybody. I do not really know what it would mean for him to hear it as "become like god." But I have some confidence that the concept "self-knowledge" had particular interest to Socrates, who lauded the soul in contrast to other aspects of oneself, and lauded knowledge in contrast to mere first or unquestioned impressions. Captivated as he was by the power of the soul and of knowledge, the idea of knowing one's soul, it seems to me, would have prompted just the right considerations for a man who said that we should strive to avoid wrong-doing and those obstacles to becoming good. In the *Cratylus*, Socrates says "I think it's necessary to keep reinvestigating whatever I say, since self-deception is the worst thing of all" (428d3). Knowing oneself advances that investigation; how so, and why, has been the topic of this book.

Bibliography

Agard, Walter, 1966. "Boreas at Athens." *Classical Journal* 61: 241–246

Allen, R.E., 1962. "Note on *Alcibiades I*, 129B 1." *American Journal of Philology* 83: 187–190

Ambury, James, 2013. "The Failed Seduction: Alcibiades, Socrates, and the Epithumetic Comportment." *Epoché* 17: 257–274

Anastasiadis, V.I., 2004. "Idealized ΣΧΟΛΗ and Disdain for Work: Aspects of Philosophy and Politics in Ancient Democracy." *Classical Quarterly* 54: 58–79

Annas, Julia, 1985. "Self-Knowledge in Early Plato." In Dominic O'Meara (ed.), *Platonic Investigations*. Washington DC: Catholic University of America Press, pp. 121–138

1999. *Platonic Ethics, Old and New*. Ithaca, NY: Cornell University Press

Austin, Emily, 2012. "Fools and Malicious Pleasure in Plato's *Philebus*." *History of Philosophy Quarterly* 29: 125–139

Avnon, D., 1995. "'Know Thyself': Socratic Companionship and Platonic Community." *Political Theory* 23: 304–329

Babbitt, Frank Cole, 1936. *Plutarch's Moralia*. Volume V. Loeb Classical Library. Cambridge, MA: Harvard University Press

Ballard, Edward, 1965. *Socratic Ignorance: An Essay on Platonic Self-Knowledge*. The Hague: Martinus Nijhoff

Barnes, Jonathan, 1982. *The Presocratic Philosophers*. Rev. edn. London: Routledge and Kegan Paul

Bartsch, Shadi, 2006. *The Mirror of the Self: Sexuality, Self-Knowledge, and the Gaze in the Early Roman Empire*. University of Chicago Press

Belfiore, Elizabeth, 2006. "Dancing with the Gods: The Myth of the Chariot in Plato's *Phaedrus*." *American Journal of Philology* 127: 185–217

2012. *Socrates' Daimonic Art: Love for Wisdom in Four Platonic Dialogues*. Cambridge University Press

Benardete, Seth, 1986. "On Interpreting Plato's *Charmides*." *Graduate Faculty Philosophy Journal* 11: 9–36

1993. *The Tragedy and Comedy of Life: Plato's Philebus*. University of Chicago Press

Benson, Hugh, 2003. "A Note on Socratic Self-Knowledge in the *Charmides*." *Ancient Philosophy* 23: 31–47

Bilgrami, Akeel, 2006. *Self-Knowledge and Resentment*. Cambridge, MA: Harvard University Press

Blakely, Sandra, 2009. "Herodoros (31)." *Brill's New Jacoby*, Editor-in-Chief Ian Worthington. Brill Online. http://brillonline.nl/brill-s-new-jacoby/herodorus-31-a31.

Bloom, Allan, 1987. "On the *Hipparchus*." In Thomas Pangle (ed.), *The Roots of Political Philosophy: Ten Forgotten Socratic Dialogues*. Ithaca, NY: Cornell University Press, pp. 32–52

Bluck, R.S., 1953. "The Origin of the *Greater Alcibiades*." *Classical Quarterly* 3: 46–52

Bollack, Jean, and Heinz Wismann (eds.), 1972. *Héraclite ou la séparation*. Paris: Les Editions de Minuit

Bowden, Hugh, 2005. *Classical Athens and the Delphic Oracle: Divination and Democracy*. Cambridge University Press

Bradley, Marshell, 2012. *Who Is Phaedrus? Keys to Plato's Dyad Masterpiece*. Eugene, OR: Pickwick

Bratman, Michael, 2000. "Reflection, Planning, and Temporally Extended Agency." *Philosophical Review* 109: 35–61

Broad, William, 2007. *The Oracle: Ancient Delphi and the Science behind Its Lost Secrets*. New York: Penguin Books

Brouwer, Rene, 2008. "Hellenistic Philosophers on *Phaedrus* 229b–30a." *Cambridge Classical Journal* 54: 30–48

Bruell, Christopher, 1977. "Socratic Politics and Self-Knowledge: An Interpretation of Plato's *Charmides*." *Interpretation* 6: 141–203

1987. "On the Original Meaning of Political Philosophy: An Interpretation of Plato's Lovers." In Thomas Pangle (ed.), *The Roots of Political Philosophy: Ten Forgotten Socratic Dialogues*. Ithaca, NY: Cornell University Press, pp. 91–110

1999. *On the Socratic Education: An Introduction to the Shorter Platonic Dialogues*. Lanham, MD: Rowman & Littlefield

Bryan, Jenny, 2012. *Likeness and Likelihood in the Presocratics and Plato*. Cambridge University Press

Burger, Ronna, 1980. *Plato's Phaedrus: A Defense of a Philosophic Art of Writing*. Tuscaloosa: University of Alabama Press

1981. "Belief, Knowledge, and Socratic Knowledge of Ignorance." *Tulane Studies in Philosophy* 30: 1–23

Burkert, Walter, 1981. *Greek Religion*. Cambridge, MA: Harvard University Press

Burnet, John, 1903. *Platonis Opera*. Volume III. Oxford Classical Texts. Oxford: Clarendon Press

Burnyeat, Myles, 1977. "Socratic Midwifery, Platonic Inspiration." *Bulletin of the Institute of Classical Studies* 24: 7–16

2003. "*Apology* 30b2–4: Socrates, Money, and the Grammar of ΓΙΓΝΕΣΘΑΙ." *Journal of Hellenic Studies* 123: 1–25

Bywater, Ingram (ed.), 1877. *Heracliti Ephesii Reliquiae*. Oxford University Press

Calder, William, 1961. "Socrates at Amphipolis (*Ap.* 28e)." *Phronesis* 6: 83–85

Carlini, Antonio (ed.), 1964. *Platone: Alcibiades, Alcibiades Secondo, Ipparco, Rivali*. Turin: Boringhieri

Carone, Gabriella, 1998. "Socrates' Human Wisdom and *Sôphrosunê* in *Charmides* 164cff." *Ancient Philosophy* 18: 267–286

Cassam, Quassim, 2014. *Self-Knowledge for Humans*. Oxford University Press

Caston, Victor, 2002. "Aristotle on Consciousness." *Mind* 111: 751–815

Chen, Chung-Hwan, 1978. "On Plato's *Charmides* 165c4–175d5." *Apeiron* 12: 13–28

Childs, William, 1993. "Herodotos, Archaic Chronology, and the Temple of Apollo at Delphi." *Jahrbuch des Deutschen Archäologischen Instituts* 108: 399–441

Chroust, Anton-Hermann, 1975. "A Tentative Outline for a Possible Reconstruction of Aristotle's Lost Dialogue *On Philosophy*." *L'Antiquité Classique* 44:2: 553–569

Clay, Diskin, 1979. "Socrates' Prayer to Pan." In G.W. Bowersock, W. Burkert, and M.C.J. Putnam (eds.), *Arktouros: Hellenic Studies Presented to B. M. W. Knox*. Berlin: De Gruyter, pp. 345–353

Clay, Jenny Strauss, 2003. *Hesiod's Cosmos*. Cambridge University Press

Cohen, Beth, 2000. *Not the Classical Ideal: Athens and the Construction of the Other in Greek Art*. Leiden: Brill

Collard, Christopher (ed.), 2009. *Aeschylus: Persians and Other Plays*. Oxford University Press

Conacher, D.J., 1980. *Aeschylus' Prometheus Bound: A Literary Commentary*. University of Toronto Press

Cook, A., 1976. "Herodotus: The Act of Inquiry as a Liberation from Myth." *Helios* 3: 23–66

Coolidge, Francis, 1993. "The Relation of Philosophy to *Sôphrosunê*: Zalmoxian Medicine in Plato's *Charmides*." *Ancient Philosophy* 13: 23–31

Cooper, John, 1977. "Plato's Theory of Human Good in the *Philebus*." *Journal of Philosophy* 74: 714–730

2012. *Pursuits of Wisdom: Six Ways of Life in Ancient Philosophy from Socrates to Plotinus*. Princeton University Press

Cooper, John (ed.), 1997. *Plato: Complete Works*. Indianapolis: Hackett

Courcelle, Pierre, 1974. *Connais-toi toi-même de Socrate à Saint Bernard*. Paris: Etudes Augustiniennes

Croiset, Alfred (ed.), 2002. *Platon: Oeuvres complètes*. Volume I. Paris: Les Belles Lettres

Daniel Parra, José, 2010. "Political Psychology in Plato's *Alcibiades I*." *Praxis Filosófica* 31: 25–44

Darwall, Stephen, 1995. *The British Moralists and the Internal "Ought," 1640–1740*. Cambridge University Press

Davis, Michael, 1980. "Socrates' Pre-Socratism: Some Remarks on the Structure of Plato's *Phaedo*." *Review of Metaphysics* 33: 559–577

2006. "Making Something from Nothing: On Plato's *Hipparchus*." *Review of Politics* 68: 547–563

Davison, J.A., 1955. "Peisistratus and Homer." *Transactions and Proceedings of the American Philological Association* 86: 1–21

de Sélincourt, Aubrey, 1996. *Herodotus: The Histories*. New edn. New York: Penguin Books

de Vries, G.J., 1969. *A Commentary on the Phaedrus of Plato*. Amsterdam: Adolf M. Hakkert

Decleva Caizzi, Fernanda, 1980. "Τῦφος: Contributo alla storia di un concetto." *Sandalion* 3: 53–66

Defradas, Jean, 1954. *Les thèmes de la propagande delphique*. Paris: Klinksieck

Denyer, Nicholas, 2001. *Plato: Alcibiades*. Cambridge University Press

2008. *Plato: Protagoras*. Cambridge University Press

Dilcher, Roman, 1995. *Studies in Heraclitus*. Hildesheim: Georg Olms Verlag

Dillon, John, 1994. "A Platonist *Ars Amatoria*." *Classical Quarterly* 44: 387–392

Dittenberger, Wilhelm (ed.), 1915–1923. *Sylloge Inscriptionum Graecarum*. Leipzig: S. Hirzel

Dorion, Louis-André, 2004. "Qu'est-ce que vivre en fonction de sa dunamis? Les deux réponses de Socrate dans les Mémorables." In *Les études philosophiques: les écrits socratiques de Xénophon*. Paris: Presses Universitaires de France, pp. 235–252

Dorion, Louis-André, 2006. "Xenophon's Socrates." In Sara Ahbel-Rappe and Rachana Kamtekar (eds.), *A Companion to Socrates*. Oxford: Blackwell, pp. 93–109

Dover, K.J. (ed.), 1968. *Aristophanes Clouds*. Oxford University Press

Dusanic, Slobodan, 2000. "Critias in the *Charmides*." *Aevum* 74: 53–63

Einarson, Benedict and Phillip De Lacy (eds.), 1967. *Plutarch: Moralia*. Volume XIV. Cambridge, MA: Harvard University Press

Eisenstadt, Michael, 1981. "A Note on *Charmides* 168e9–169a1." *Hermes* 109: 126–128

Evans, Dale, 1976. "Plato's *Minos*, *Hipparchus*, *Theages* and *Lovers*: A Philosophical Interpretation." PhD dissertation. The Pennsylvania State University

Evans, Gareth, 1982. *The Varieties of Reference*. Oxford University Press
Evans, Matthew, 2007. "Plato's Rejection of Thoughtless and Pleasureless Lives." *Phronesis* 52: 337–363
Ferrari, G.R.F., 1987. *Listening to the Cicadas: A Study of Plato's Phaedrus*. Cambridge University Press
Fine, Gail, 2008. "Does Socrates Claim to Know that He Knows Nothing?" *Oxford Studies in Ancient Philosophy* 35: 49–85
Finkelstein, David, 2003. *Expression of the Inner*. Cambridge, MA: Harvard University Press
Finlay, John, 1994. "The Night of Alcibiades." *Hudson Review* 47: 57–79
Fletcher, Richard, 2007. "Legwork: Ion's Socrates." In Victoria Jennings and Andrea Katsaros (eds.) *The World of Ion of Chios*. Leiden: Brill, pp. 319–330
Fontenrose, Joseph, 1978. *The Delphic Oracle: Its Responses and Operations, with a Catalog of Responses*. Berkeley: University of California Press
Ford, Andrew, 2002. *The Origins of Criticism: Literary Culture and Poetic Theory in Classical Greece*. Princeton University Press
Forster, Michael, 2007. "Socratic Ignorance." *Oxford Studies in Ancient Philosophy* 32: 1–35
Foucault, Michel, 2006. *The Hermeneutics of the Subject: Lectures at the Collège de France, 1981–1982*. ed. Frédéric Gros. New York: Picador
Frankfurt, Harry, 1988. *The Importance of What We Care About: Philosophical Essays*. Cambridge University Press
2006. *The Reasons of Love*. Princeton University Press
Frede, Dorothea, 1993. *Plato: Philebus*. Indianapolis: Hackett
2000. "The Hedonist's Conversion: The Role of Socrates in the *Philebus*." In Christopher Gill and M.M. McCabe (eds.) *Form and Argument in Late Plato*. Oxford University Press, pp. 213–248
Freese, J.H., 1926. *Aristotle: Art of Rhetoric*. Loeb Classical Library 193. Cambridge, MA: Harvard University Press
Gadamer, Hans-Georg, 1986. *The Idea of the Good in Platonic-Aristotelian Philosophy*. New Haven: Yale University Press
1991. *Plato's Dialectical Ethics: Phenomenological Interpretations Relating to the Philebus*. New Haven: Yale University Press
Gagarin, Michael, and Paul Woodruff (eds.), 1995. *Early Greek Political Thought from Homer to the Sophists*. Cambridge University Press
Gehrke, Hans-Joachim, 2011. "Myth, History, Politics – Ancient and Modern." In John Marincola (ed.) *Greek and Roman Historiography*. Oxford University Press, pp. 40–71
Gerson, Lloyd, 2003. *Knowing Persons: A Study in Plato*. Oxford University Press

2008. Review of: J.-F. Pradeau, *Etudes platoniciennes IV. Les puissances de l'âme selon Platon. Bryn Mawr Classical Review*. http://bmcr.brynmawr.edu/2014/2014-01-43.html

Gertler, Brie, 2011. *Self-Knowledge*. London: Routledge

Gill, Christopher, 2007. "Self-Knowledge in Plato's *Alcibiades*." In Suzanne Stern-Gillet and Kevin Corrigan (eds.), *Reading Ancient Texts*: Volume I: *Presocratics and Plato. Essays in Honour of Denis O'Brien*. Leiden: Brill, pp. 97–112

Goldman, Harvey, 2004. "Reexamining the 'Examined Life' in Plato's *Apology of Socrates*." *Philosophical Forum* 35: 1–33

González, Francisco, 1998. *Dialectic and Dialogue: Plato's Practice of Philosophical Inquiry*. Evanston, IL: Northwestern University Press

Gordon, Jill, 2003. "Eros and Philosophical Seduction in *Alcibiades I*." *Ancient Philosophy* 23: 11–30

Goslin, Owen, 2010. "Hesiod's Typhonomachy and the Ordering of Sound." *Transactions of the American Philological Association* 140: 351–373

Gosling, J.C.B., 1973. "Knowledge as Vision." In *Plato*. London: Routledge and Kegan Paul, pp. 120–139

1975. *Plato: Philebus*. Oxford University Press

Graham, Daniel, 1997. "What Socrates Knew." *Apeiron* 30: 25–36

2008. "Socrates on Samos." *Classical Quarterly* 58: 308–313

2010. *The Texts of Early Greek Philosophy: The Complete Fragments and Selected Testimonies of the Major Presocratics*. Cambridge University Press

Granger, Herbert, 2004. "Argumentation and Heraclitus' Book." *Oxford Studies in Ancient Philosophy* 26: 1–17

Griffith, Mark, 2006. "Horsepower and Donkeywork: Equids and the Ancient Greek Imagination." *Classical Philology* 101: 185–246, 307–358

Griffiths, J. Gwyn, 1955. "The Delphic E: A New Approach." *Hermes* 83: 237–245

Griswold, Charles, 1986. *Self-Knowledge in Plato's Phaedrus*. New Haven: Yale University Press

Guthrie, William, 1971. *Socrates*. Cambridge University Press

1986. *A History of Greek Philosophy*: Volume V, *The Later Plato and the Academy*. Cambridge University Press

Hackforth, Reginald, 1913. *The Authorship of the Platonic Epistles*. University of Manchester Press

1952. *Plato's Phaedrus*. Cambridge University Press

Hadot, Pierre, 2004. *What Is Ancient Philosophy?* Cambridge, MA: Harvard University Press

Halper, Edward, 2000. "Is Knowledge of Knowledge Possible? *Charmides* 167a–169d." In Thomas Robinson and Luc Brisson (eds.), *Plato: Euthydemus, Lysis, Charmides. Proceedings of the Fifth Symposium Platonicum*. Sankt Augustin: Akademia Verlag, pp. 309–316

Hampton, Cynthia, 1990. *Pleasure, Knowledge, and Being: An Analysis of Plato's Philebus*. Albany: State University of New York Press

Harte, Verity, 2014. "The Life of Protarchus' Choosing: Plato *Philebus* 20b–22c." In Mi-Kyoung Lee (ed.), *Strategies of Argument: Essays in Ancient Ethics, Epistemology, and Logic*. Oxford University Press, pp. 3–20

Hasluck, Frederick, 1907. "Inscriptions from the Cyzicus District, 1906." *Journal of Hellenic Studies* 27: 61–67

Hatzimoysis, Anthony, 2011. *Self-Knowledge*. Oxford University Press

Havelock, Eric, 1972. "The Socratic Self as It Is Parodied in Aristophanes' *Clouds*." *Yale Classical Studies* 22: 1–18

Heidel, W.H., 1896. "Pseudo-Platonica." PhD dissertation. University of Chicago

1913. "On Certain Fragments of the Pre-Socratics: Critical Notes and Elucidations." *Proceedings of the American Academy of Arts and Sciences* 4:19: 681–734

Hornblower, Simon, 1997. *A Commentary on Thucydides*: Volume I: *Books I–III*. Oxford University Press

Hunter, Richard, 2012. *Plato and the Traditions of Ancient Literature*. Cambridge University Press

Ioppolo, Anna, 1995. "Socrate nelle tradizioni accademico-scettica e pirroniana." In Gabriele Giannantoni (ed.), *La tradizione socratica*. Naples: Bibliopolis, pp. 89–123

Irby-Massie, Georgia, 2008. "Prometheus Bound and Contemporary Trends in Greek Natural Philosophy." *Greek, Roman, and Byzantine Studies* 48: 133–157

Jacoby, Felix, 1947. "Some Remarks on Ion of Chios." *Classical Quarterly* 41: 1–17

Jeremiah, Edward, 2012. *The Emergence of Reflexivity in Greek Language and Thought: From Homer to Plato and Beyond*. Leiden: Brill

Jirsa, Jakub, 2009. "Authenticity of the *Alcibiades I*: Some Reflections." *Listy filologické* 132: 225–244

Johnson, David, 1999. "God as the True Self: Plato's *Alcibiades I*." *Ancient Philosophy* 19: 1–19

2005. "Xenophon at His Most Socratic (*Memorabilia* 4.2)." *Oxford Studies in Ancient Philosophy* 29: 39–73

Johnston, Richard and David Mulroy, 2004. "Simonides' Use of the Term *Tetragonos*." *Arethusa* 37: 1–10

Joosse, Albert, 2014. "Dialectic and Who We Are in the *Alcibiades*." *Phronesis* 59: 1–21

Joyal, Mark, 2003. Review of Nicholas Denyer, *Plato: Alcibiades*. *Bryn Mawr Classical Review*. http://bmcr.brynmawr.edu/2003/2003-01-28.html

Kaempf-Dimitriadou, Sophia, 1979. *Die Liebe der Götter in der Attischen Kunst des 5. Jahrhunderts V. Chr.* Bern: Hrsg. von der Vereinigung der Freunde antiker Kunst

Kahn, Charles, 1979. *The Art and Thought of Heraclitus*. Cambridge University Press

1996. *Plato and the Socratic Dialogue: The Philosophical Use of a Literary Form*. Cambridge University Press

Kantzios, Ippokratis, 2005. "Tyranny and the Symposion of Anacreon." *Classical Journal* 100: 227–245

Kaufmann, Walter, 1979. *Tragedy and Philosophy*. Princeton University Press

Kechagia, Eleni, 2011. *Plutarch against Colotes: A Lesson in History of Philosophy*. Oxford University Press

Ketchum, R., 1991. "Plato on the Uselessness of Epistemology: *Charmides* 166e–172a." *Apeiron* 24: 81–98

Keuls, Eva, 1993. *The Reign of the Phallus: Sexual Politics in Ancient Athens*. Berkeley: University of California Press

Kirk, G.S., 1962. *Heraclitus: The Cosmic Fragments*. Cambridge University Press

Kleve, Knut, 1983. "Scurra Atticus: The Epicurean View of Socrates." In G.P. Carratelli (ed.) *Syzêtêsis, studi sull'epicureismo greco e romano efferti a Marcello Gigante*. Naples: G. Macchiaroli, pp. 227–253

Kolb, David, 1983. "Pythagoras Bound: Limit and Unlimited in Plato's *Philebus*." *Journal of the History of Philosophy* 21: 497–511

Korsgaard, Christine, 1999. "Self-Constitution in the Ethics of Plato and Kant." *Journal of Ethics* 3: 1–29

2009. *Self-Constitution: Agency, Identity, and Integrity*. Oxford University Press

Kosman, Aryeh, 1975. "Perceiving that We Perceive: *On the Soul* III, 2." *Philosophical Review* 84: 499–519

1983. "Charmides' First Definition: Sophrosyne as Quietness." In John Anton and Anthony Preus (eds.) *Essays in Ancient Greek Philosophy*. Albany: State University of New York Press, pp. 203–216

Kurihara, Yuji, 2012. "Socratic Ignorance, or the Place of *Alcibiades I* in Plato's Early Works." In Marguerite Johnson and Harold Tarrant (eds.)

Alcibiades and the Socratic Lover-Educator. London: Bloomsbury, pp. 77–89

Kurke, Leslie, 2011. *Aesopic Conversations: Popular Tradition, Cultural Dialogue, and the Invention of Greek Prose.* Princeton University Press

Lamb, W.R.M. (ed.), 1927. *Plato VIII: Charmides, Alcibiades I and II, Hipparchus, The Lovers, Theages, Minos, Epinomis.* Loeb Classical Library, New York: G.P. Putnam's Sons

Lampert, Laurence, 2010. *How Philosophy Became Socratic: A Study of Plato's Protagoras, Charmides, and Republic.* University of Chicago Press

Landy, Tucker, 1999. "Limitations of Political Philosophy: An Interpretation of Plato's *Charmides*." *Interpretation* 26: 183–199

Lane, Nicholas, 2005. "Plato, *Apology* 26d6–e2." *Illinois Classical Studies* 30: 23–29

Larmore, Charles, 2010. *The Practices of the Self.* University of Chicago Press

Lattimore, Steven, 1998. *Thucydides: The Peloponnesian War.* Indianapolis: Hackett

Lauriello, Christopher, 2010. "Political Science and the Irrational: Plato's *Alcibiades*." *Interpretation* 37: 237–258

Lear, Jonathan, 1988. *Aristotle: The Desire to Understand.* Cambridge University Press

Lenfant, Dominique, 1999. "Monsters in Greek Ethnography and Society in the Fifth and Fourth Centuries BCE." In Richard Buxton (ed.), *From Myth to Reason? Studies in the Development of Greek Thought.* Oxford University Press, pp. 198–214

Lesher, James, 1987. "Socrates' Disavowal of Knowledge." *Journal of the History of Philosophy* 25: 275–288

Lipsey, Roger, 2001. *Have You Been to Delphi? Tales of the Ancient Oracle for Modern Minds.* Albany: State University of New York Press

Liu, JeeLoo and John Perry (eds.), 2012. *Consciousness and the Self: New Essays.* Cambridge University Press

Long, Anthony, 1978. "Timon of Phlius: Pyrrhonist and Satirist." *Cambridge Classical Journal* 24: 68–91

1988. "Socrates in Hellenistic Philosophy." *Classical Quarterly* 38: 150–171

2001. "Ancient Philosophy's Hardest Question: What to Make of Oneself?" *Representations* 74: 19–36

2009. "Heraclitus on Measure and the Explicit Emergence of Rationality." In Dorothea Frede and Burkhard Reis (eds.), *Body and Soul in Ancient Philosophy.* Berlin: De Gruyter, pp. 87–110

2014. *Greek Models of Mind and Self.* Cambridge, MA: Harvard University Press

Long, Herbert, 1958. "Notes on Aeschylus' *Prometheus Bound*." *Proceedings of the American Philosophical Association* 102: 229–280

Loraux, Nicole, 2006. *The Invention of Athens: The Funeral Oration in the Classical City*. New York: Zone Books

Lovibond, Sabina, 2002. *Ethical Formation*. Cambridge, MA: Harvard University Press

Lyons, John, 1963. *Structural Semantics: An Analysis of Part of the Vocabulary of Plato*. Oxford: Blackwell

Mackenzie, M.M., 1988a. "Heraclitus and the Art of Paradox." *Oxford Studies in Ancient Philosophy* 6: 1–37

1988b. "The Virtues of Socratic Ignorance." *Classical Quarterly* 38: 331–350

MacLachlan, Bonnie, 1993. *The Age of Grace: Charis in Early Greek Poetry*. Princeton University Press

Mahoney, Timothy, 1996. "The *Charmides*: Socratic *Sôphrosunê*, Human *Sôphrosunê*." *Southern Journal of Philosophy* 34: 183–198

Marcovich, M., 1967. *Heraclitus: Greek Text*. Santiago: Los Andes University Press

Matthews, Gareth, 2003. *Socratic Perplexity and the Nature of Philosophy*. Oxford University Press

McAvoy, Martin, 1996. "Carnal Knowledge in the *Charmides*." *Apeiron* 29: 63–103

McCabe, M.M., 1994. *Plato's Individuals*. Princeton University Press

2007a. "Looking Inside Charmides' Cloak: Seeing Others and Oneself in Plato's *Charmides*." In Dominic Scott (ed.), *Maieusis: Essays on Ancient Philosophy in Honor of Myles Burnyeat*. Oxford University Press, pp. 1–19

2007b. "Perceiving that We See and Hear: Aristotle on Plato on Judgment and Reflection." In M.M. McCabe and Markus Textor (eds.), *Perspectives on Perception*. Frankfurt: Ontos Verlag, pp. 143–177

2009. "Escaping One's Own Notice Knowing: Meno's Paradox Again." *Proceedings of the Aristotelian Society* 109: 233–256

2010. "Banana Skins and Custard Pies: Plato on Comedy and Self-Knowledge." In John M. Dillon and Luc Brisson (eds.). *Plato's Philebus: Selected Papers from the Eighth Symposium Platonicum*. Sankt Augustin: Academia Verlag, pp. 194–203

2011. "'It Goes Deep with Me': Plato's *Charmides* on Knowledge, Self-Knowledge and Integrity." In Christopher Cordner (ed.), *Philosophy, Ethics and a Common Humanity: Essays in Honour of Raimond Gaita*. London: Routledge, pp. 161–180

2013. "Waving or Drowning? Socrates and the Sophists on Self-Knowledge in the *Euthydemus*." In G. Boys-Stones, C. Gill, and D. el Murr (eds),

The Platonic Art of Philosophy: Festschrift for Christopher Rowe. Cambridge University Press, pp. 130–149

McCoy, Marina, 2005. "Philosophy, Elenchus, and Charmides' Definitions of ΣΩΦΡΟΣΥΝΗ." *Arethusa* 38: 133–159

McInerney, Jay, 2004. "'Do You See What I See?' Plutarch and Pausanias at Delphi." In Lukas De Blois (ed.), *The Statesman in Plutarch's Works: Proceedings of the Sixth International Conference of the International Plutarch Society*. Leiden: Brill, pp. 43–55

McKim, Richard, 1985. "Socratic Self-Knowledge and 'Knowledge of Knowledge' in Plato's *Charmides*." *Transactions of the American Philological Association* 115: 59–77

McKirahan, Richard, 1994. *Philosophy Before Socrates*. Indianapolis: Hackett

Meinwald, Constance, 2008. "The *Philebus*." In Gail Fine (ed.) *Oxford Handbook to Plato*. Oxford University Press, pp. 484–503

Michelini, Ann, 1998. "ΠΟΛΛΗ ΑΓΡΟΙΚΙΑ: Rudeness and Irony in Plato's *Gorgias*." *Classical Philology* 93: 50–59

Mikalson, Jon, 2010. *Greek Popular Religion in Greek Philosophy*. Oxford University Press

Miller, Mitchell, 2008. "The Pleasures of the Comic and of Socratic Inquiry: Aporetic Reflections on *Philebus* 48A–50B." *Arethusa* 41: 263–289

Moore, Christopher, 2012a. "Socrates and Clitophon in the Platonic *Clitophon*." *Ancient Philosophy* 32: 257–278

2012b. "The Myth of Theuth in the *Phaedrus*." In Catherine Collobert, Pierre Destrée, and Francisco González (eds.), *Plato and Myths*. Leiden: Brill, pp. 279–304

2013a. "Chaerephon the Socratic." *Phoenix* 67: 284–300

2013b. "Socrates Psychagogos (*Birds* 1555, *Phaedrus* 261a7)." In Alessandro Stavru and Fulvia de Luisa (eds.), *Socratica III: Studies on Socrates, the Socratics, and the Ancient Socratic Literature*. Sankt Augustin: Akademie Verlag, pp. 41–55

2013c. "Deception and Knowledge in the *Phaedrus*." *Ancient Philosophy* 33: 97–110

2013d. "Socrates among the Mythographers." *Polis* 30: 106–117

2014a. "Arguing for the Immortality of the Soul in the Palinode of Plato's *Phaedrus*." *Philosophy & Rhetoric* 47: 179–208

2014b. "Pindar's Charioteer in Plato's *Phaedrus*." *Classical Quarterly* 64: 525–532

2015a. "Socrates and Self-Knowledge in Aristophanes' *Clouds*." *Classical Quarterly* 65: 2

2015b. "Self-Knowledge in Xenophon's *Memorabilia* 4.2," *Classical Journal* 110:4: 397–417

2016. "Spartan Philosophy and Sage Wisdom in Plato's *Protagoras*," *Epochê* 20: 2

Moore, G.E., 1903. *Principia Ethica*. Cambridge University Press

Moran, Richard, 2001. *Authority and Estrangement: An Essay on Self-Knowledge*. Princeton University Press

Morgan, Kathryn, 2000. *Myth and Philosophy from the Presocratics to Plato*. Cambridge University Press

Morris, T.F., 1989. "Knowledge of Knowledge and Lack of Knowledge in the *Charmides*." *International Studies in Philosophy* 21: 49–61

Morrison, Donald, 1994. "Xenophon's Socrates as Teacher." In Paul Vander Waerdt (ed.), *The Socratic Movement*. Ithaca, NY: Cornell University Press, pp. 181–208

Mouraviev, Serge, 1999. *Héraclite d'Ephèse, édition critique complète des témoignages sur la vie et l'œuvre d'Héraclite d'Ephèse et des vestiges de son livre*. Sankt Augustin: Academia Verlag

Mueller, Gustav, 1957. "Unity of the *Phaedrus*." *Classical Bulletin* 33: 50–53

Mulroy, David, 2007. "The Concealed Artistry of the *Minos* and the *Hipparchus*." *Transactions of the American Philological Association* 137: 115–131

Munn, Mark, 2000. *The School of History: Athens in the Age of Socrates*. Berkeley: University of California Press

Murphy, David, 2007. "Critical Notes on Plato's *Charmides*." *Mnemosyne* 60: 213–234

Neer, Richard, 2007. "Delphi, Olympia, and the Art of Politics." In H.A. Shapiro (ed.), *The Cambridge Companion to Archaic Greece*. Cambridge University Press, pp. 225–264

Nichols, James, 1998. *Plato: Phaedrus*. Ithaca, NY: Cornell University Press

Nicholson, Graeme, 1999. *Plato's Phaedrus: The Philosophy of Love*. West Lafayette, IN: Purdue University Press

Nightingale, Andrea, 2010. "Plato on Aporia and Self-Knowledge." In Andrea Nightingale and David Sedley (eds.), *Ancient Models of Mind: Studies in Human and Divine Rationality*. Cambridge University Press, pp. 8–26

Nilsson, Martin, 1948. *Greek Piety*. Oxford University Press

North, Helen, 1966. *Sôphrosunê: Self-Knowledge and Self-Restraint in Greek Literature*. Ithaca, NY: Cornell University Press

Nussbaum, Martha, 2001. *Upheavals of Thought: The Intelligence of Emotions*. Cambridge University Press

Ogden, Daniel, 2013. *Drakon: Dragōn Myth and Serpent Cult in the Greek and Roman Worlds*. Oxford University Press

Oikonomides, A.N., 1980. "The Lost Delphic Inscription with the Commandments of the Seven and P. Univ. Athen 2782." *Zeitschrift für Papyrologie und Epigraphik* 37: 179–183

1987. "Records of 'The Commandments of the Seven Wise Men' in the 3rd century B.C.: The Revered 'Greek Reading-Book' of the Hellenistic World." *Classical Bulletin* 63: 67–76

Oldfather, C.H. (tr.), 1989. *Diodorus Siculus: The Library of History*, Volume IV: *Books IX–XII.40*. Cambridge, MA: Harvard University Press

O'Neill, William (ed.), 1971. *Proclus: Alcibiades I.* 2nd edn. The Hague: Martinus Nijhoff

Osborne, Catherine, 1983. "Aristotle, *De Anima* 3.2: How Do We Perceive That We See and Hear?" *Classical Quarterly* 33: 401–411

Owens, Ron, 2010. *Solon of Athens: Poet, Philosopher, Soldier, Statesman.* Portland, OR: Sussex Academic Press

Page, Denys, 1972. *Aeschyli: Septem quae Supersunt Tragoedias.* Oxford University Press

Parke, Herbert and Donald Wormell, 1956. *The Delphic Oracle.* Oxford: Blackwell

Pearson, Lionel, 1939. *Early Ionian Historians.* Oxford University Press

Peterson, Sandra, 2011. *Socrates and Philosophy in the Dialogues of Plato.* Cambridge University Press

Phillips, John, 1989. "Xenophon's *Memorabilia* 4.2." *Hermes* 117: 366–370

Plax, Martin, 2005. "Profit and Envy: The *Hipparchus*." *Polis* 22: 85–108

Podlecki, Anthony, 1969. "Reciprocity in *Prometheus Bound*." *Greek, Roman, and Byzantine Studies* 10: 287–292

2005. *Aeschylus: Prometheus Bound.* Oxford: Aris & Phillips

Politis, Vasilis, 2007. "The *Aporia* in the *Charmides* about Reflexive Knowledge, and the Contribution to Its Solution in the Sun-Analogy of the *Republic*." In Douglas Cairns, Fritz-Gregor Herrmann, and Terry Penner (eds.), *Pursuing the Good: Ethics and Metaphysics in Plato's Republic.* Edinburgh University Press, pp. 231–250

2008. "The Place of *aporia* in Plato's *Charmides*." *Phronesis* 53: 1–34

Pradeau, J.-F. (ed.), 2002. *Héraclite: Fragments.* Paris: Flammarion

Press, Gerald, 2002. "The Elenchos in the *Charmides*, 162–175." In Gary Alan Scott (ed.), *Does Socrates Have a Method? Rethinking the Elenchus.* University Park: Pennsylvania State University Press, pp. 252–265

Race, William, 1982. "Aspects of Rhetoric and Form in Greek Hymns." *Greek, Roman, and Byzantine Studies* 23: 5–14

Rademaker, Adriaan, 2005. *Sophrosyne and the Rhetoric of Self-Restraint: Polysemy and Persuasive Use of an Ancient Greek Value Term.* Leiden: Brill

Rapp, Jennifer, 2014. *Ordinary Oblivion and the Self Unmoored: Reading Plato's Phaedrus and Writing the Soul.* New York: Fordham University Press

Rappe, Sara, 1995. "Socrates and Self-Knowledge." *Apeiron* 28: 1–24

Reece, Andrew, 1998. "Drama, Narrative, and Socratic Eros in Plato's *Charmides*." *Interpretation* 26: 65–76

Reeve, C.D.C., 2013. *Blindness and Reorientation: Problems in Plato's Republic*. Oxford University Press

Rider, Benjamin, 2011. "Self-Care, Self-Knowledge, and Politics in the *Alcibiades I*." *Epoché* 15: 395–413

Riegel, Nicholas, 2011. "Beauty, *To Kalon*, and Its Relation to the Good in the Works of Plato." PhD dissertation. University of Toronto

Riley, Mark, 1980. "The Epicurean Criticism of Socrates." *Phoenix* 34: 55–68

Rinella, M.A., 2000. "Supplementing the Ecstatic: Plato, the Eleusinian Mysteries and the *Phaedrus*." *Polis* 17: 61–78

Rives, James, 2004. "Aristotle, Antisthenes of Rhodes, and the Magikos." *Rheinisches Museum für Philologie* 147: 35–54

Robert, Louis, 1968. "De Delphes à l'Oxus: Inscriptions grecques nouvelles de la Bactriane." *Comptes rendus des scéances l'Academie des Inscriptions et Belles Lettres* 112: 416–457

Robinson, T.M., 1987. *Heraclitus: Fragments*. University of Toronto Press

Roochnik, David, 2002. "Self-Recognition in the *Theaetetus*." *Ancient Philosophy* 22: 37–51

Roscher, W.H., 1900. "Die Bedeutung des E zu Delphi und die übrigen Grammata Delphika." *Philologus* 59: 21–41

1901. "Weiteres über die Bedeutung des E zu Delphi und die übrigen Grammata Delphika." *Philologus* 60: 81–102

Rose, H.J., 1940. "Some Herodotean Rationalisms." *Classical Quarterly* 34: 78–84

Rosivach, Vincent, 1977. "Earthborns and Olympians: The Parodos of the *Ion*." *Classical Quarterly* 27: 284–294

Ross, W.D., 1952. *The Works of Aristotle: Selected Fragments*. Volume XII. Oxford: Clarendon Press

Rossetti, Livio, 2011. "L'*Euthydème* de Xénophon." In *Le dialogue socratique*. Paris: Encre Marine/Les Belles Lettres, pp. 55–99

Rouse, W.H.D., 1902. *The Votive Offerings*. Cambridge University Press

Rowe, Christopher, 1986. *Plato Phaedrus*. Warminster: Aris & Phillips

2005. *Plato Phaedrus*. New York: Penguin Books

2011. "Self-Examination." In Donald Morrison (ed.), *The Cambridge Companion to Socrates*. Cambridge University Press, pp. 201–214

Russell, D., 2005. *Plato on Pleasure and the Good Life*. Oxford University Press

Rutherford, Ian, 2001. *Pindar's Paeans: A Reading of the Fragments with a Survey of the Genre*. Oxford University Press

Ryan, Paul, 2012. *Plato's Phaedrus: A Commentary for Greek Readers*. Norman: University of Oklahoma Press

Samad, Joy, 2010. "Is Greed Good? An Interpretation of Plato's *Hipparchus*." *Polis* 27: 25–37

Sanders, Kirk, 2011. "Don't Blame Socrates (Xen. *Mem*. 1.2.40–46)." *Classical Philology* 106: 349–356

Santas, Gerasimos, 1973. "Socrates at Work on Virtue and Knowledge in Plato's *Charmides*." In E.N. Lee, A.P.D. Mourelatos, and R.M. Rorty (eds.), *Exegesis and Argument: Essays in Honor of Gregory Vlastos*. Assen, the Netherlands: Van Gorcum, 105–132

Schapiro, Tamar, 1999. "What Is a Child?" *Ethics* 109: 715–738

Schefer, Christina, 2003. "Rhetoric as Part of an Initiation into the Mysteries: A New Interpretation of the Platonic *Phaedrus*." In Ann Michelini (ed.), *Plato as Author: The Rhetoric of Philosophy*. Leiden: Brill, 175–196

Schleiermacher, Friedrich, 1836. *Introductions to the Dialogues of Plato*. Cambridge: Deighton

Schmid, Walter, 1998. *Plato's Charmides and the Socratic Ideal of Rationality*. Albany: State University of New York Press

Schwitzgebel, Eric, 2011. "Knowing Your Own Beliefs." *Canadian Journal of Philosophy* 35: 41–62

Scott, Dominic, 2011. "Philosophy and Madness in the *Phaedrus*." *Oxford Studies in Ancient Philosophy* 41: 169–200

Scott, William, 1981. *Aeschylus' Prometheus Bound*. 2nd edn. Bryn Mawr College, Department of Greek

Searby, Denis M., 1998. *Aristotle in the Greek Gnomological Tradition*. Uppsala Universitet

Segonds, A. Ph. (ed.), 2003. *Proclus: sur le premier Alcibiade de Platon*. 2nd edn. Paris: Les Belles Lettres

Shoemaker, Sydney, 1963. *Self-Knowledge and Self-Identity*. Ithaca, NY: Cornell University Press

Slings, S.R., 1999. *Plato, Clitophon*. Cambridge University Press

Smith, Joel, 2012. Review of Liu and Perry 2012. *Notre Dame Philosophical Reviews*. http://ndpr.nd.edu/news/32138-consciousness-and-the-self-new-essays/

Smith, Nicholas, 2004. "Did Plato Write the *Alcibiades I*?" *Apeiron* 37: 93–108

Steinbock, Bernd, 2012. *Social Memory in Athenian Public Discourse: Uses and Meanings of the Past*. Ann Arbor: University of Michigan Press

Stern, Jacob, 1989. "Demythologization in Herodotus 5.92." *Eranos* 87: 13–20

1996. *Palaephatus: On Unbelievable Tales.* Mundelein, IL: Bolchazy-Carducci Publishers

2003. "Heraclitus the Paradoxographer: Περὶ Ἀπίστων, *On Unbelievable Tales.*" *Transactions of the American Philological Association* 133: 51–97

Stern, Paul, 1999. "Tyranny and Self-Knowledge: Critias and Socrates in Plato's *Charmides.*" *American Political Science Review* 9:2: 399–412

Strauss, Leo, 1966. *Socrates and Aristophanes.* University of Chicago Press

Tarrant, Harold, 2000a. "Naming Socratic Interrogation in the *Charmides.*" In Thomas Robinson and Luc Brisson (eds.), *Plato: Euthydemus, Lysis, Charmides. Proceedings of the Fifth Symposium Platonicum.* Sankt Augustin: Academia Verlag, pp. 251–258

2000b. *Plato's First Interpreters.* Ithaca, NY: Cornell University Press

2007. "Olympiodorus and Proclus on the Climax of the *Alcibiades.*" *International Journal of the Platonic Tradition* 1: 3–29

Taylor, A.E., 1911. "The Phrontisterion." In *Varia Socratica, first series.* Oxford: J. Parker, pp. 129–177

1927. *Plato, the Man and His Work.* London: Methuen

Tell, Håkan, 2010. *Plato's Counterfeit Sophists.* Washington DC: Center for Hellenic Studies

Thein, Karel, 2011. "L'âme, l'homme et la connaissance de soi dans le *Premier Alcibiade.*" *Chôra* 9–10: 171–202

Thesleff, Holger, 1982. *Studies in Platonic Chronology.* Helsinki: Societas Scientiarum Fennica

Thomas, C.J., 2006. "Plato's Prometheanism." *Oxford Studies in Ancient Philosophy* 31: 203–231

Thompson, W.H., 1868. *The Phaedrus of Plato, with English Notes and Dissertations.* London: Whittaker

Tipton, James, 1998. "Love of Gain, Philosophy and Tyranny: A Commentary on Plato's *Hipparchus.*" *Interpretation* 26: 201–216

Tonelli, Angelo (ed.), 1993. *Eraclito: Dell'origine.* Milan: Feltrinelli

Too, Yun Lee, 1998. "*Krisis* and *Agôn*: The Etymology of Criticism." In *The Idea of Ancient Literary Criticism.* Oxford University Press, pp. 18–50

Tortzen, Chr. Gorm, 2002. "Know Thyself – A Note on the Success of a Delphic Saying." In Bettina Amden, Pernille Flensted-Jensen, Thomas Heine Nielsen, Adam Schwartz, and Chr. Gorm Tortzen (eds.), *Noctes Atticae.* Copenhagen: Museum Tusculanum Press, pp. 2–14

Tränkle, H., 1985. "Gnothi seauton. Zu Ursprung und Deutungsgeschichte des delphischen Spruchs." *Würzburger Jahrbücher für die Altertumswissenschaft* 11: 19–31

Trypanis, C.A., 1951. "The Epigrams of Anacreon on Hermae." *Classical Quarterly* 1: 31–34

Tsouna, Voula, 2001. "Socrate et la connaissance de soi: quelques interprétations." In André Laks and Michel Narcy (eds.), *Figures de Socrate*, Villeneuve d'Ascq: Presses Universitaires du Septentrion, pp. 37–64

Tuckey, T.G., 1951. *Plato's Charmides*. Cambridge University Press

Tulli, Mauro, 2010. "Weak Ignorance: The Γελοῖον from the Scenes of Aristophanes to the Dialogue of Plato." In John Dillon and Luc Brisson (eds.), *Plato's Philebus: Selected Papers from the Eighth Symposium Platonicum*. Sankt Augustin: Academia Verlag, pp. 194–203

Tuozzo, Thomas, 1996. "The General Account of Pleasure in Plato's *Philebus*." *Journal of the History of Philosophy* 34: 495–513

2000. "Greetings from Apollo: *Charmides* 164c–165b, *Epistle* III, and the Structure of the *Charmides*." In Thomas Robinson and Luc Brisson (eds.), *Plato: Euthydemus, Lysis, Charmides. Proceedings of the Fifth Symposium Platonicum*. Sankt Augustin: Academia Verlag, pp. 296–305

2011. *Plato's Charmides: Positive Elenchus in a "Socratic" Dialogue*. Cambridge University Press

Usacheva, Anna, 2010. "Concerning the Date of Plato's *Phaedrus*." *Hermathena* 189: 53–70

Van der Ben, N., 1985. *The Charmides of Plato: Problems and Interpretations*. Amsterdam: B.R. Grüner

Vander Waerdt, Paul, 1989. "Colotes and the Epicurean Refutation of Skepticism." *Greek, Roman, and Byzantine Studies* 30: 225–267

1993. "Socratic Justice and Self-Sufficiency: The Story of the Delphic Oracle in Xenophon's *Apology of Socrates*." *Oxford Studies in Ancient Philosophy* 11: 1–48

Veith, Jerome, 2013. "Concerned with Oneself as One Person: Self-Knowledge in *Phronesis*." *Epoché* 18: 17–27

Velleman, J. David, 1989. *Practical Reflection*. Princeton University Press

Verdenius, W.J., 1955. "Notes on Plato's *Phaedrus*." *Mnemosyne* 8: 265–289

Warnek, Peter, 2005. *Descent of Socrates: Self-Knowledge and Cryptic Nature in the Platonic Dialogues*. Bloomington: Indiana University Press

Warren, James, 2002. "Socratic Skepticism in Plutarch's *Adversus Colotem*." *Elenchos* 23: 333–356

Waterfield, Robin (ed.), 2002. *Plato: Phaedrus*. Oxford University Press

Węowski, Marek, 2009. "Hippias of Elis (6)." *Brill's New Jacoby*. Editor-in-Chief Ian Worthington. Brill Online. http://brillonline.nl/brill-s-new-jacoby/hippias-of-elis-6-a6

Wellman, R.R., 1964. "The Question Posed at *Charmides* 165a–166c." *Phronesis* 9: 107–113

Werner, Daniel, 2012. *Myth and Philosophy in Plato's Phaedrus*. Cambridge University Press

2013. "The Self-Seeing Soul in the *Alcibiades I*." *Ancient Philosophy* 33:1–5

West, Martin, 1999. "The Invention of Homer." *Classical Quarterly* 49: 364–382

West, Martin (ed.), 1966. *Hesiod: Theogony*. Oxford University Press

West, T.G., and G.S. West, 1986. *Plato: Charmides*. Indianapolis: Hackett

Westra, Laura, 1992. "Knowing the Self in Plato, Plotinus and Avicenna." In Parviz Morewedge (ed.), *Neoplatonism and Islamic Thought*. Albany: State University of New York Press, pp. 89–110

White, David, 1993. *Rhetoric and Reality in Plato's Phaedrus*. Albany: State University of New York Press

Wilkins, Eliza, 1917. *"Know Thyself" in Greek and Latin Literature*. PhD Dissertation. University of Chicago

1929. *The Delphic Maxims in Literature*. University of Chicago Press

Witte, Bernd, 1970. *Die Wissenschaft von Guten und Bosen: Interpretationen zu Platons Charmides*. Berlin: de Gruyter

Wohl, Victoria, 2012. "The Eye of the Beloved: Opsis and Eros in Socratic Pedagogy." In Marguerite Johnson and Harold Tarrant (eds.), *Alcibiades and the Socratic Lover-Educator*. London: Bloomsbury, pp. 77–89

Wolfsdorf, David, 1997. "The Dramatic Date of Plato's *Protagoras*." *Rheinisches Museum für Philologie* 140: 223–230

Wollheim, Richard, 1984. *The Tread of Life*. New Haven: Yale University Press

Wood, James, 2007. "Comedy, Malice, and Philosophy in Plato's *Philebus*." *Ancient Philosophy* 27: 77–94

Woodbury, Leonard, 1971. "Socrates and Archelaus." *Phoenix* 25: 299–309

Woolf, Raphael, 2008. "Socratic Authority." *Archiv für Geschichte der Philosophie* 90: 1–38

Worthington, Ian. 2006. *Demosthenes: Speeches 60 and 61, Prologues, Letters*. Austin: University of Texas Press

Yunis, Harvey, 2011. *Plato: Phaedrus*. Cambridge University Press

Zacharia, Katerina, 2003. *Converging Truths: Euripides' Ion and the Athenian Quest for Self-Definition*. Leiden: Brill

Zuckert, Catherine, 1998. "Plato's *Parmenides*: A Dramatic Reading." *Review of Metaphysics* 51: 875–906

2004. "The Socratic Turn." *History of Political Thought* 25: 189–219

2009. *Plato's Philosophers: The Coherence of the Dialogues*. University of Chicago Press

Index

Printed in Great Britain
by Amazon

17060499R00167